I took this photo in the incredibly hot summer of 2010. I drew the material in this volume during the spring, and this volume will come out in November*, and right now it's October... I never know what time to talk about!! But my favorite time is the morning in a scorching summer.

—HIROSHI SHIIBASHI,
2010

*Japanese tankobon release date

HIROSHI SHIIBASHI debuted in BUSINESS JUMP magazine with *Aratama*. NURA: RISE OF THE YOKAI CLAN is his breakout hit. He was an assistant to manga artist Hirohiko Araki, the creator of *Jojo's Bizarre Adventure*. *Steel Ball Run* by Araki is one of his favorite manga.

NURA: RISE OF THE YOKAI CLAN
VOLUME 13
SHONEN JUMP Manga Edition

Story and Art by HIROSHI SHIIBASHI

Translation – John Werry
Touch-up Art and Lettering – Gia Cam Luc
Graphics and Cover Design – Fawn Lau
Editor – Joel Enos

NURARIHYON NO MAGO © 2008 by Hiroshi Shiibashi. All rights reserved. First published in Japan in 2008 by SHUEISHA Inc., Tokyo. English translation rights arranged by SHUEISHA Inc.

The rights of the author(s) of the work(s) in this publication to be so identified have been asserted in accordance with the Copyright, Designs and Patents Act 1988. A CIP catalogue record for this book is available from the British Library.

The stories, characters and incidents mentioned in this publication are entirely fictional.

Printed in the U.S.A.

Published by VIZ Media, LLC
P.O. Box 77010
San Francisco, CA 94107

10 9 8 7 6 5 4 3 2 1
First printing, February 2013

www.viz.com   www.shonenjump.com

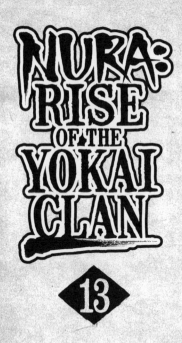

NURA: RISE OF THE YOKAI CLAN

13

CONFLICT

STORY AND ART BY
HIROSHI SHIIBASHI

CHARACTERS

NURARIHYON

Rikuo's grandfather and the Lord of Pandemonium. He intends to pass leadership of the Nura clan—leaders of the yokai world—to Rikuo. He's mischievous and likes to dine and ditch.

RIKUO NURA

Though he appears to be a human boy, he's actually the grandson of Nurarihyon, a yokai. His grandfather's blood makes him one-quarter yokai, and he transforms into a yokai at times.

KIYOTSUGU

Rikuo's classmate. He has adored yokai ever since Rikuo saved him in his yokai form, leading him to form the Kiyojuji Paranormal Patrol.

KANA IENAGA

Rikuo's classmate and a childhood friend. Even though she hates scary things, she's a member of the Kiyojuji Paranormal Patrol for some reason.

YUKI-ONNA

A yokai of the Nura clan who is in charge of looking after Rikuo. She disguises herself as a human and attends the same school as Rikuo to protect him from danger. When in human form, she goes by the name Tsurara Oikawa.

YURA KEIKAIN

Rikuo's classmate and a descendant of the Keikain family of onmyoji. She transferred into Ukiyoe Middle School to do field training in yokai exorcism. She has the power to control her shikigami and uses them to destroy yokai.

HAGOROMO-GITSUNE

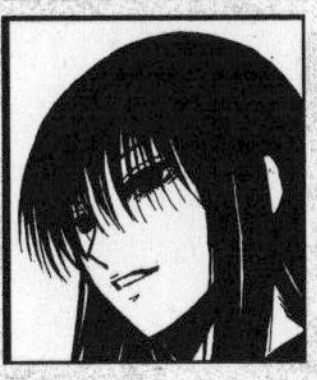

A great yokai in Kyoto who has a connection to Nurarihyon and the Keikain clan. She possesses humans and then commits foul deeds. She has returned to life after a 400-year absence.

GYUKI

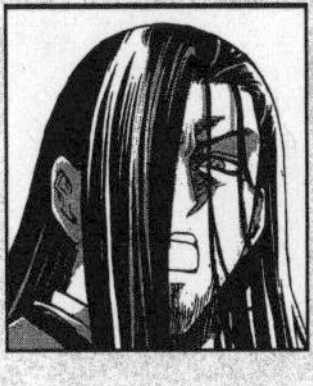

The leader of the Gyuki clan, an affiliate of the Nura clan. He established the clan base atop Mt. Nejireme in the far western area where the Nura clan holds sway. He is wise and cool-headed.

TSUCHIGUMO

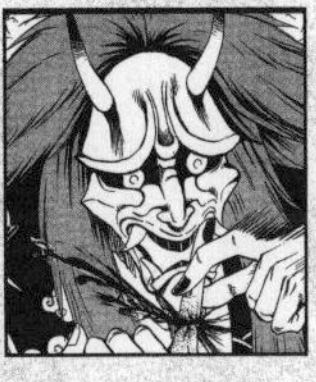

One of the Kyoto yokai, but instead of obeying Hagoromo-Gitsune, he does what he wants. He is so strong that people say he is an ayakashi you definitely don't want to meet!

IBARAKI-DOJI

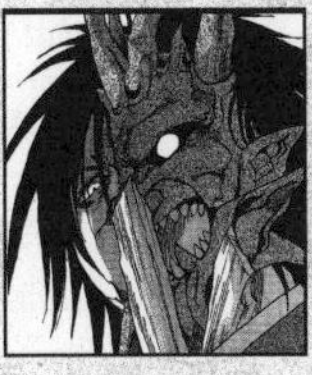

A person of high status among the Kyoto yokai. He is ill-tempered and loves a fight. When the stupa covering half of his face comes off, his violent nature grows even more violent and he displays his true power.

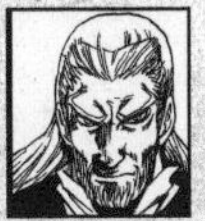

KIDOMARU

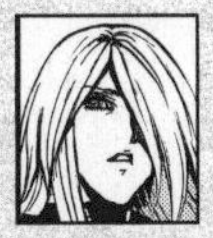

SHOKERA

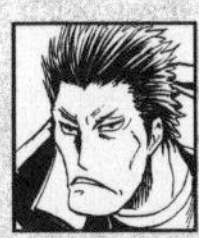

AOTABO

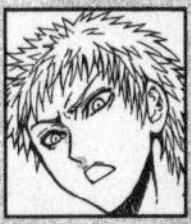

ZEN

STORY SO FAR

Rikuo Nura is a seventh-grader at Ukiyoe Middle School. At a glance, he appears to be just another average, normal boy. But he's actually the grandson of the yokai Overlord Nurarihyon. He's also the Underboss of the powerful Nura clan. He spends his days as a human, despite the clan's hopes that he will someday become a great Overlord like his grandfather.

When his comrades get hurt, Rikuo grows angry and faces the yokai Tsuchigumo. However, Tsuchigumo's Fear, known as Destroyer of the Parade of the Hundred Demons, defeats him. What's worse, Tsuchigumo takes Tsurara as his captive to Sokokuji Temple. Gyuki shows up to train Rikuo in preparation for resolving this predicament. Gyuki orders him to attain a technique worthy of the Lord of a Hundred Demons in just three days, but Rikuo has trouble grasping his meaning. Nonetheless, he tackles his training with a strong desire to save his friends.

Meanwhile, Kubinashi clashes with Ibaraki-Doji at Ryuenji Temple, site of the Sixth Seal of Hidemoto! Overcome with anger at himself for failing to save Rikuo from Tsuchigumo, Kubinashi rages out of control, but Kejoro helps him regain himself. Then Ibaraki-Doji reveals his true power, Kidomaru joins the fight, and the two display their superiority in battle. Now, Yura and Hidemoto show up to join the excitement!!

TABLE OF CONTENTS

NURA:RISE OF THE YOKAI CLAN

Act 104: The Invader Who Parted the Sky

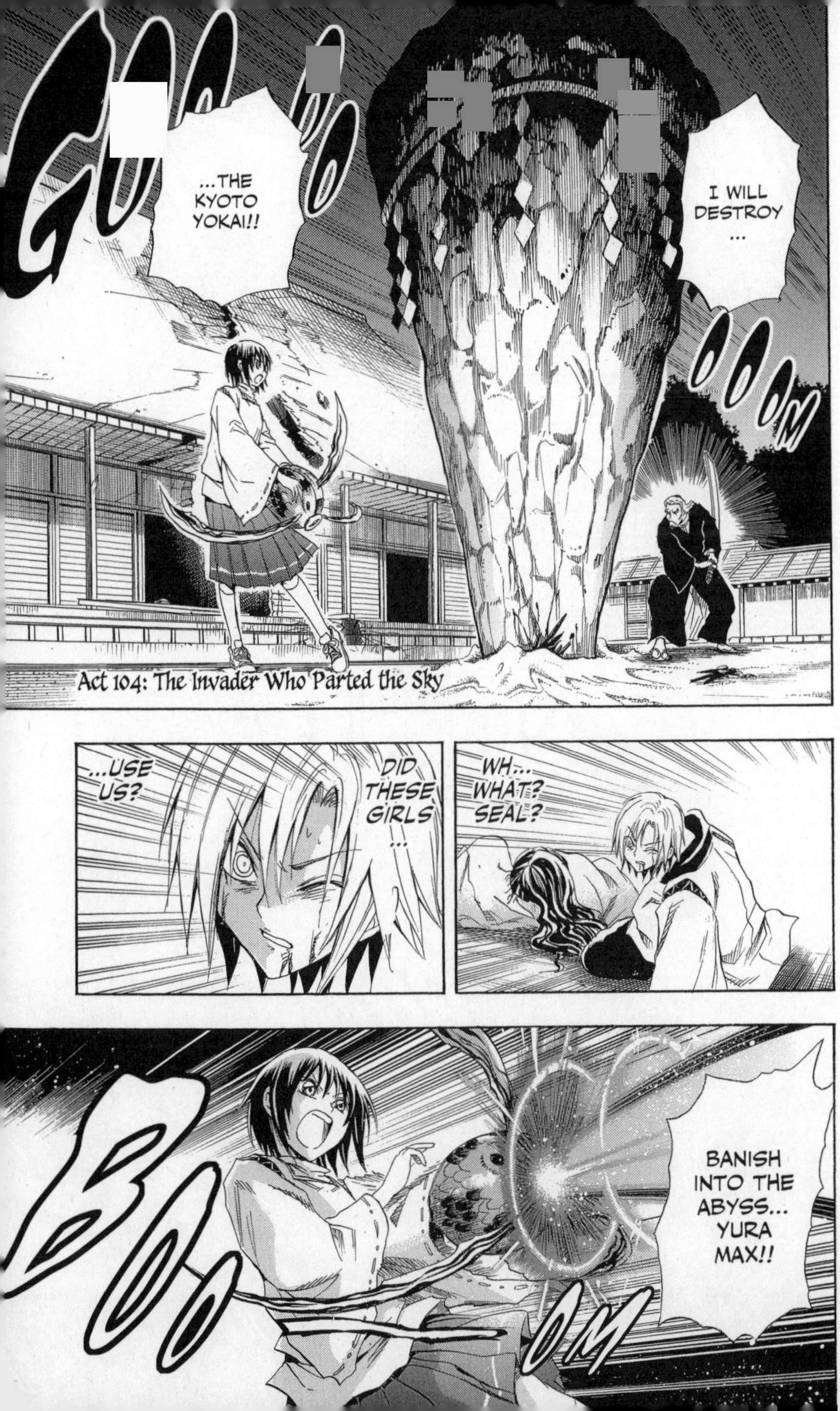

I WILL DESTROY ...
...THE KYOTO YOKAI!!
GOOOOOM
WH... WHAT? SEAL?
DID THESE GIRLS ...
...USE US?
BANISH INTO THE ABYSS... YURA MAX!!
BOOOOOM

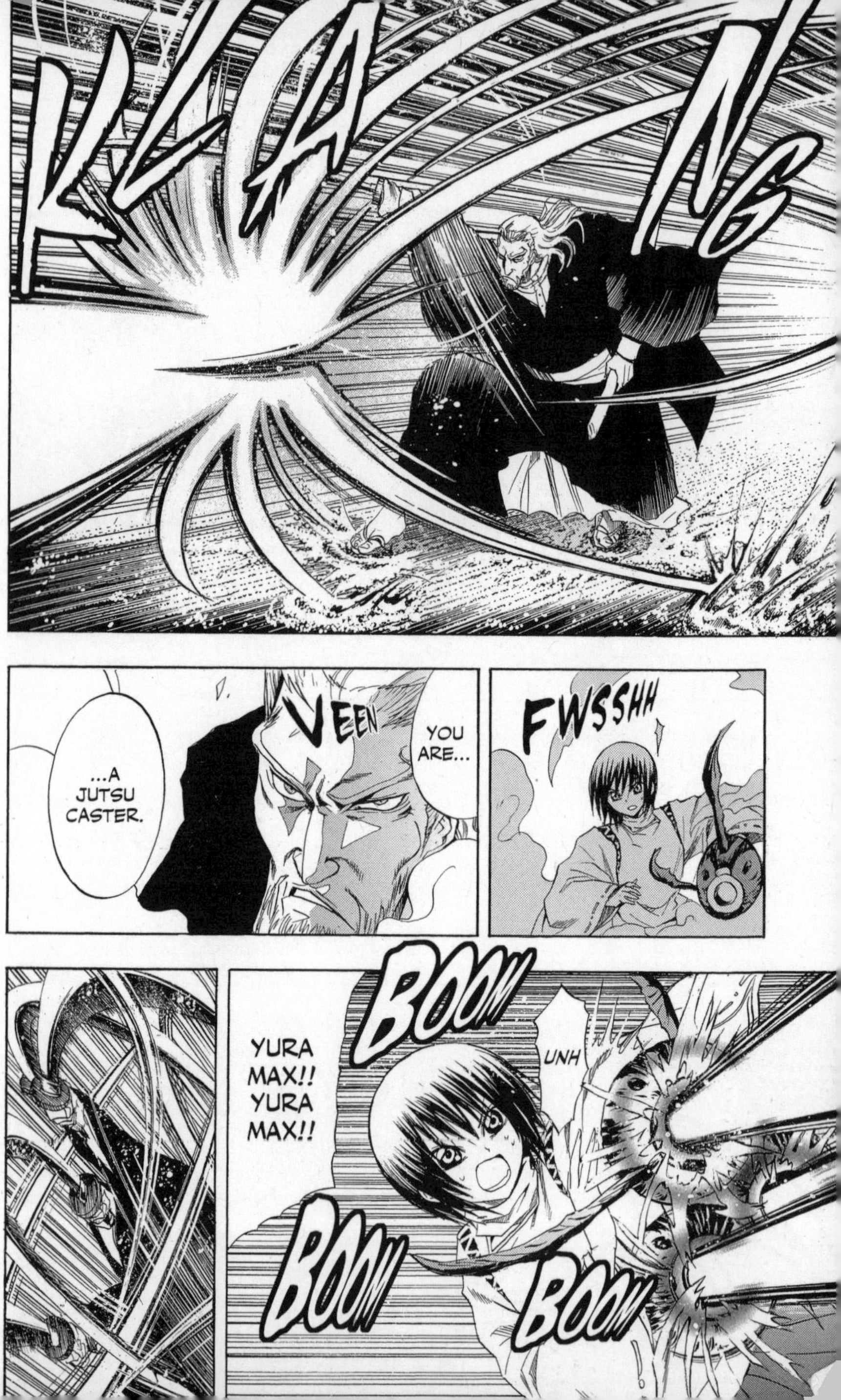
KLANG
FWSSHH
VEEN
YOU ARE...
...A JUTSU CASTER.
BOOM
UNH
YURA MAX!! YURA MAX!!
BOOM
BOOM

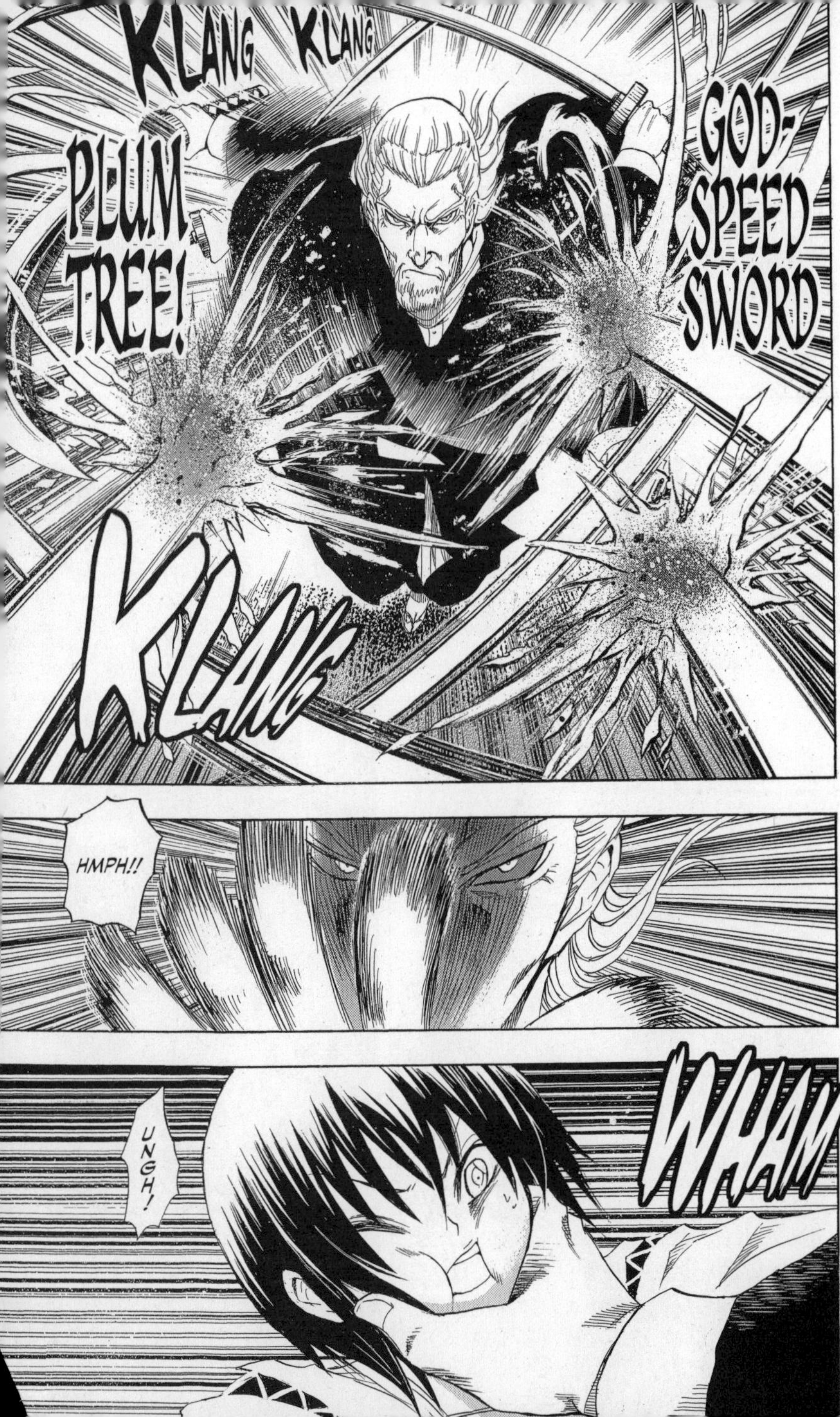
GOD-SPEED SWORD
KLANG KLANG
PLUM TREE!
KLANG
HMPH!!
WHAM
UNGH!

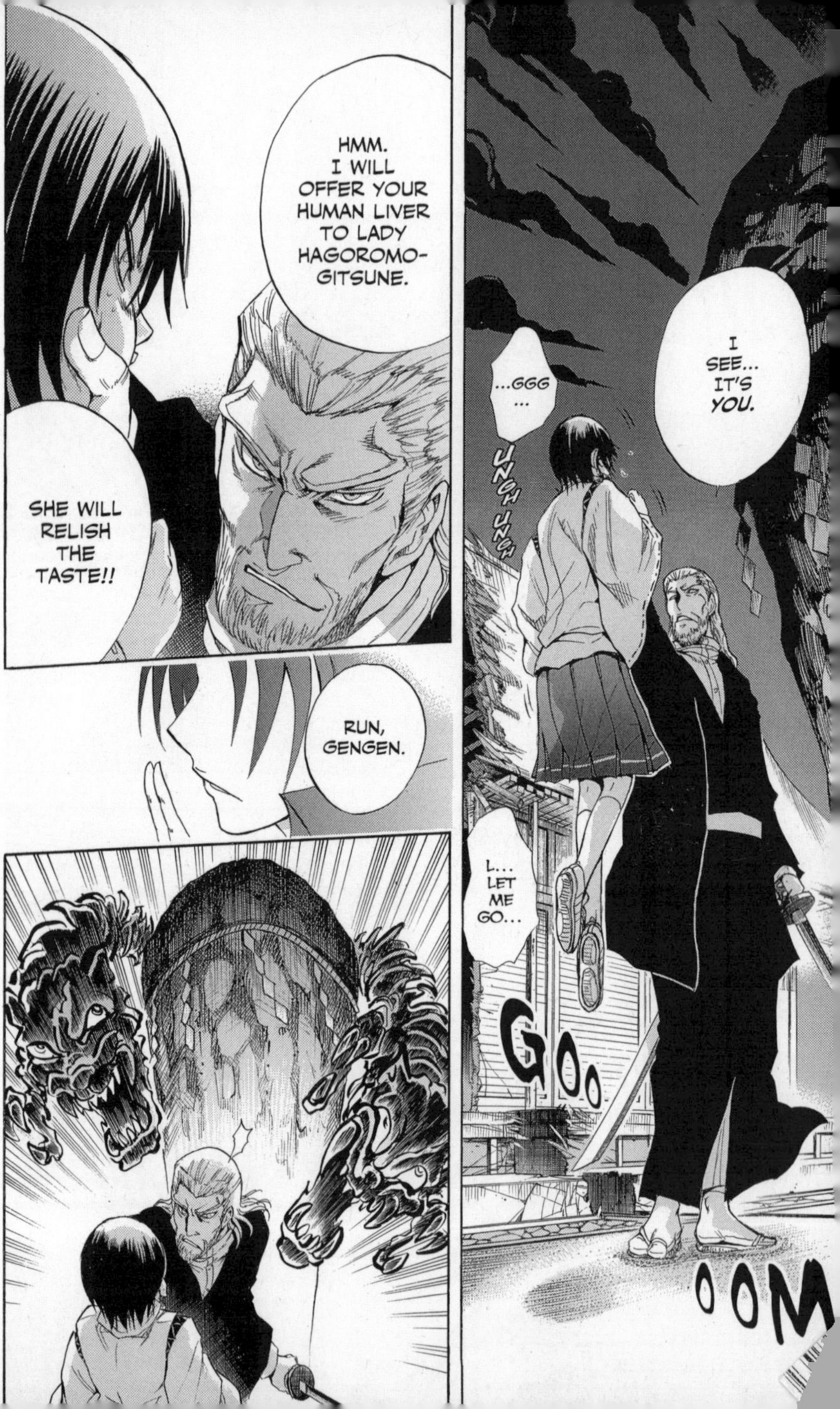
I SEE... IT'S YOU.
...GGG ...
UNGH UNGH
L... LET ME GO...
GOO
OOM
HMM. I WILL OFFER YOUR HUMAN LIVER TO LADY HAGOROMO-GITSUNE.
SHE WILL RELISH THE TASTE!!
RUN, GENGEN.

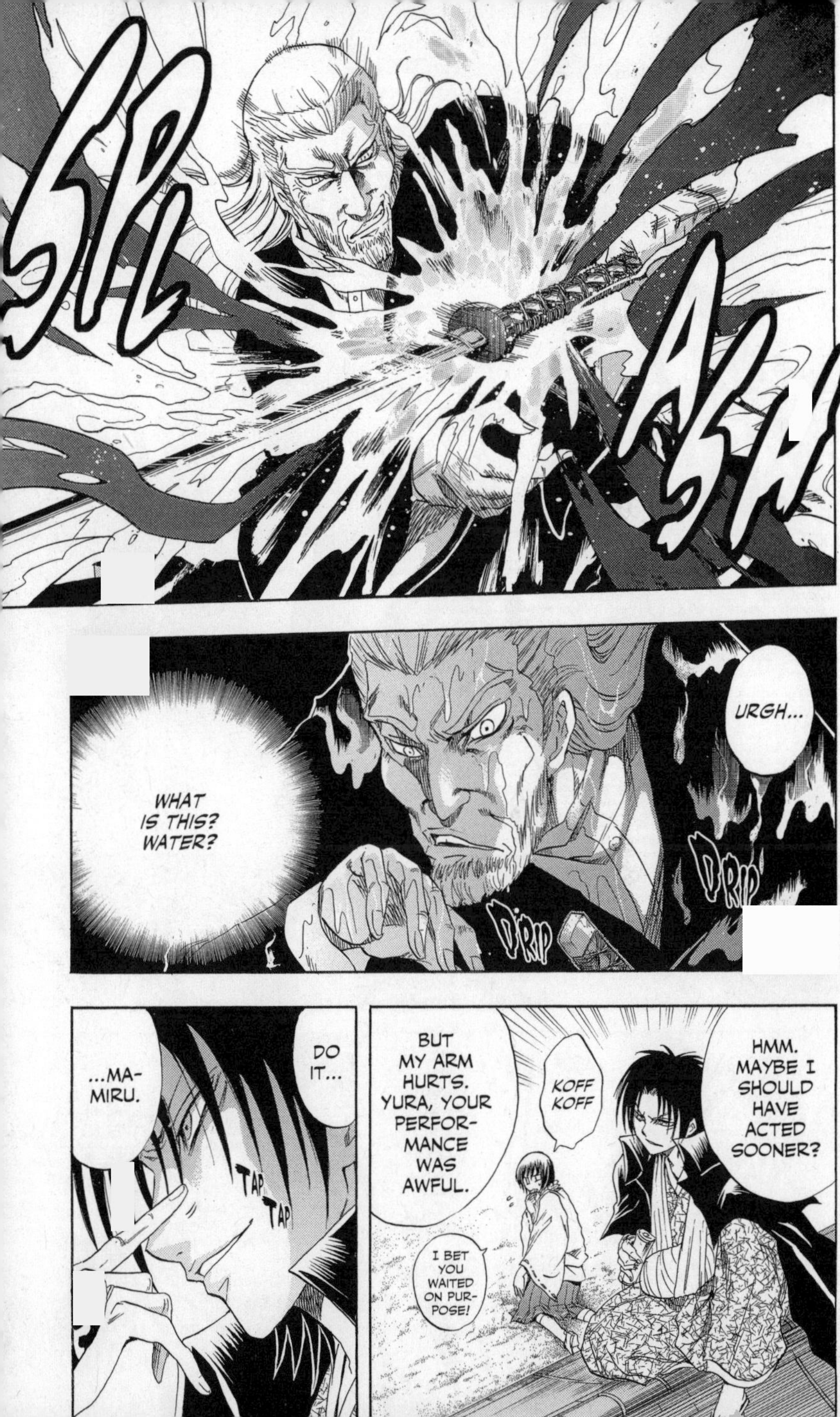
SPLASH
URGH...
DRIP
WHAT IS THIS? WATER?
DRIP
HMM. MAYBE I SHOULD HAVE ACTED SOONER?
KOFF KOFF
BUT MY ARM HURTS. YURA, YOUR PERFOR-MANCE WAS AWFUL.
I BET YOU WAITED ON PUR-POSE!
DO IT...
...MA-MIRU.
TAP TAP

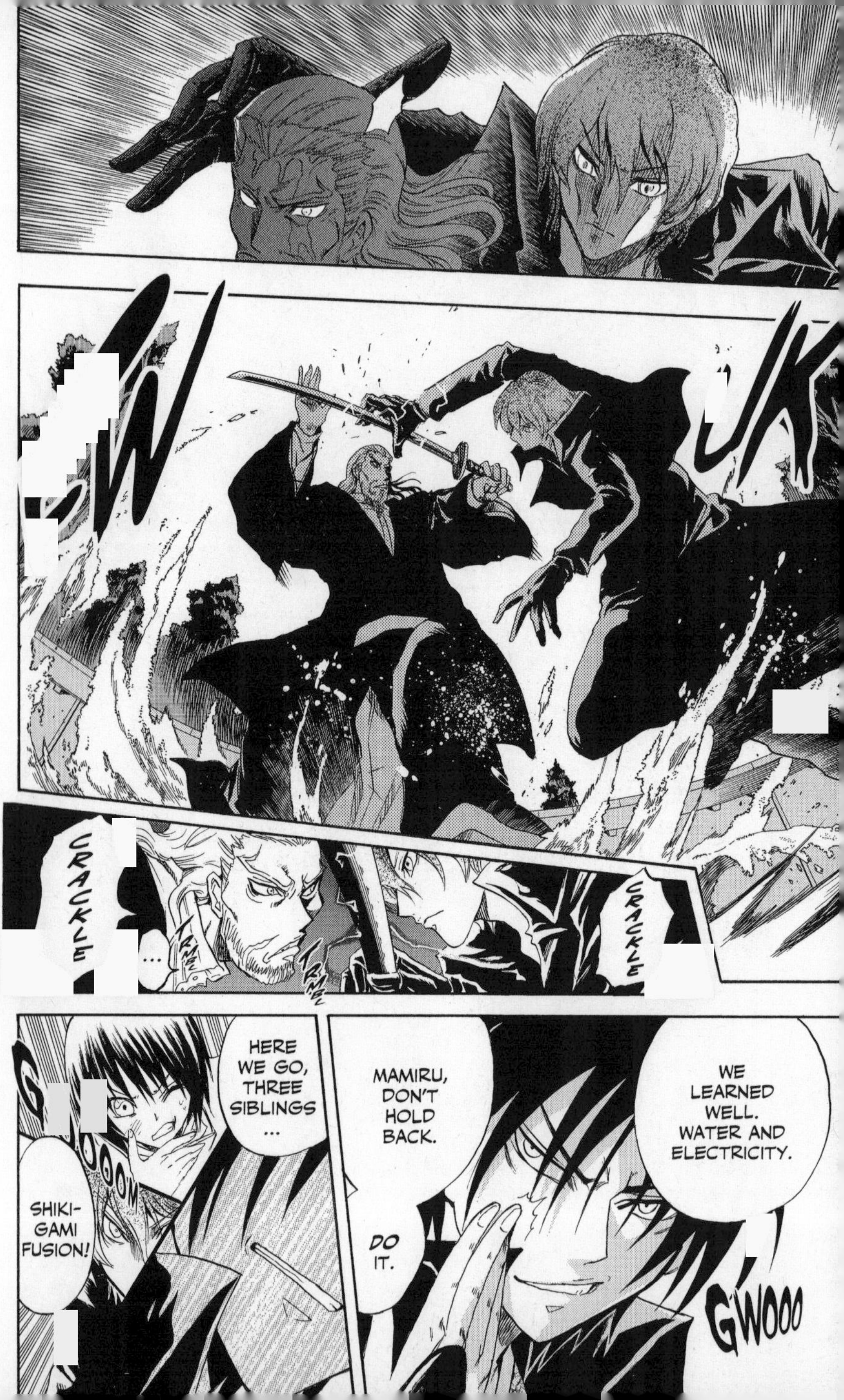
CRACKLE
TRMBL
...
TRMBL
CRACKLE
WE LEARNED WELL. WATER AND ELECTRICITY.
MAMIRU, DON'T HOLD BACK.
DO IT.
GWOOO
HERE WE GO, THREE SIBLINGS ...
SHIKI-GAMI FUSION!

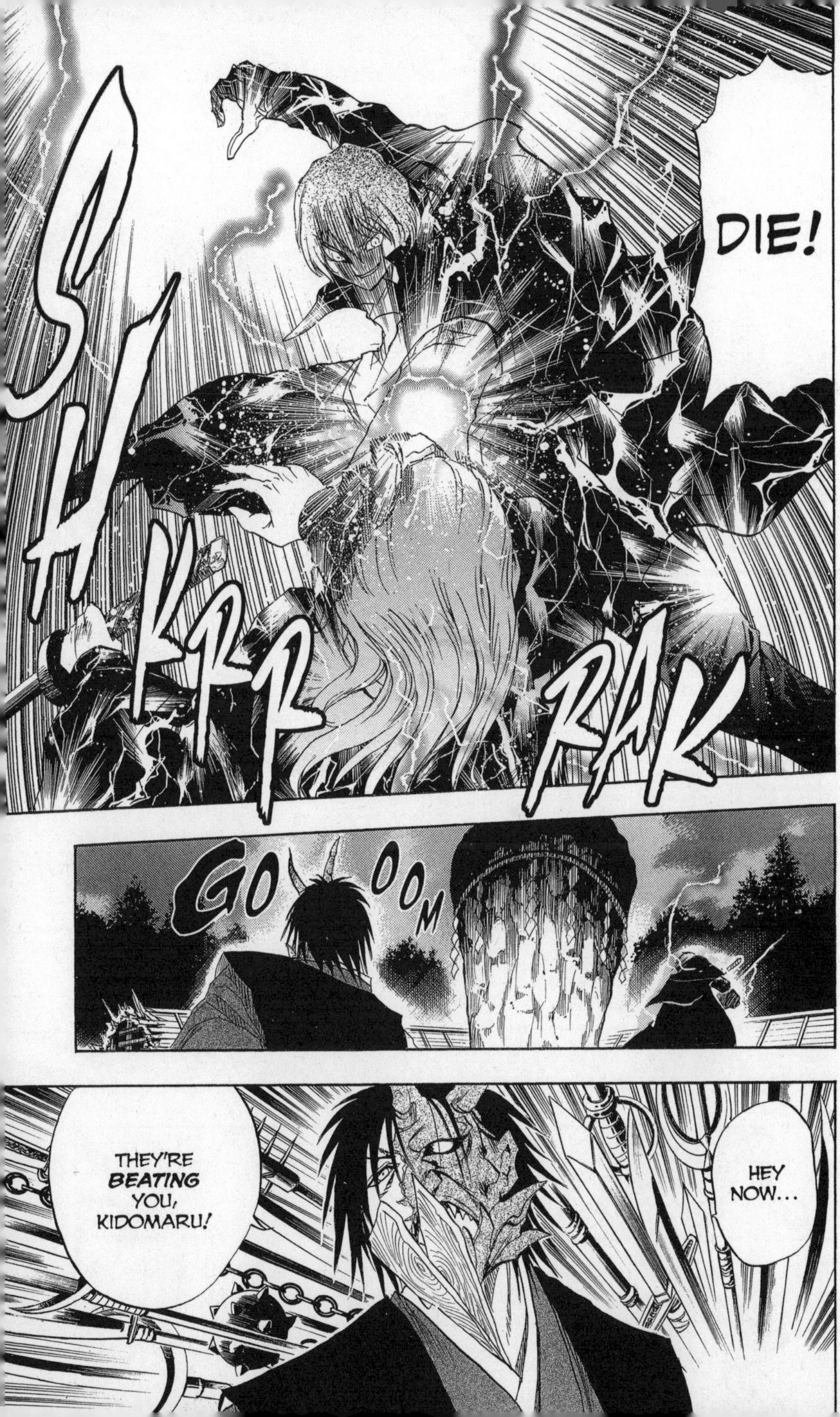
DIE!
SHKRRRAK
GOOOM
HEY NOW...
THEY'RE BEATING YOU, KIDOMARU!

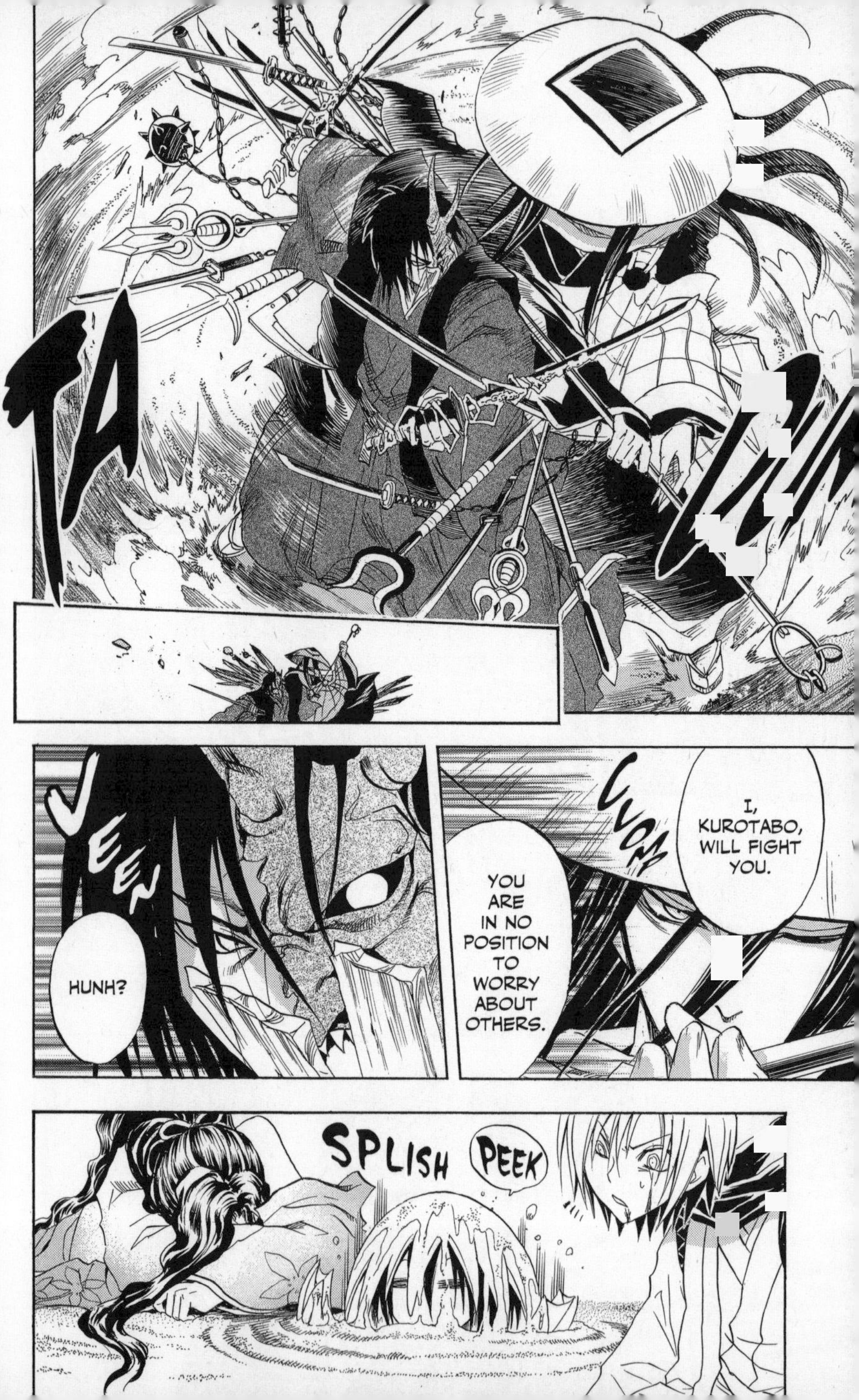
I, KUROTABO, WILL FIGHT YOU.
YOU ARE IN NO POSITION TO WORRY ABOUT OTHERS.
HUNH?
PEEK
SPLISH

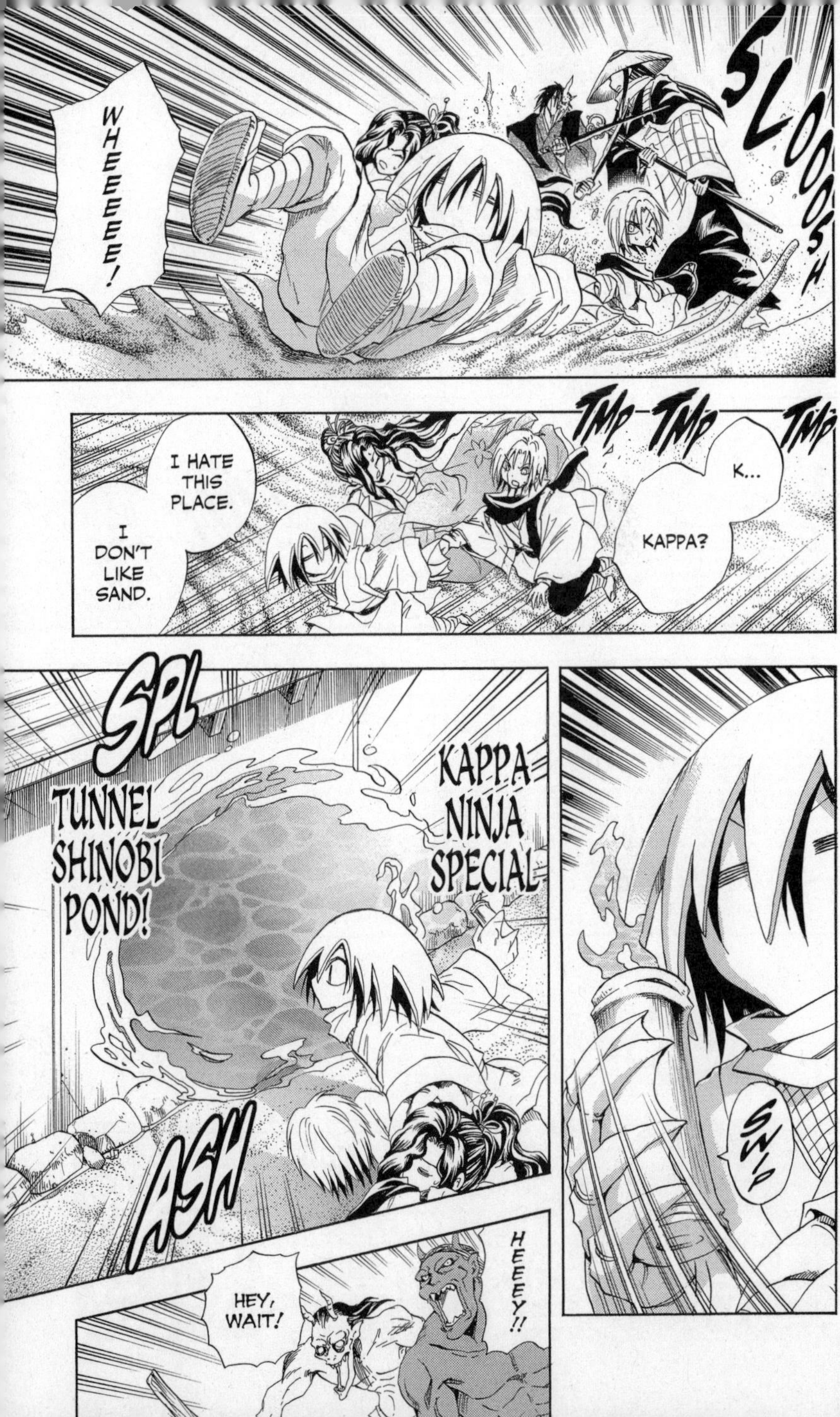
SLOOOOSH
WHEEEEEE!
TMP TMP TMP
K...
KAPPA?
I HATE THIS PLACE.
I DON'T LIKE SAND.
SWIP
KAPPA NINJA SPECIAL
TUNNEL SHINOBI POND!
SPL
ASH
HEEEEY!!
HEY, WAIT!

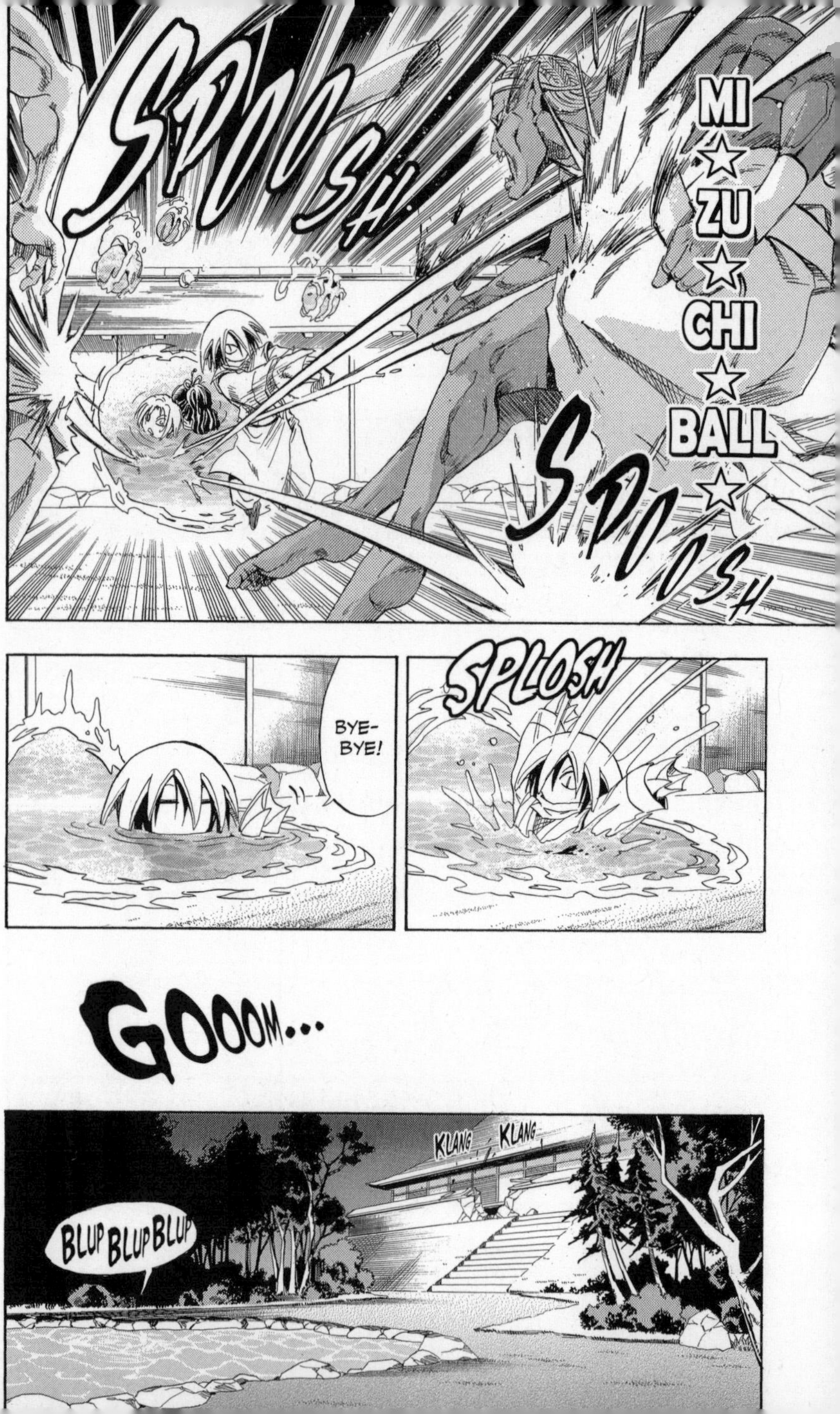
MI☆ZU☆CHI☆BALL☆
SPLOOSH
SPLOOSH
SPLOSH
BYE-BYE!
GOOOM...
KLANG KLANG
BLUP BLUP BLUP

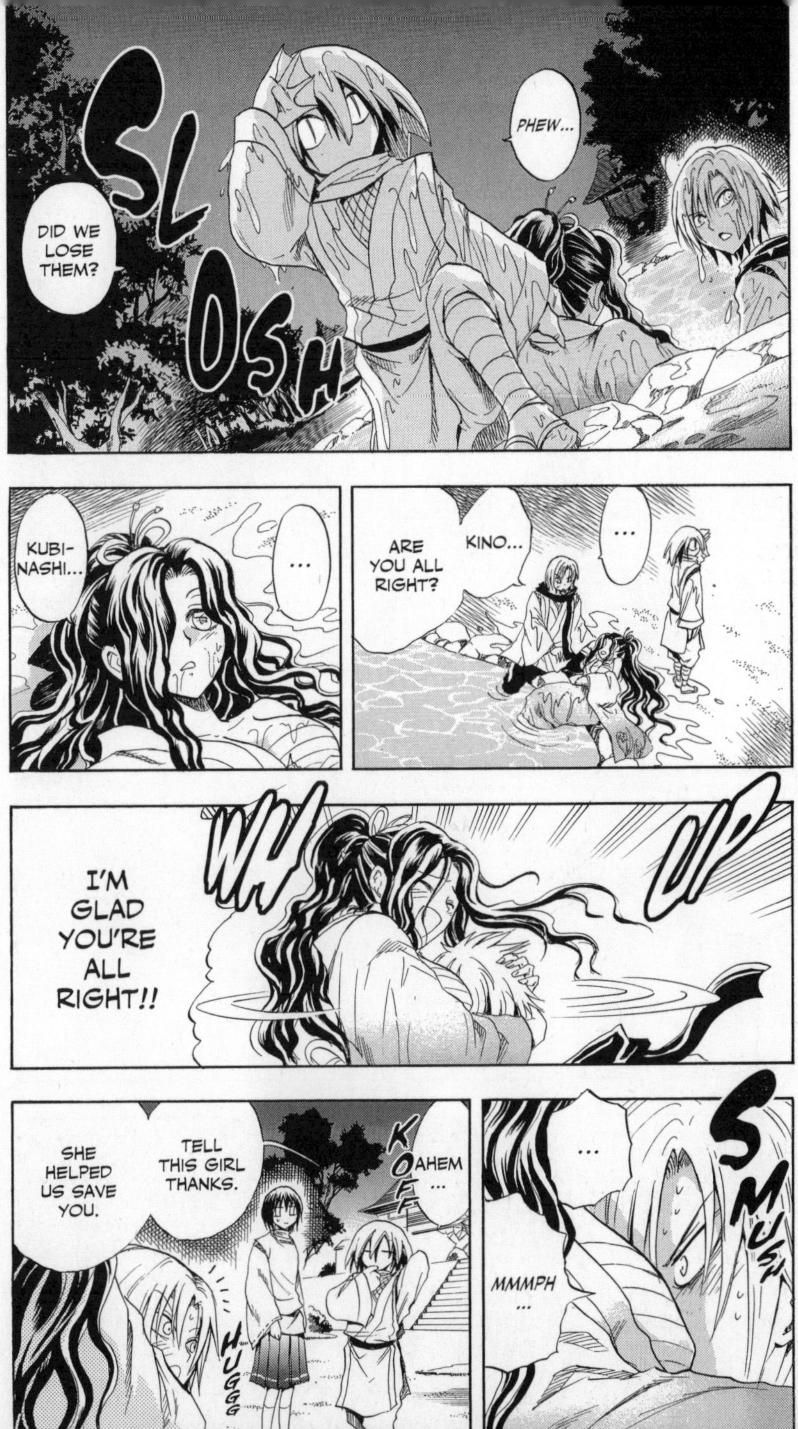
PHEW...
SLOSH
DID WE LOSE THEM?
...
KINO...
ARE YOU ALL RIGHT?
...
KUBI-NASHI...
WHUP
I'M GLAD YOU'RE ALL RIGHT!!
SMUSH
...
MMMPH ...
KOFF
AHEM ...
TELL THIS GIRL THANKS.
SHE HELPED US SAVE YOU.
HUGGG

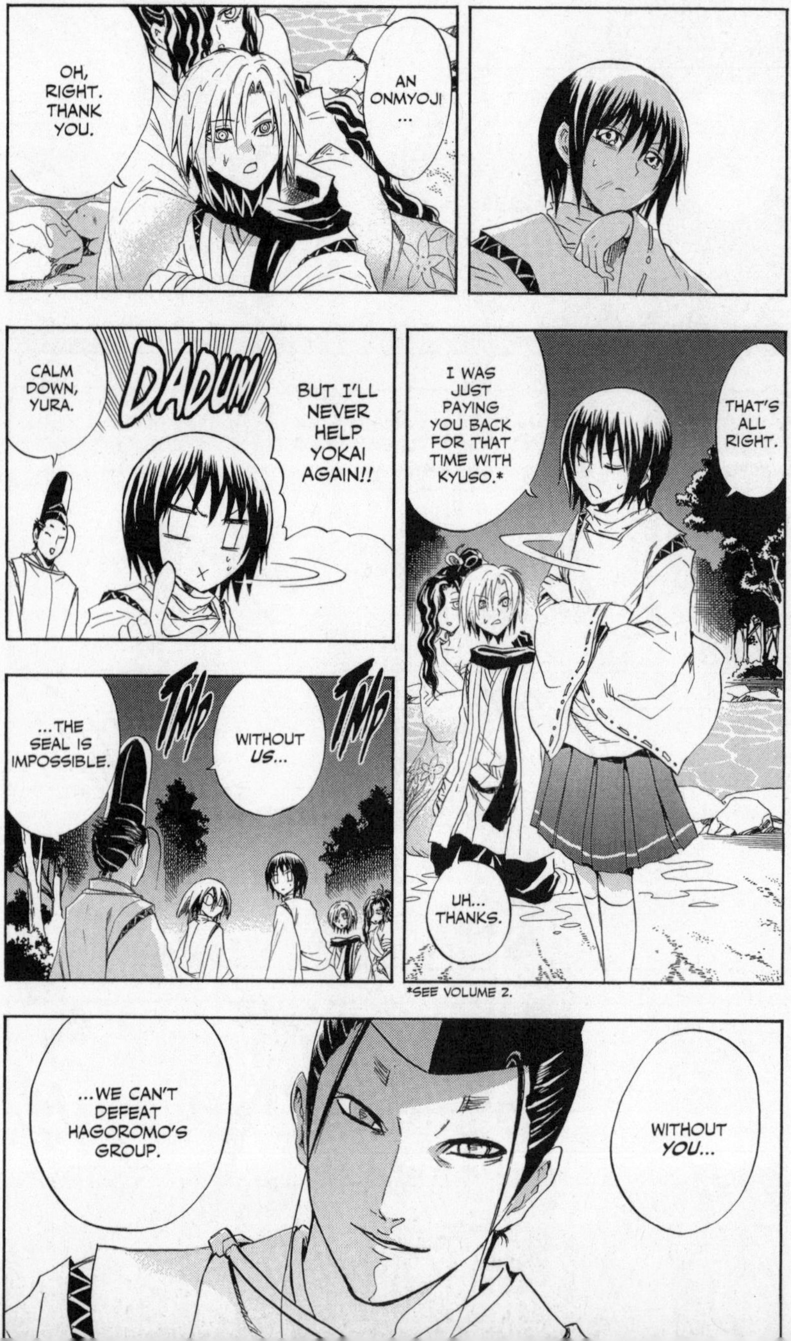
AN ONMYOJI ...
OH, RIGHT. THANK YOU.
THAT'S ALL RIGHT.
I WAS JUST PAYING YOU BACK FOR THAT TIME WITH KYUSO.*
UH... THANKS.
BUT I'LL NEVER HELP YOKAI AGAIN!!
DADUM
CALM DOWN, YURA.
TMP
WITHOUT *US*...
TMP
...THE SEAL IS IMPOSSIBLE.
WITHOUT *YOU*...
...WE CAN'T DEFEAT HAGOROMO'S GROUP.

*SEE VOLUME 2.

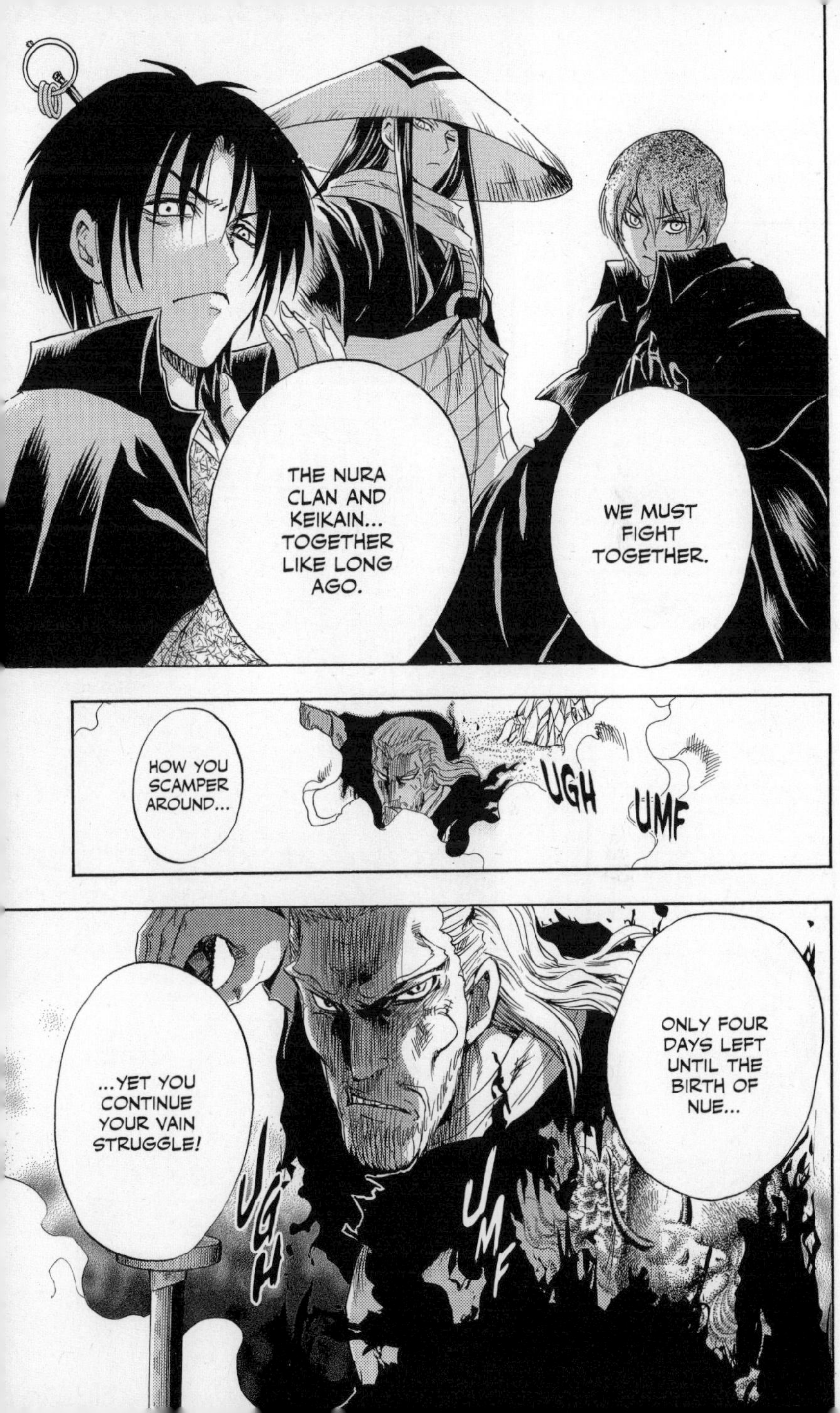
THE NURA CLAN AND KEIKAIN... TOGETHER LIKE LONG AGO.
WE MUST FIGHT TOGETHER.
UMF
UGH
HOW YOU SCAMPER AROUND...
ONLY FOUR DAYS LEFT UNTIL THE BIRTH OF NUE...
UMF
UGH
...YET YOU CONTINUE YOUR VAIN STRUGGLE!

Act 104: The Invader Who Parted the Sky

Keikain Clan Main Family
RRMMMM
LOOK AT THAT!
IS THAT NIJO CASTLE?

A GIANT CASTLE SUDDENLY APPEARED...

STRANGE PHENOMENA ARE OCCURRING THROUGHOUT THE CITY. PEOPLE ARE DISAPPEARING ...
WHAT HAS HAPPENED TO KYO--

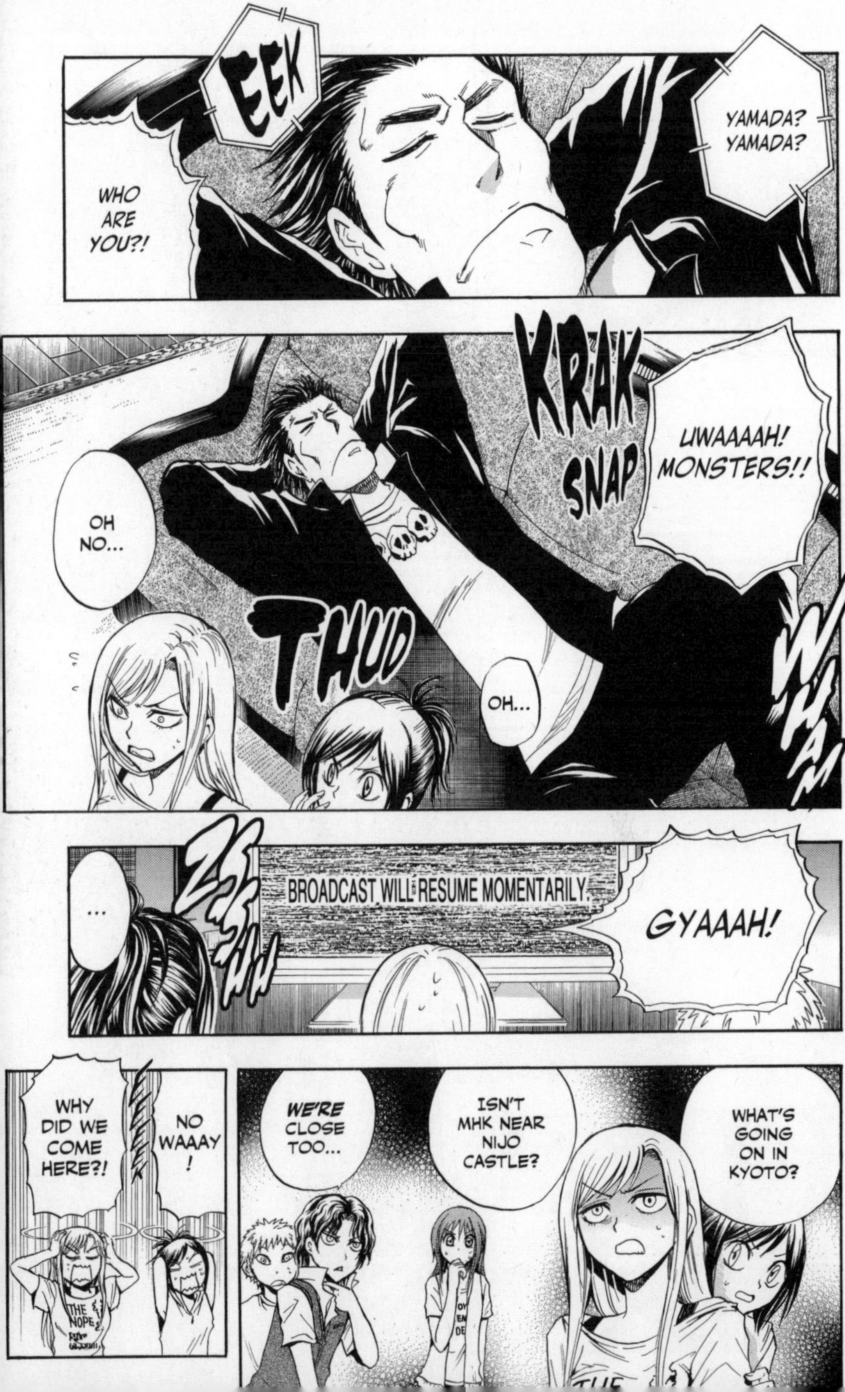
YAMADA? YAMADA?
EEK
WHO ARE YOU?!
UWAAAAH! MONSTERS!!
KRAK
SNAP
OH...
THUD
OH NO...
GYAAAH!
BROADCAST WILL RESUME MOMENTARILY.
...
WHAT'S GOING ON IN KYOTO?
ISN'T MHK NEAR NIJO CASTLE?
WE'RE CLOSE TOO...
NO WAAAY!
WHY DID WE COME HERE?!

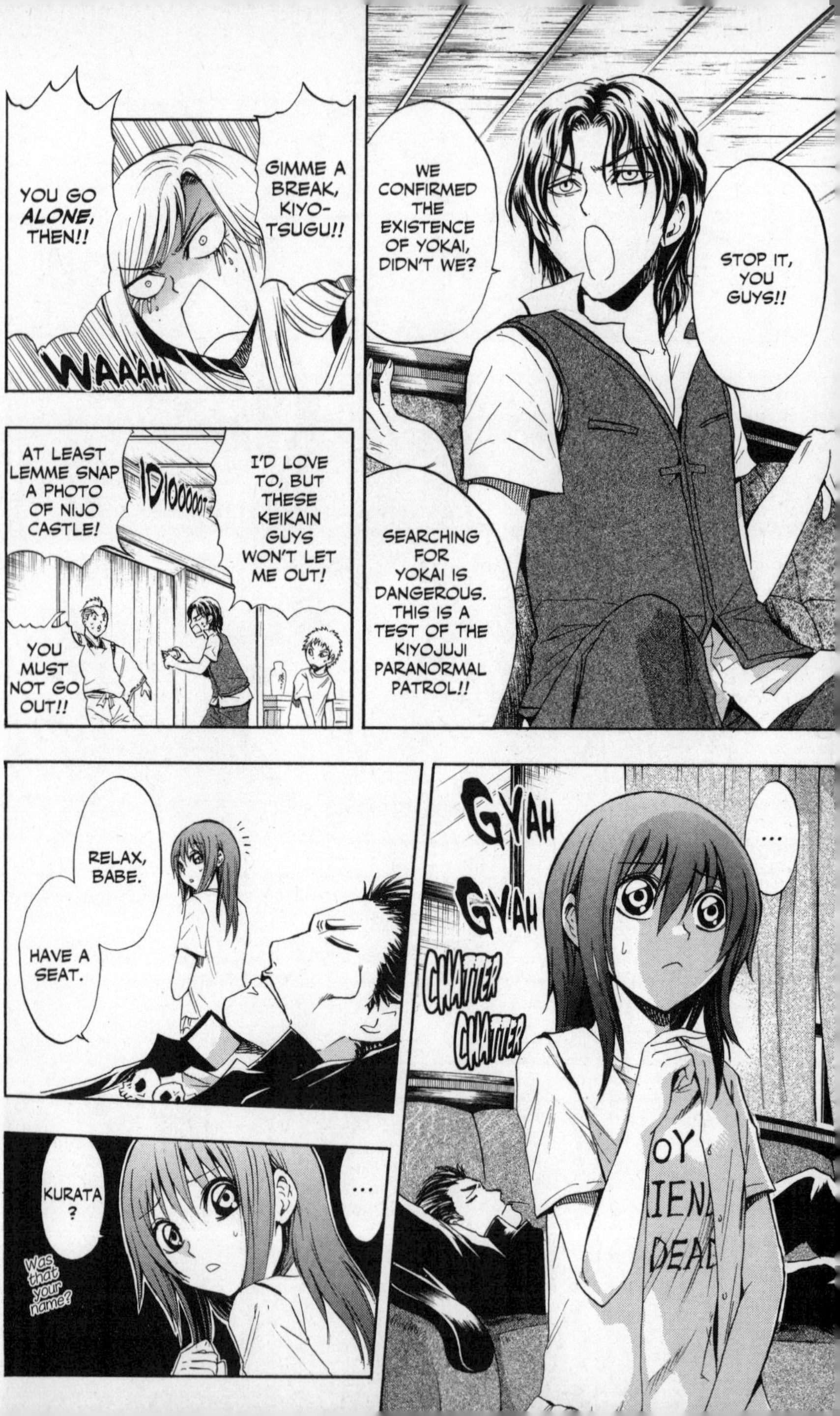
STOP IT, YOU GUYS!!
WE CONFIRMED THE EXISTENCE OF YOKAI, DIDN'T WE?
SEARCHING FOR YOKAI IS DANGEROUS. THIS IS A TEST OF THE KIYOJUJI PARANORMAL PATROL!!
GIMME A BREAK, KIYO-TSUGU!!
YOU GO ALONE, THEN!!
WAAAH
I'D LOVE TO, BUT THESE KEIKAIN GUYS WON'T LET ME OUT!
IDIOOOOOT
AT LEAST LEMME SNAP A PHOTO OF NIJO CASTLE!
YOU MUST NOT GO OUT!!
...
GYAH
GYAH
CHATTER
CHATTER
RELAX, BABE.
HAVE A SEAT.
...
KURATA?
Was that your name?

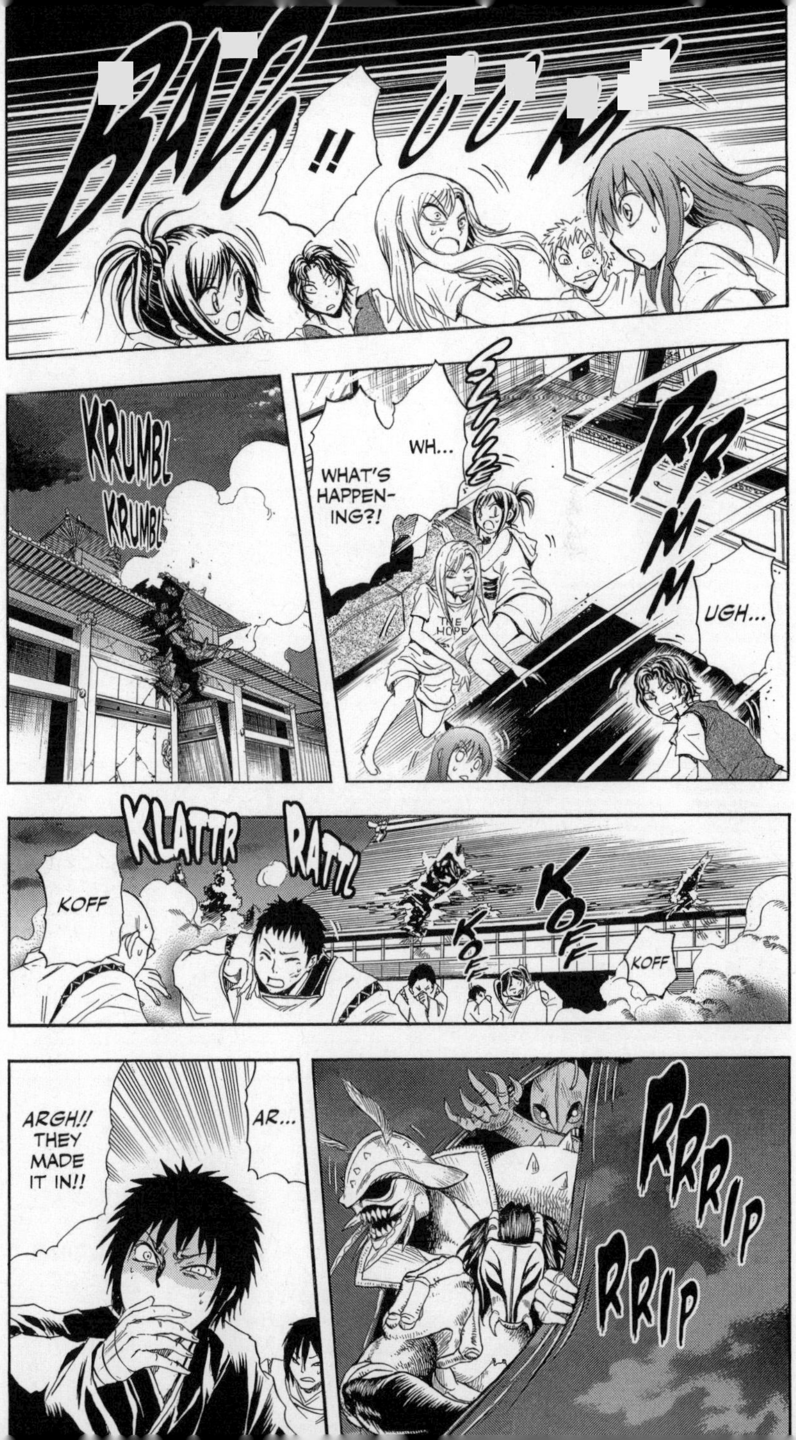

BRAOO!! OOM
UGH...
WH...
WHAT'S HAPPEN-ING?!
KRUMBL KRUMBL
KOFF
KOFF KOFF
KLATTR RATTL
KOFF
RRRIP RRIP
AR...
ARGH!! THEY MADE IT IN!!

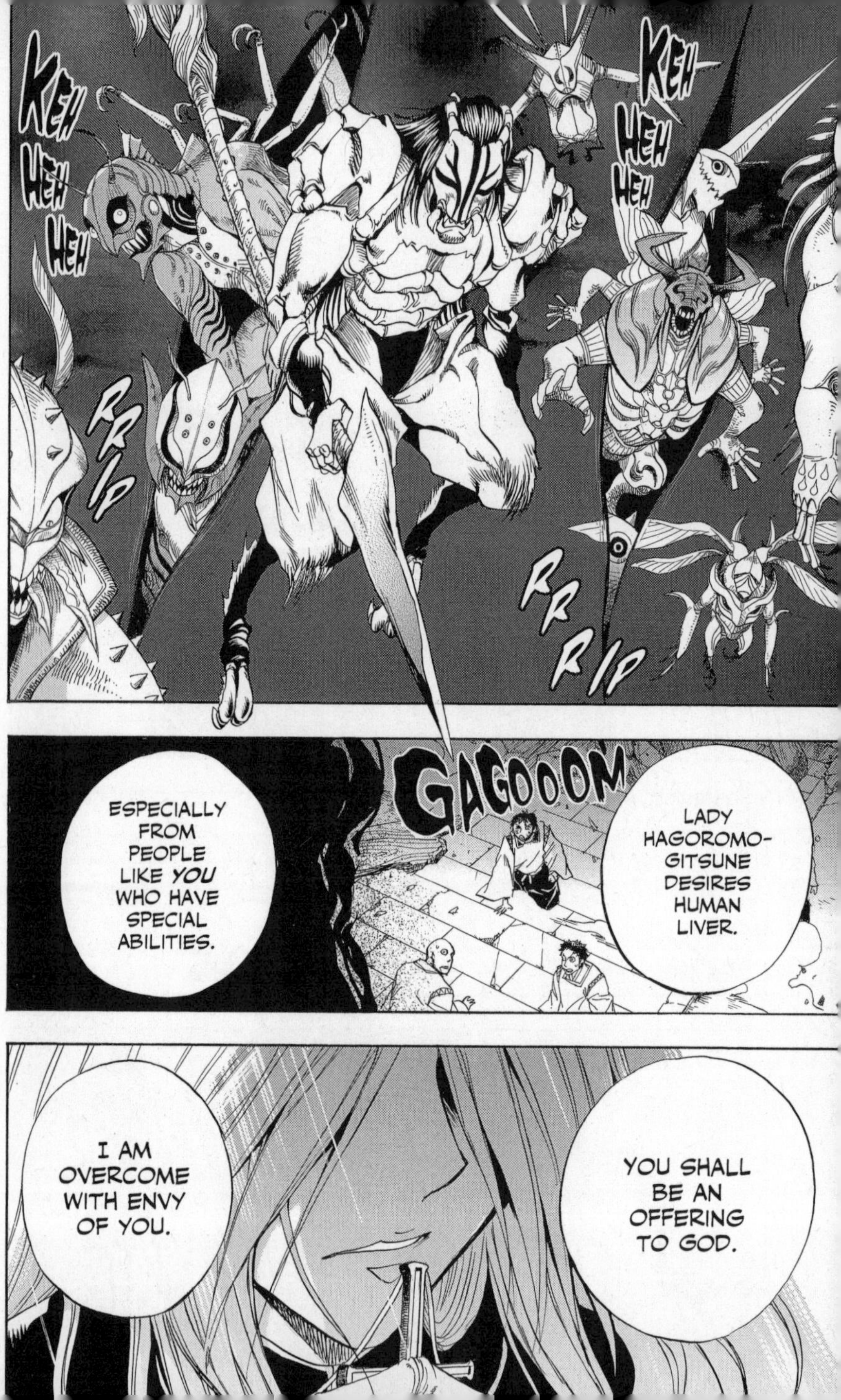
KEH HEH HEH
RRRIP
KEH HEH HEH HEH
RRIP
GAGOOOM
LADY HAGOROMO-GITSUNE DESIRES HUMAN LIVER.
ESPECIALLY FROM PEOPLE LIKE *YOU* WHO HAVE SPECIAL ABILITIES.
YOU SHALL BE AN OFFERING TO GOD.
I AM OVERCOME WITH ENVY OF YOU.

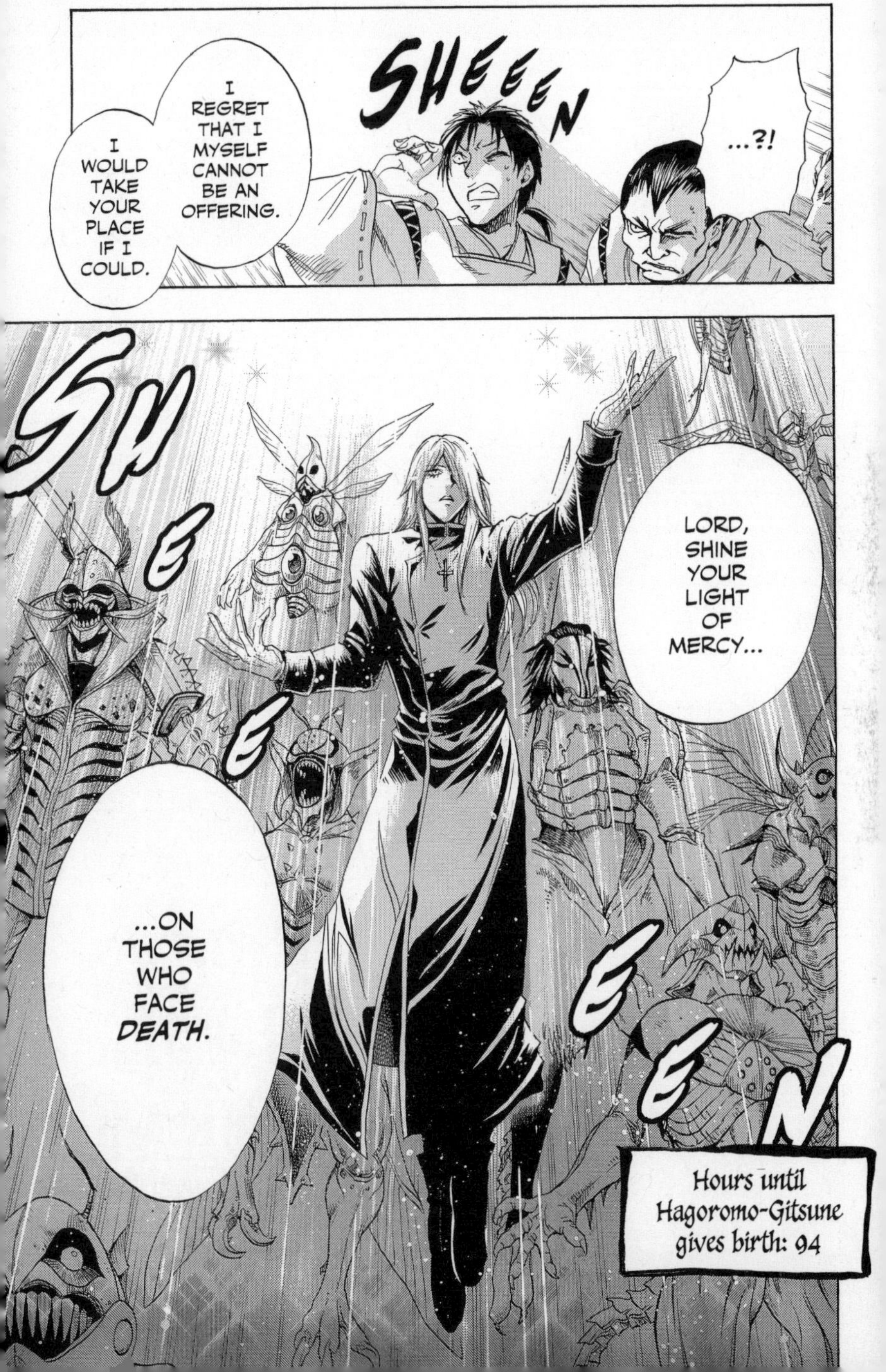
...?!
SHEEEN
I REGRET THAT I MYSELF CANNOT BE AN OFFERING.
I WOULD TAKE YOUR PLACE IF I COULD.
SHEEEEN
LORD, SHINE YOUR LIGHT OF MERCY...
...ON THOSE WHO FACE *DEATH.*
Hours until Hagoromo-Gitsune gives birth: 94

NURA: RISE OF THE YOKAI CLAN

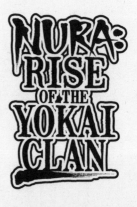

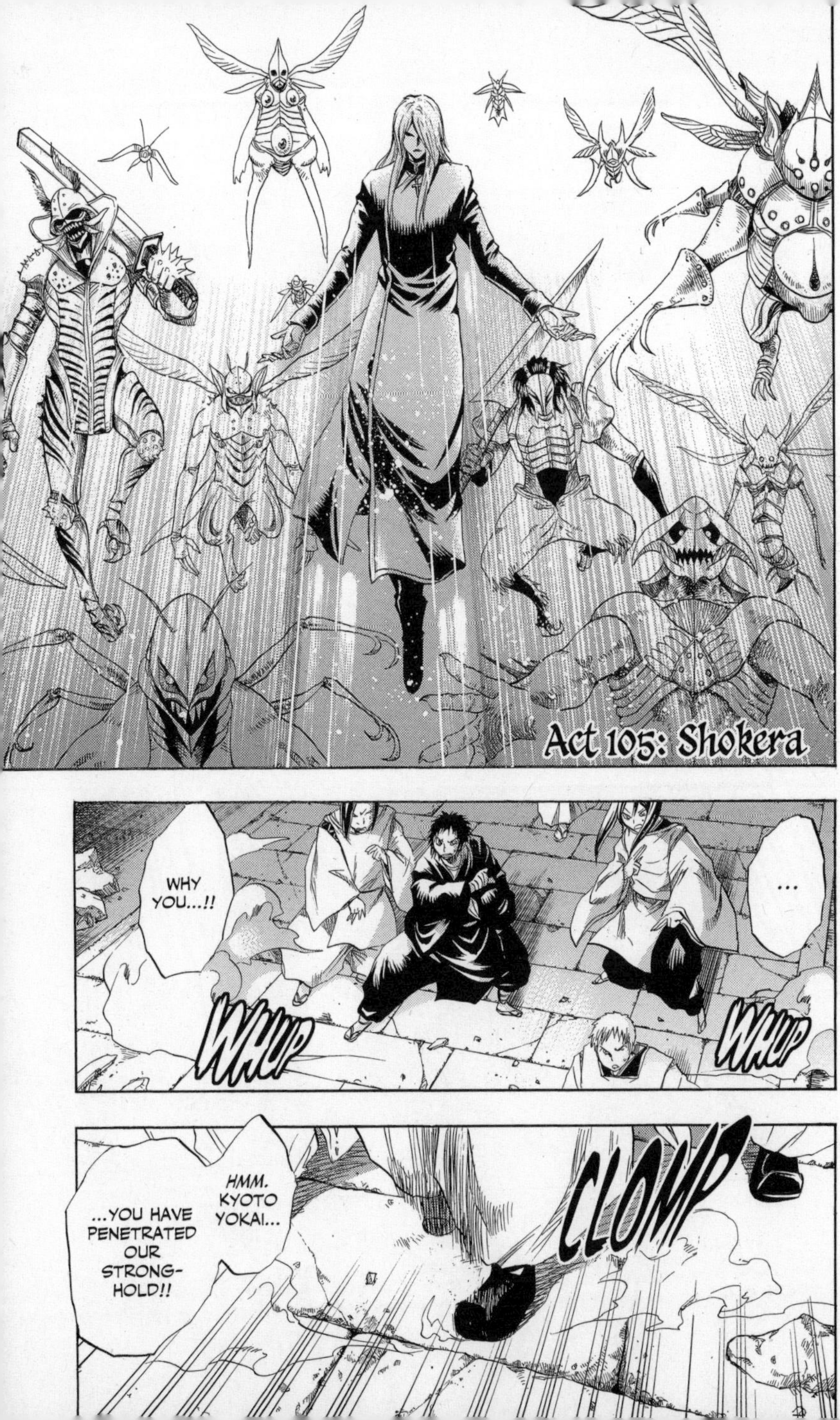
Act 105: Shokera
...
WHUP
WHY YOU...!!
WHUP
CLOMP
HMM. KYOTO YOKAI...
...YOU HAVE PENETRATED OUR STRONGHOLD!!

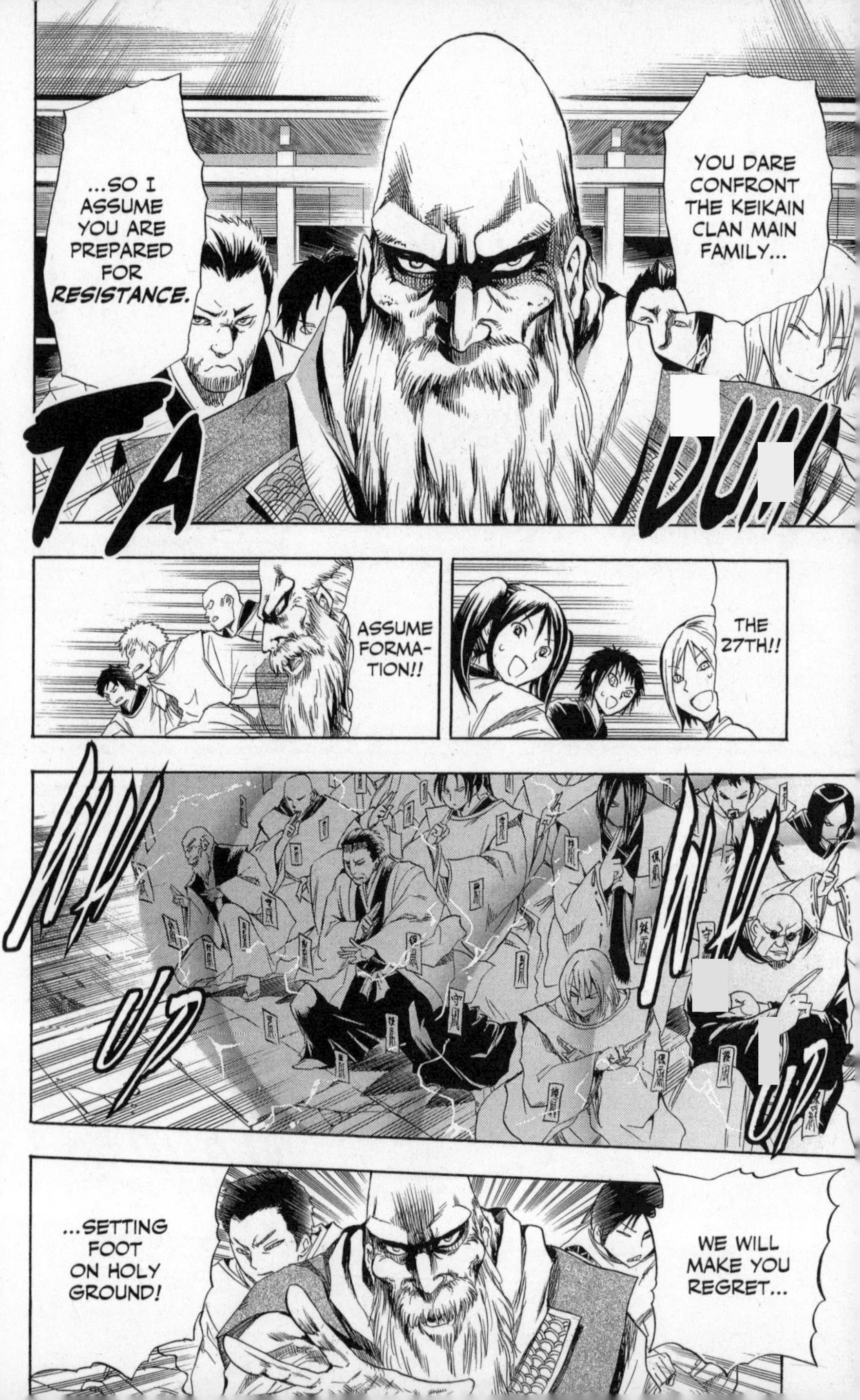
YOU DARE CONFRONT THE KEIKAIN CLAN MAIN FAMILY...
...SO I ASSUME YOU ARE PREPARED FOR RESISTANCE.
TA DUM
THE 27TH!!
ASSUME FORMATION!!
WE WILL MAKE YOU REGRET...
...SETTING FOOT ON HOLY GROUND!

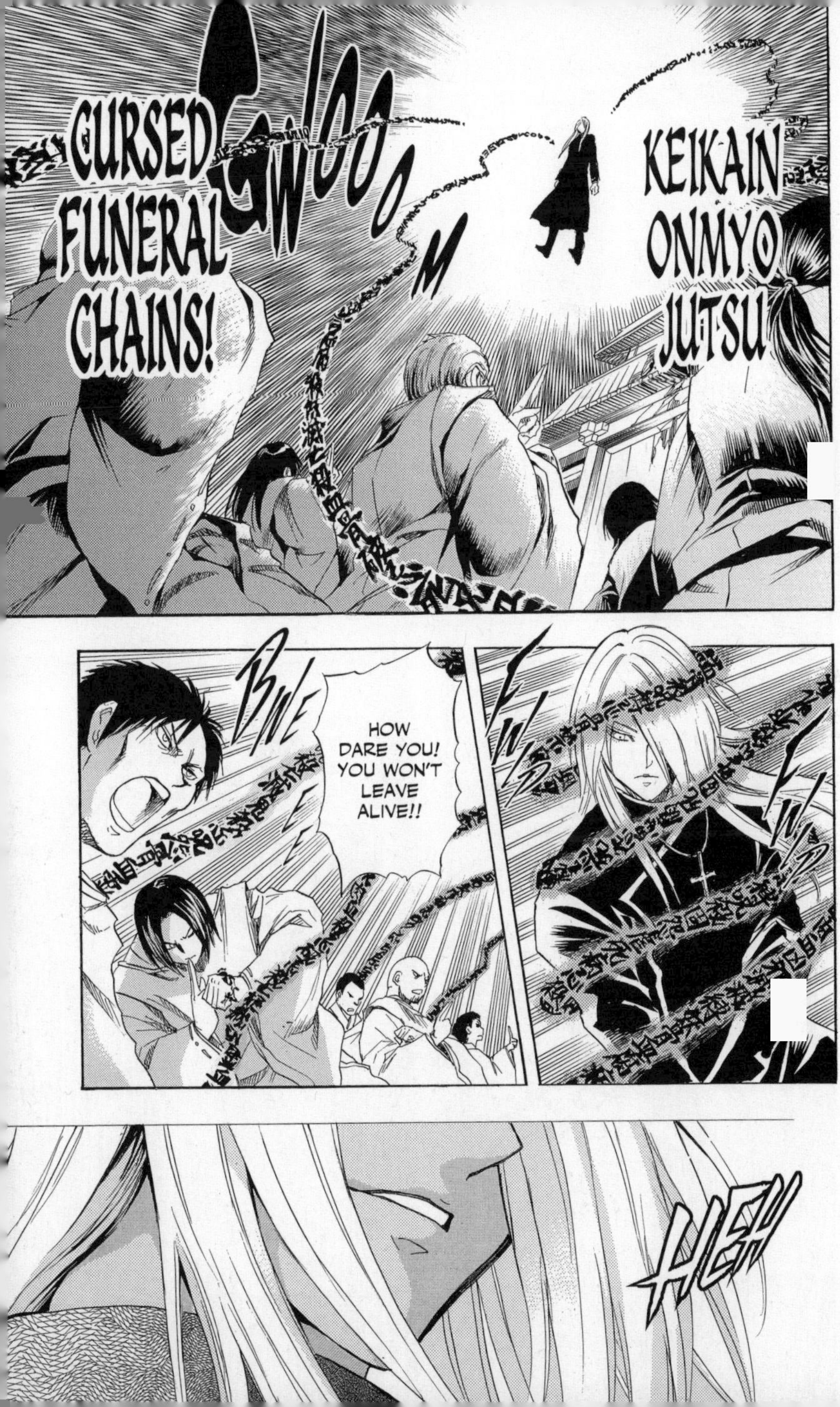
KEIKAIN ONMYO JUTSU
GWOOOOM
CURSED FUNERAL CHAINS!
HOW DARE YOU! YOU WON'T LEAVE ALIVE!!

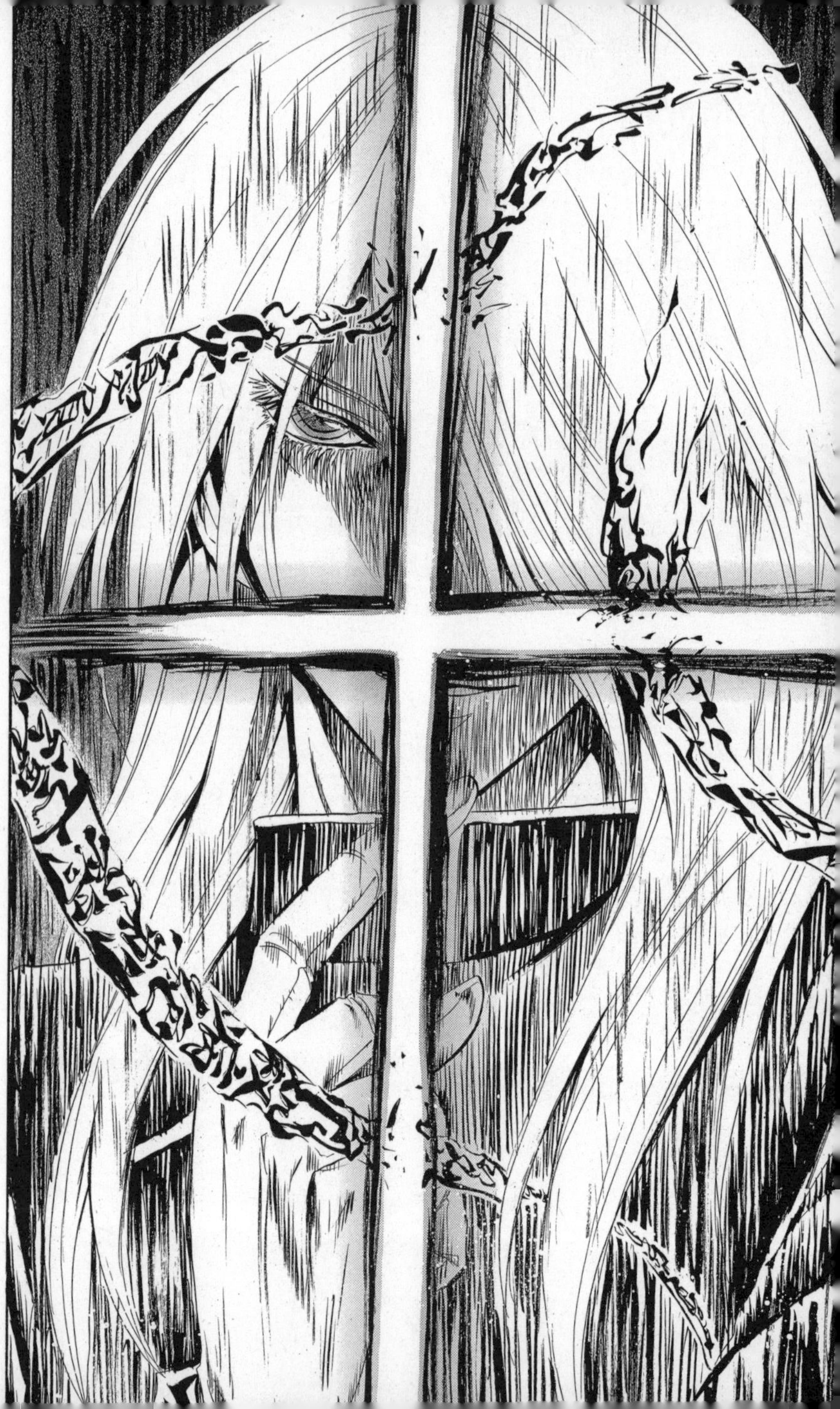

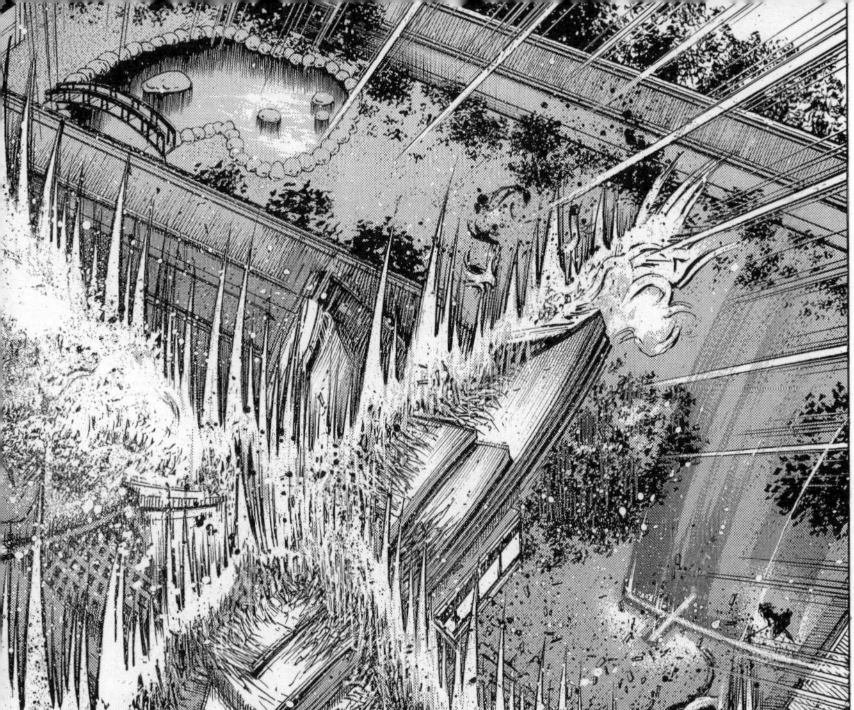

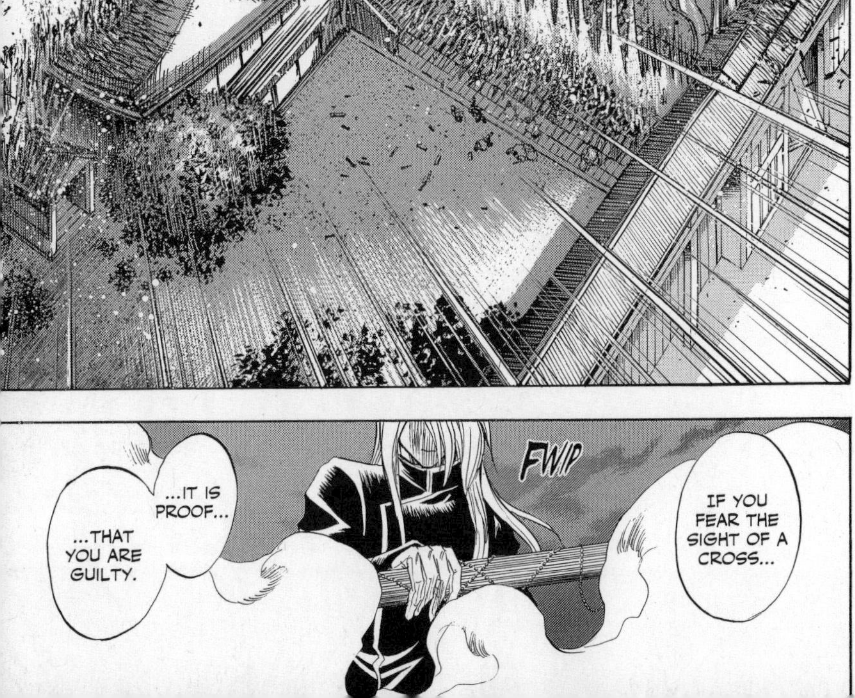
IF YOU FEAR THE SIGHT OF A CROSS...
FWIP
...IT IS PROOF...
...THAT YOU ARE GUILTY.

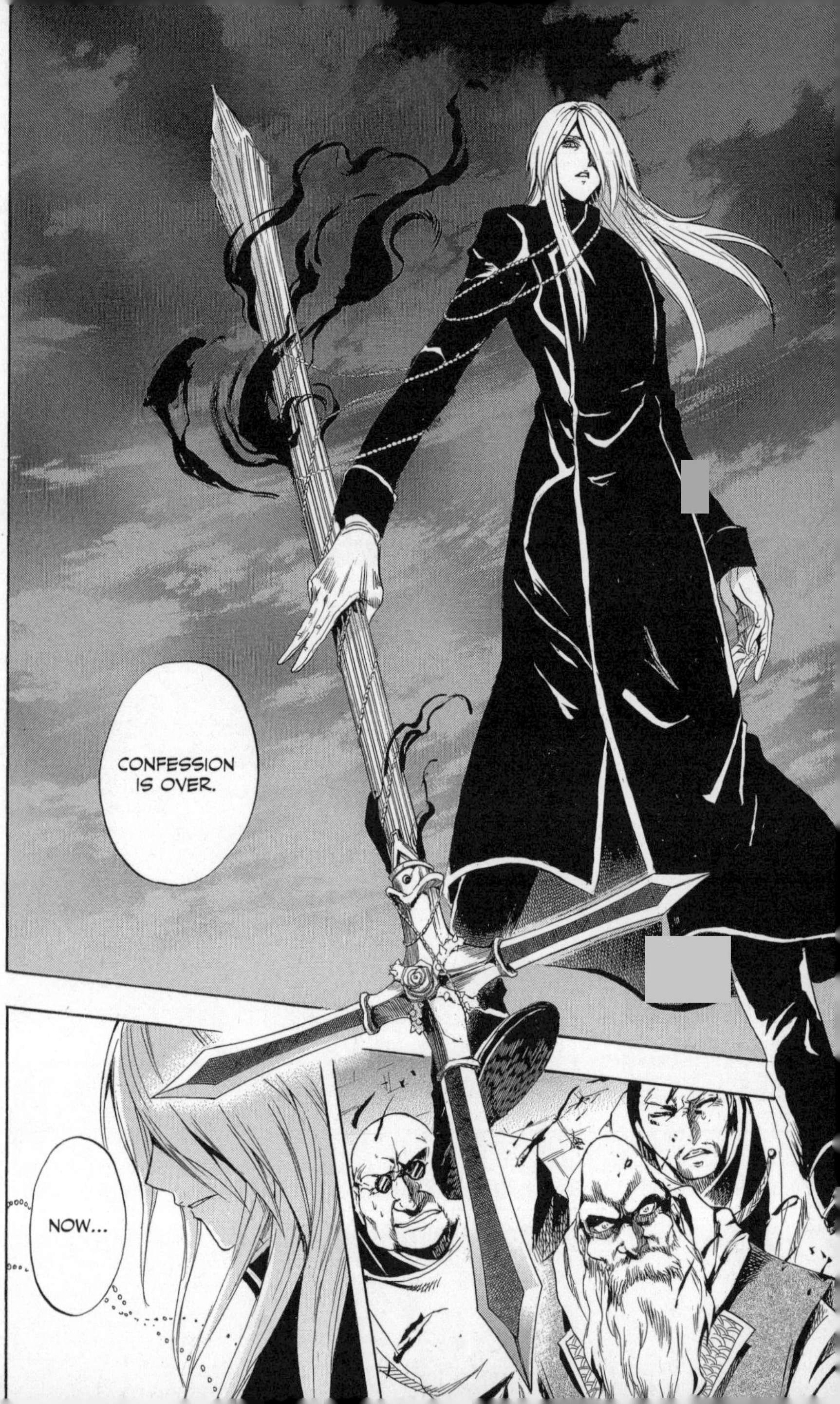
CONFESSION IS OVER.
NOW...

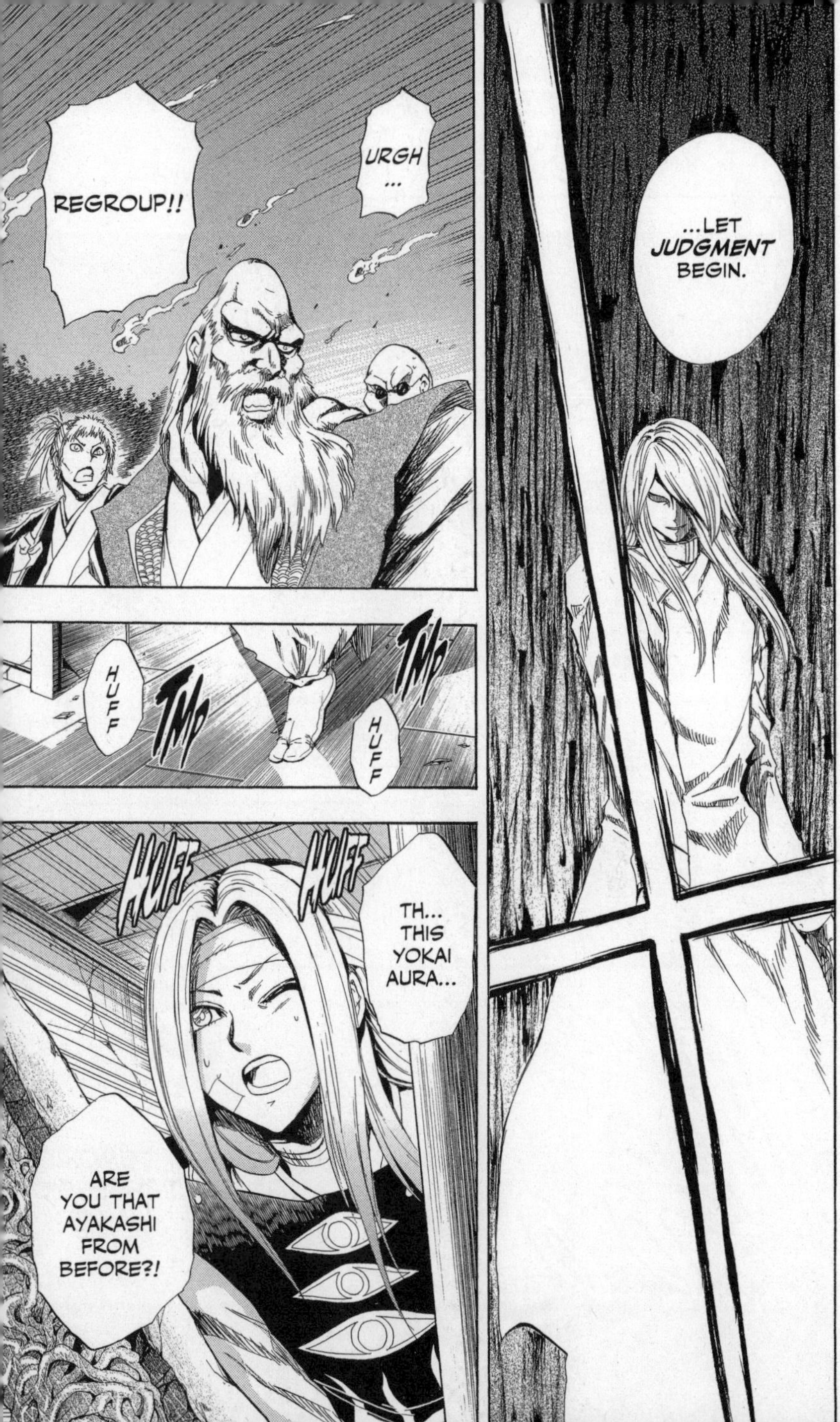
...LET JUDGMENT BEGIN.
URGH ...
REGROUP!!
TMP
HUFF
HUFF
TMP
HUFF
HUFF
TH... THIS YOKAI AURA...
ARE YOU THAT AYAKASHI FROM BEFORE?!

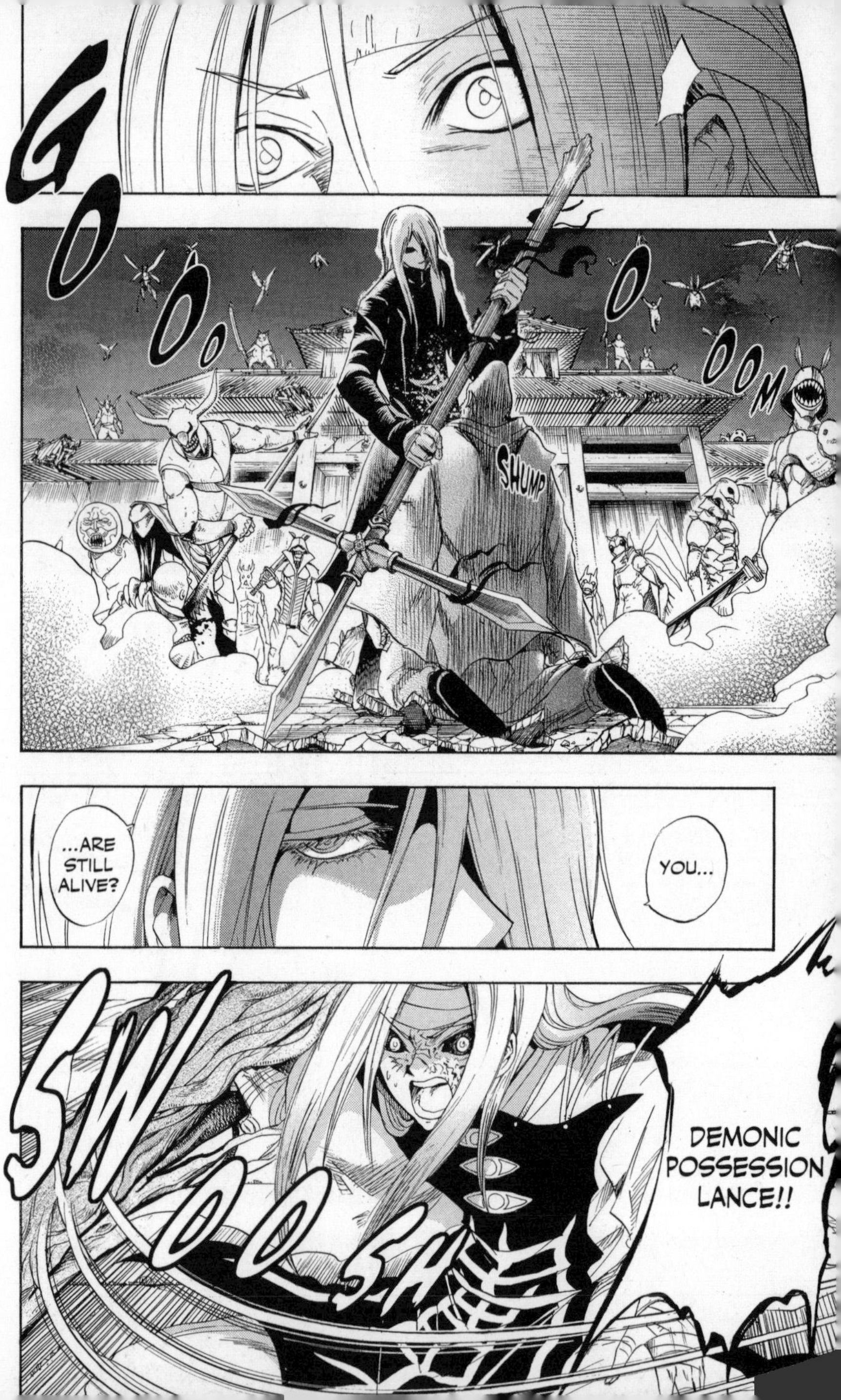
GOOOOOOM
SHUMP
YOU...
...ARE STILL ALIVE?
SWOOOSH
DEMONIC POSSESSION LANCE!!

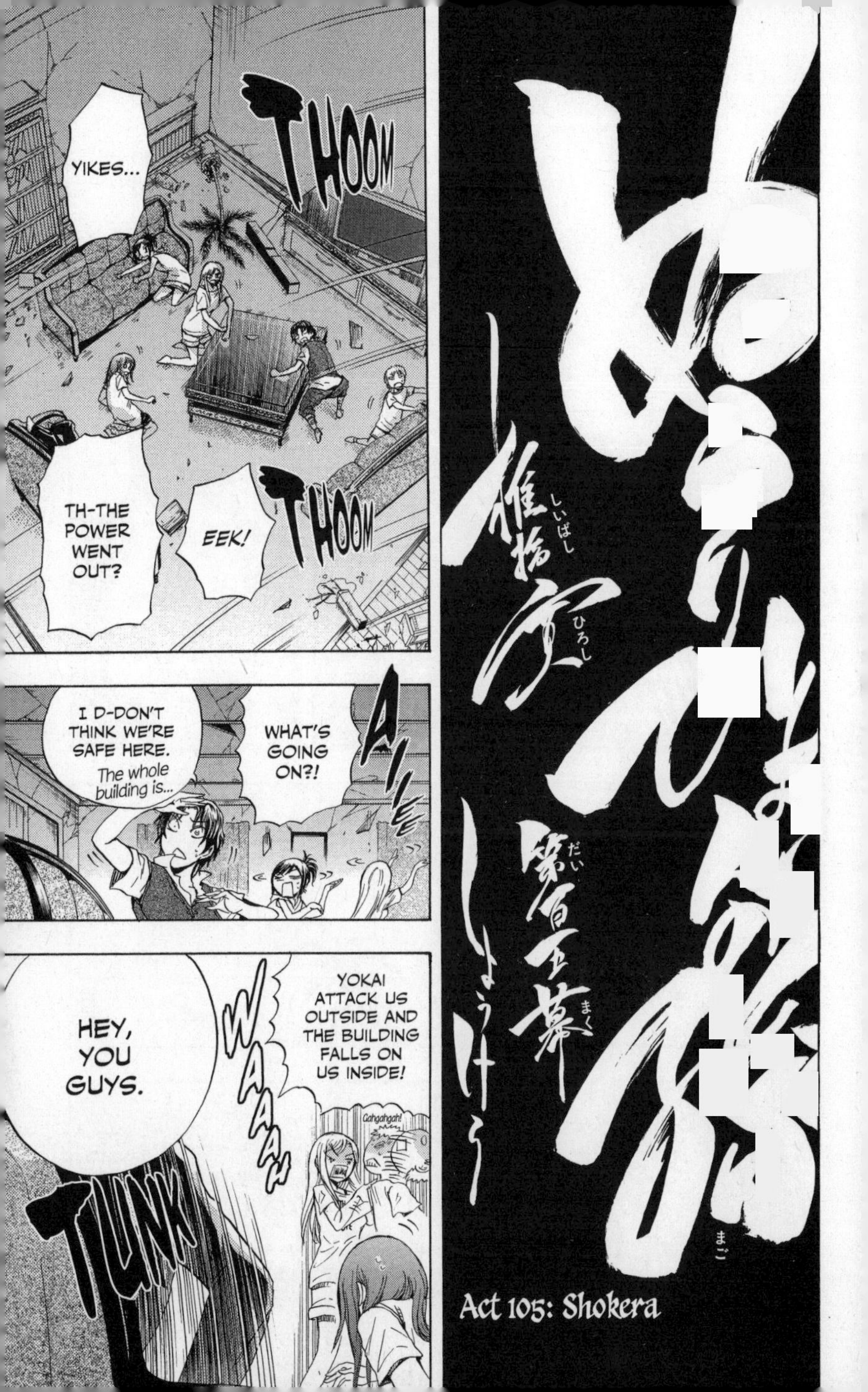

椎橋寛
しいばし ひろし
第百五幕
だい まく
しょうけら
まご
Act 105: Shokera
THOOM
YIKES...
THOOM
EEK!
TH-THE POWER WENT OUT?
AIIEE
WHAT'S GOING ON?!
I D-DON'T THINK WE'RE SAFE HERE.
The whole building is...
YOKAI ATTACK US OUTSIDE AND THE BUILDING FALLS ON US INSIDE!
WAAAAH
Gahgahgah!
HEY, YOU GUYS.
TUNK

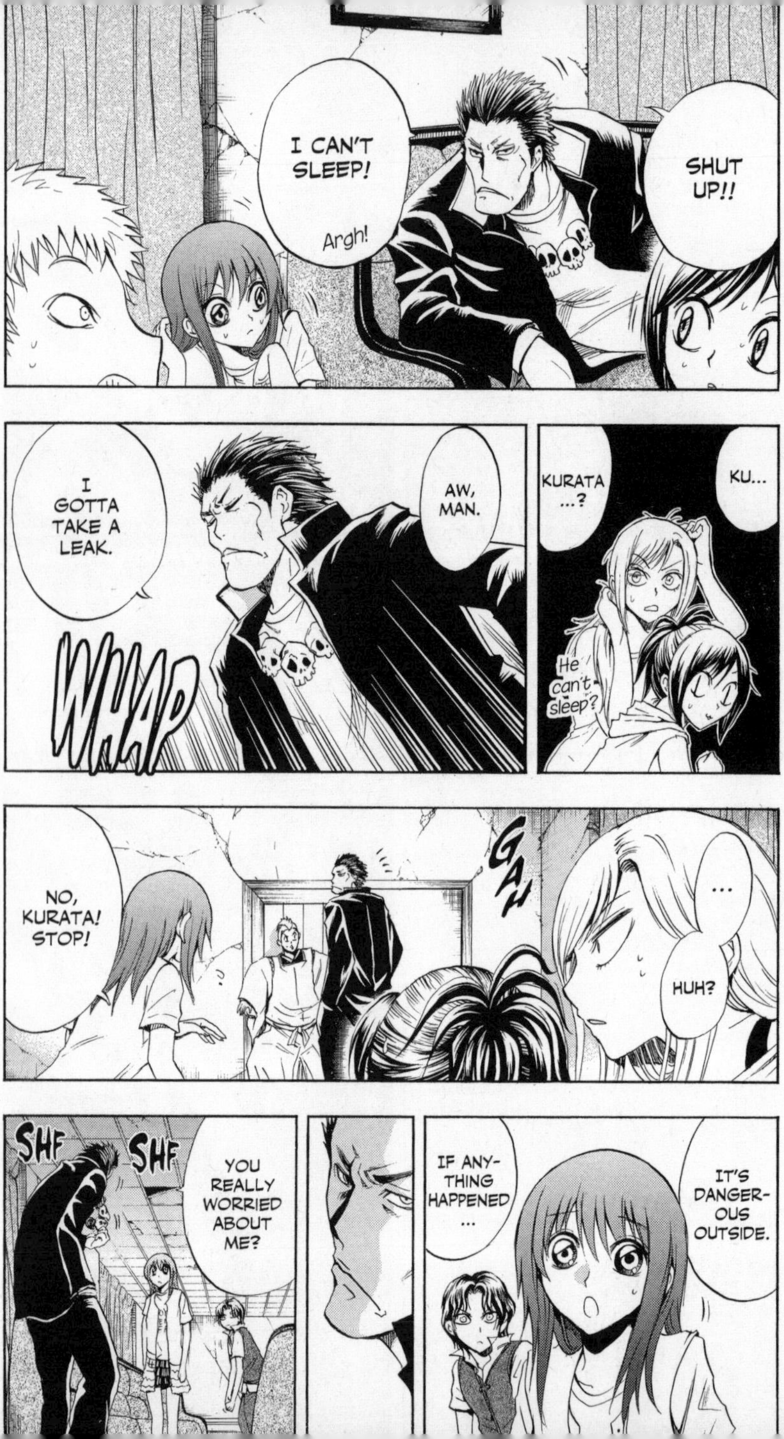
I CAN'T SLEEP!
Argh!
SHUT UP!!
KU...
KURATA ...?
He can't sleep?
AW, MAN.
I GOTTA TAKE A LEAK.
WHAP
...
HUH?
GAH
NO, KURATA! STOP!
IT'S DANGER-OUS OUTSIDE.
IF ANY-THING HAPPENED ...
YOU REALLY WORRIED ABOUT ME?
SHF
SHF

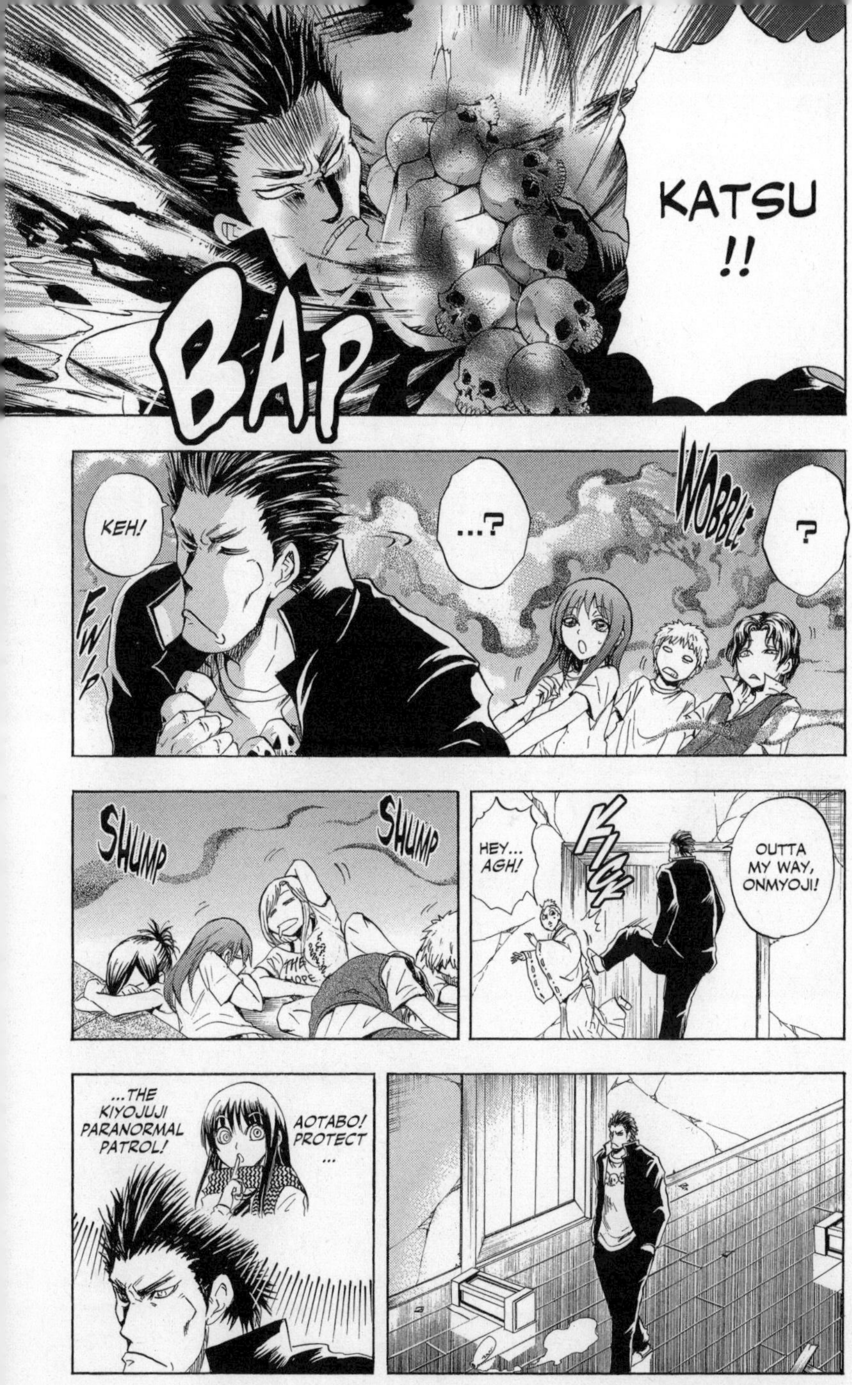
KATSU !!
BAP
?
WOBBLE
...?
KEH!
FWIP
OUTTA MY WAY, ONMYOJI!
KICK
HEY... AGH!
SHUMP
SHUMP
AOTABO! PROTECT ...
...THE KIYOJUJI PARANORMAL PATROL!

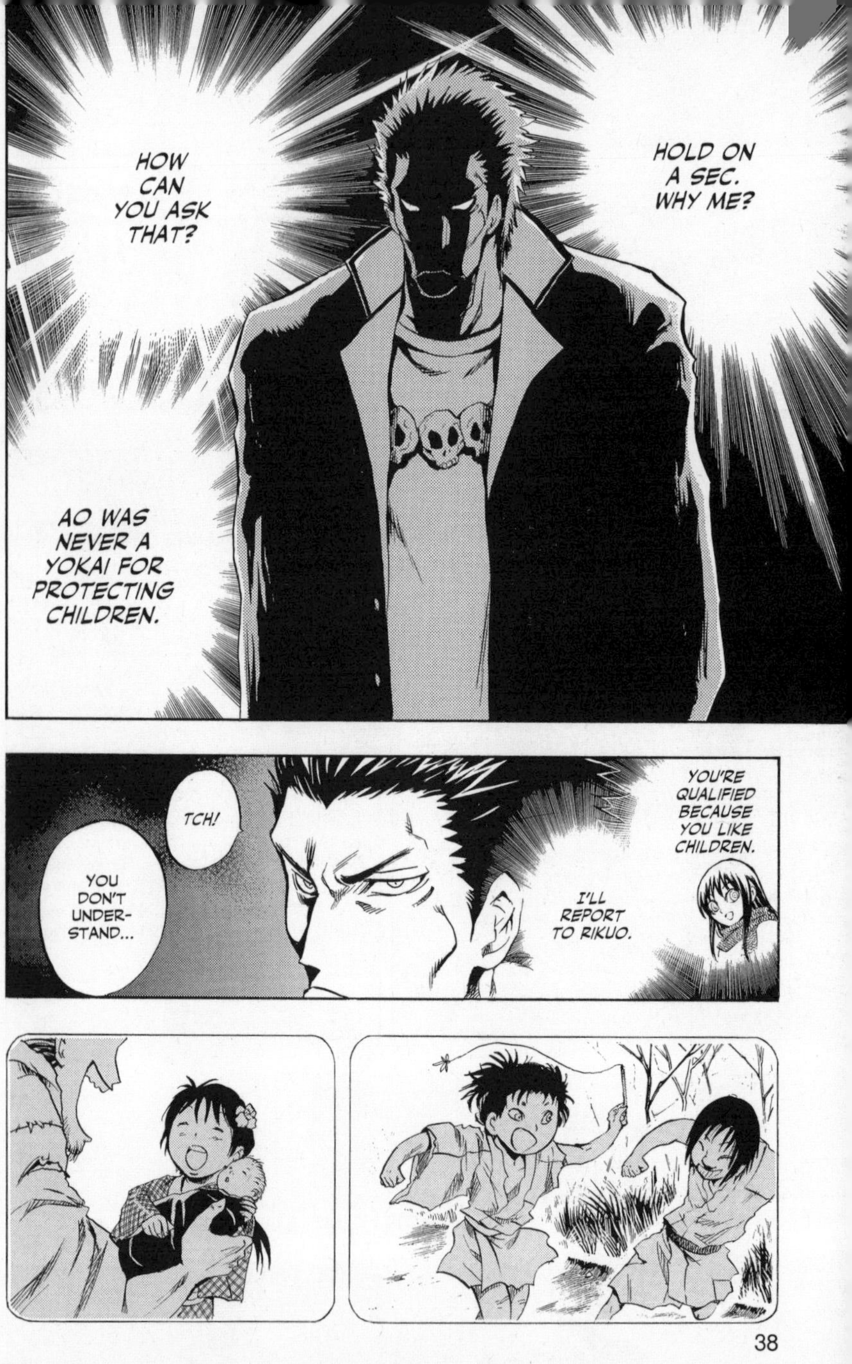
HOLD ON A SEC. WHY ME?
HOW CAN YOU ASK THAT?
AO WAS NEVER A YOKAI FOR PROTECTING CHILDREN.
YOU'RE QUALIFIED BECAUSE YOU LIKE CHILDREN.
I'LL REPORT TO RIKUO.
TCH!
YOU DON'T UNDER-STAND...

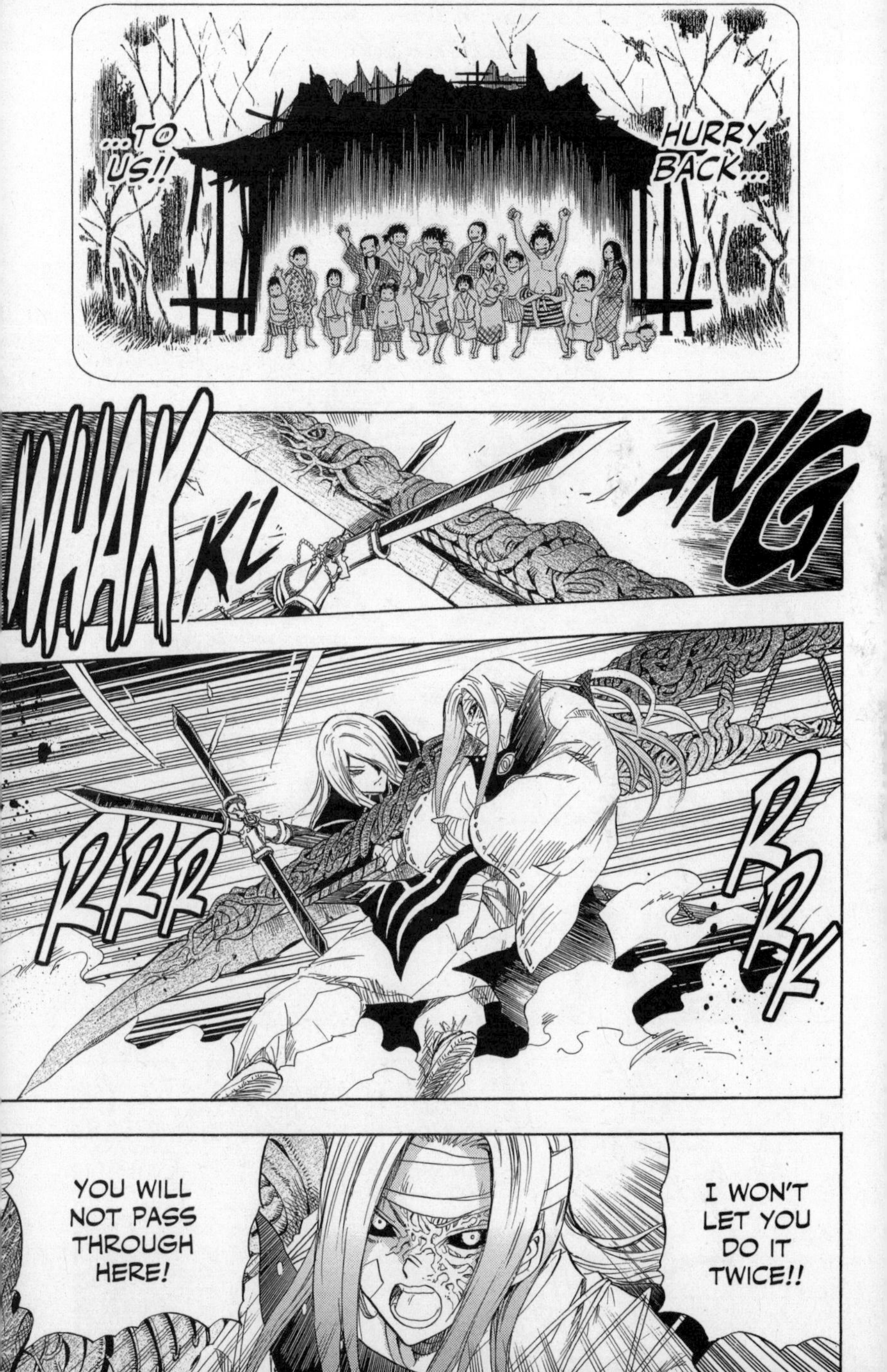
HURRY BACK...
...TO US!!
WHAK
KL
ANG
RRRK
RRR
I WON'T LET YOU DO IT TWICE!!
YOU WILL NOT PASS THROUGH HERE!

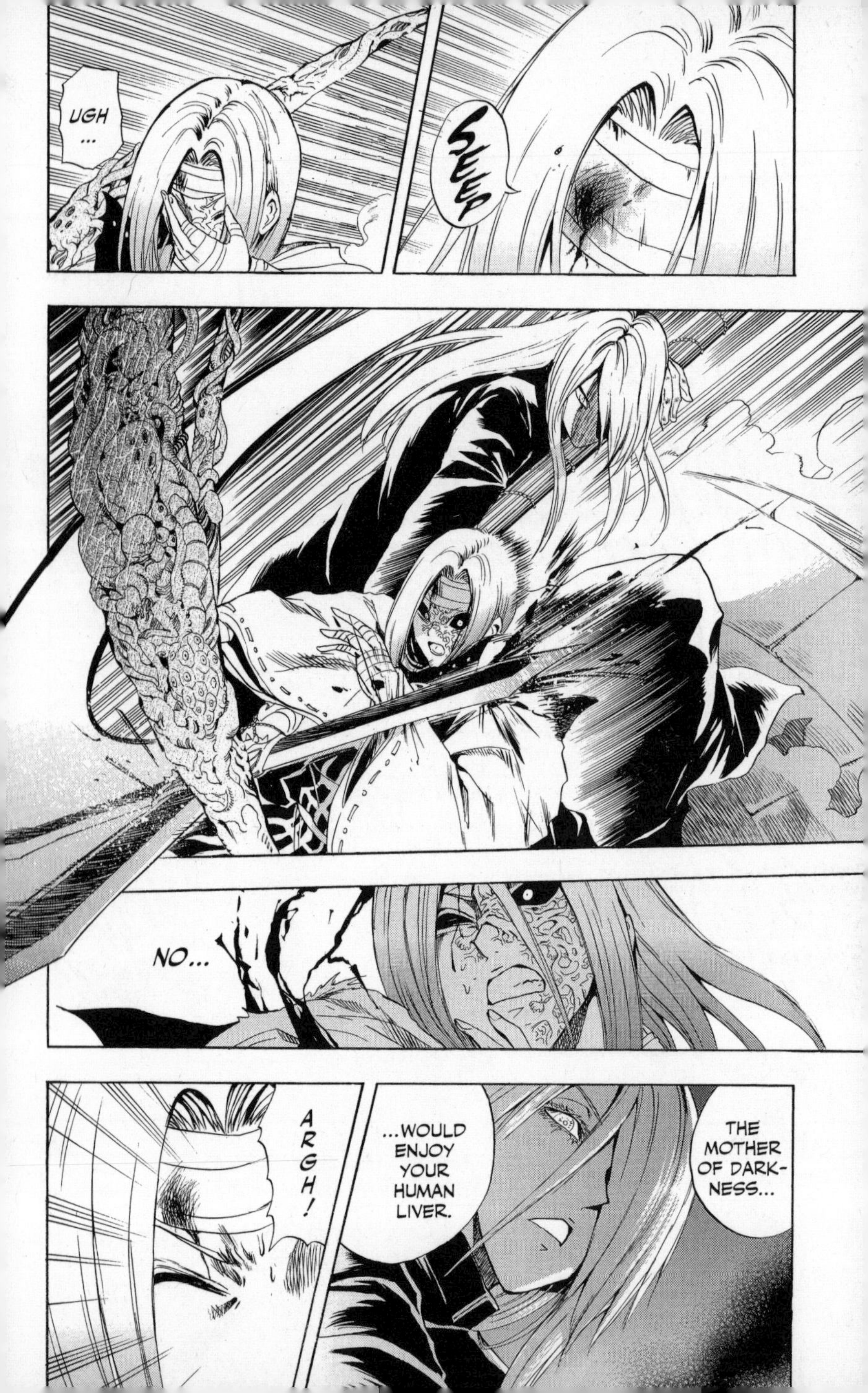
SEEP
UGH ...
NO...
THE MOTHER OF DARK-NESS...
...WOULD ENJOY YOUR HUMAN LIVER.
ARGH!

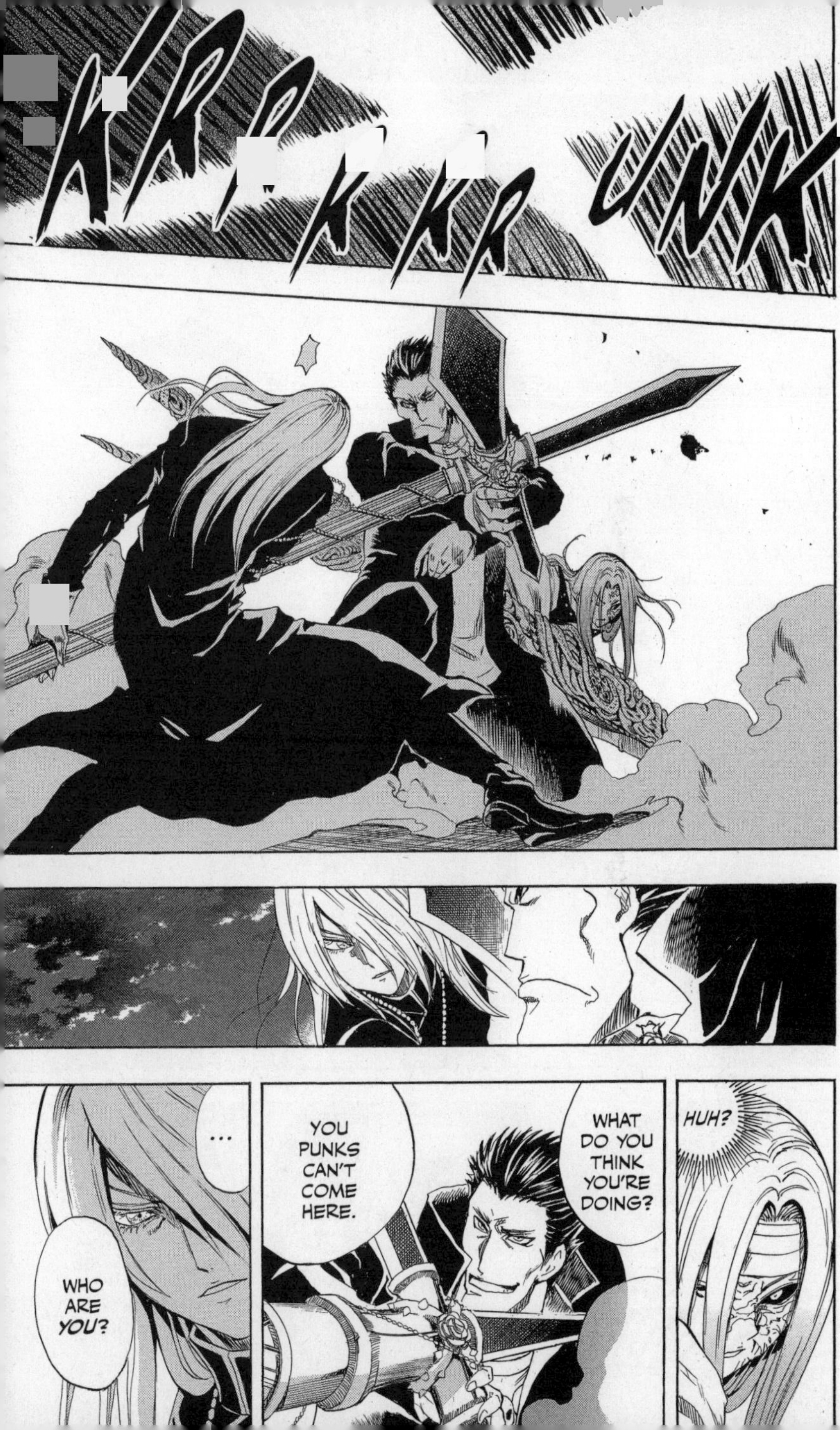
HUH?
WHAT DO YOU THINK YOU'RE DOING?
YOU PUNKS CAN'T COME HERE.
...
WHO ARE *YOU*?

HUMANS AND AYAKASHI EACH HAVE THEIR OWN DOMAIN.
I DON'T LIKE NEEDLESSLY TAKING LIFE.
YOU SEEM LIKE A YOKAI...
...SO HOW CAN YOU SAY THAT?
FUMP
YOU!
FUMP
STAY OUT OF THIS!
FUMP

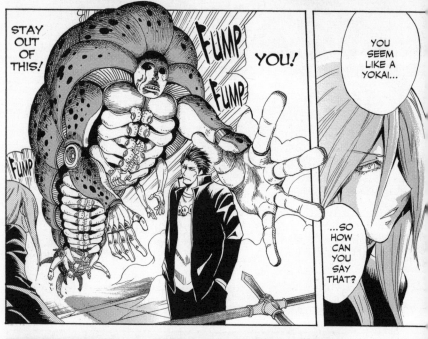

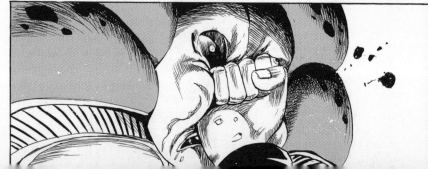

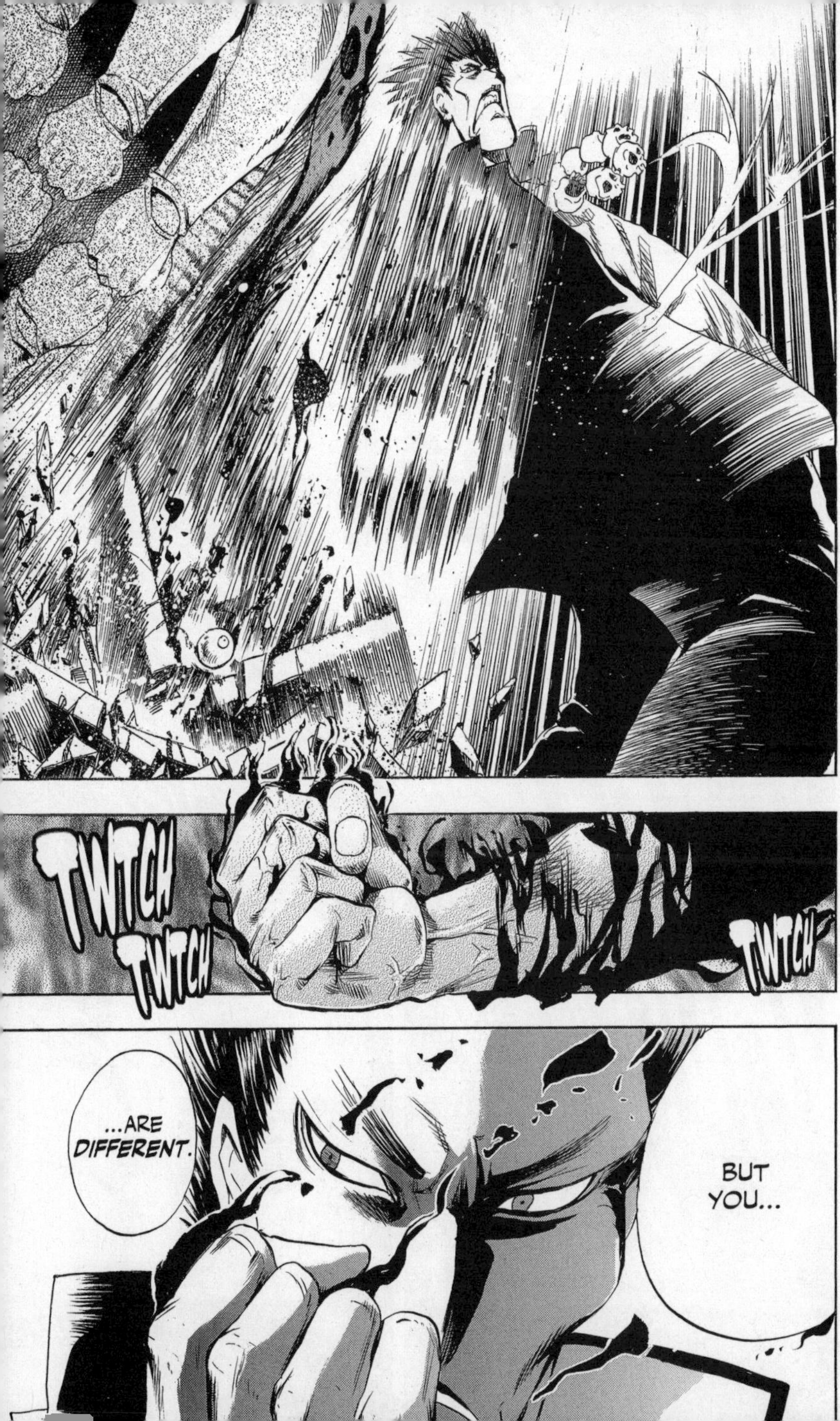
TWTCH
TWTCH TWTCH
BUT YOU...
...ARE DIFFERENT.

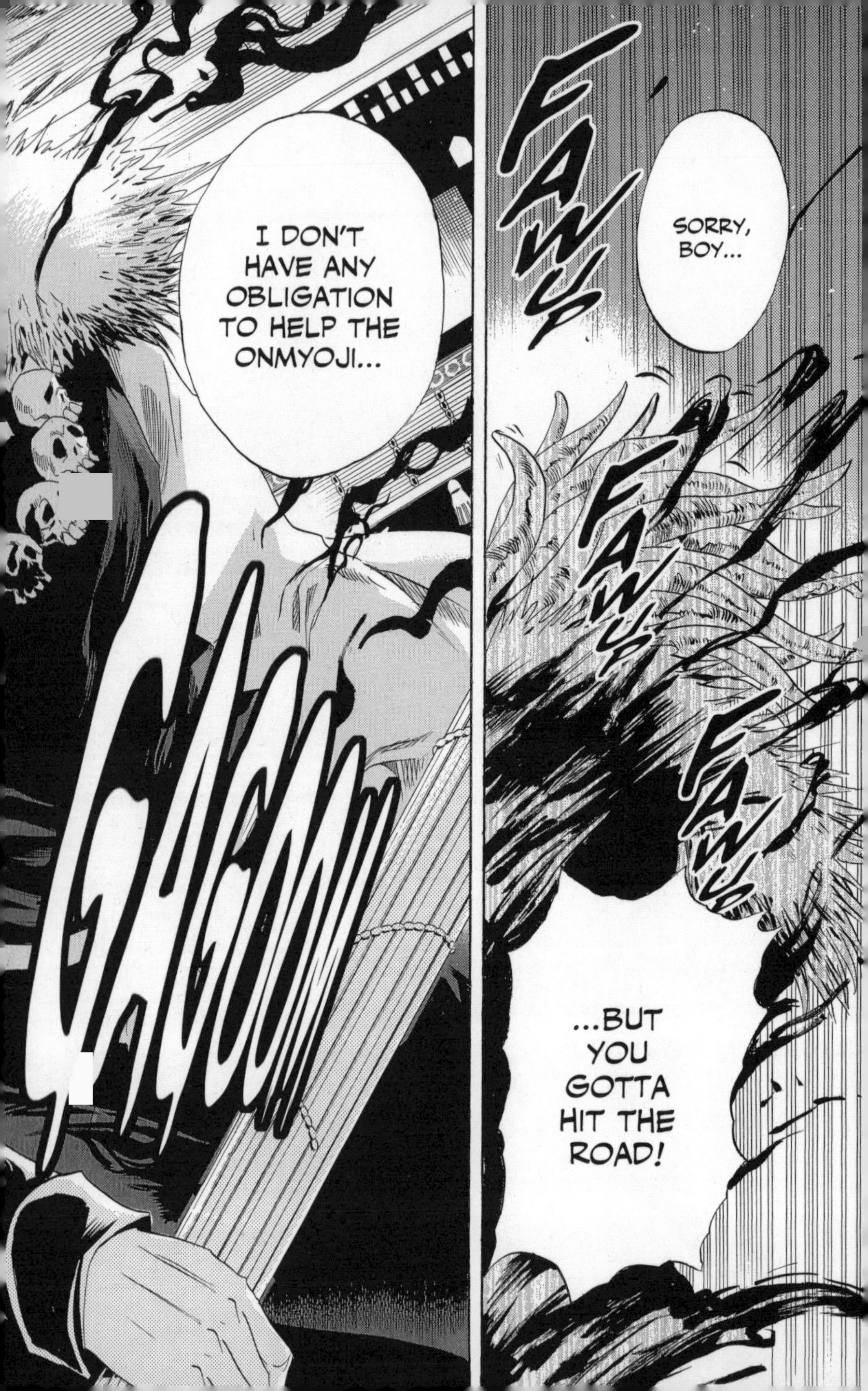
SORRY, BOY...
FAWUP
FAWUP
FAWUP
FAWUP
...BUT YOU GOTTA HIT THE ROAD!
I DON'T HAVE ANY OBLIGATION TO HELP THE ONMYOJI...

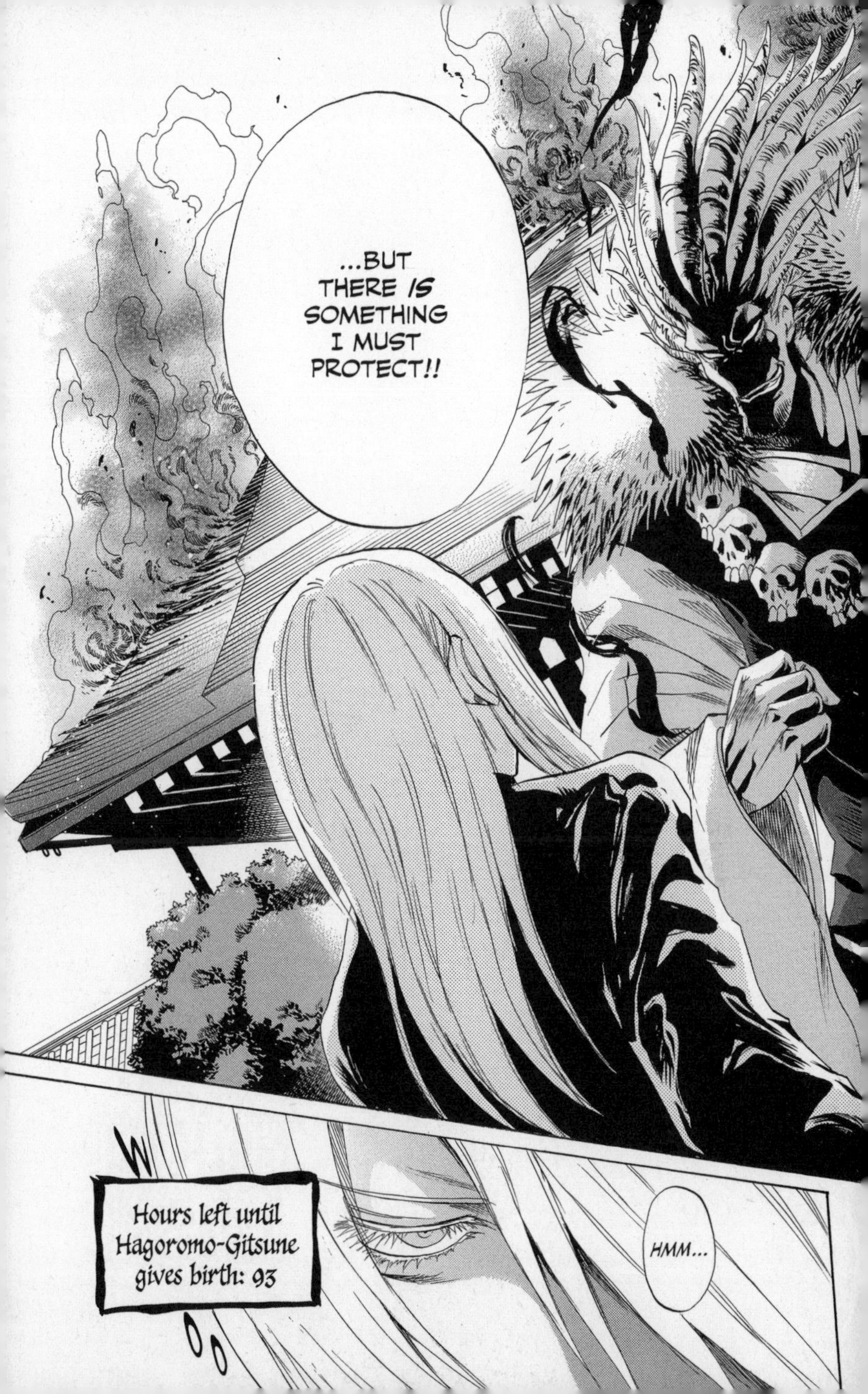
...BUT THERE IS SOMETHING I MUST PROTECT!!
HMM...
Hours left until Hagoromo-Gitsune gives birth: 93

NURA: RISE OF THE YOKAI CLAN

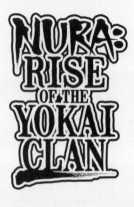

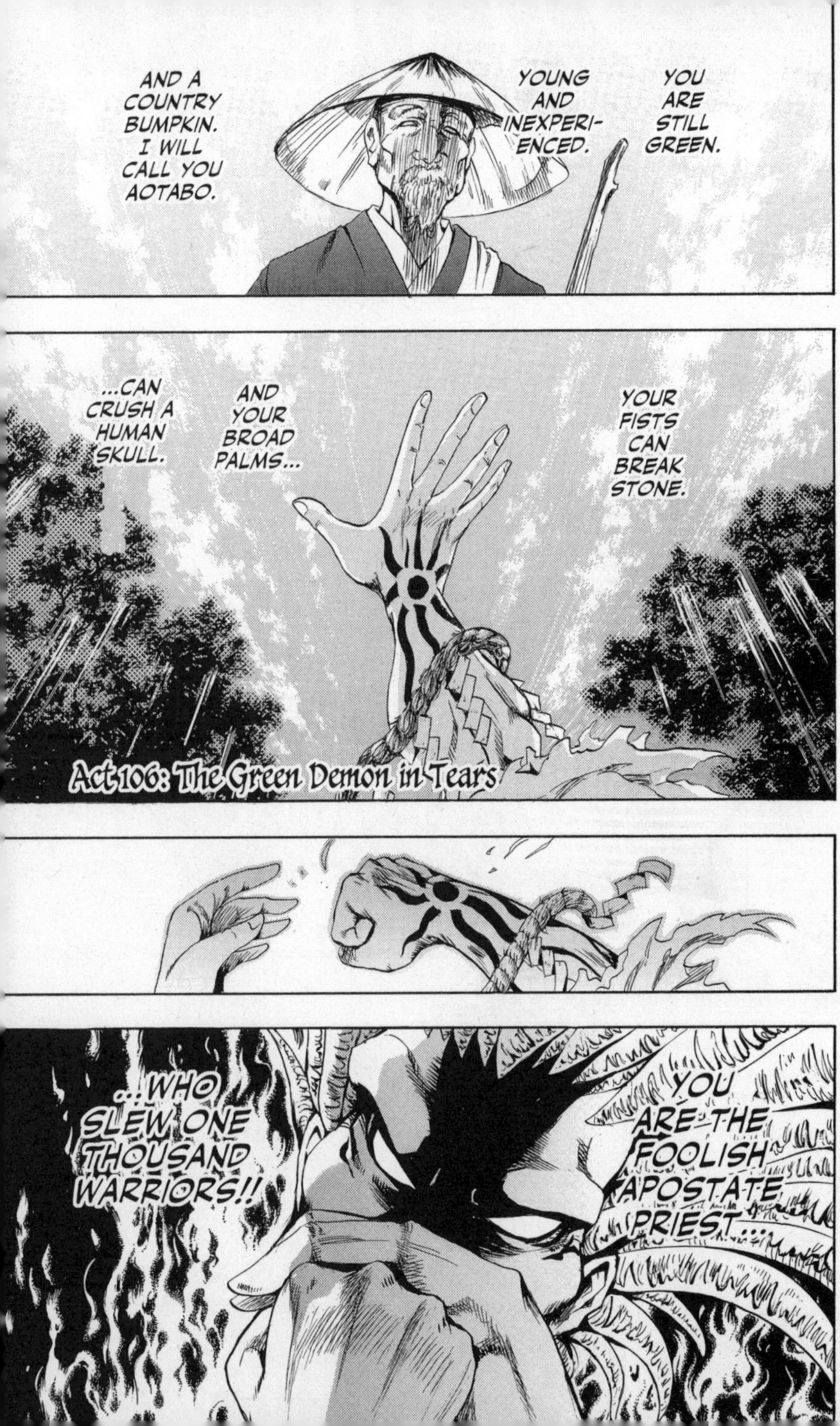
YOU ARE STILL GREEN.
YOUNG AND INEXPERIENCED.
AND A COUNTRY BUMPKIN. I WILL CALL YOU AOTABO.
YOUR FISTS CAN BREAK STONE.
AND YOUR BROAD PALMS...
...CAN CRUSH A HUMAN SKULL.
Act 106: The Green Demon in Tears
YOU ARE THE FOOLISH APOSTATE PRIEST...
...WHO SLEW ONE THOUSAND WARRIORS!!

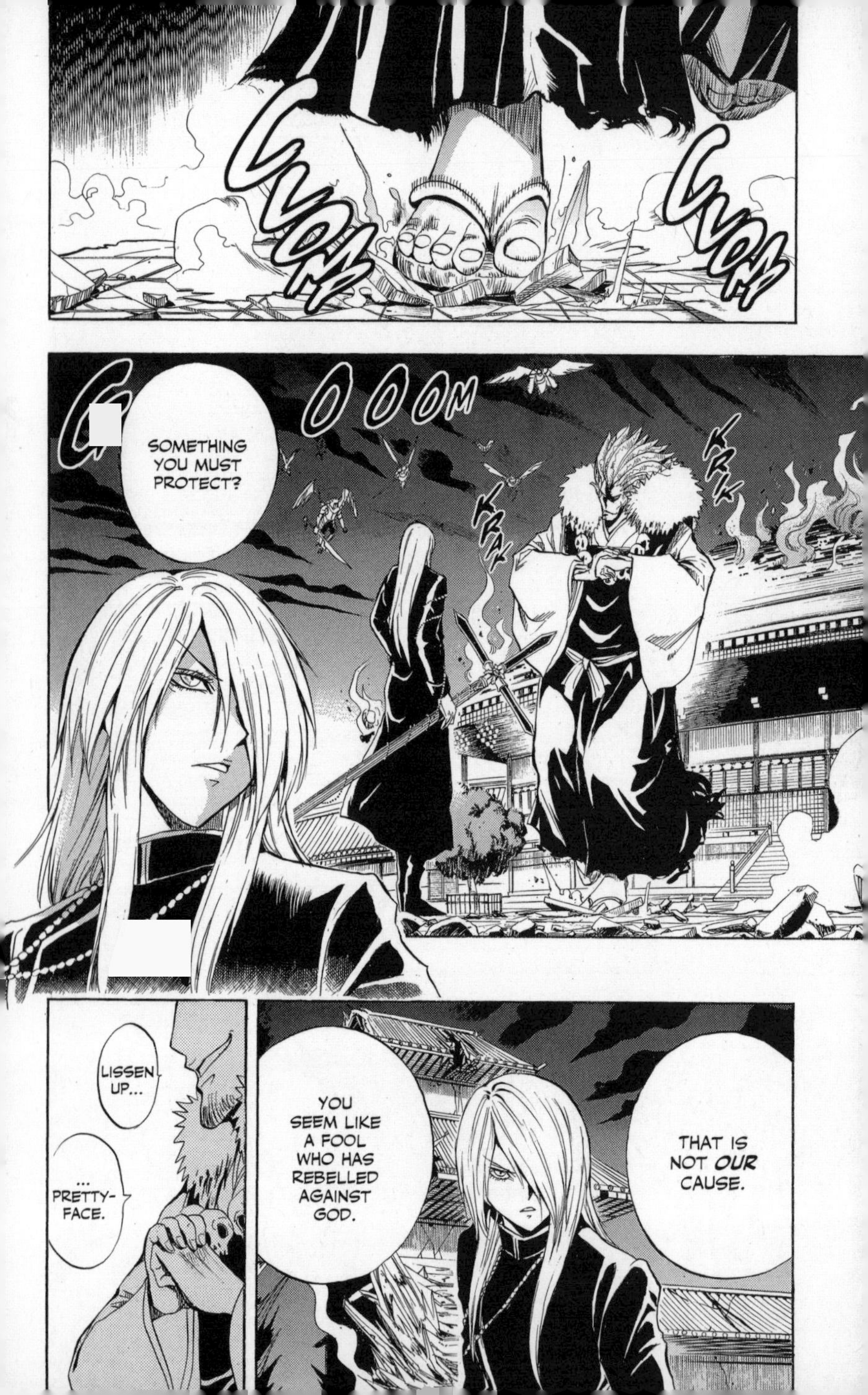
VVOM
VVOM
GOOOM
SOMETHING YOU MUST PROTECT?
KRAK
KRAK
THAT IS NOT *OUR* CAUSE.
YOU SEEM LIKE A FOOL WHO HAS REBELLED AGAINST GOD.
LISSEN UP...
...PRETTY-FACE.

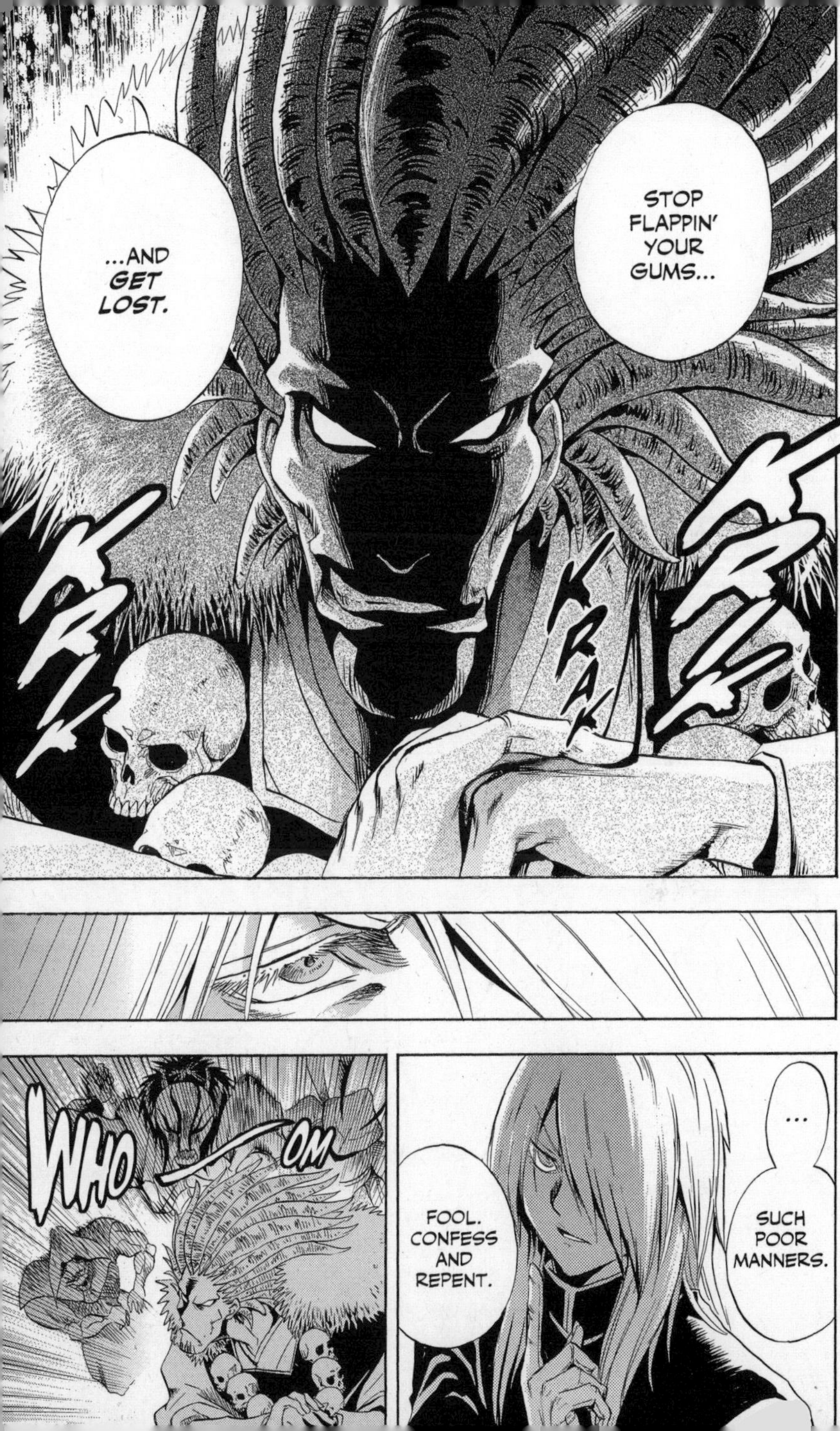
STOP FLAPPIN' YOUR GUMS...
...AND GET LOST.
KRAK
...
SUCH POOR MANNERS.
FOOL. CONFESS AND REPENT.
WHO—OM

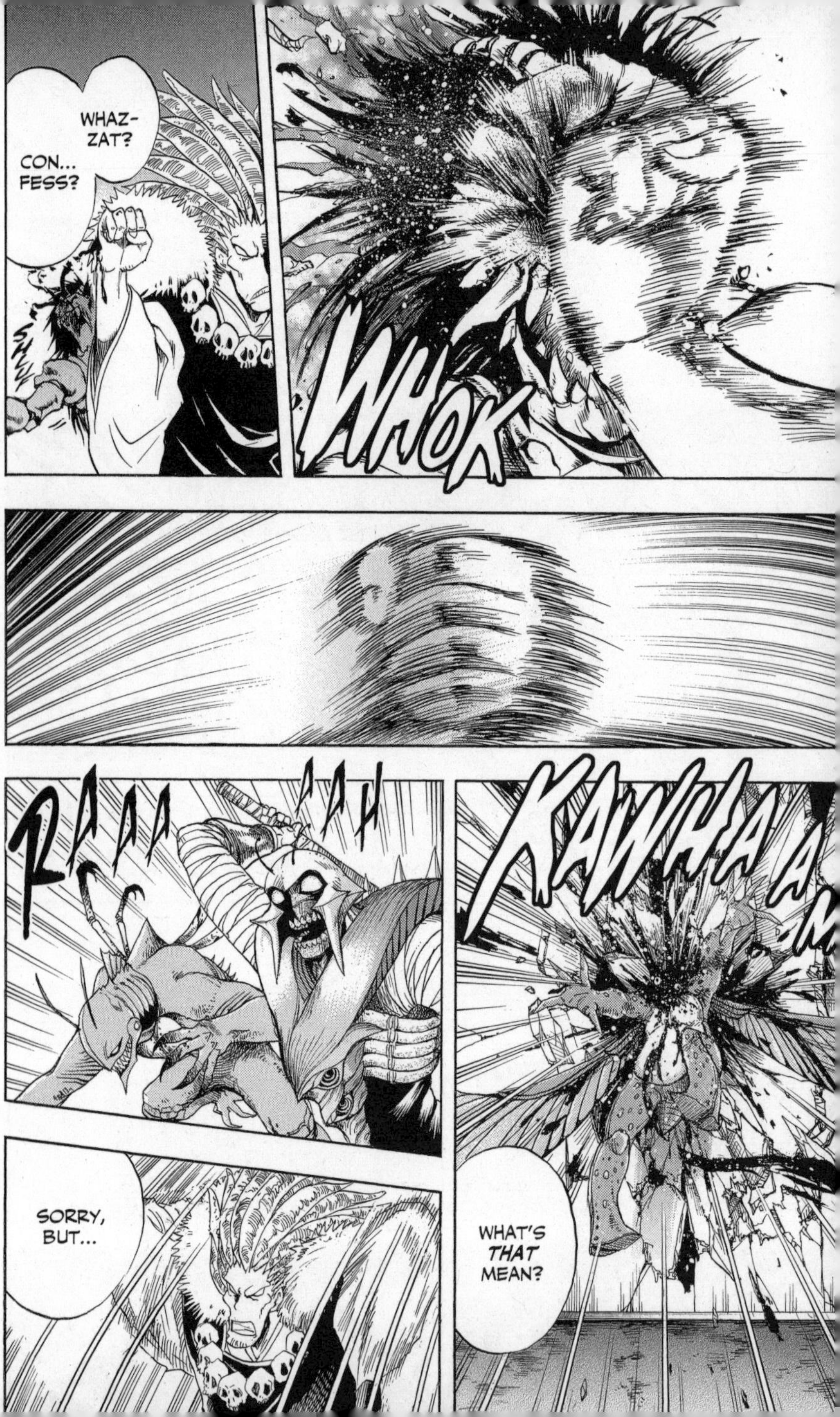
WHOK
WHAZ-ZAT? CON... FESS?
KAWHAAAM
RAAAAAH
WHAT'S *THAT* MEAN?
SORRY, BUT...

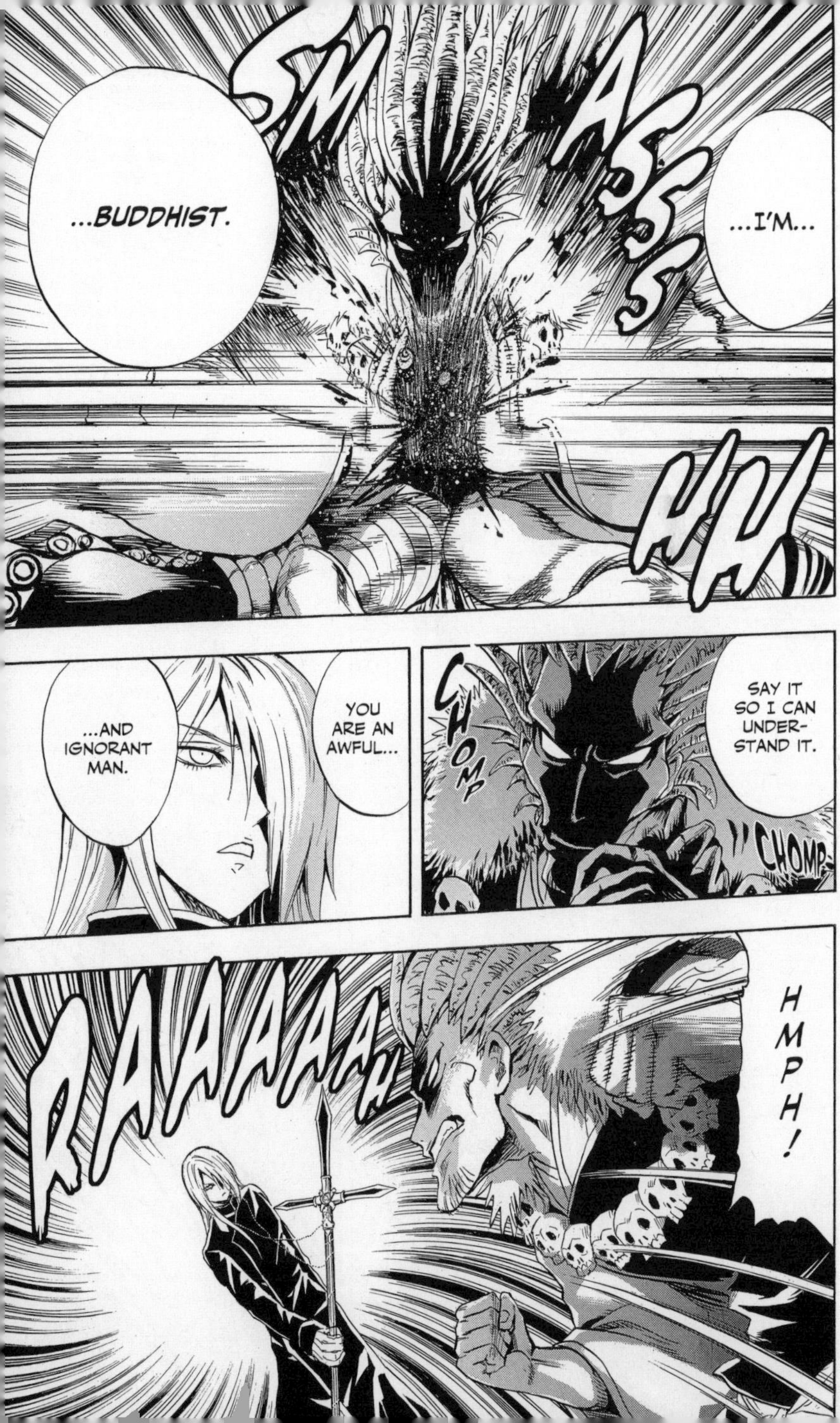
...I'M...
...BUDDHIST.
SMASSSSHH
SAY IT SO I CAN UNDER-STAND IT.
CHOMP
CHOMP
YOU ARE AN AWFUL...
...AND IGNORANT MAN.
HMPH!
RAAAAAAH

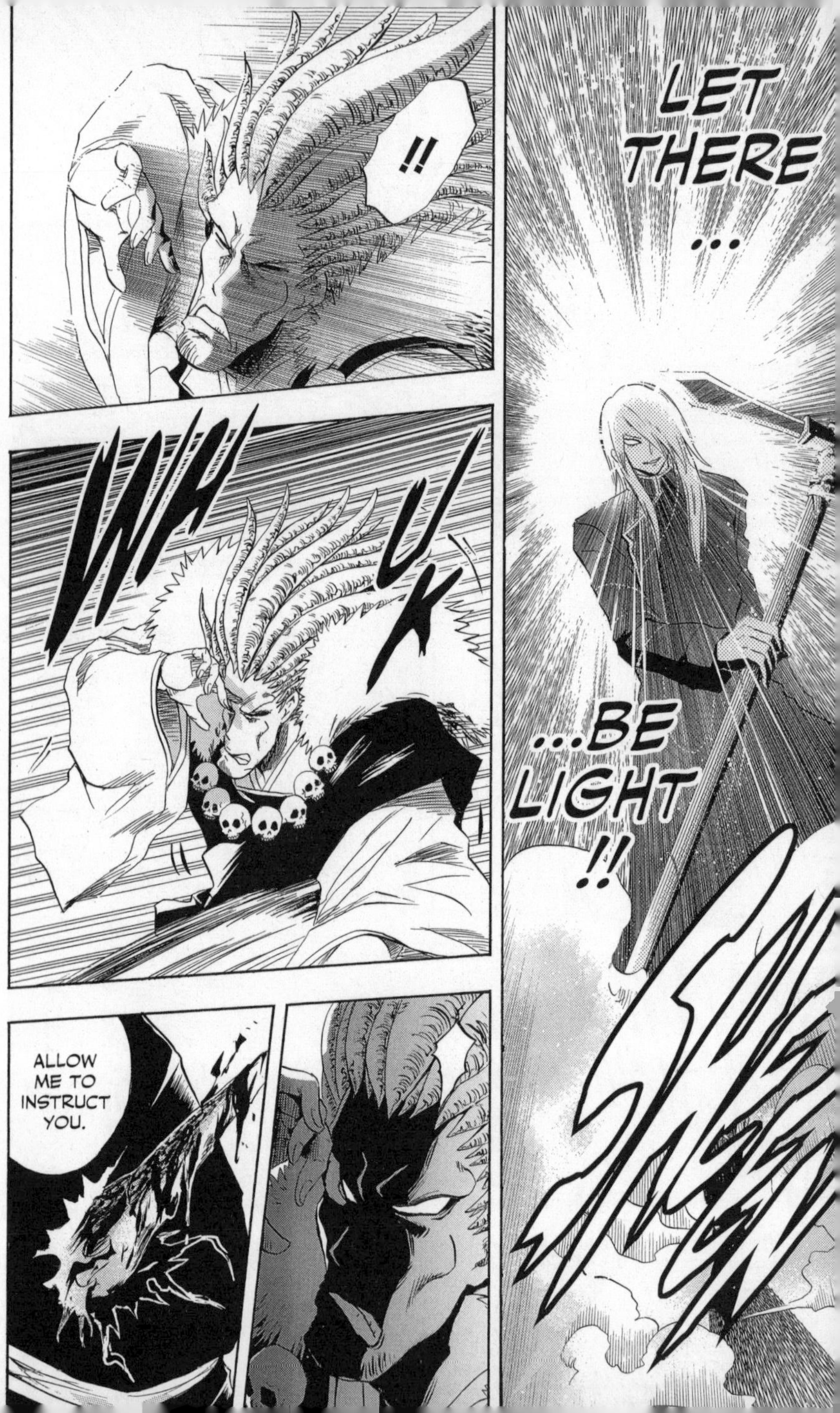
LET THERE ...
...BE LIGHT !!
!!
WHUK
ALLOW ME TO INSTRUCT YOU.

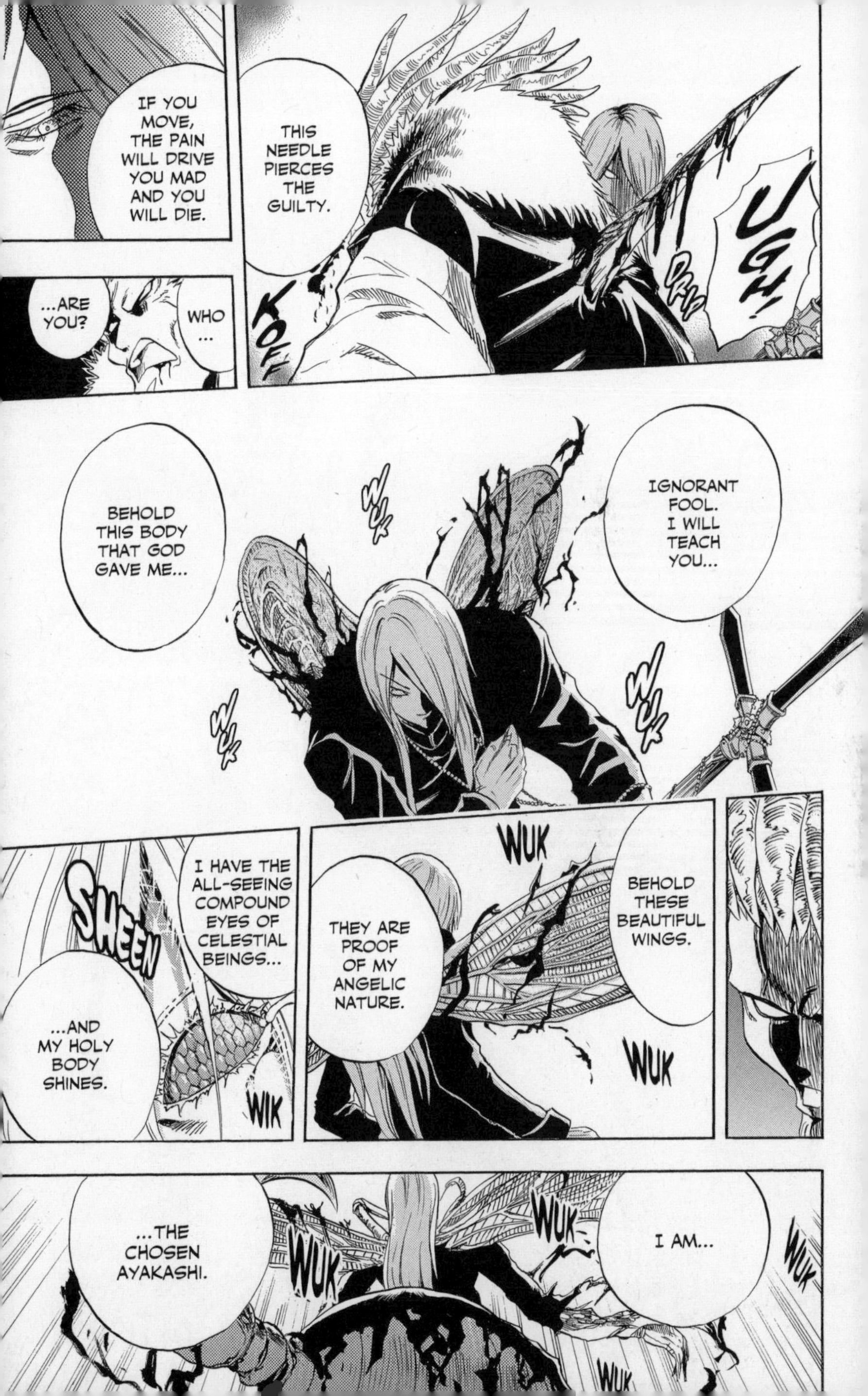
UGH!
THIS NEEDLE PIERCES THE GUILTY.
KOFF
IF YOU MOVE, THE PAIN WILL DRIVE YOU MAD AND YOU WILL DIE.
WHO...
...ARE YOU?
IGNORANT FOOL. I WILL TEACH YOU...
WUK
BEHOLD THIS BODY THAT GOD GAVE ME...
WUK
WUK
BEHOLD THESE BEAUTIFUL WINGS.
WUK
THEY ARE PROOF OF MY ANGELIC NATURE.
WUK
I HAVE THE ALL-SEEING COMPOUND EYES OF CELESTIAL BEINGS...
SHEEN
...AND MY HOLY BODY SHINES.
WIK
WUK
I AM...
WUK
WUK
...THE CHOSEN AYAKASHI.
WUK

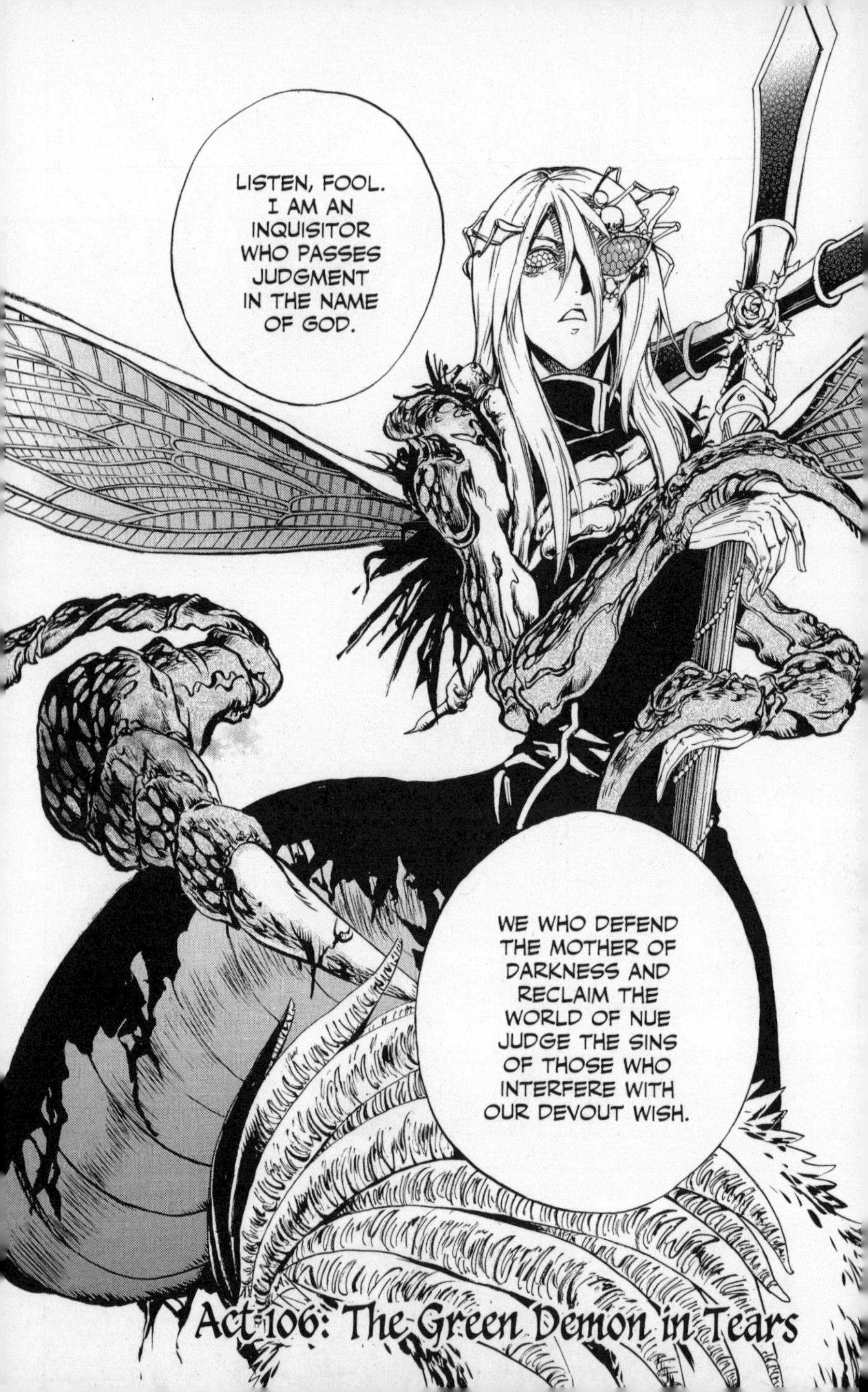
LISTEN, FOOL. I AM AN INQUISITOR WHO PASSES JUDGMENT IN THE NAME OF GOD.
WE WHO DEFEND THE MOTHER OF DARKNESS AND RECLAIM THE WORLD OF NUE JUDGE THE SINS OF THOSE WHO INTERFERE WITH OUR DEVOUT WISH.
Act 106: The Green Demon in Tears

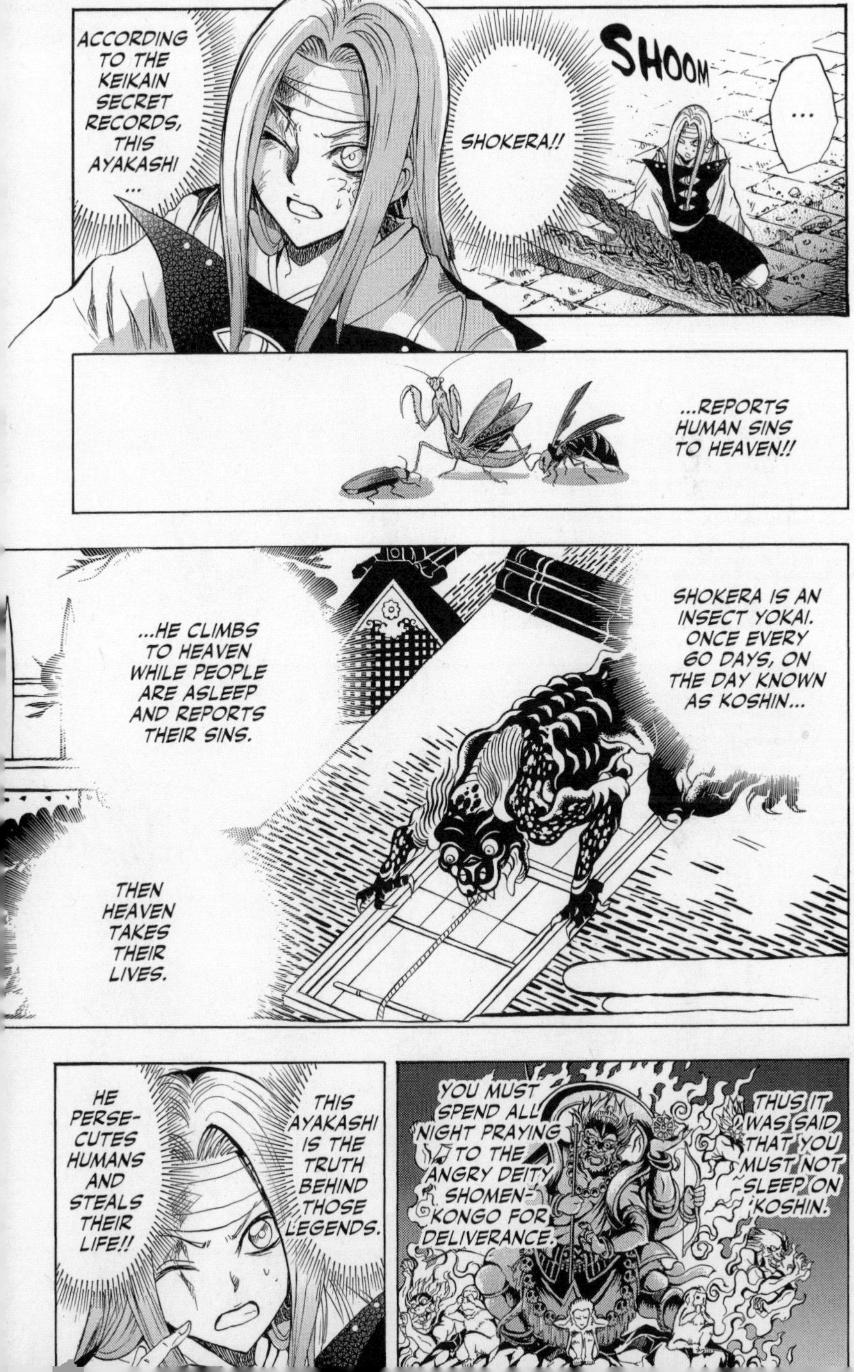
SHOOM
...
SHOKERA!!
ACCORDING TO THE KEIKAIN SECRET RECORDS, THIS AYAKASHI ...
...REPORTS HUMAN SINS TO HEAVEN!!
SHOKERA IS AN INSECT YOKAI. ONCE EVERY 60 DAYS, ON THE DAY KNOWN AS KOSHIN...
...HE CLIMBS TO HEAVEN WHILE PEOPLE ARE ASLEEP AND REPORTS THEIR SINS.
THEN HEAVEN TAKES THEIR LIVES.
THUS IT WAS SAID THAT YOU MUST NOT SLEEP ON KOSHIN.
YOU MUST SPEND ALL NIGHT PRAYING TO THE ANGRY DEITY SHOMEN-KONGO FOR DELIVERANCE.
THIS AYAKASHI IS THE TRUTH BEHIND THOSE LEGENDS.
HE PERSE-CUTES HUMANS AND STEALS THEIR LIFE!!

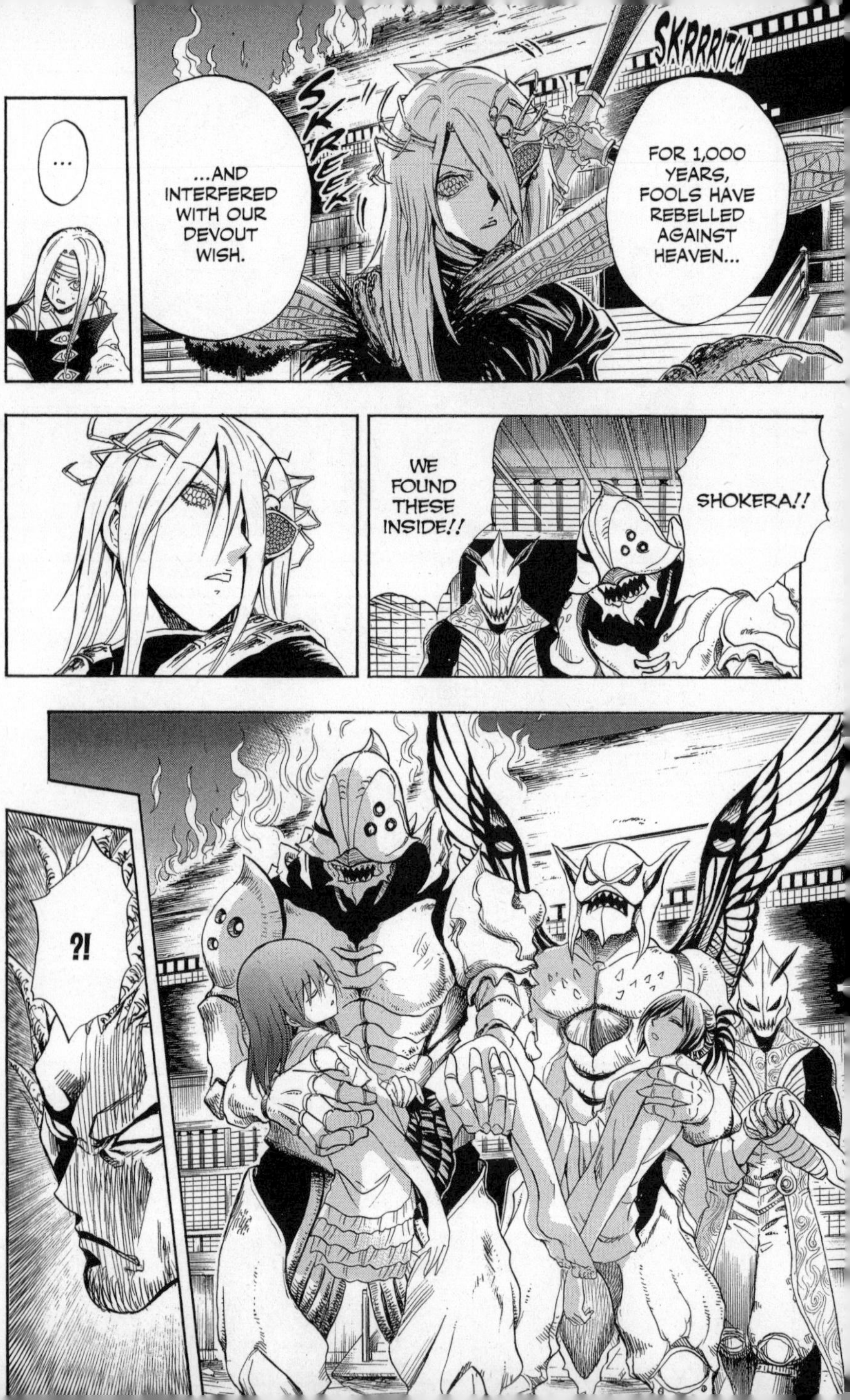
SKRRRITCH
FOR 1,000 YEARS, FOOLS HAVE REBELLED AGAINST HEAVEN...
SKREEK
...AND INTERFERED WITH OUR DEVOUT WISH.
...
SHOKERA!!
WE FOUND THESE INSIDE!!
?!

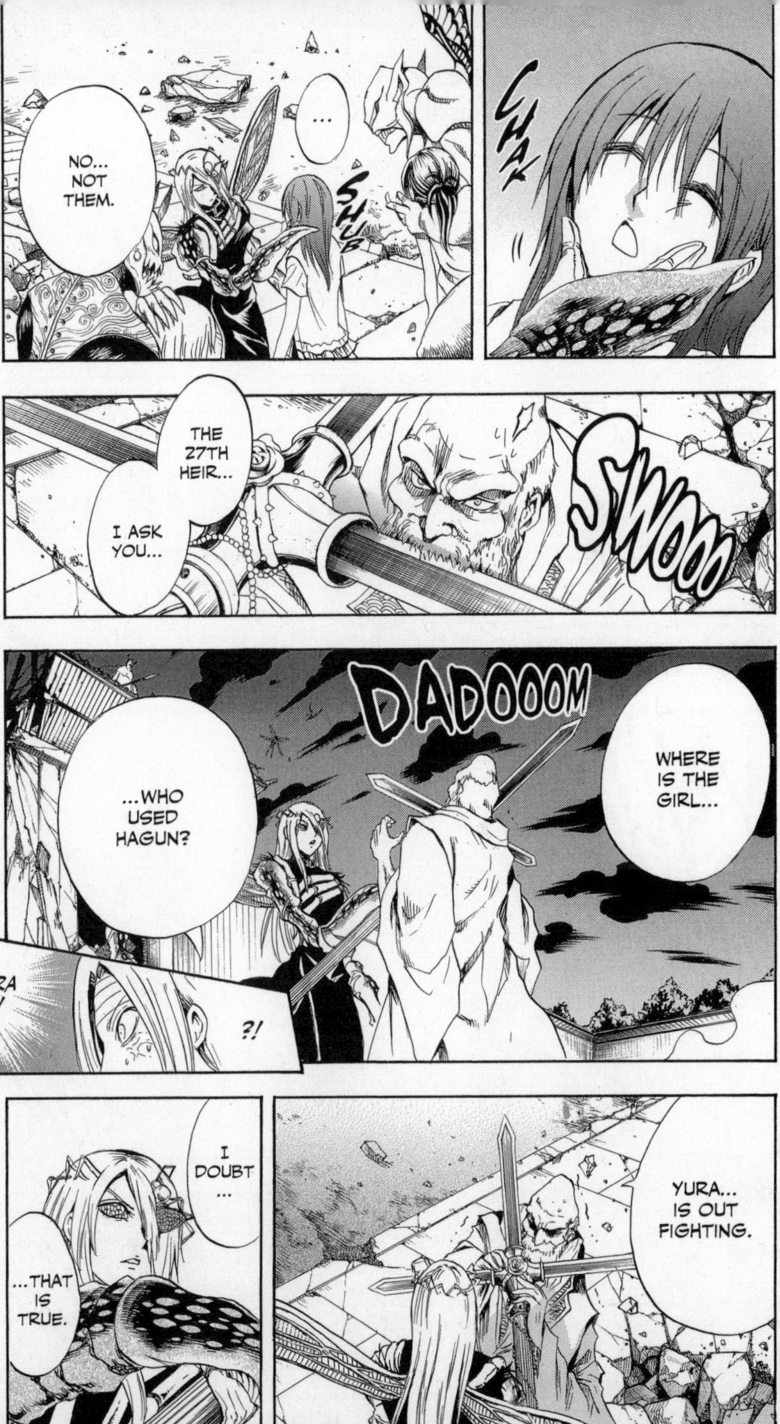
CHAK
...
SHUB
NO... NOT THEM.
SWOOO
THE 27TH HEIR...
I ASK YOU...
DADOOOM
WHERE IS THE GIRL...
...WHO USED HAGUN?
?!
YURA ?!
YURA... IS OUT FIGHTING.
I DOUBT ...
...THAT IS TRUE.

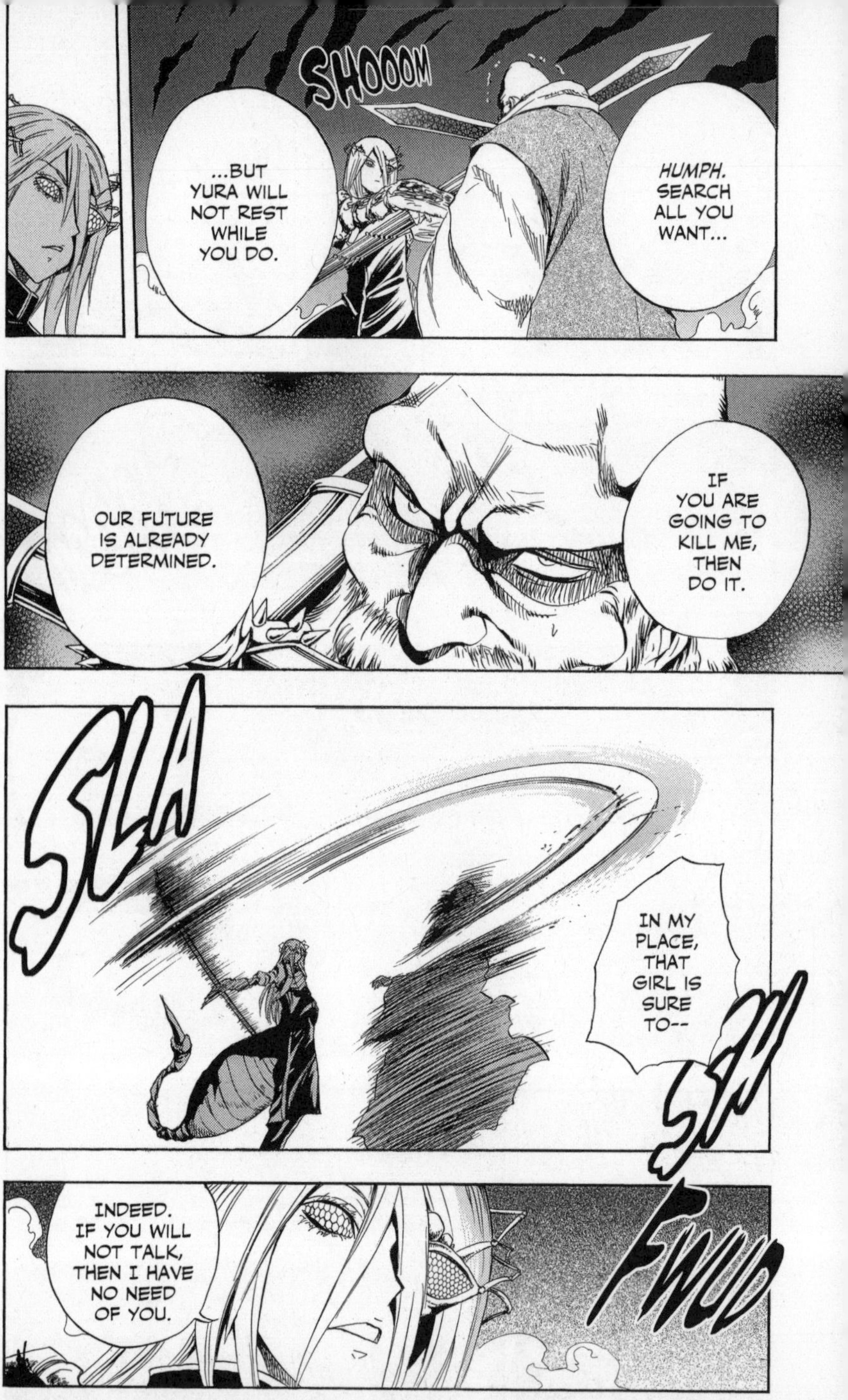
HUMPH. SEARCH ALL YOU WANT...
SHOOOM
...BUT YURA WILL NOT REST WHILE YOU DO.
IF YOU ARE GOING TO KILL ME, THEN DO IT.
OUR FUTURE IS ALREADY DETERMINED.
IN MY PLACE, THAT GIRL IS SURE TO--
SLA
SPH
FWUD
INDEED. IF YOU WILL NOT TALK, THEN I HAVE NO NEED OF YOU.

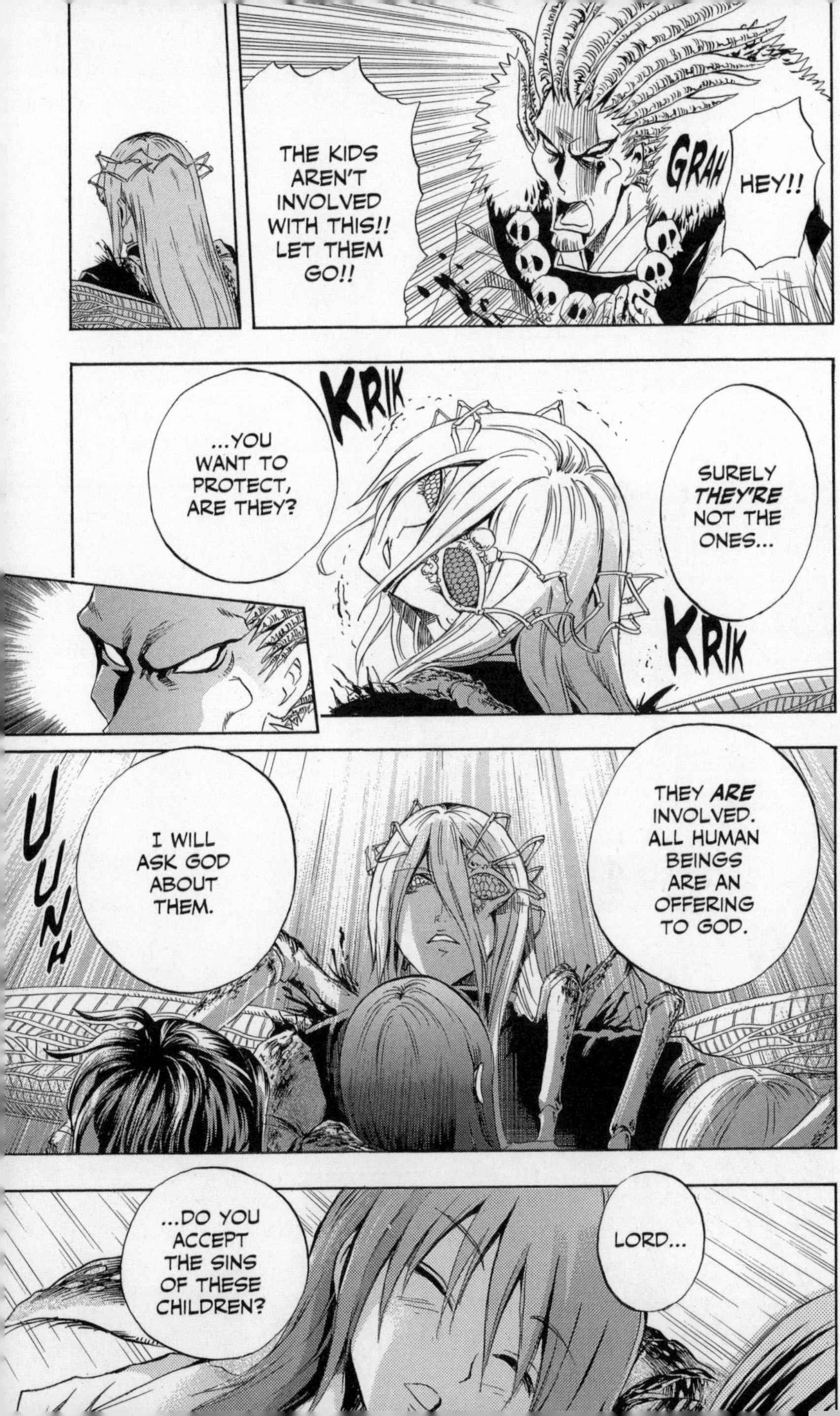
HEY!!
GRAH
THE KIDS AREN'T INVOLVED WITH THIS!! LET THEM GO!!
KRIK
SURELY *THEY'RE* NOT THE ONES...
...YOU WANT TO PROTECT, ARE THEY?
KRIK
THEY *ARE* INVOLVED. ALL HUMAN BEINGS ARE AN OFFERING TO GOD.
I WILL ASK GOD ABOUT THEM.
UUNH
LORD...
...DO YOU ACCEPT THE SINS OF THESE CHILDREN?

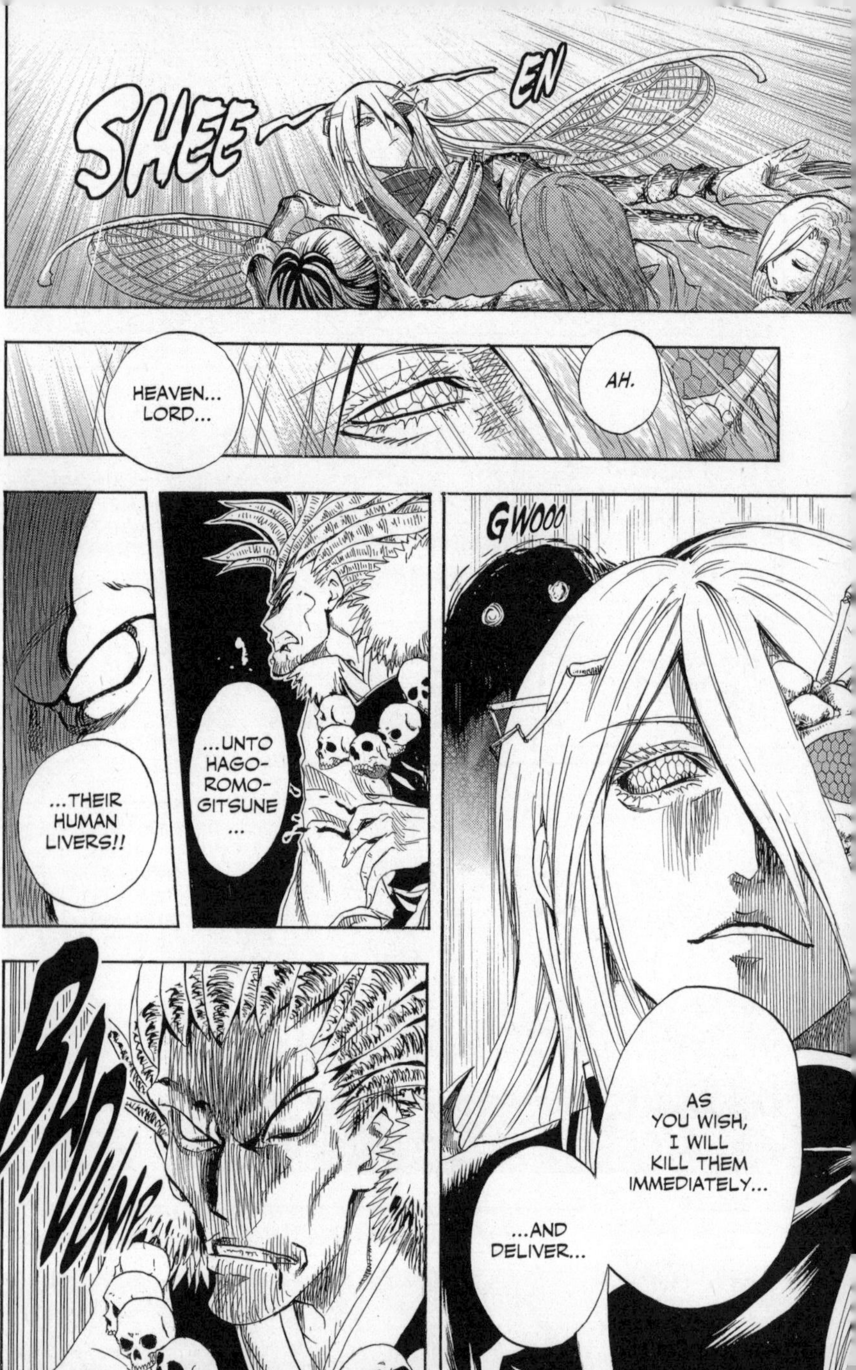
SHEE~EN
AH.
HEAVEN... LORD...
GWOOO
AS YOU WISH, I WILL KILL THEM IMMEDIATELY...
...AND DELIVER...
...UNTO HAGO-ROMO-GITSUNE...
...THEIR HUMAN LIVERS!!
BADUMP

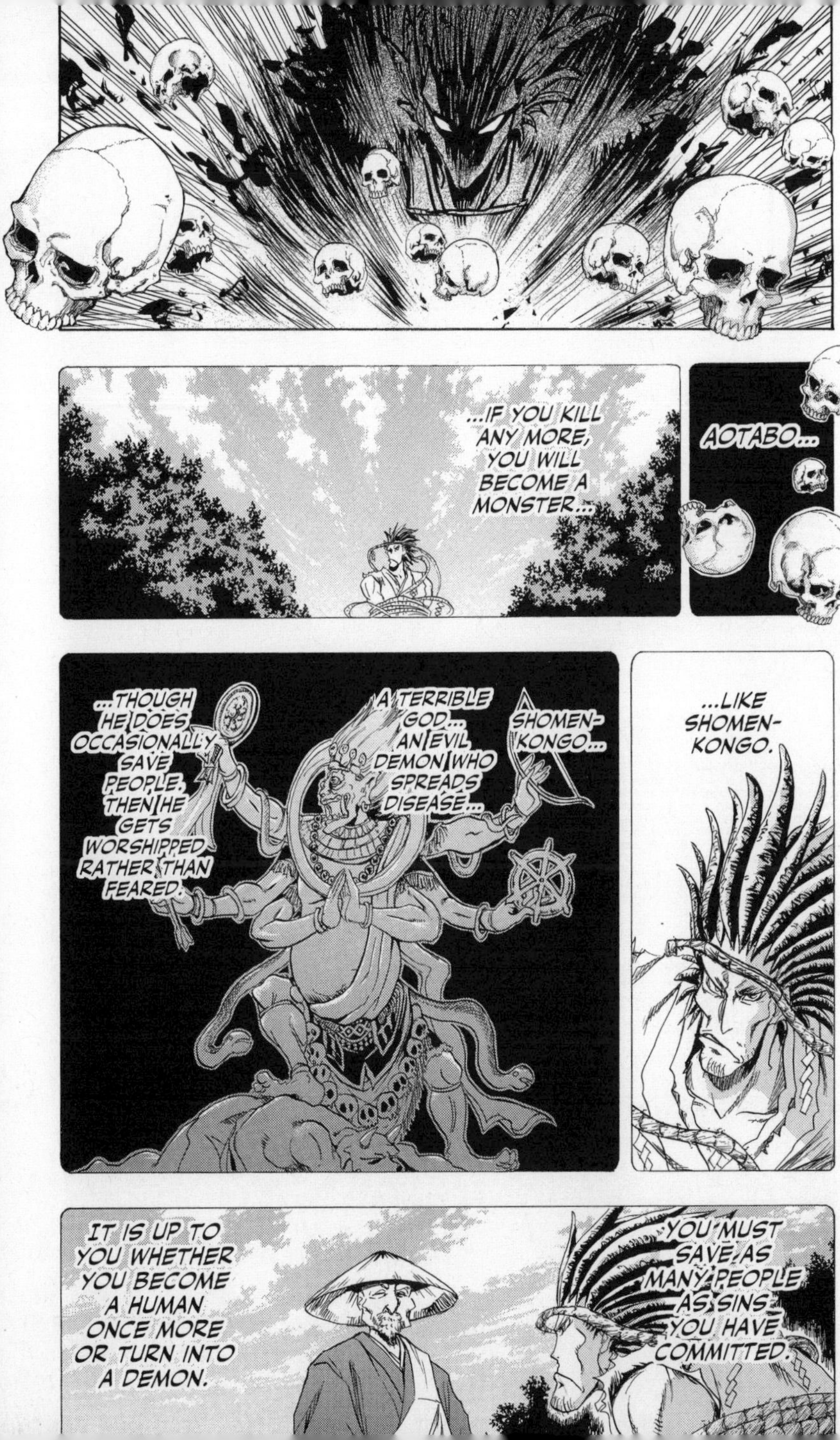
AOTABO...
...IF YOU KILL ANY MORE, YOU WILL BECOME A MONSTER...
...LIKE SHOMEN-KONGO.
SHOMEN-KONGO...
A TERRIBLE GOD... AN EVIL DEMON WHO SPREADS DISEASE...
...THOUGH HE DOES OCCASIONALLY SAVE PEOPLE. THEN HE GETS WORSHIPPED RATHER THAN FEARED.
YOU MUST SAVE AS MANY PEOPLE AS SINS YOU HAVE COMMITTED.
IT IS UP TO YOU WHETHER YOU BECOME A HUMAN ONCE MORE OR TURN INTO A DEMON.

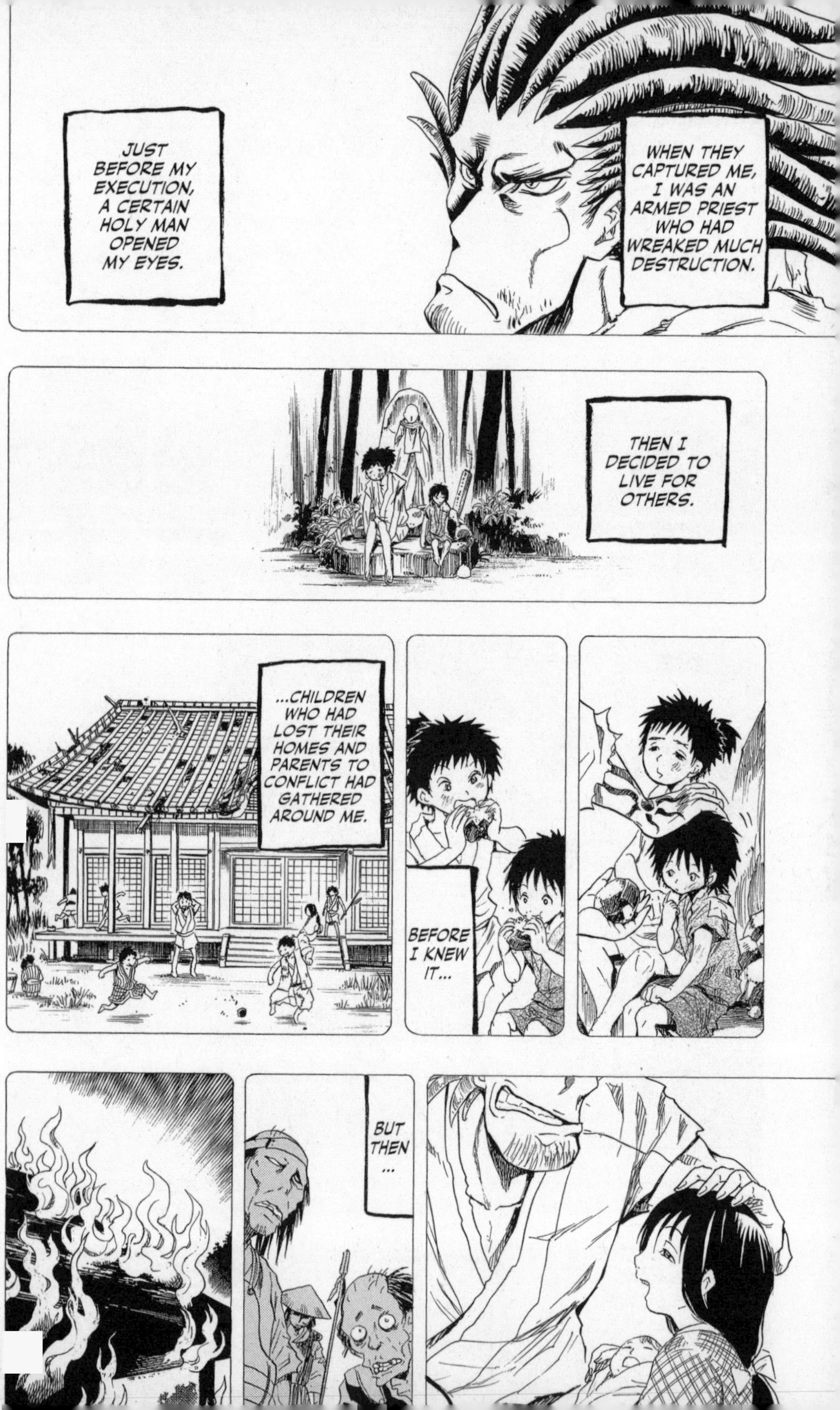
WHEN THEY CAPTURED ME, I WAS AN ARMED PRIEST WHO HAD WREAKED MUCH DESTRUCTION.
JUST BEFORE MY EXECUTION, A CERTAIN HOLY MAN OPENED MY EYES.
THEN I DECIDED TO LIVE FOR OTHERS.
BEFORE I KNEW IT...
...CHILDREN WHO HAD LOST THEIR HOMES AND PARENTS TO CONFLICT HAD GATHERED AROUND ME.
BUT THEN ...

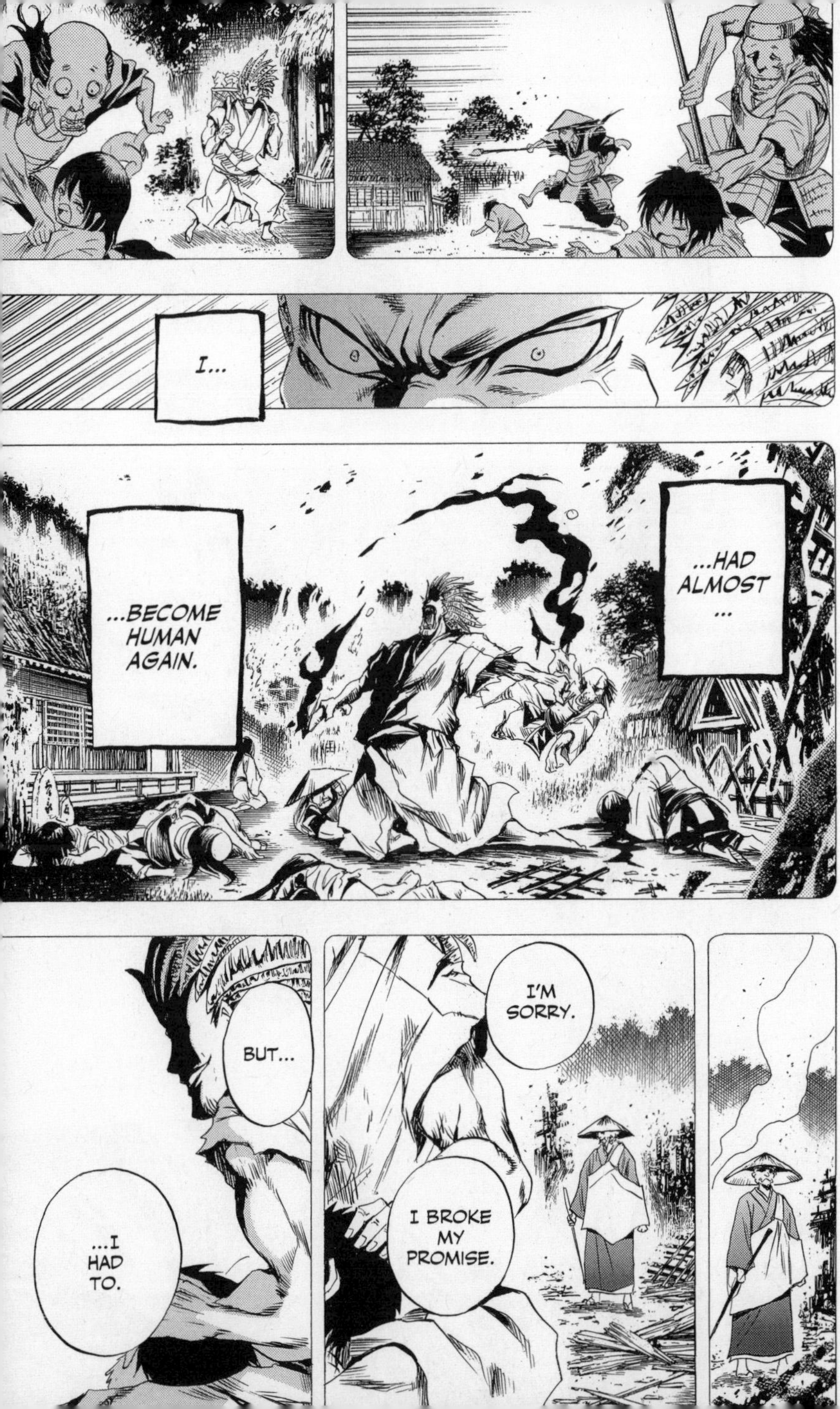
I...
...HAD ALMOST ...
...BECOME HUMAN AGAIN.
I'M SORRY.
I BROKE MY PROMISE.
BUT...
...I HAD TO.

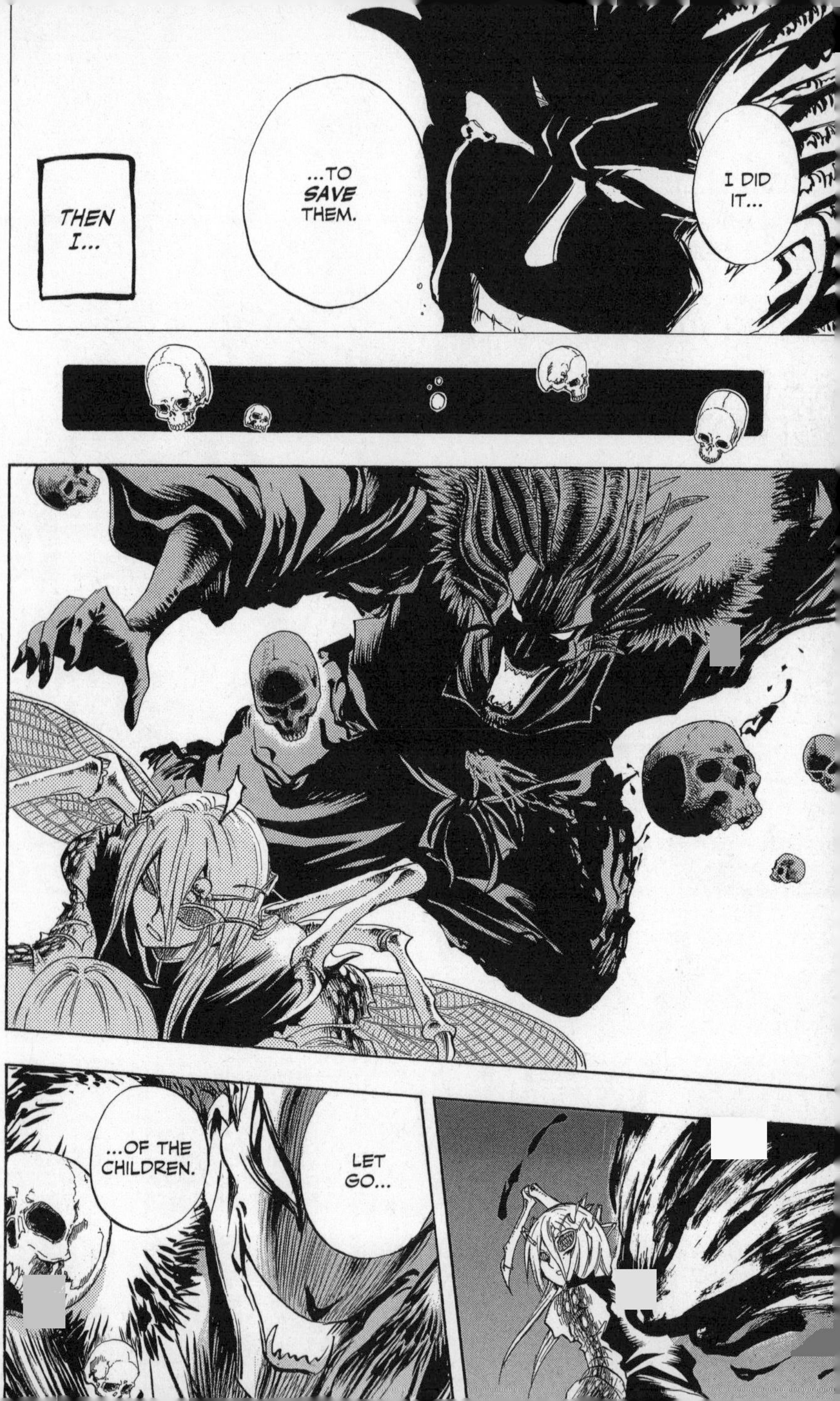
I DID IT...
...TO SAVE THEM.
THEN I...
LET GO...
...OF THE CHILDREN.

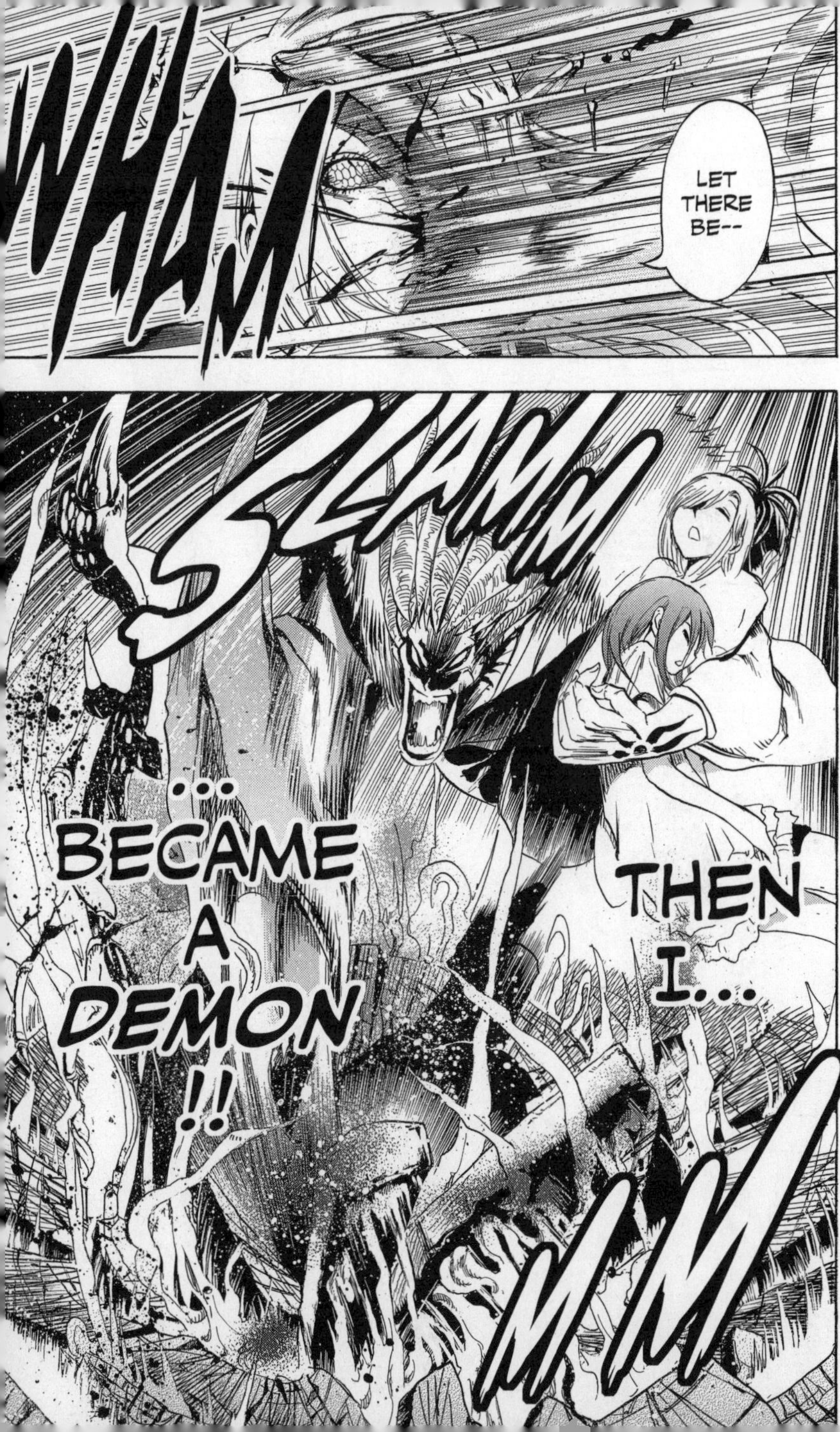
LET THERE BE--
THEN I...
...BECAME A DEMON!!

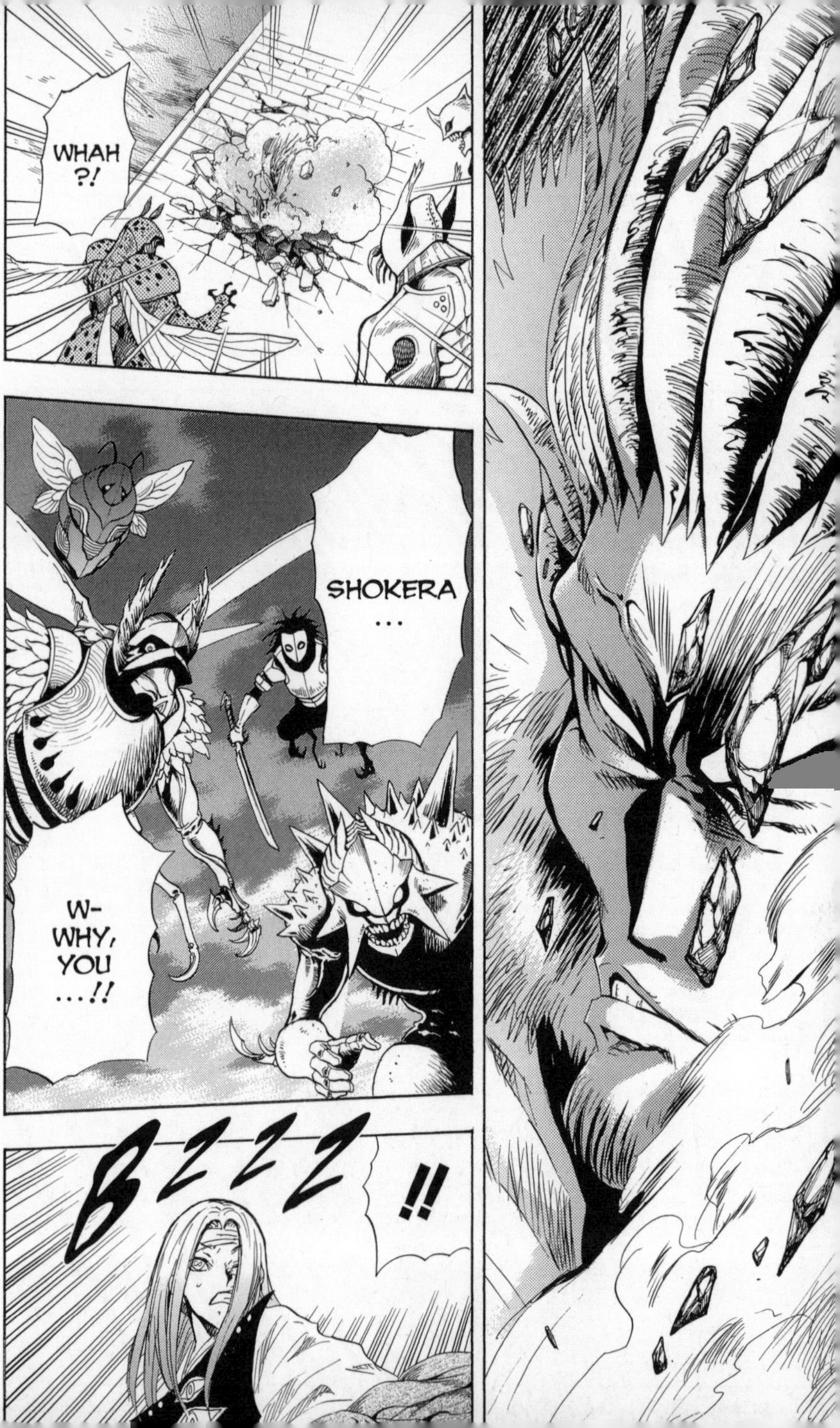
WHAH ?!
SHOKERA ...
W- WHY, YOU ...!!
BZZZ !!

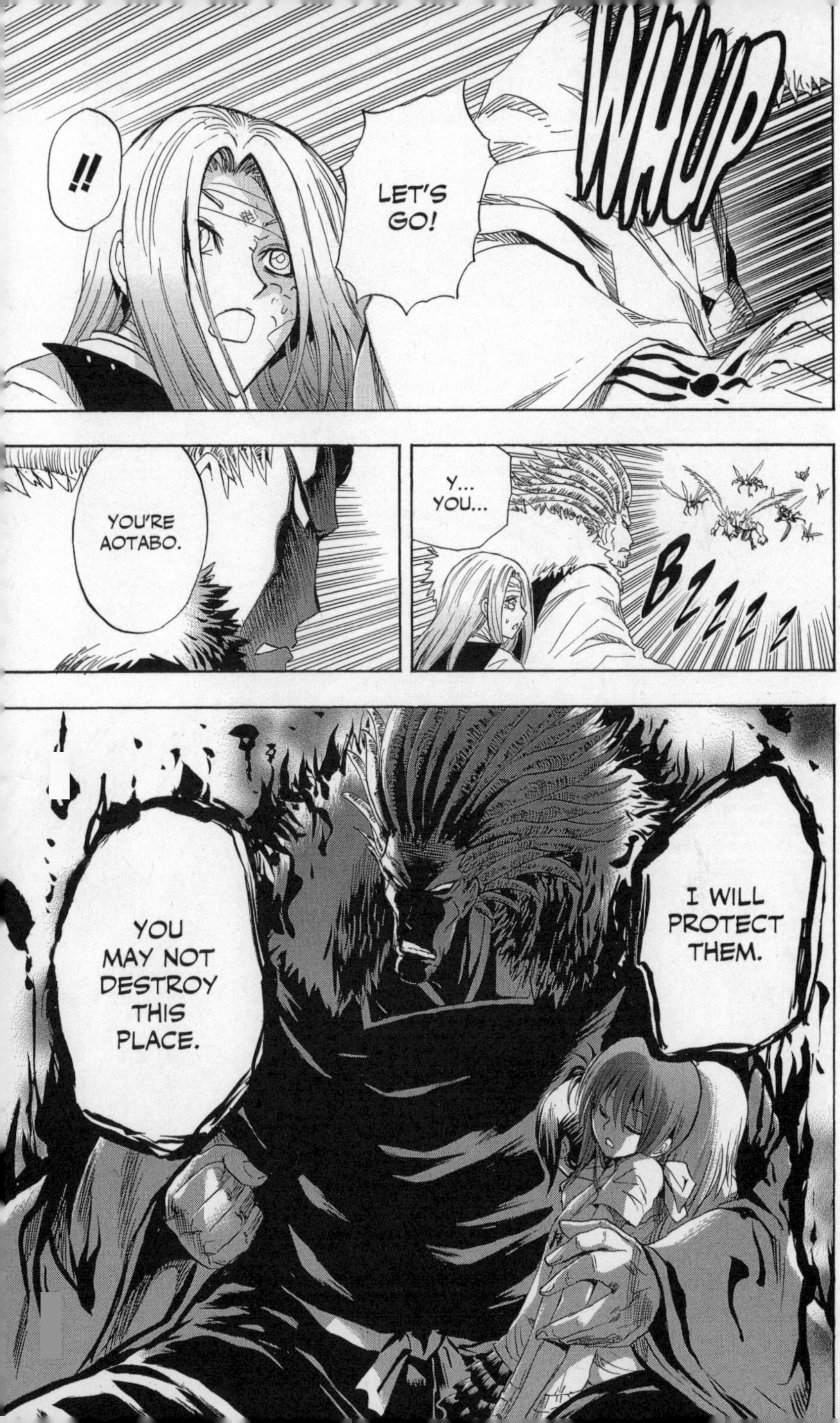
WHOP
LET'S GO!
!!
Y... YOU...
BZZZZZ
YOU'RE AOTABO.
I WILL PROTECT THEM.
YOU MAY NOT DESTROY THIS PLACE.

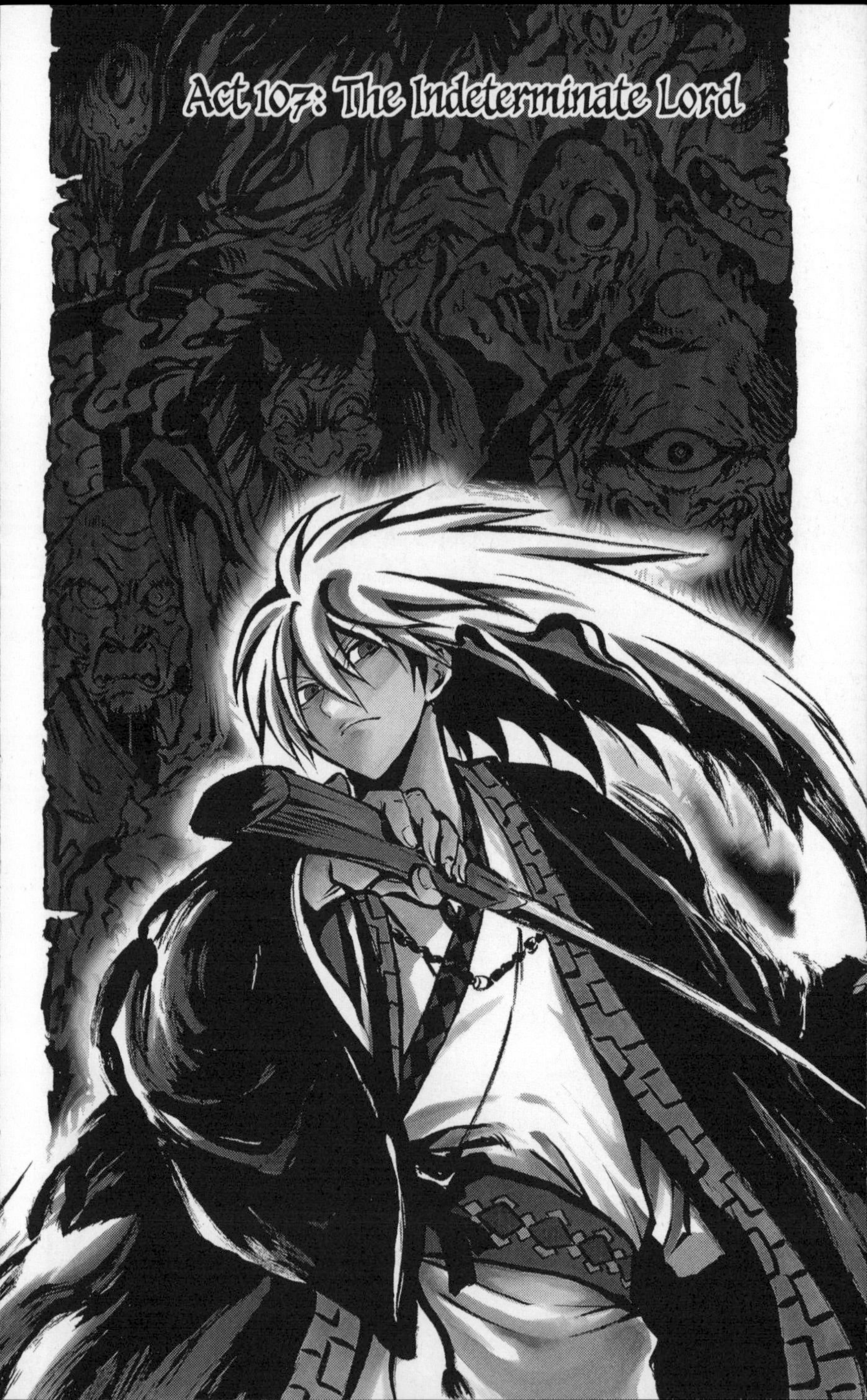
Act 107: The Indeterminate Lord

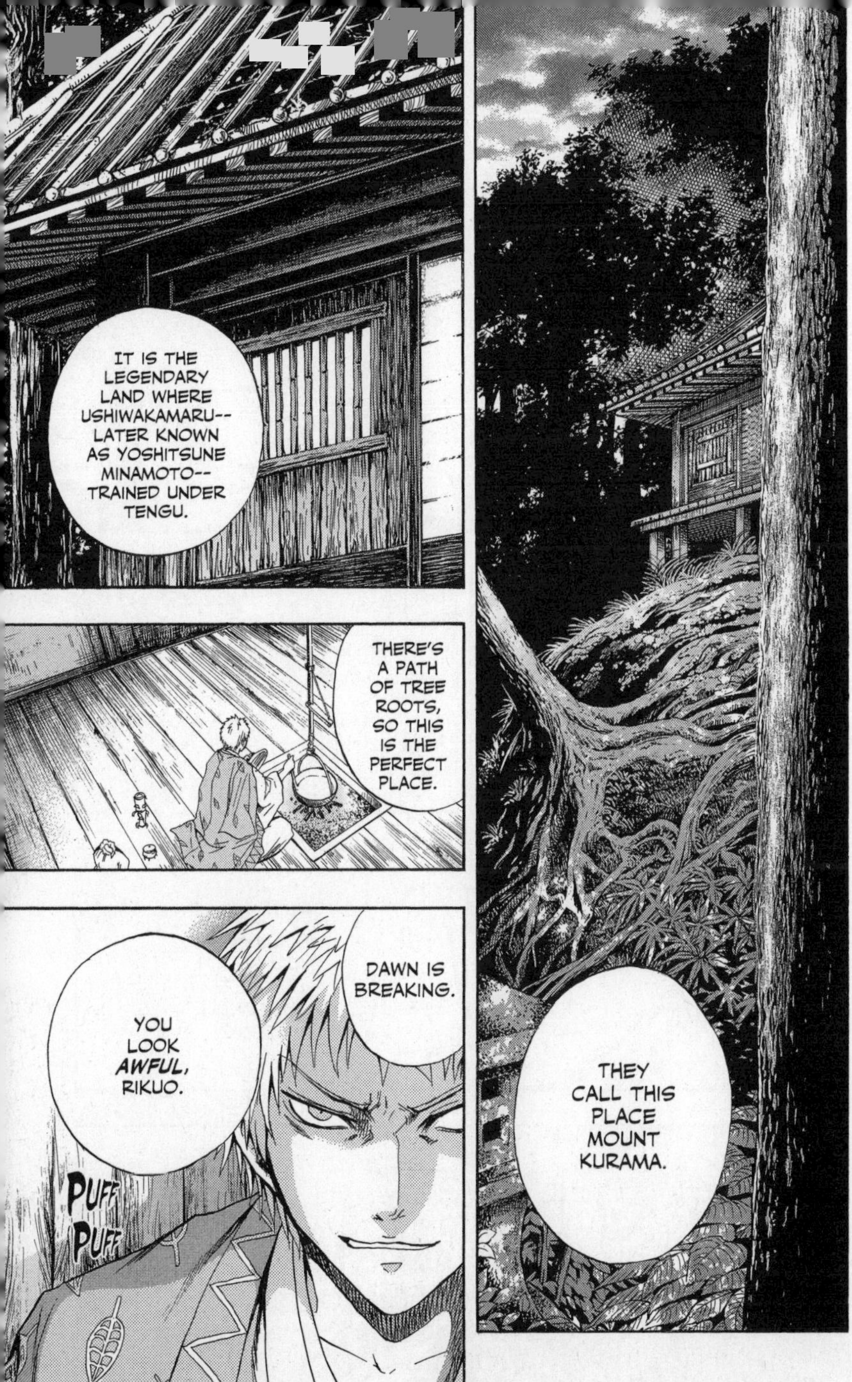
THEY CALL THIS PLACE MOUNT KURAMA.
IT IS THE LEGENDARY LAND WHERE USHIWAKAMARU-- LATER KNOWN AS YOSHITSUNE MINAMOTO-- TRAINED UNDER TENGU.
THERE'S A PATH OF TREE ROOTS, SO THIS IS THE PERFECT PLACE.
DAWN IS BREAKING.
YOU LOOK *AWFUL*, RIKUO.
PUFF PUFF

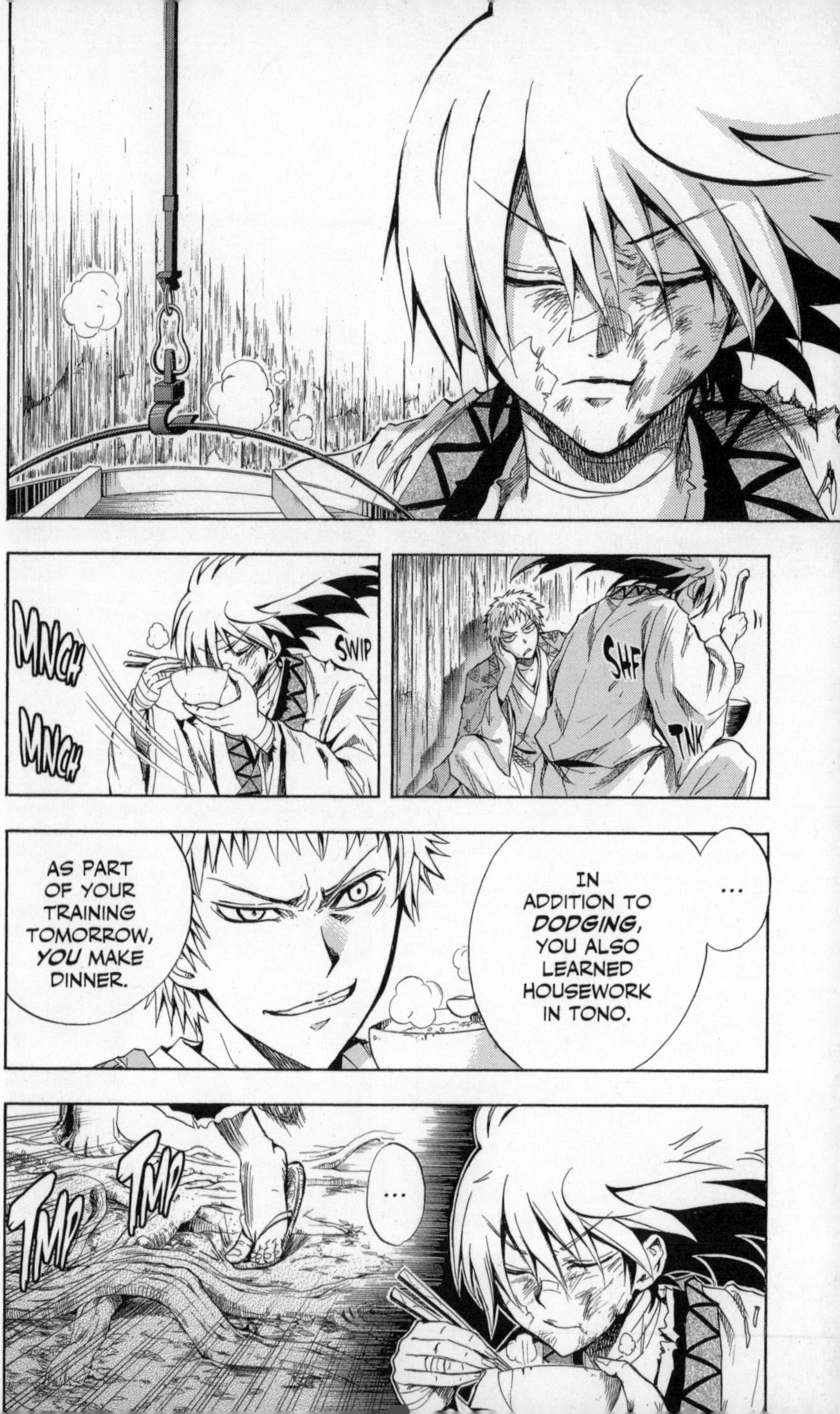
SHF
TNK
SWIP
MNCH
MNCH
...
IN ADDITION TO *DODGING*, YOU ALSO LEARNED HOUSEWORK IN TONO.
AS PART OF YOUR TRAINING TOMORROW, *YOU* MAKE DINNER.
...
TMP
TMP

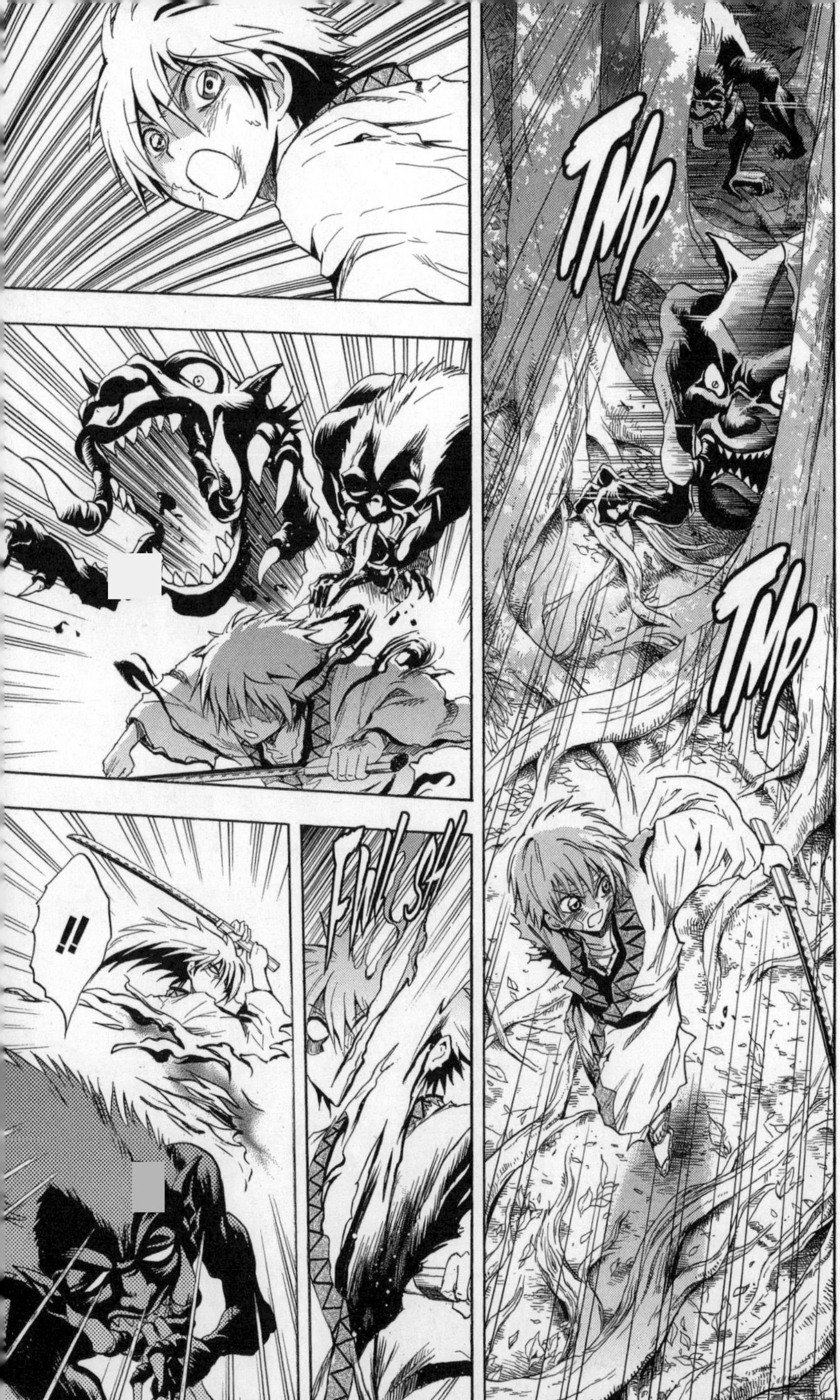
TMP
TMP
!!

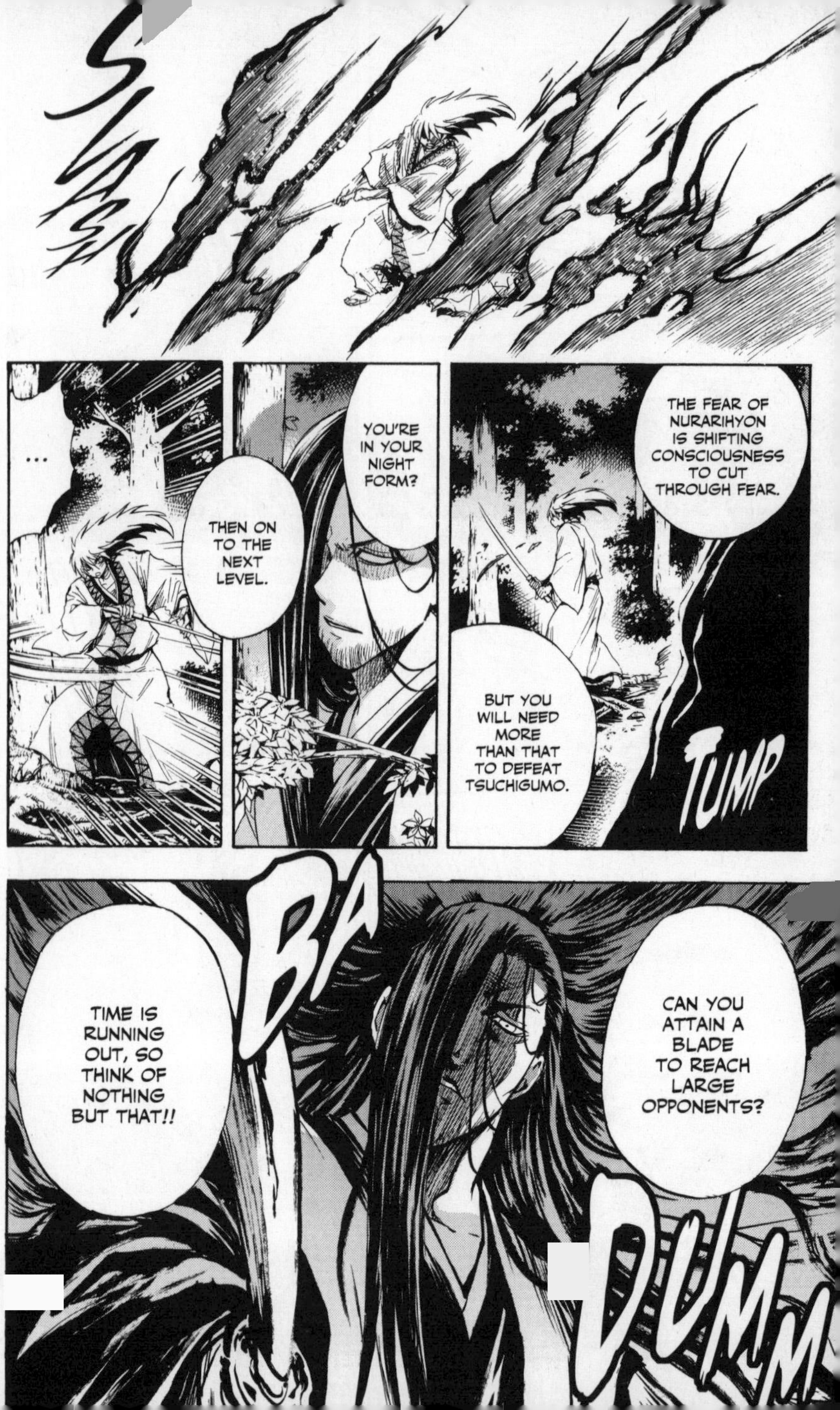
SLASH
THE FEAR OF NURARIHYON IS SHIFTING CONSCIOUSNESS TO CUT THROUGH FEAR.
BUT YOU WILL NEED MORE THAN THAT TO DEFEAT TSUCHIGUMO.
TUMP
YOU'RE IN YOUR NIGHT FORM?
THEN ON TO THE NEXT LEVEL.
...
BA
DUMM
CAN YOU ATTAIN A BLADE TO REACH LARGE OPPONENTS?
TIME IS RUNNING OUT, SO THINK OF NOTHING BUT THAT!!

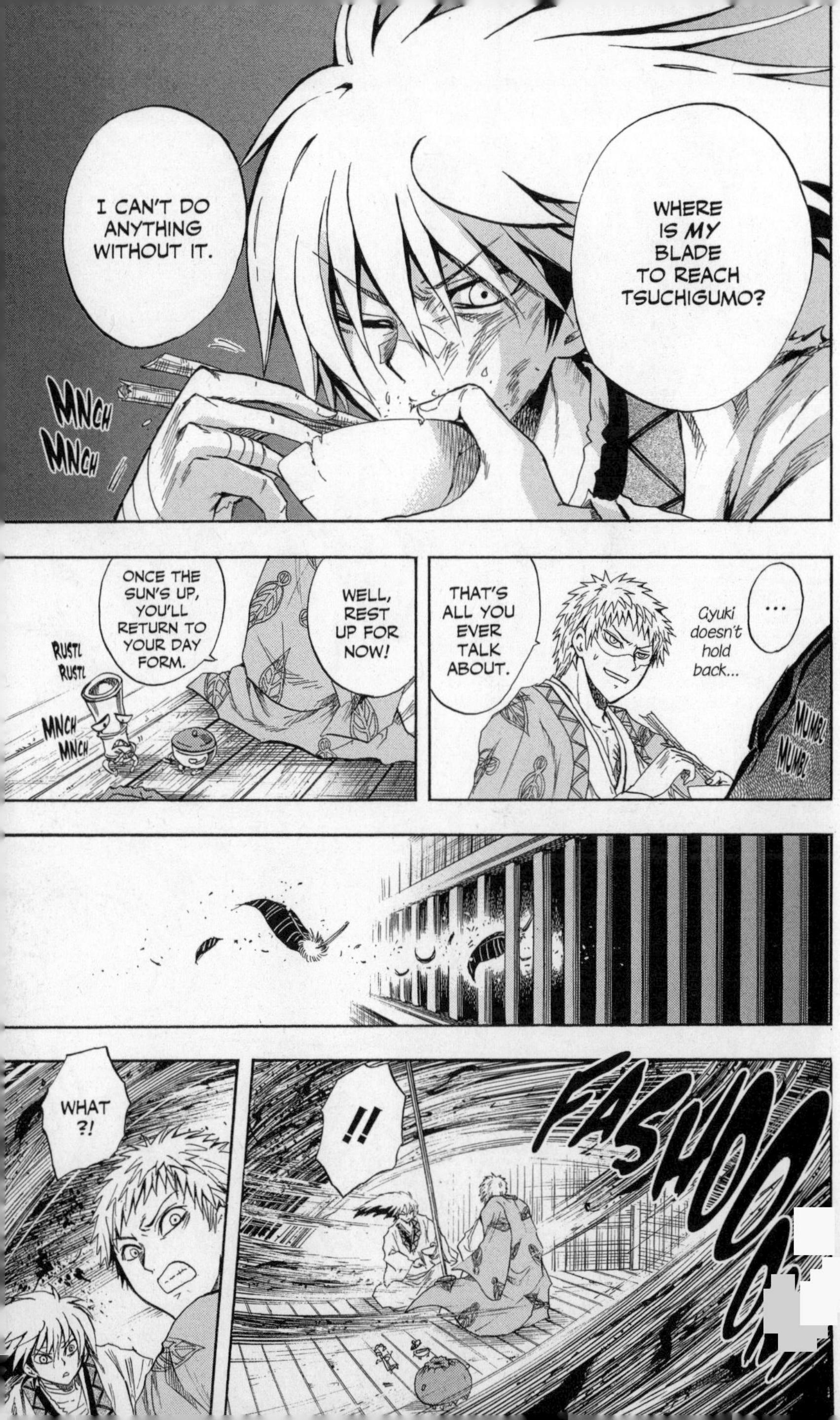
WHERE IS MY BLADE TO REACH TSUCHIGUMO?
I CAN'T DO ANYTHING WITHOUT IT.
MNCH MNCH
...
Gyuki doesn't hold back...
THAT'S ALL YOU EVER TALK ABOUT.
MUMBL MUMBL
WELL, REST UP FOR NOW!
ONCE THE SUN'S UP, YOU'LL RETURN TO YOUR DAY FORM.
RUSTL RUSTL
MNCH MNCH
FASHOOO
!!
WHAT ?!

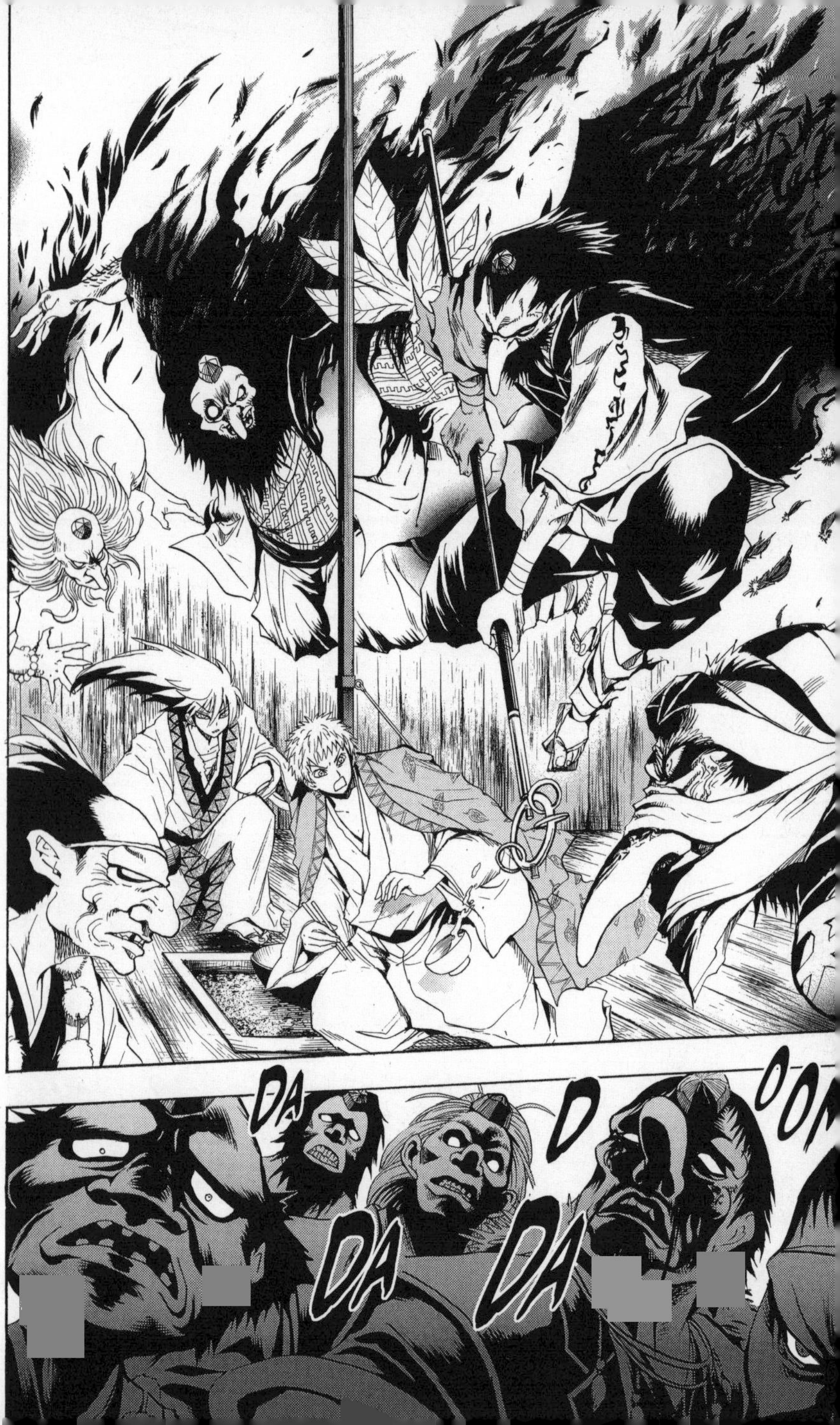

DA D OOM
DA DA

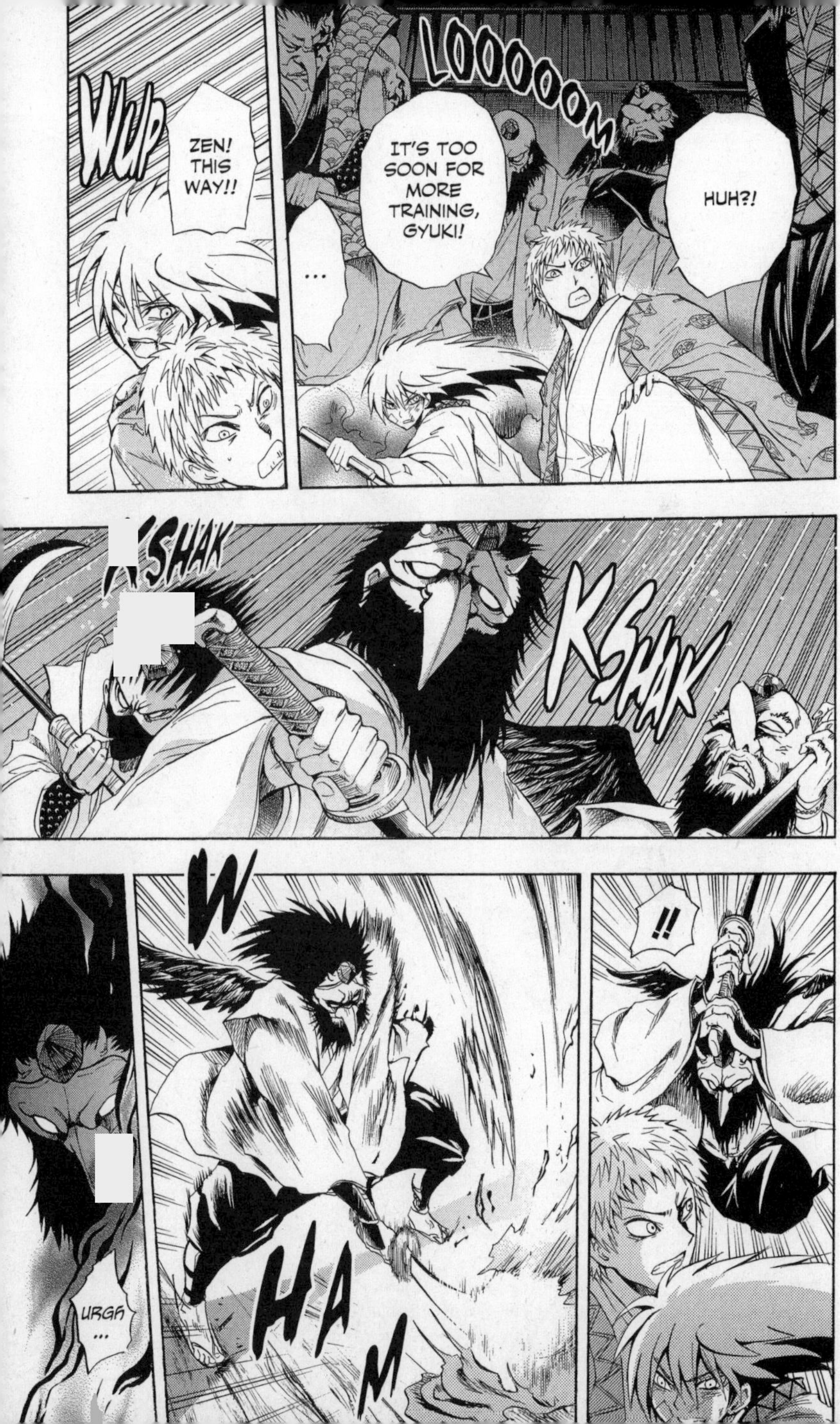
LOOOOOOM
HUH?!
IT'S TOO SOON FOR MORE TRAINING, GYUKI!
...
WUP
ZEN! THIS WAY!!
KSHAK
SHAK
!!
WHAM
URGH ...

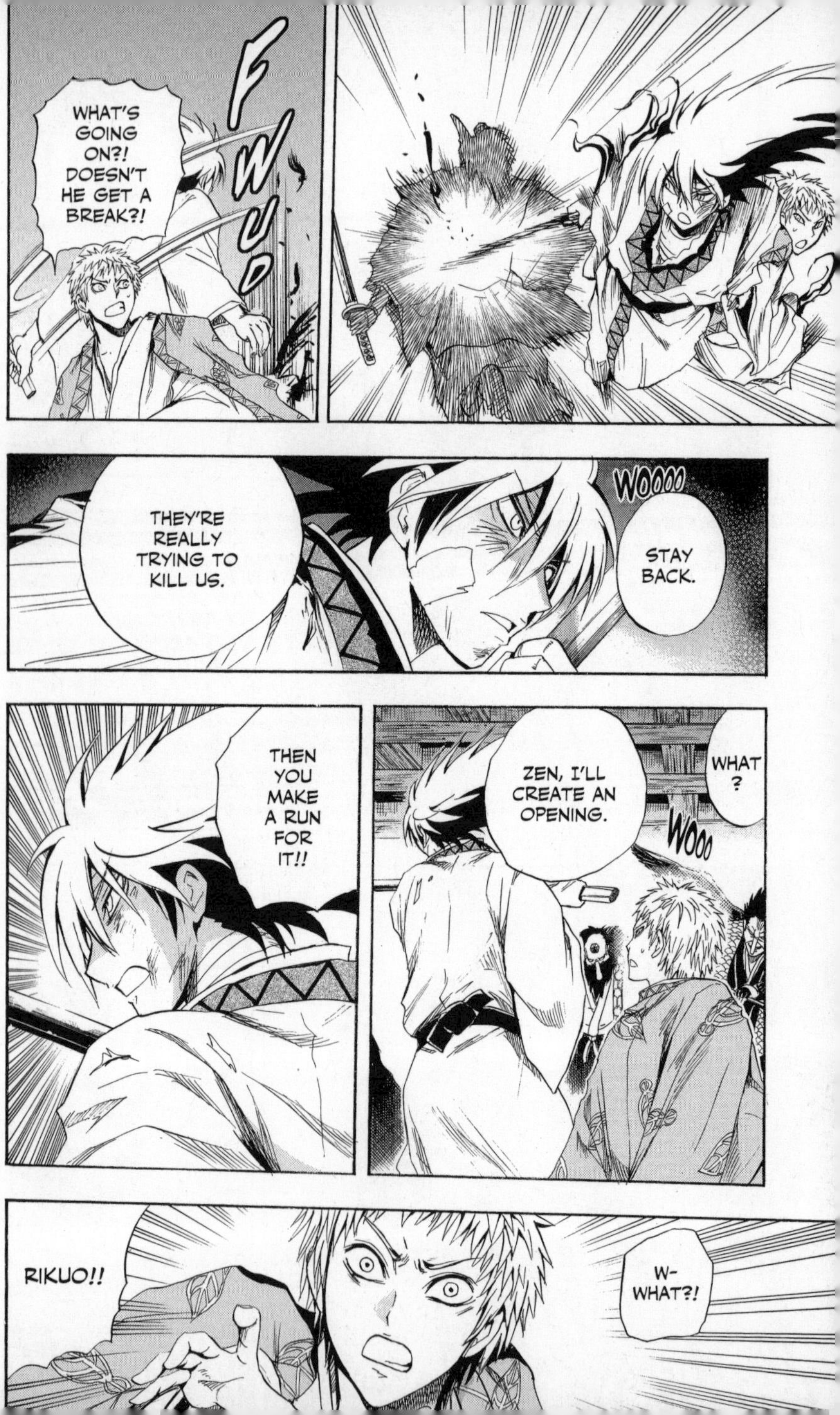
FWUD
WHAT'S GOING ON?! DOESN'T HE GET A BREAK?!
WOOOO
STAY BACK.
THEY'RE REALLY TRYING TO KILL US.
WHAT?
ZEN, I'LL CREATE AN OPENING.
WOOO
THEN YOU MAKE A RUN FOR IT!!
W-WHAT?!
RIKUO!!

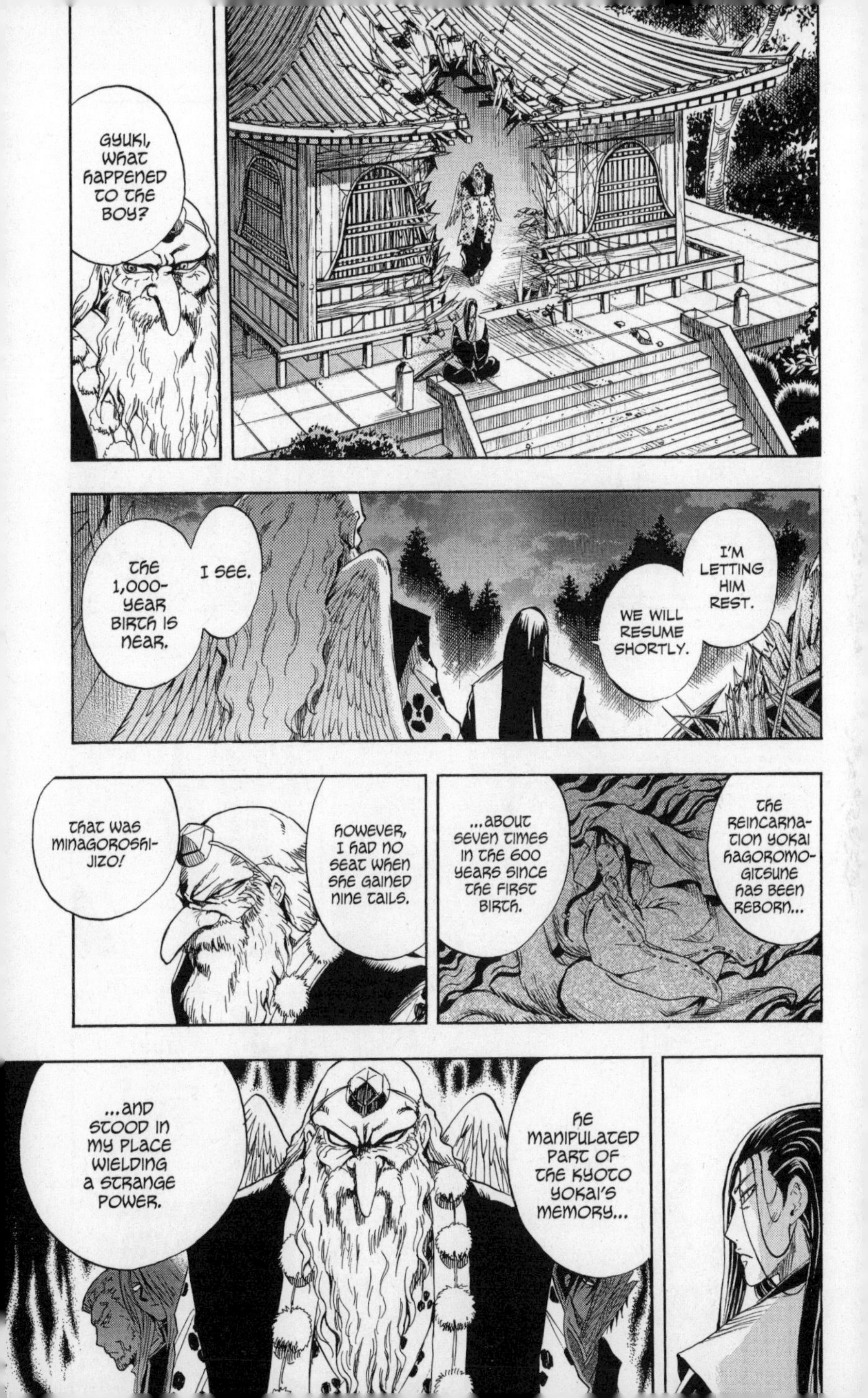
GYUKI, WHAT HAPPENED TO THE BOY?
I'M LETTING HIM REST.
WE WILL RESUME SHORTLY.
I SEE.
THE 1,000-YEAR BIRTH IS NEAR.
THE REINCARNATION YOKAI HAGOROMO-GITSUNE HAS BEEN REBORN...
...ABOUT SEVEN TIMES IN THE 600 YEARS SINCE THE FIRST BIRTH.
HOWEVER, I HAD NO SEAT WHEN SHE GAINED NINE TAILS.
THAT WAS MINAGOROSHI-JIZO!
HE MANIPULATED PART OF THE KYOTO YOKAI'S MEMORY...
...AND STOOD IN MY PLACE WIELDING A STRANGE POWER.

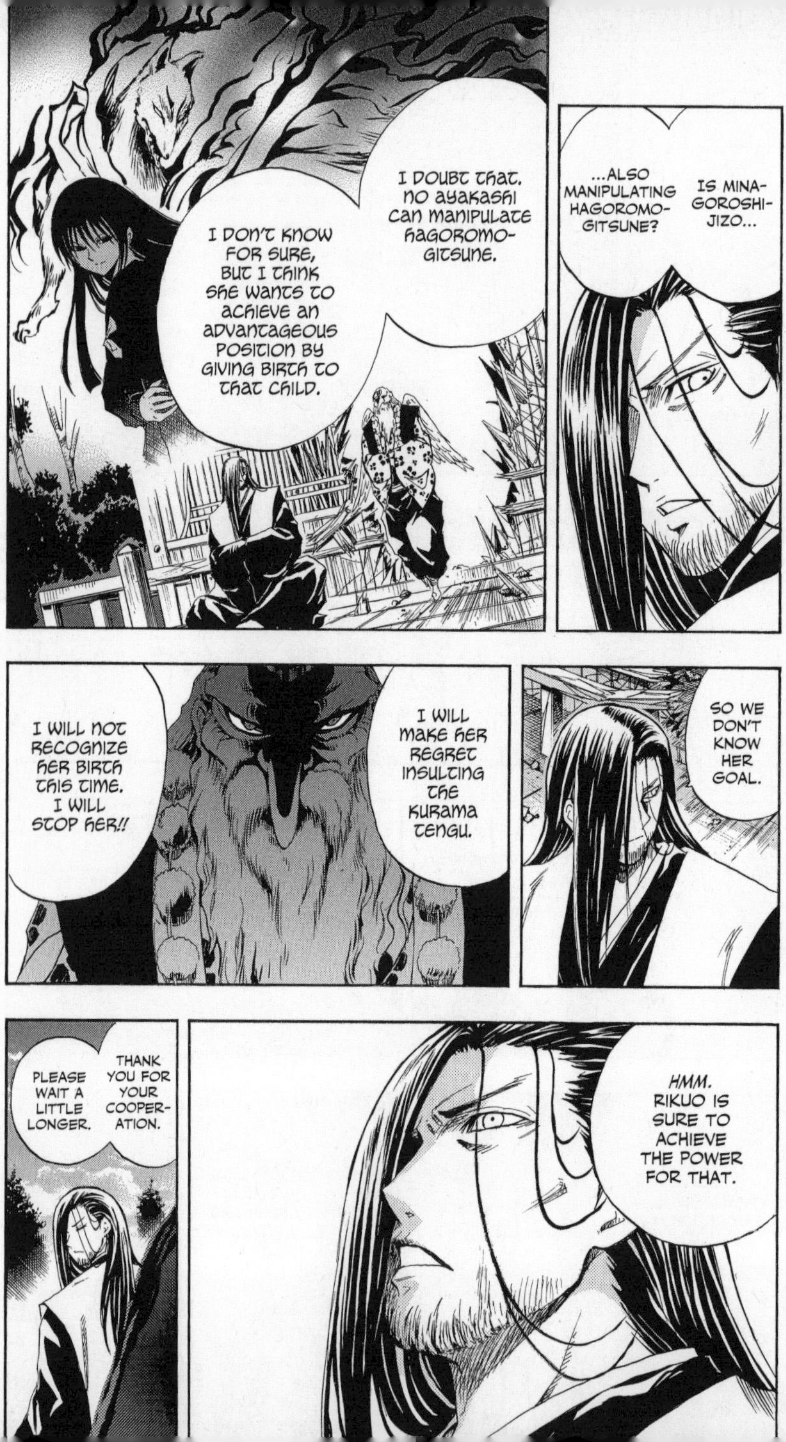
IS MINAGOROSHI-JIZO...
...ALSO MANIPULATING HAGOROMO-GITSUNE?
I DOUBT THAT. NO AYAKASHI CAN MANIPULATE HAGOROMO-GITSUNE.
I DON'T KNOW FOR SURE, BUT I THINK SHE WANTS TO ACHIEVE AN ADVANTAGEOUS POSITION BY GIVING BIRTH TO THAT CHILD.
SO WE DON'T KNOW HER GOAL.
I WILL MAKE HER REGRET INSULTING THE KURAMA TENGU.
I WILL NOT RECOGNIZE HER BIRTH THIS TIME. I WILL STOP HER!!
HMM. RIKUO IS SURE TO ACHIEVE THE POWER FOR THAT.
THANK YOU FOR YOUR COOPERATION.
PLEASE WAIT A LITTLE LONGER.

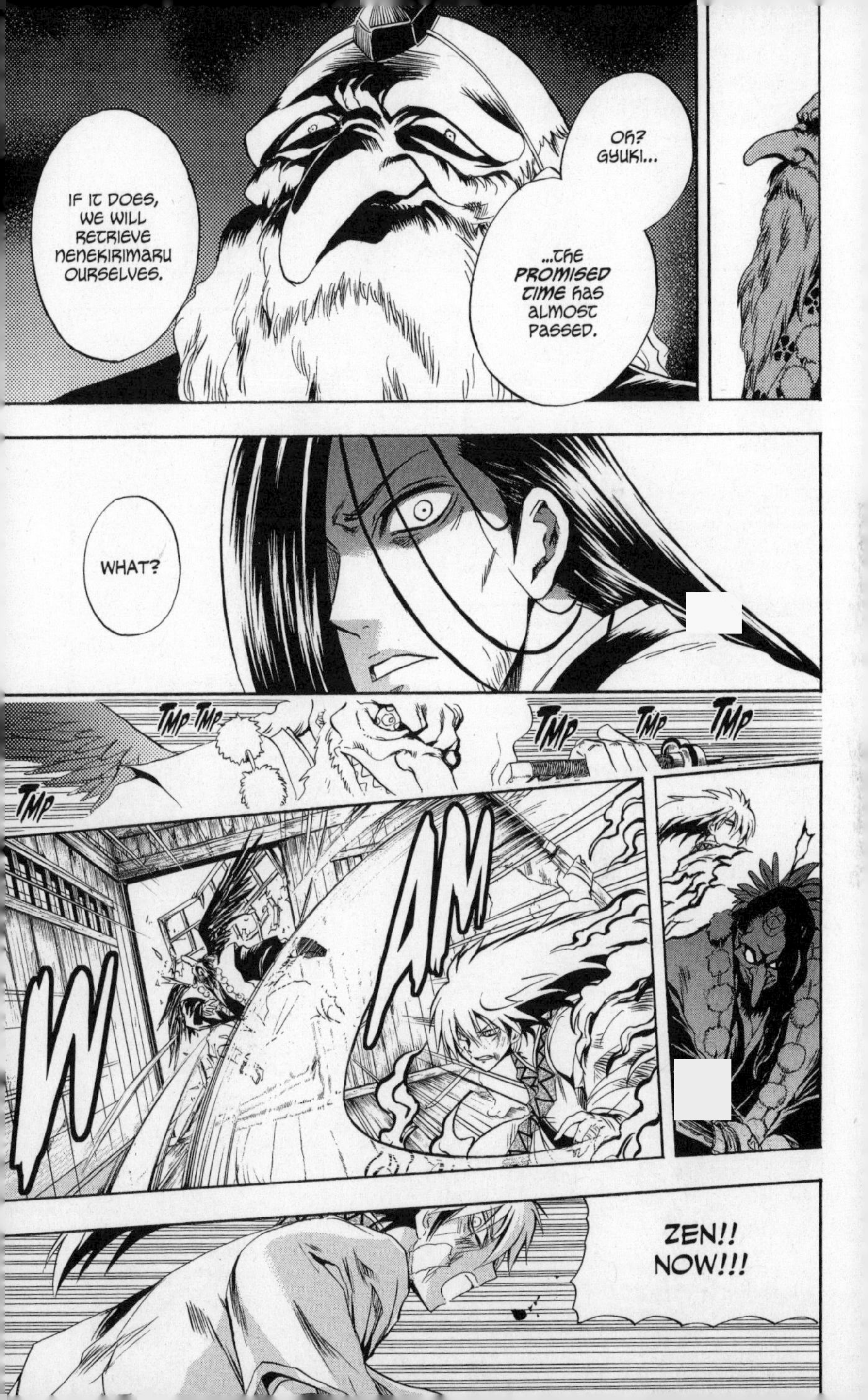
OH? GYUKI...
...THE PROMISED TIME HAS ALMOST PASSED.
IF IT DOES, WE WILL RETRIEVE NENEKIRIMARU OURSELVES.
WHAT?
TMP TMP TMP
TMP TMP
TMP
W
AM
ZEN!! NOW!!!

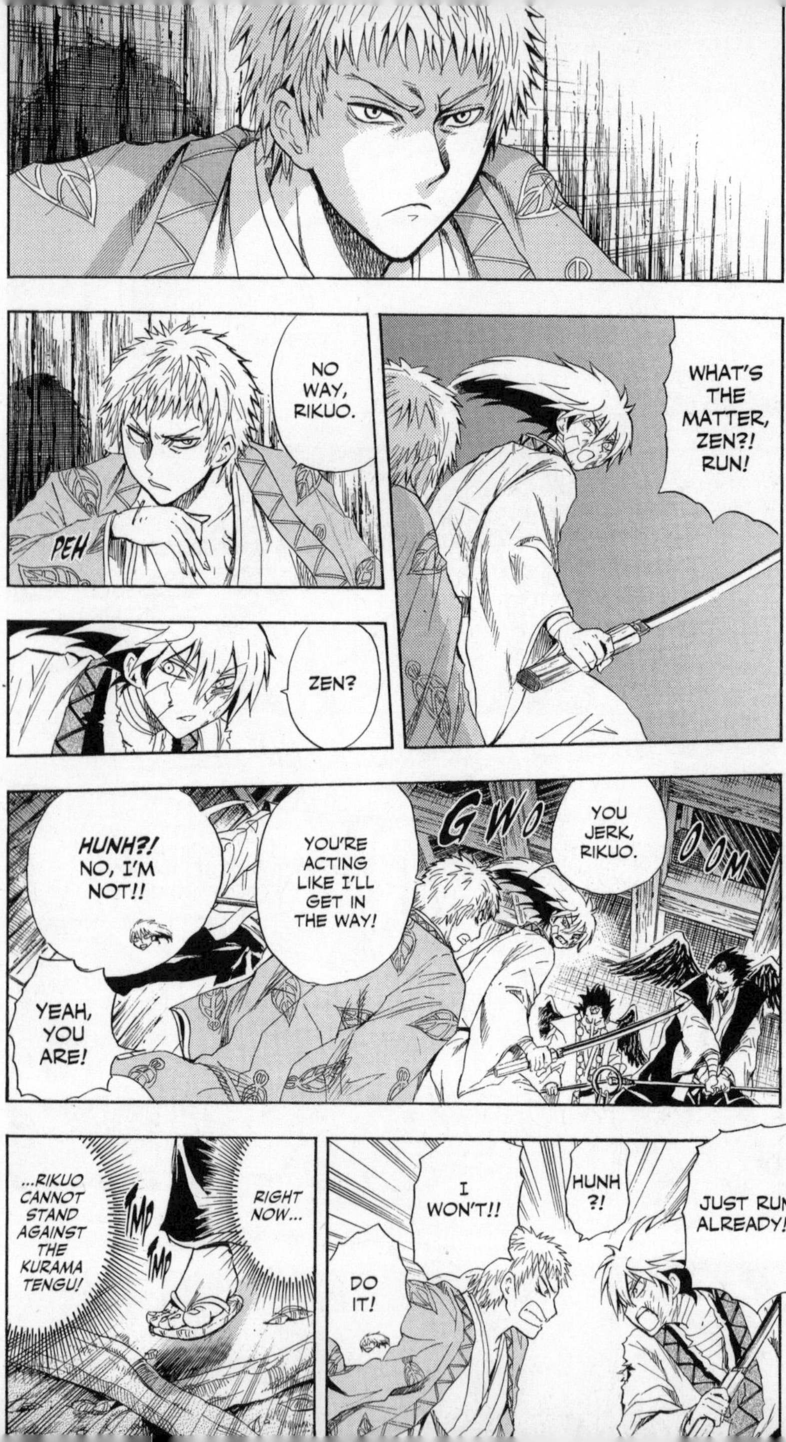
WHAT'S THE MATTER, ZEN?! RUN!
NO WAY, RIKUO.
PEH
ZEN?
YOU JERK, RIKUO.
GWOOOM
YOU'RE ACTING LIKE I'LL GET IN THE WAY!
HUNH?! NO, I'M NOT!!
YEAH, YOU ARE!
JUST RUN ALREADY!!
HUNH?!
I WON'T!!
DO IT!
RIGHT NOW...
...RIKUO CANNOT STAND AGAINST THE KURAMA TENGU!
TMP
TMP

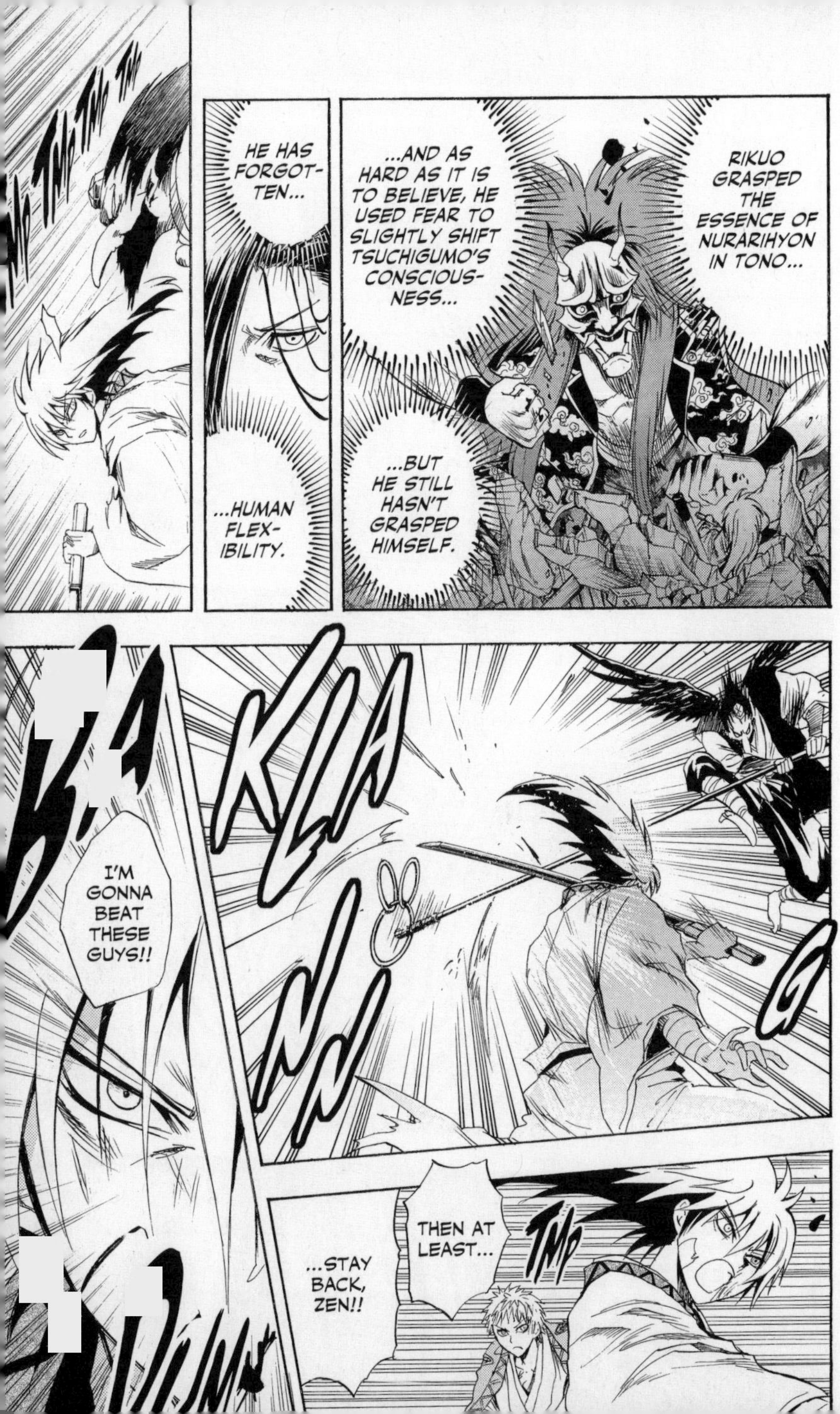
RIKUO GRASPED THE ESSENCE OF NURARIHYON IN TONO...
...AND AS HARD AS IT IS TO BELIEVE, HE USED FEAR TO SLIGHTLY SHIFT TSUCHIGUMO'S CONSCIOUSNESS...
...BUT HE STILL HASN'T GRASPED HIMSELF.
HE HAS FORGOTTEN...
...HUMAN FLEXIBILITY.
KLA
THEN AT LEAST...
...STAY BACK, ZEN!!
TMP
I'M GONNA BEAT THESE GUYS!!

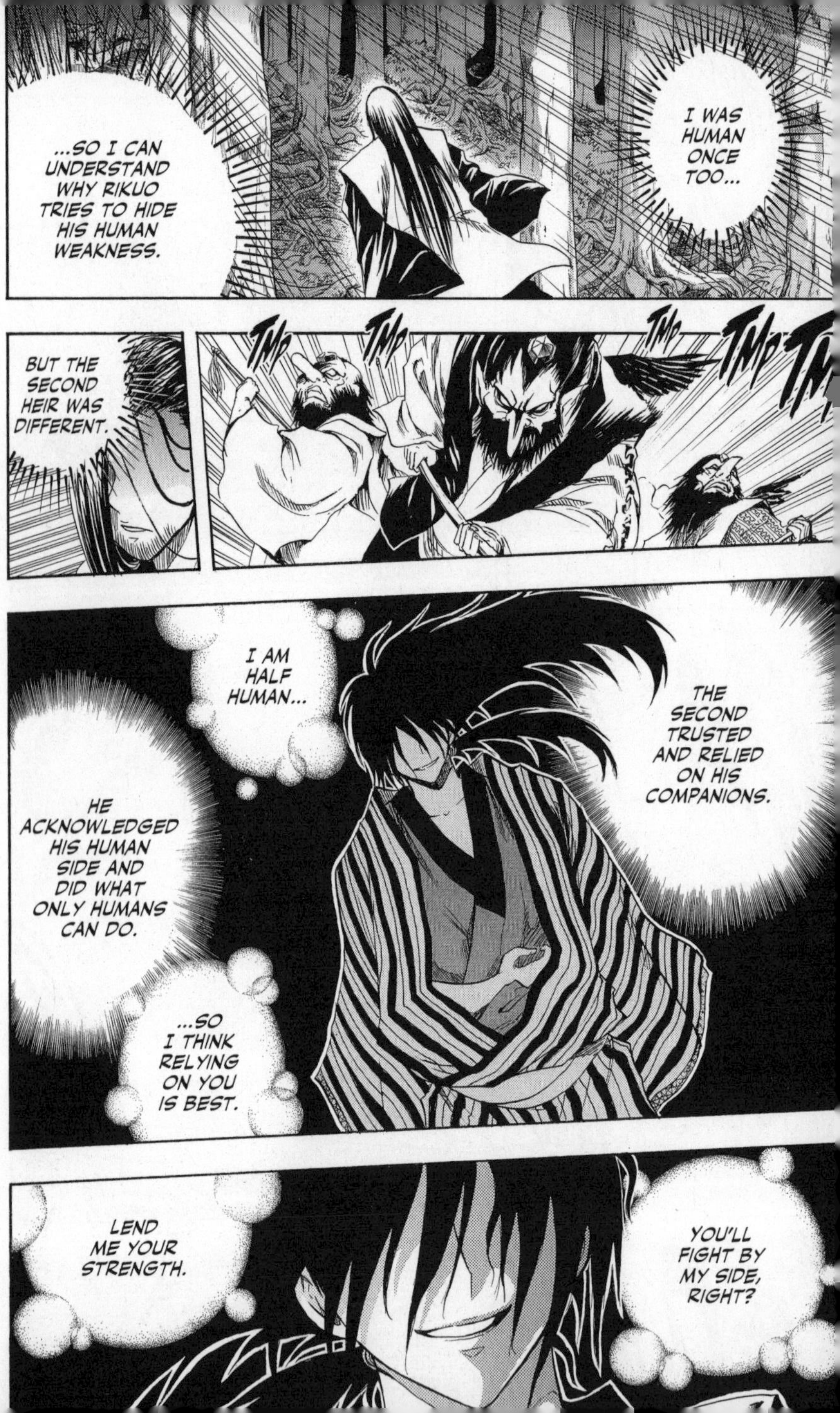
I WAS HUMAN ONCE TOO...
...SO I CAN UNDERSTAND WHY RIKUO TRIES TO HIDE HIS HUMAN WEAKNESS.
TMP TMP TMP TMP
BUT THE SECOND HEIR WAS DIFFERENT.
THE SECOND TRUSTED AND RELIED ON HIS COMPANIONS.
HE ACKNOWLEDGED HIS HUMAN SIDE AND DID WHAT ONLY HUMANS CAN DO.
I AM HALF HUMAN...
...SO I THINK RELYING ON YOU IS BEST.
YOU'LL FIGHT BY MY SIDE, RIGHT?
LEND ME YOUR STRENGTH.

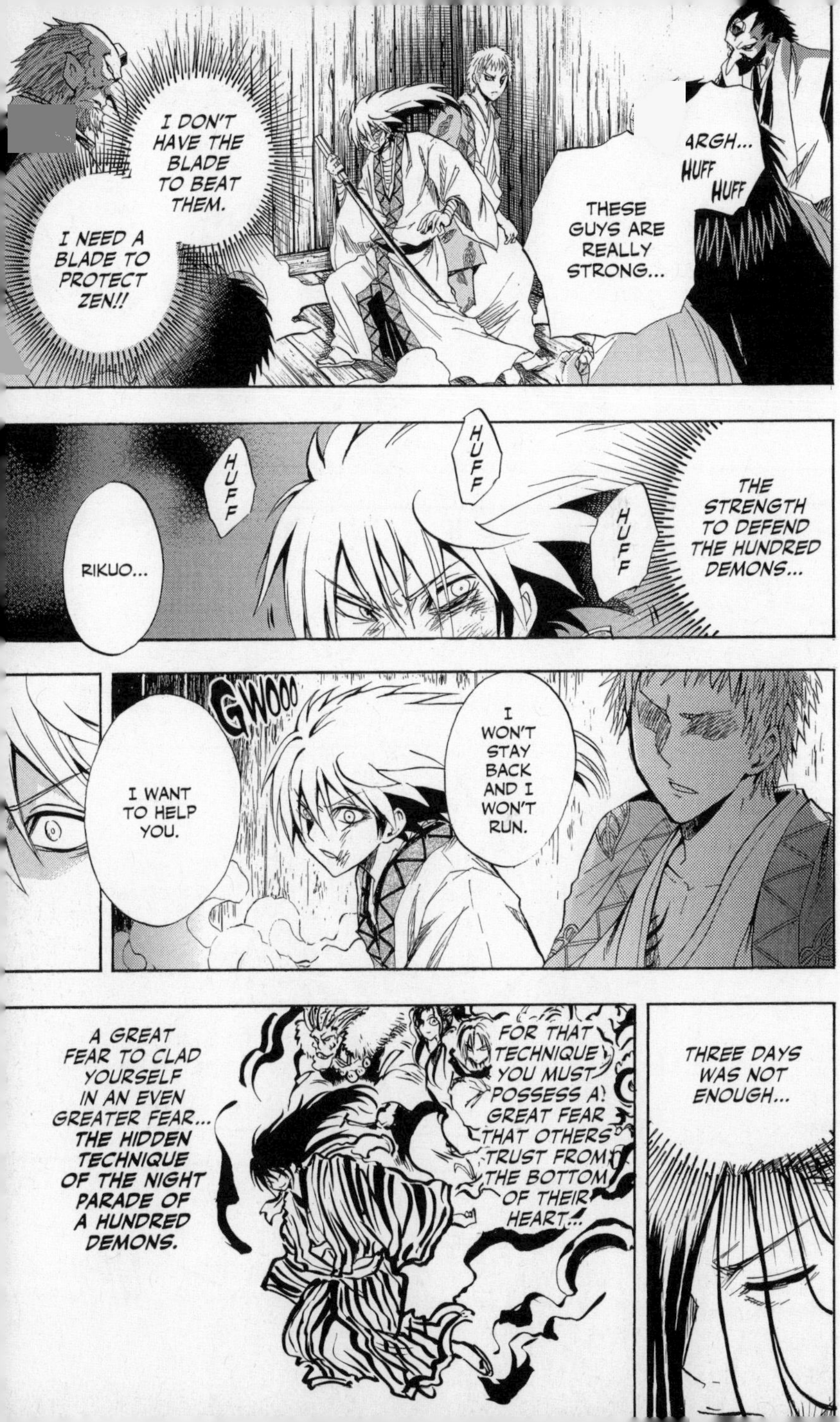
ARGH... HUFF HUFF
THESE GUYS ARE REALLY STRONG...
I DON'T HAVE THE BLADE TO BEAT THEM.
I NEED A BLADE TO PROTECT ZEN!!
THE STRENGTH TO DEFEND THE HUNDRED DEMONS...
HUFF
HUFF
HUFF
RIKUO...
I WON'T STAY BACK AND I WON'T RUN.
GWOOO
I WANT TO HELP YOU.
THREE DAYS WAS NOT ENOUGH...
FOR THAT TECHNIQUE YOU MUST POSSESS A GREAT FEAR THAT OTHERS TRUST FROM THE BOTTOM OF THEIR HEART...
A GREAT FEAR TO CLAD YOURSELF IN AN EVEN GREATER FEAR... THE HIDDEN TECHNIQUE OF THE NIGHT PARADE OF A HUNDRED DEMONS.

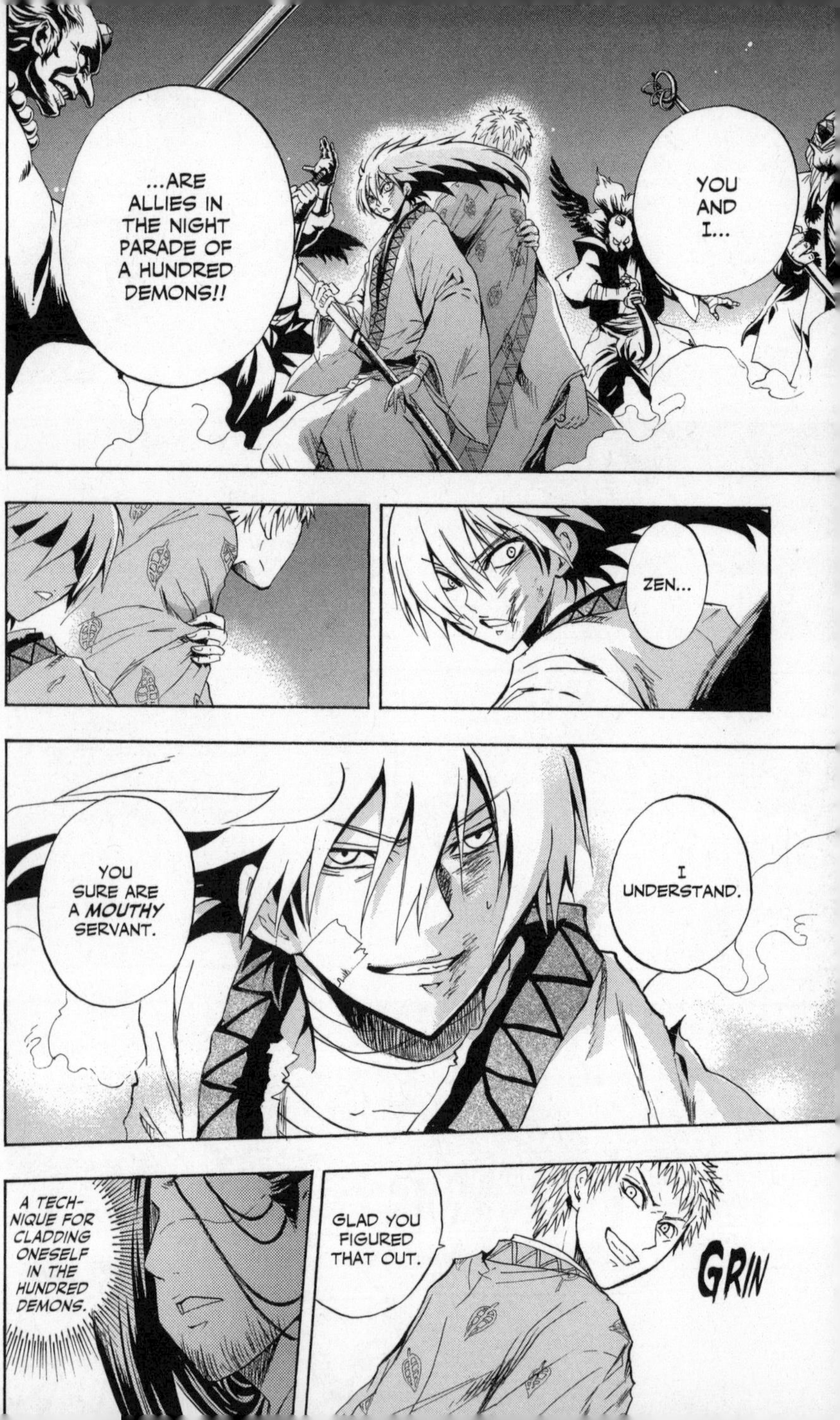

YOU AND I...
...ARE ALLIES IN THE NIGHT PARADE OF A HUNDRED DEMONS!!
ZEN...
I UNDERSTAND.
YOU SURE ARE A *MOUTHY* SERVANT.
GLAD YOU FIGURED THAT OUT.
GRIN
A TECHNIQUE FOR CLADDING ONESELF IN THE HUNDRED DEMONS.

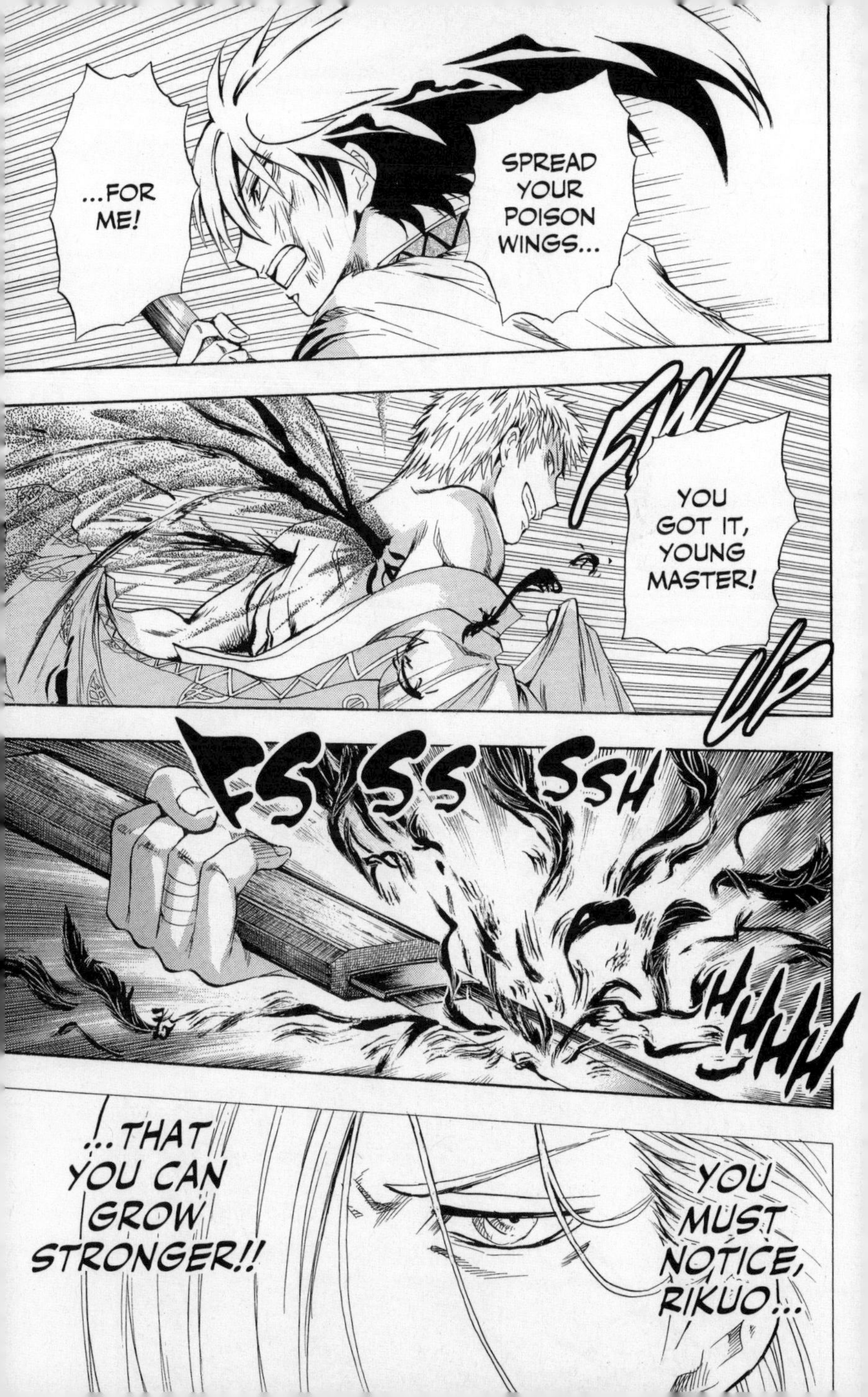
SPREAD YOUR POISON WINGS...
...FOR ME!
YOU GOT IT, YOUNG MASTER!
YOU MUST NOTICE, RIKUO!...
...THAT YOU CAN GROW STRONGER!!

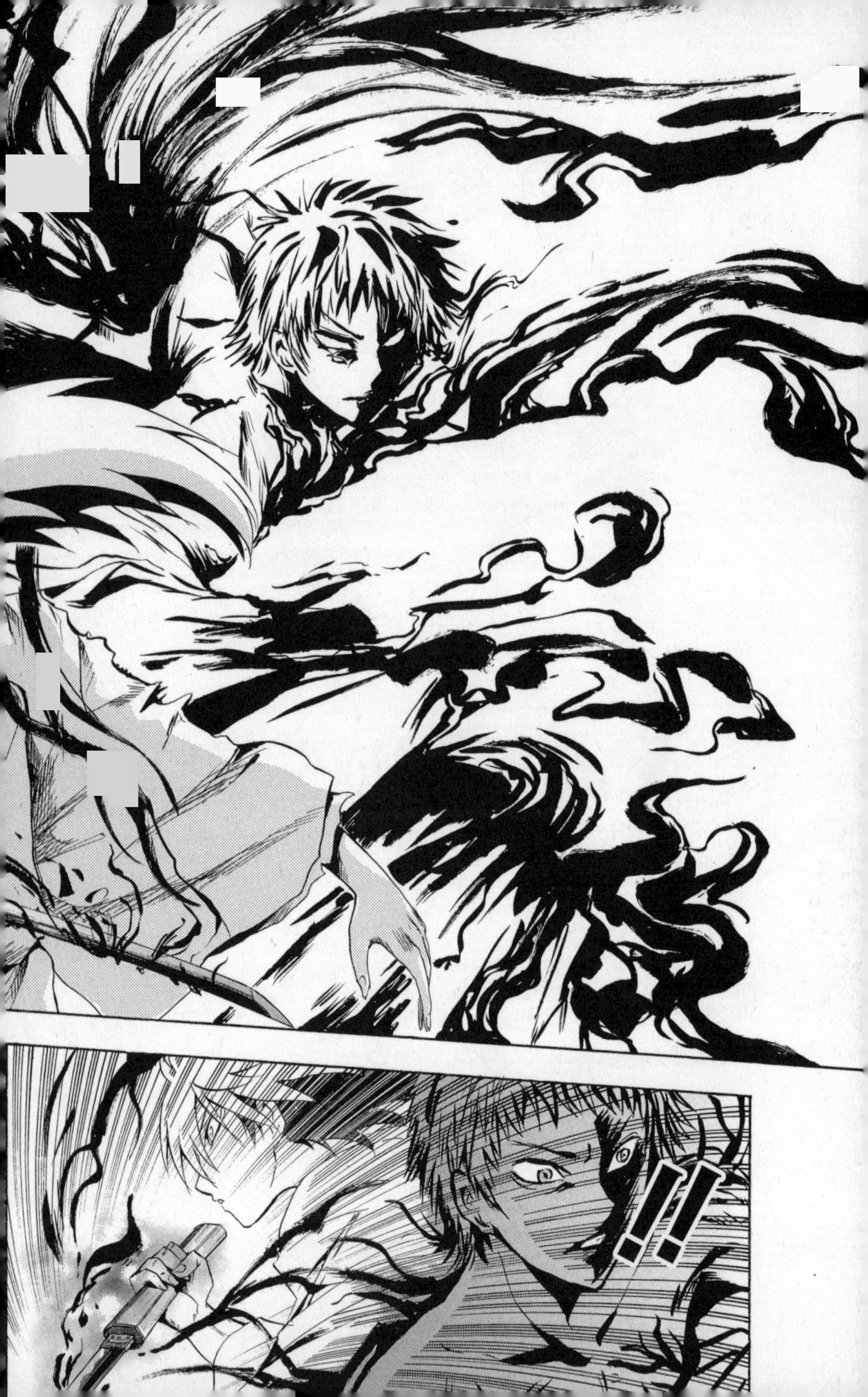
!!

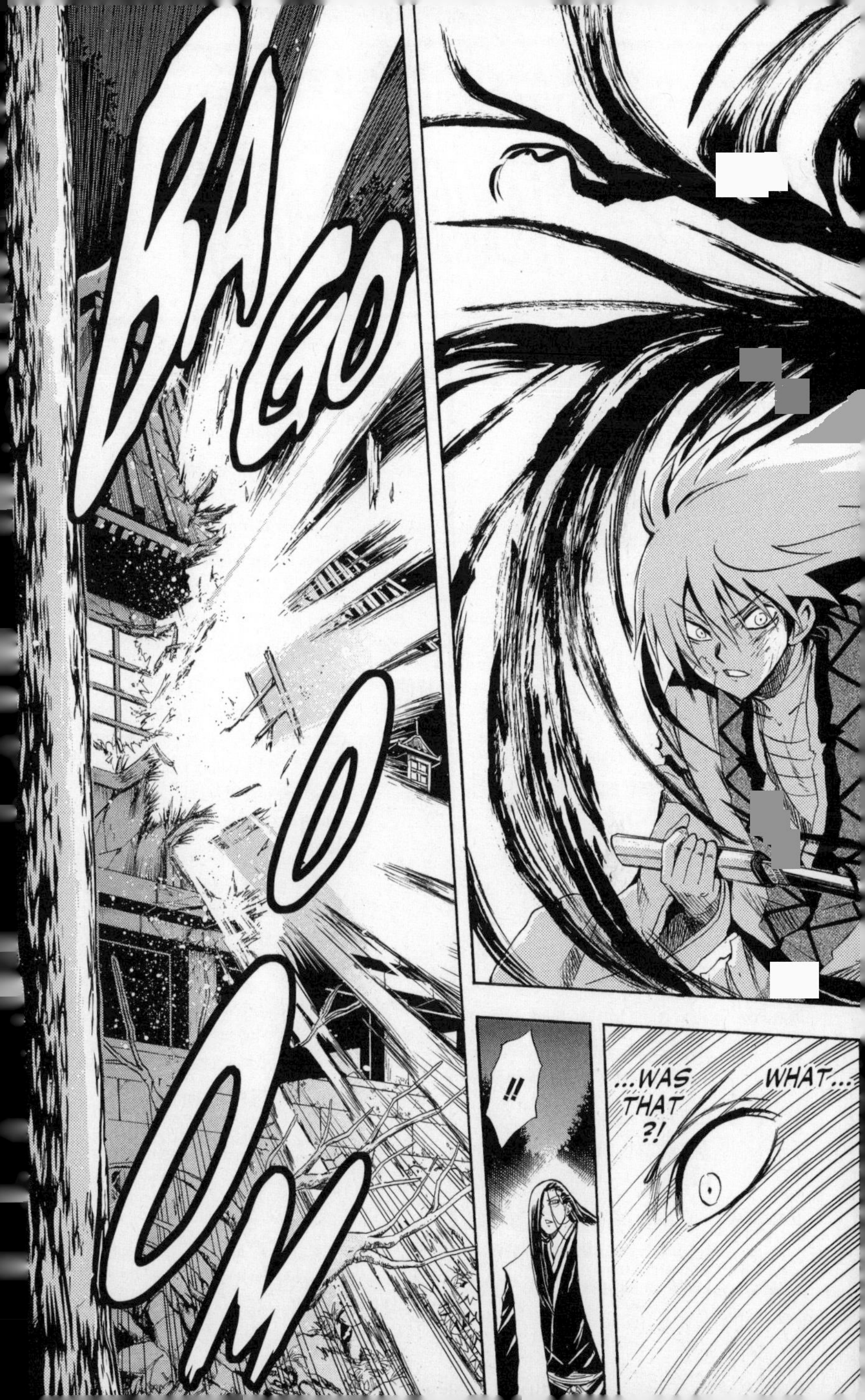
WHAT...
...WAS THAT ?!
!!

KIYOTSUGU'S
#12 BY KIYO
YOKAI BRAIN
YOH-KWAI-NOH!
LEADS TO THE RIVER

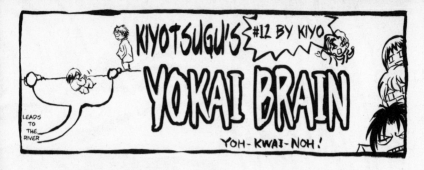

Question: Why is Ryuji so cool? I just gotta know.
—Ayaka, Hokkaido

Yura: Huuuuuh?! Ryuji is coooool? What're you talking about? I don't think so!

Mamiru: Yura, you shouldn't talk like that about Ryuji.

Yura: But I mean, come on! He's too mean! Don't let him fool you!

Ryuji: Lay off, would ya?!

Question: How much medicine does Zen always walk around with?
—Maki Tanaka, Osaka

Zen: I don't carry that much on me. My servants carry it. Thanks to them, I can move around freely. I suppose I've got enough to last me each time I go out.

Question: Who is the least of the Sanba-Garasu? Sasami? Tosakamaru?
—Yurika Takase, Akita Prefecture

Sasami: Me!! After Kuromaru is Tosakamaru, and then there's me! (bluntly)

Tosakamaru: But you're not like a little sister. Big Bro is like a big bro, though.

Sasami: I think so too! (bluntly)

Question: Do they ever change the water in Kappa's pond?
—The Seventh, Toyama Prefecture

Kappa: That pond is actually connected to a nearby river. I dug it myself.

Rikuo: That pond is where the little yokai go to kick back and relax. I love that pond!

Question: How many chores does Rikuo do each day at school?
—Kaoringo, Osaka

Tsurara: Lord Rikuo does all kinds of work depending on what day it is, from being class helper in the morning to performing odd jobs for the student council. I'm really worried about him!! But at least we can wait on him hand and foot back at the clan.

Rikuo: Yesterday, I carried out a record-breaking two tons of garbage! (eyes ablaze)

Aotabo: Lord Rikuo...

Question: I wrote a letter to Kuromaru. Would you give it to him for me?
—Yukina Imafuku, Kanagawa Prefecture

Kuromaru: Huh...? Uh, yeah. I got it. Thanks.

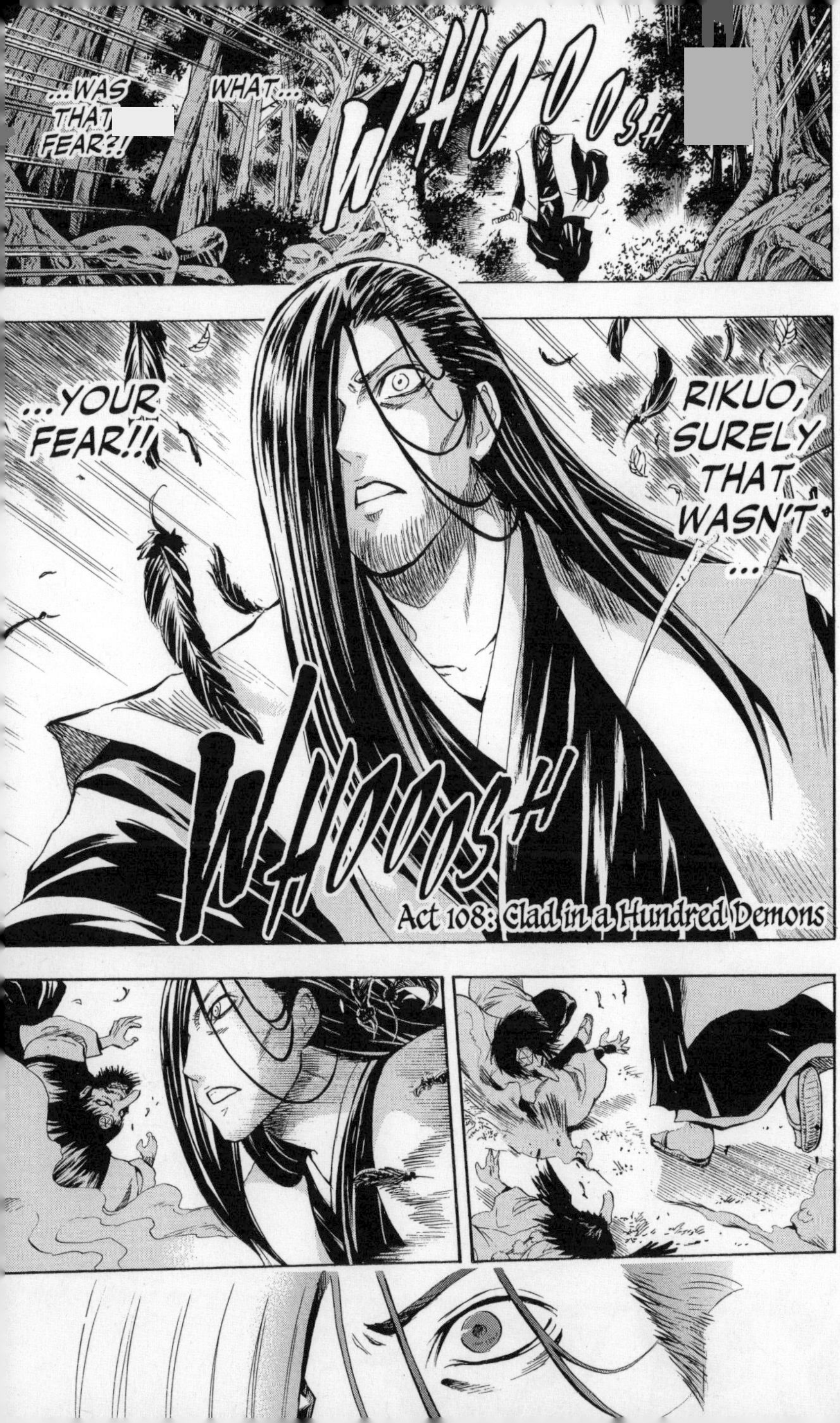
WHOOOSH
WHAT...
...WAS THAT FEAR?!
RIKUO, SURELY THAT WASN'T ...
...YOUR FEAR!!
WHOOOSH
Act 108: Clad in a Hundred Demons

Act 108: Clad in a Hundred Demons

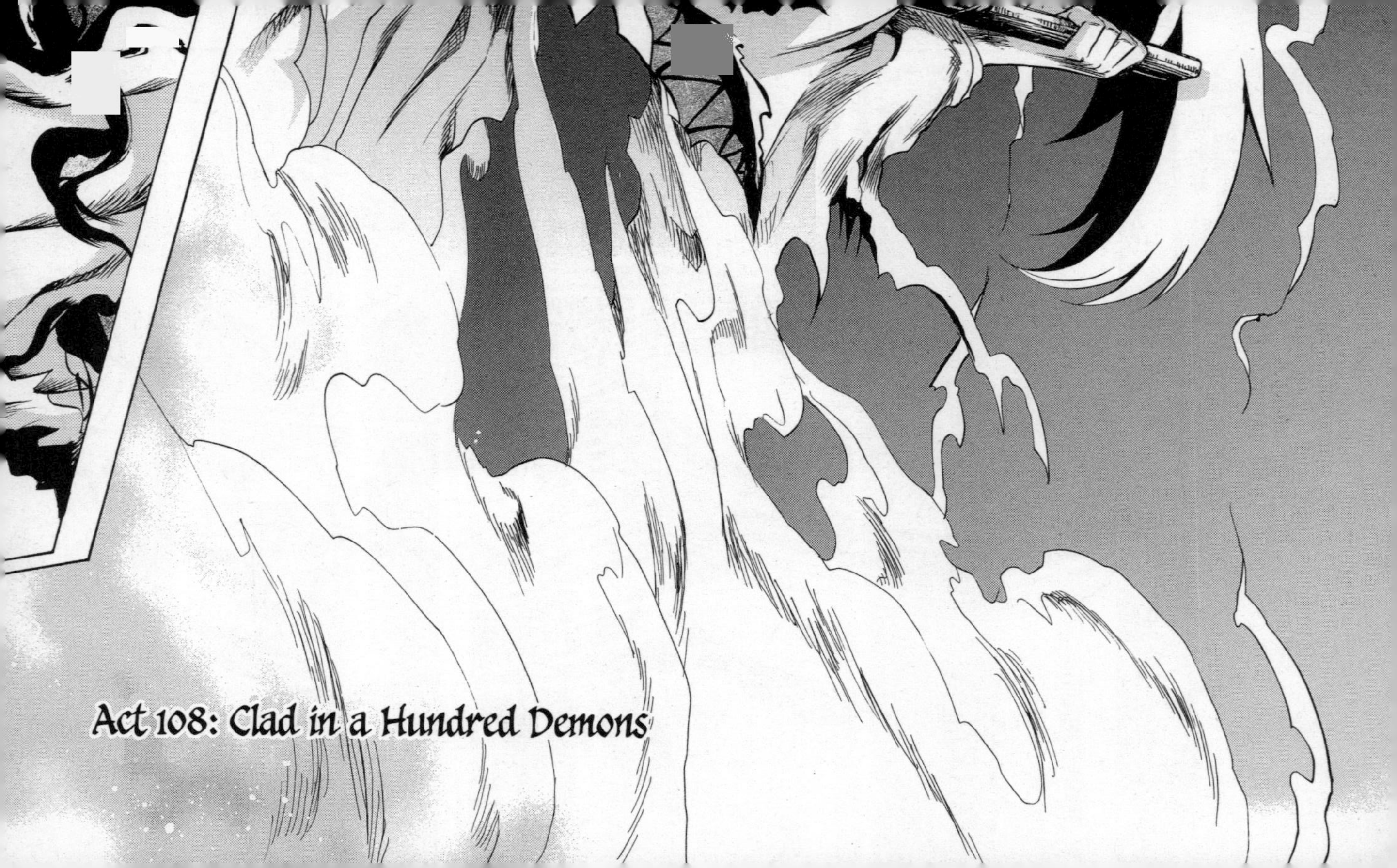

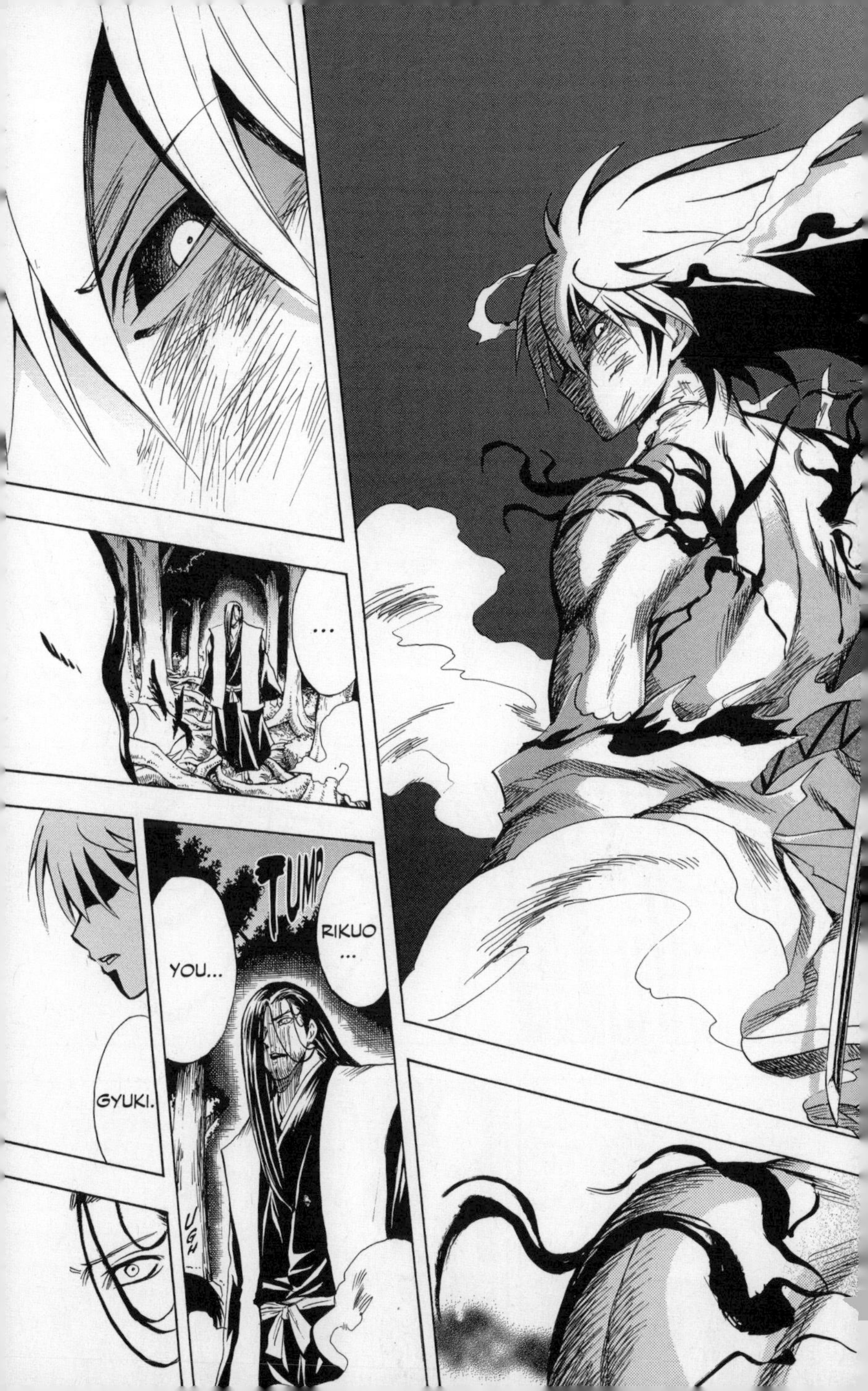
...
TUMP
RIKUO ...
YOU...
GYUKI.
UGH...

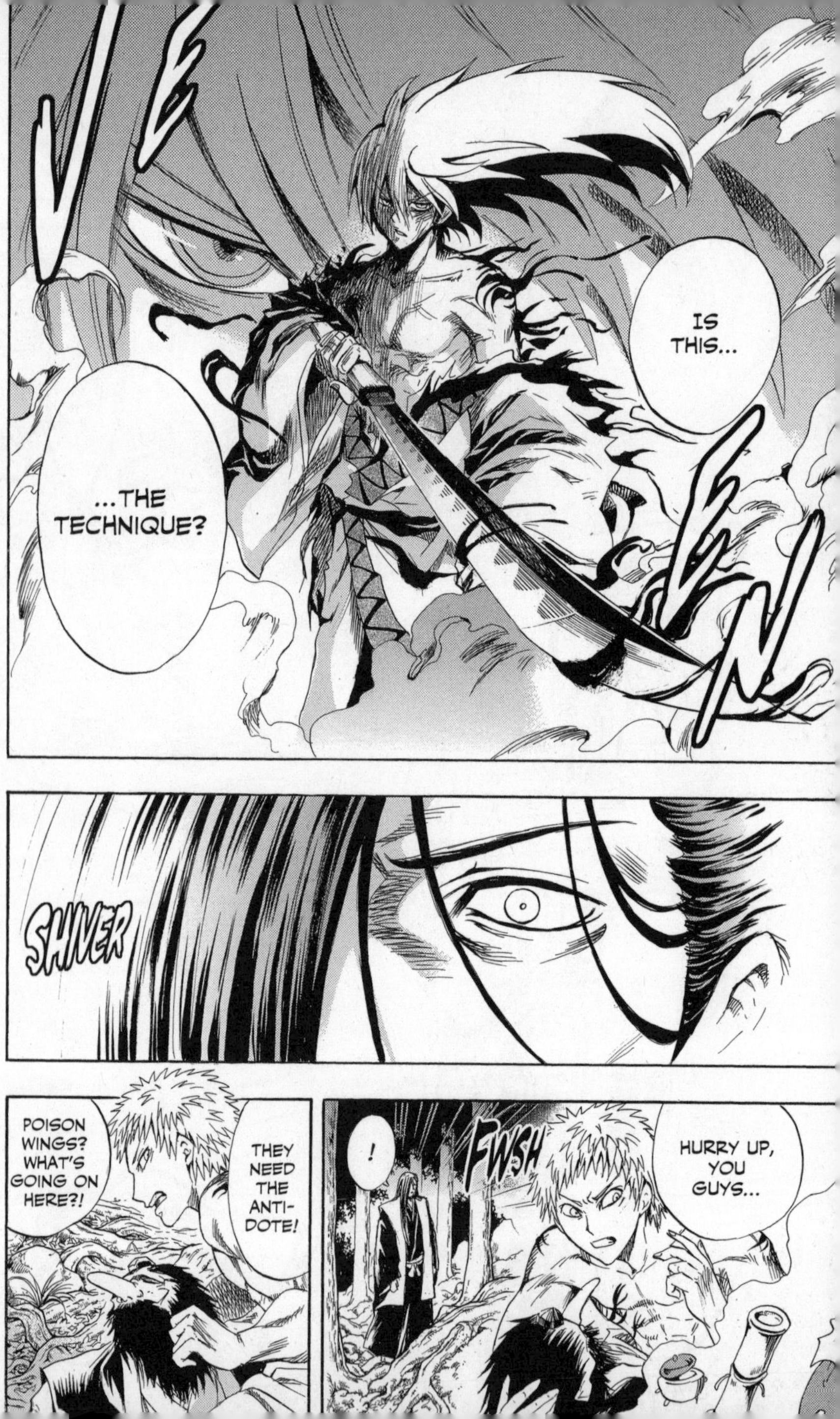
IS THIS...
...THE TECHNIQUE?
SHIVER
HURRY UP, YOU GUYS...
FWSH
!
THEY NEED THE ANTI-DOTE!
POISON WINGS? WHAT'S GOING ON HERE?!

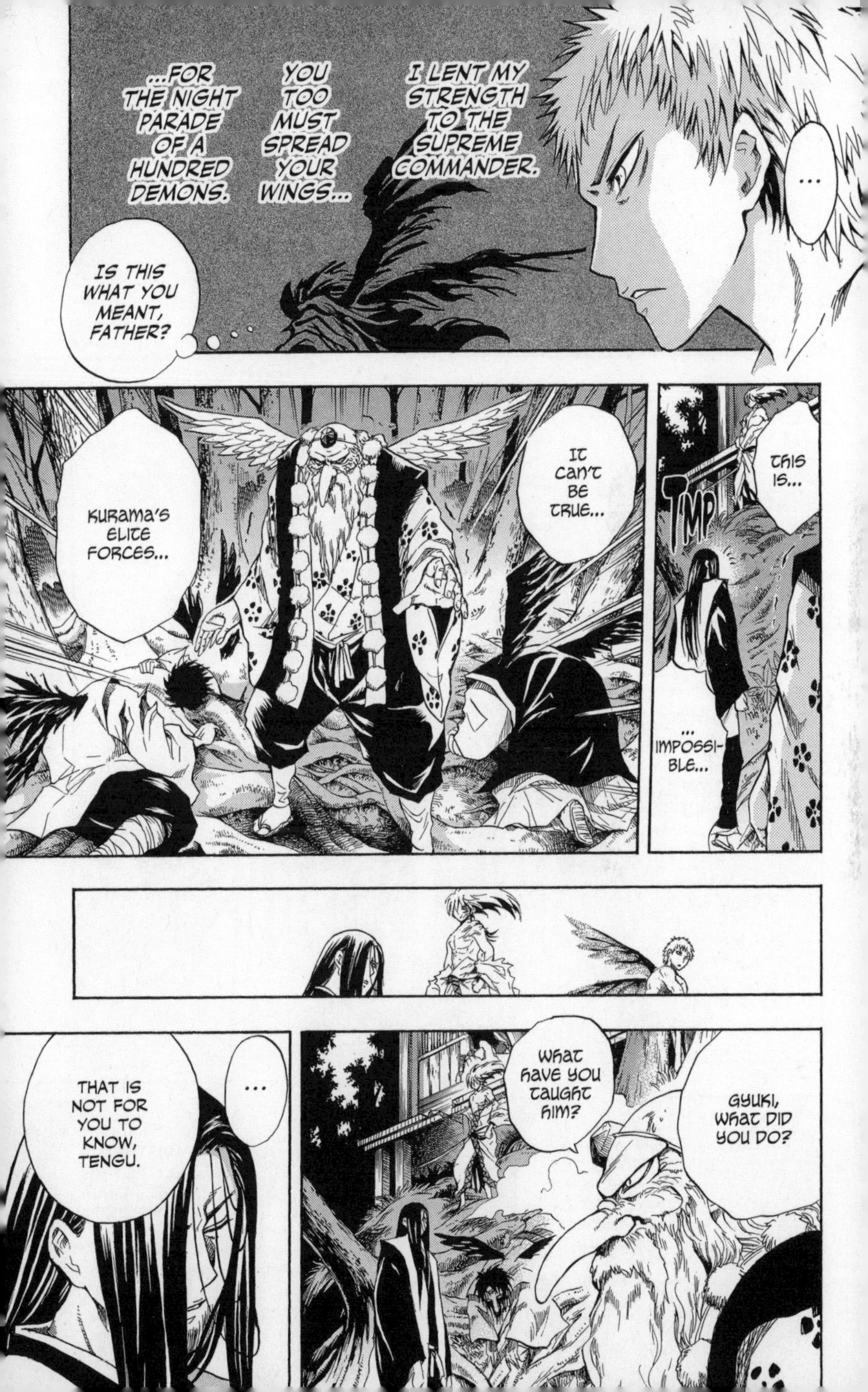
...
I LENT MY STRENGTH TO THE SUPREME COMMANDER.
YOU TOO MUST SPREAD YOUR WINGS...
...FOR THE NIGHT PARADE OF A HUNDRED DEMONS.
IS THIS WHAT YOU MEANT, FATHER?
TMP
This is...
...impossible...
It can't be true...
Kurama's elite forces...
Gyuki, what did you do?
What have you taught him?
...
THAT IS NOT FOR YOU TO KNOW, TENGU.

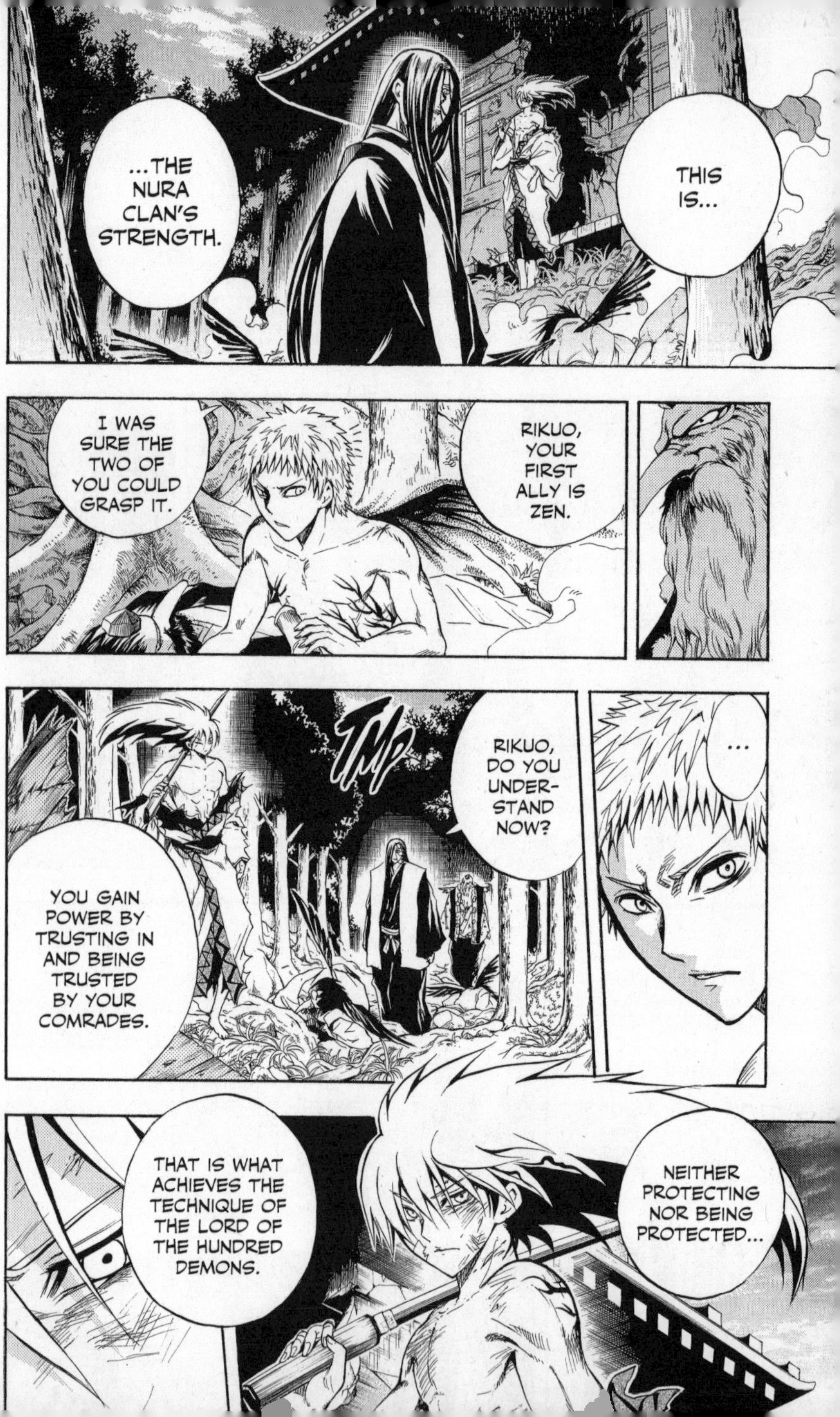
THIS IS...
...THE NURA CLAN'S STRENGTH.
RIKUO, YOUR FIRST ALLY IS ZEN.
I WAS SURE THE TWO OF YOU COULD GRASP IT.
...
RIKUO, DO YOU UNDER-STAND NOW?
TMP
YOU GAIN POWER BY TRUSTING IN AND BEING TRUSTED BY YOUR COMRADES.
NEITHER PROTECTING NOR BEING PROTECTED...
THAT IS WHAT ACHIEVES THE TECHNIQUE OF THE LORD OF THE HUNDRED DEMONS.

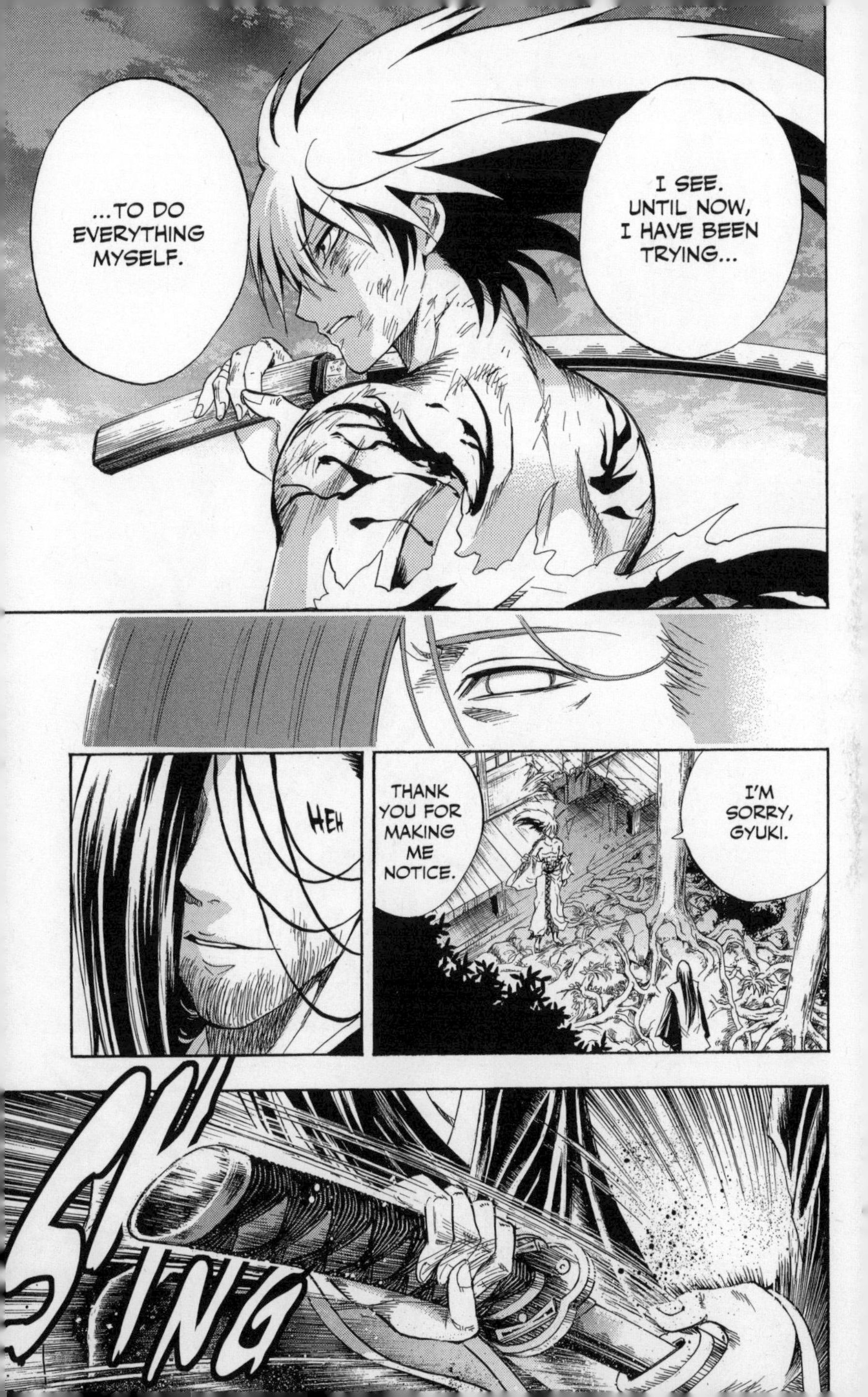
I SEE. UNTIL NOW, I HAVE BEEN TRYING...
...TO DO EVERYTHING MYSELF.
I'M SORRY, GYUKI.
THANK YOU FOR MAKING ME NOTICE.
HEH
SHING

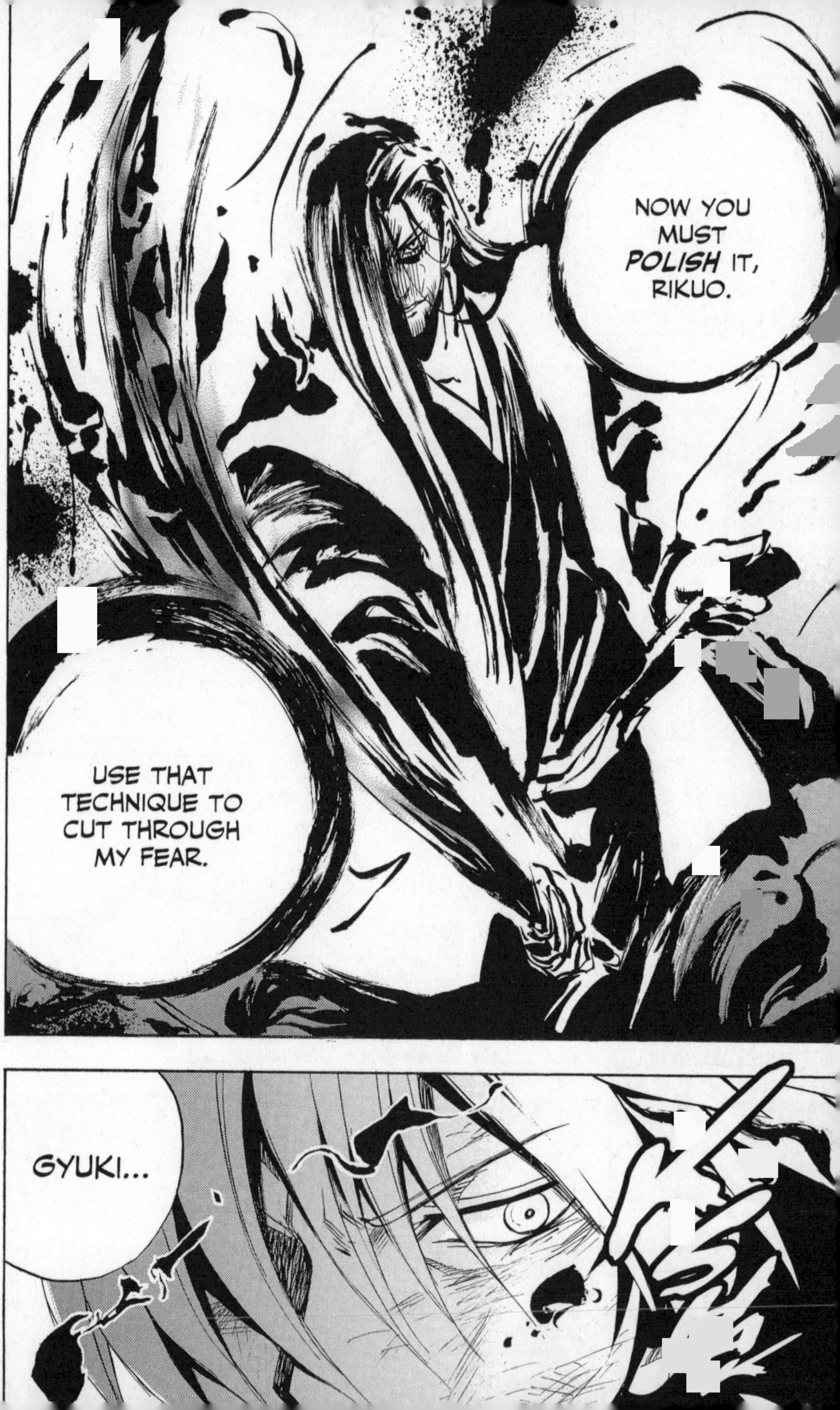
NOW YOU MUST POLISH IT, RIKUO.
USE THAT TECHNIQUE TO CUT THROUGH MY FEAR.
GYUKI...

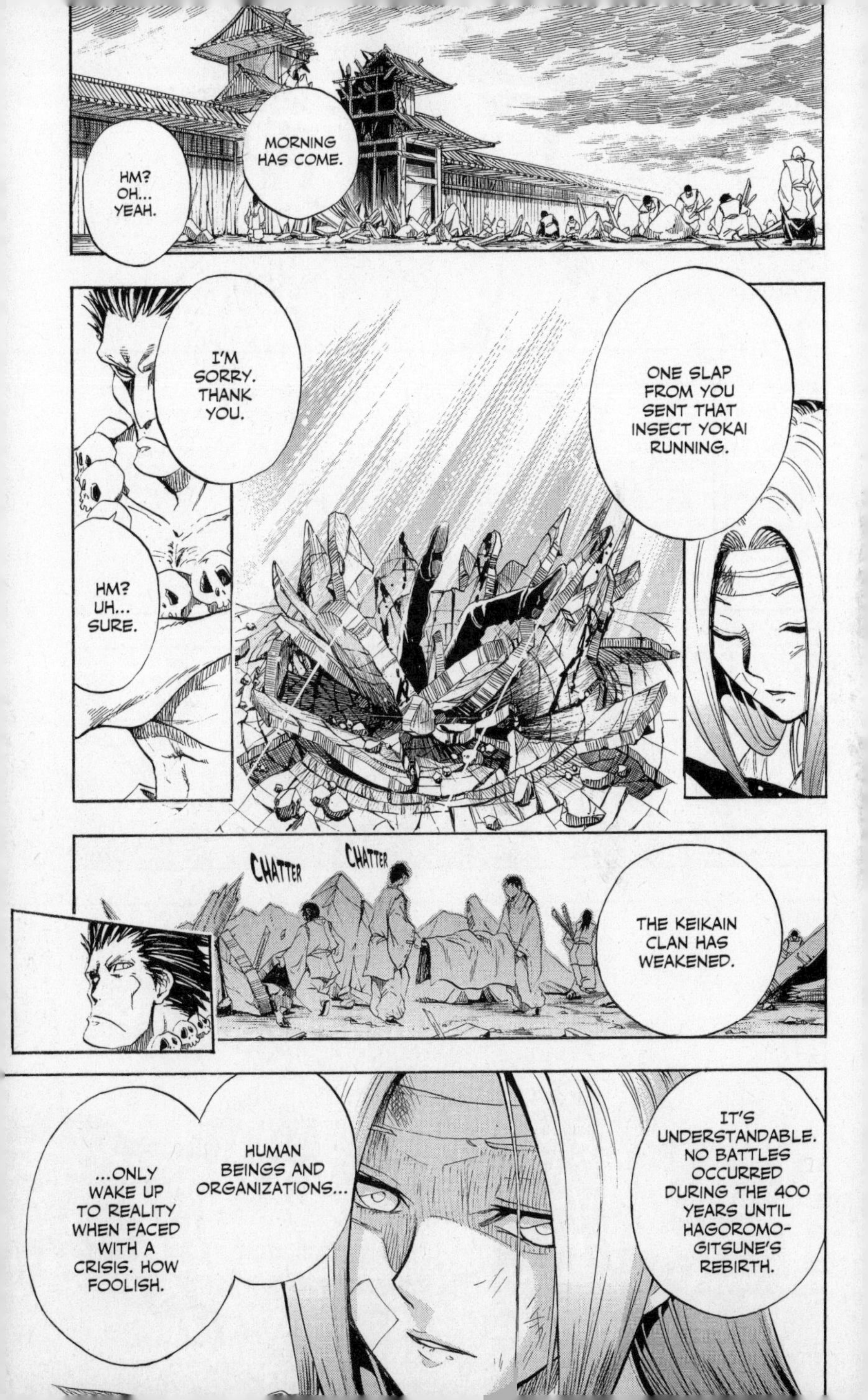
MORNING HAS COME.
HM? OH... YEAH.
ONE SLAP FROM YOU SENT THAT INSECT YOKAI RUNNING.
I'M SORRY. THANK YOU.
HM? UH... SURE.
THE KEIKAIN CLAN HAS WEAKENED.
CHATTER
CHATTER
IT'S UNDERSTANDABLE. NO BATTLES OCCURRED DURING THE 400 YEARS UNTIL HAGOROMO-GITSUNE'S REBIRTH.
HUMAN BEINGS AND ORGANIZATIONS...
...ONLY WAKE UP TO REALITY WHEN FACED WITH A CRISIS. HOW FOOLISH.

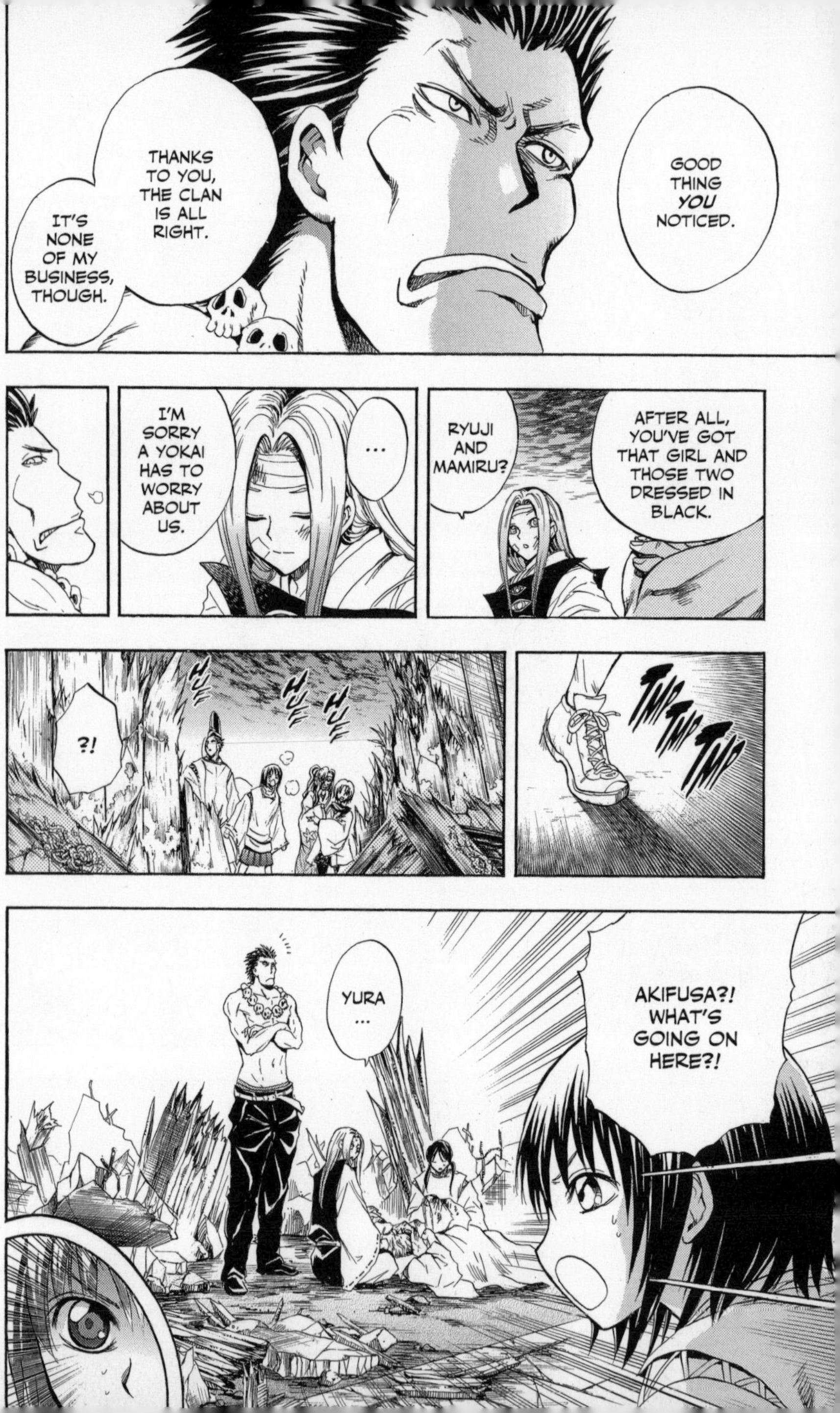
GOOD THING *YOU* NOTICED.
THANKS TO YOU, THE CLAN IS ALL RIGHT.
IT'S NONE OF MY BUSINESS, THOUGH.
AFTER ALL, YOU'VE GOT THAT GIRL AND THOSE TWO DRESSED IN BLACK.
RYUJI AND MAMIRU?
...
I'M SORRY A YOKAI HAS TO WORRY ABOUT US.
TMP TMP TMP
HUF HUF HUF
?!
AKIFUSA?! WHAT'S GOING ON HERE?!
YURA ...

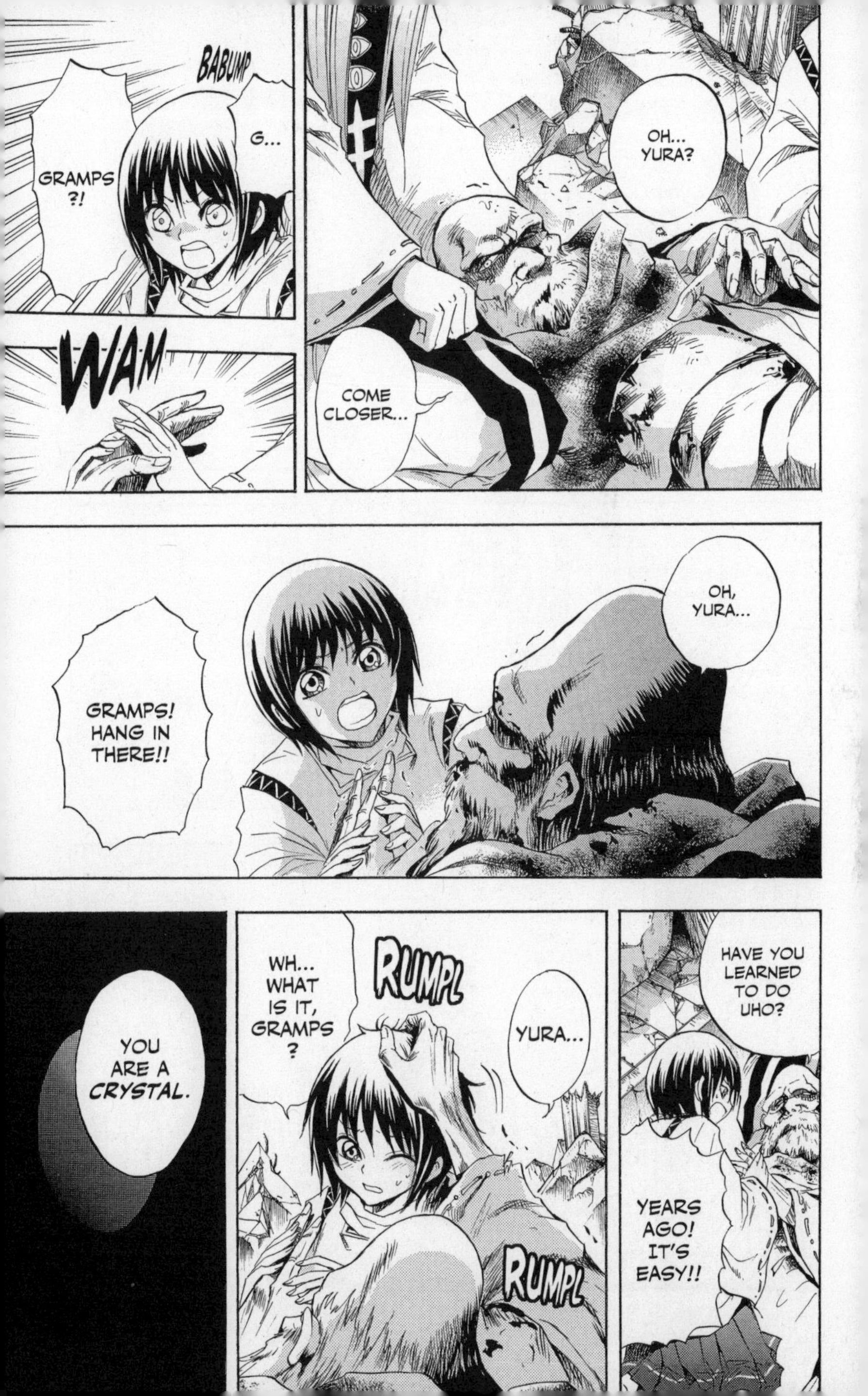
OH... YURA?
COME CLOSER...
BABUMP
G...
GRAMPS ?!
WAM
OH, YURA...
GRAMPS! HANG IN THERE!!
HAVE YOU LEARNED TO DO UHO?
YEARS AGO! IT'S EASY!!
RUMPL
YURA...
WH... WHAT IS IT, GRAMPS?
RUMPL
YOU ARE A CRYSTAL.

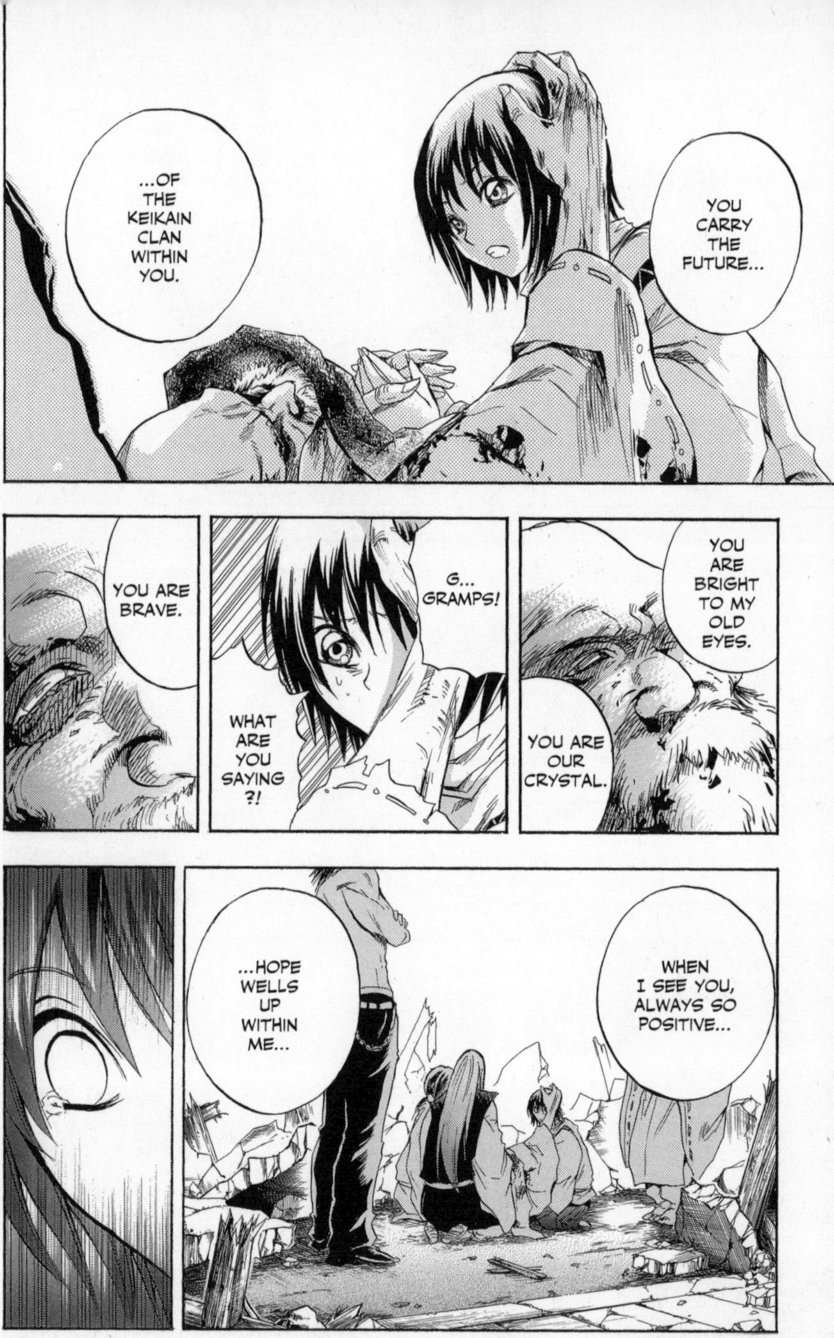
YOU CARRY THE FUTURE...
...OF THE KEIKAIN CLAN WITHIN YOU.
YOU ARE BRIGHT TO MY OLD EYES.
YOU ARE OUR CRYSTAL.
G... GRAMPS!
WHAT ARE YOU SAYING?!
YOU ARE BRAVE.
WHEN I SEE YOU, ALWAYS SO POSITIVE...
...HOPE WELLS UP WITHIN ME...

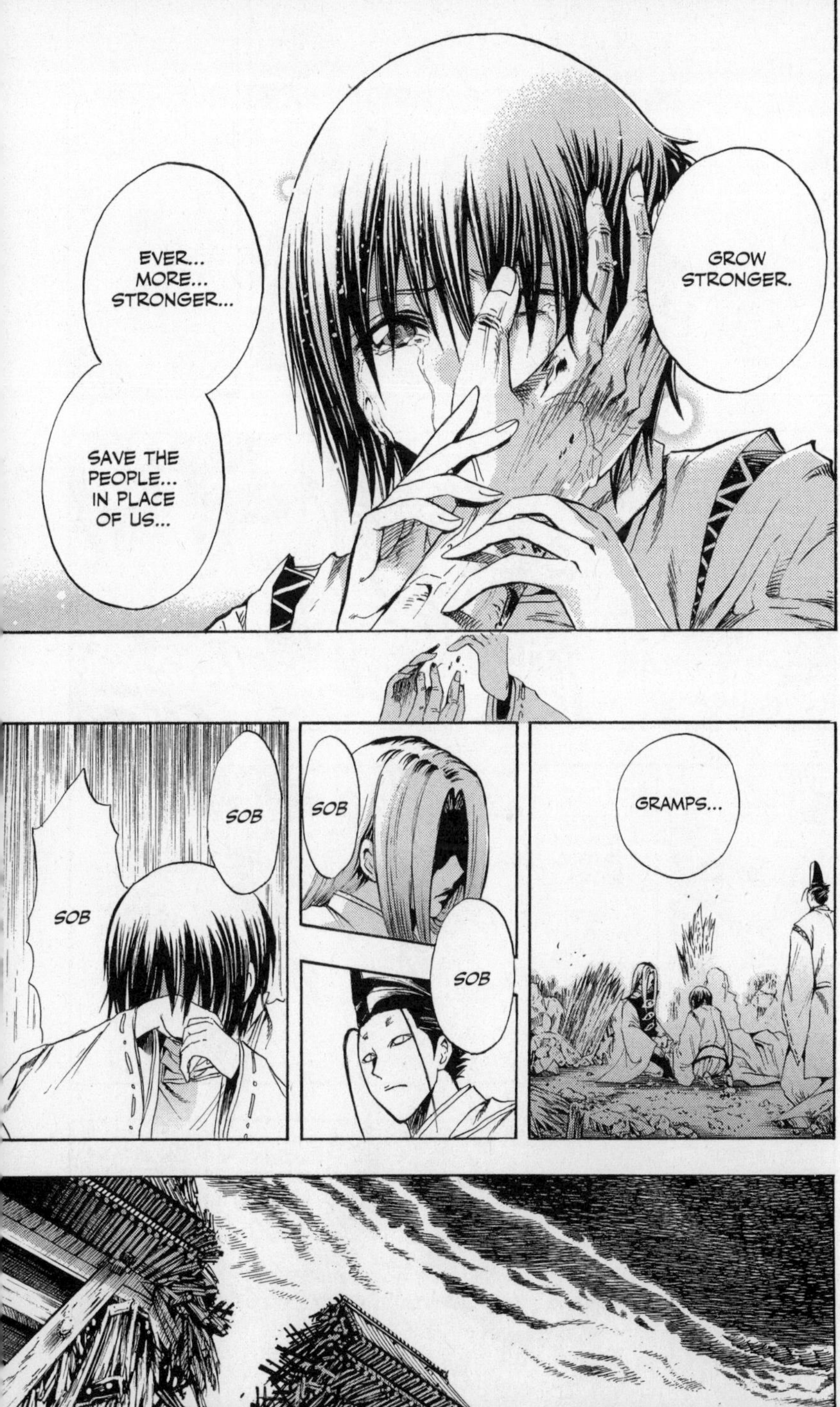
GROW STRONGER.
EVER... MORE... STRONGER...
SAVE THE PEOPLE... IN PLACE OF US...
GRAMPS...
SOB
SOB
SOB
SOB

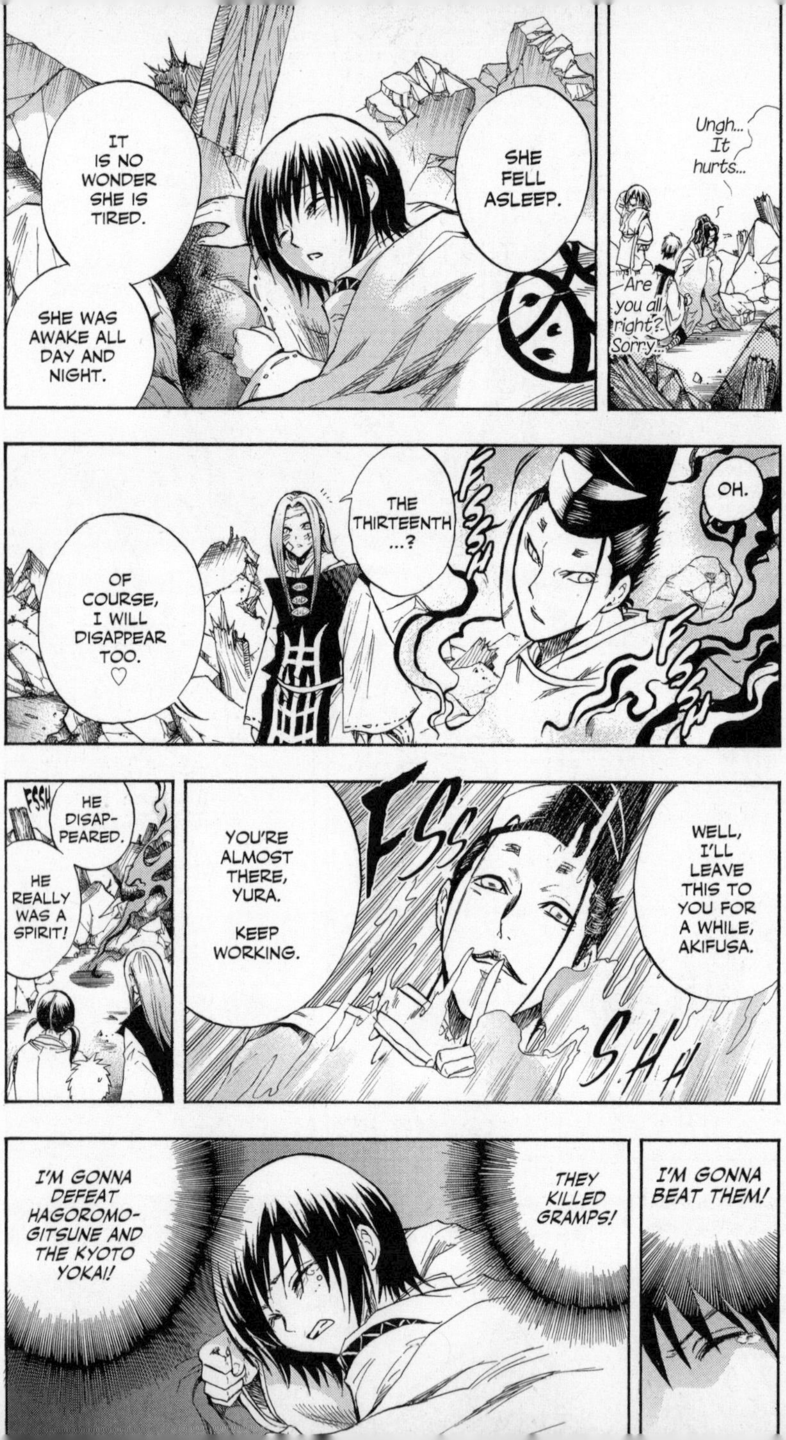
Ungh... It hurts...
Are you all right? Sorry...
SHE FELL ASLEEP.
IT IS NO WONDER SHE IS TIRED.
SHE WAS AWAKE ALL DAY AND NIGHT.
OH.
THE THIRTEENTH ...?
OF COURSE, I WILL DISAPPEAR TOO. ♡
WELL, I'LL LEAVE THIS TO YOU FOR A WHILE, AKIFUSA.
YOU'RE ALMOST THERE, YURA.
KEEP WORKING.
SHH
FSSH
HE DISAP-PEARED.
HE REALLY WAS A SPIRIT!
I'M GONNA BEAT THEM!
THEY KILLED GRAMPS!
I'M GONNA DEFEAT HAGOROMO-GITSUNE AND THE KYOTO YOKAI!

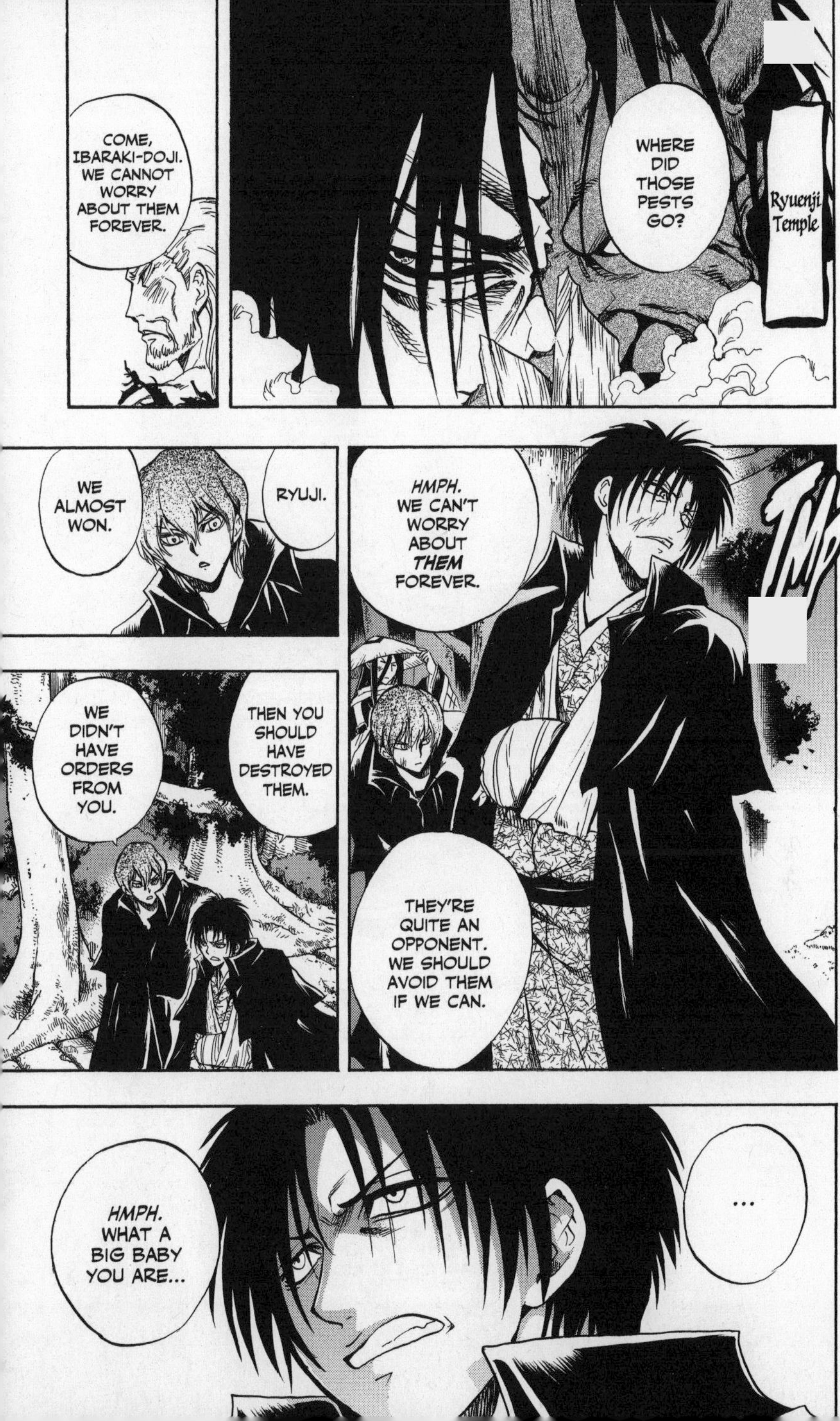
Ryuenji Temple
WHERE DID THOSE PESTS GO?
COME, IBARAKI-DOJI. WE CANNOT WORRY ABOUT THEM FOREVER.
HMPH. WE CAN'T WORRY ABOUT *THEM* FOREVER.
THEY'RE QUITE AN OPPONENT. WE SHOULD AVOID THEM IF WE CAN.
RYUJI.
WE ALMOST WON.
THEN YOU SHOULD HAVE DESTROYED THEM.
WE DIDN'T HAVE ORDERS FROM YOU.
...
HMPH. WHAT A BIG BABY YOU ARE...

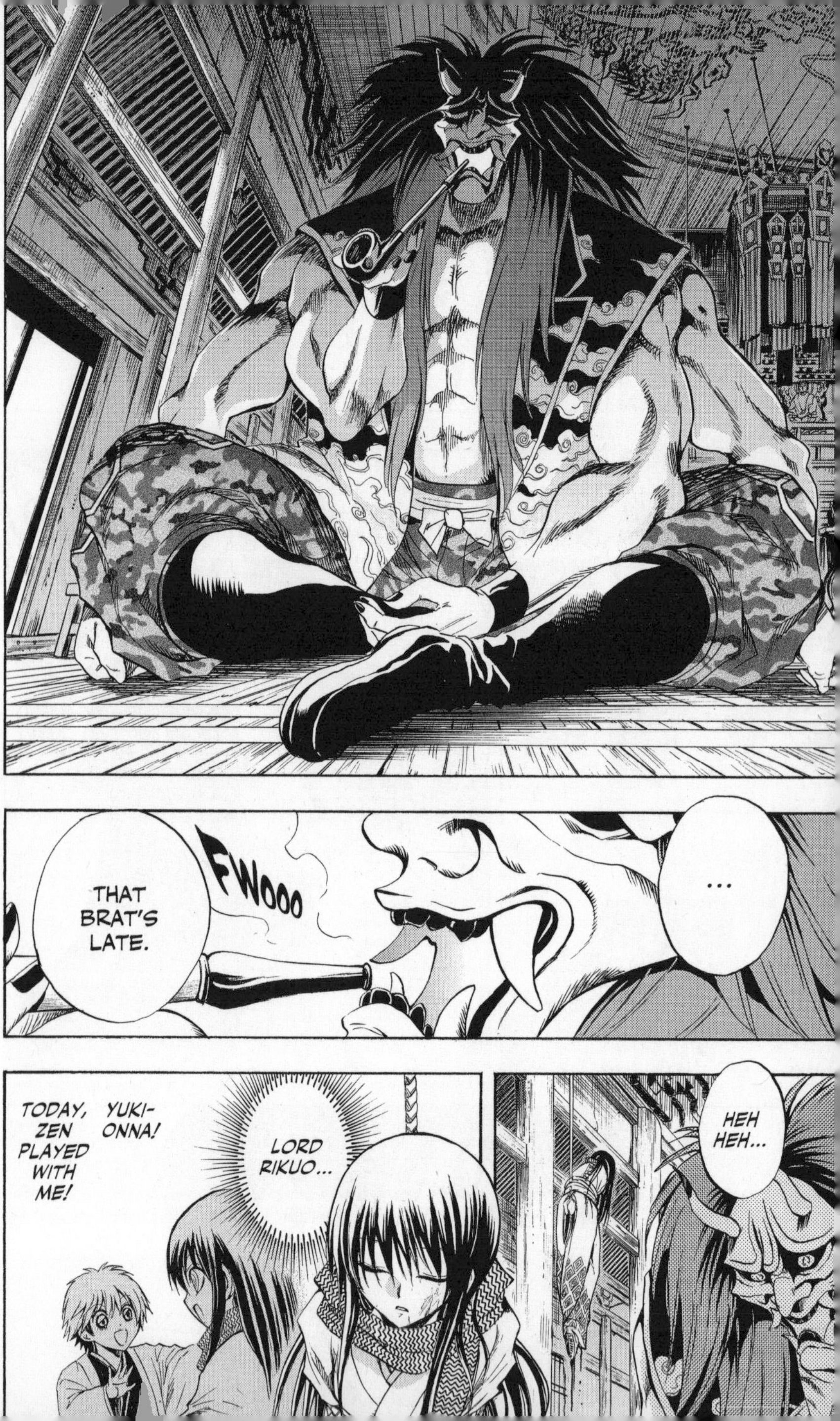
...
FWOOO
THAT BRAT'S LATE.
HEH HEH...
LORD RIKUO...
YUKI-ONNA!
TODAY, ZEN PLAYED WITH ME!

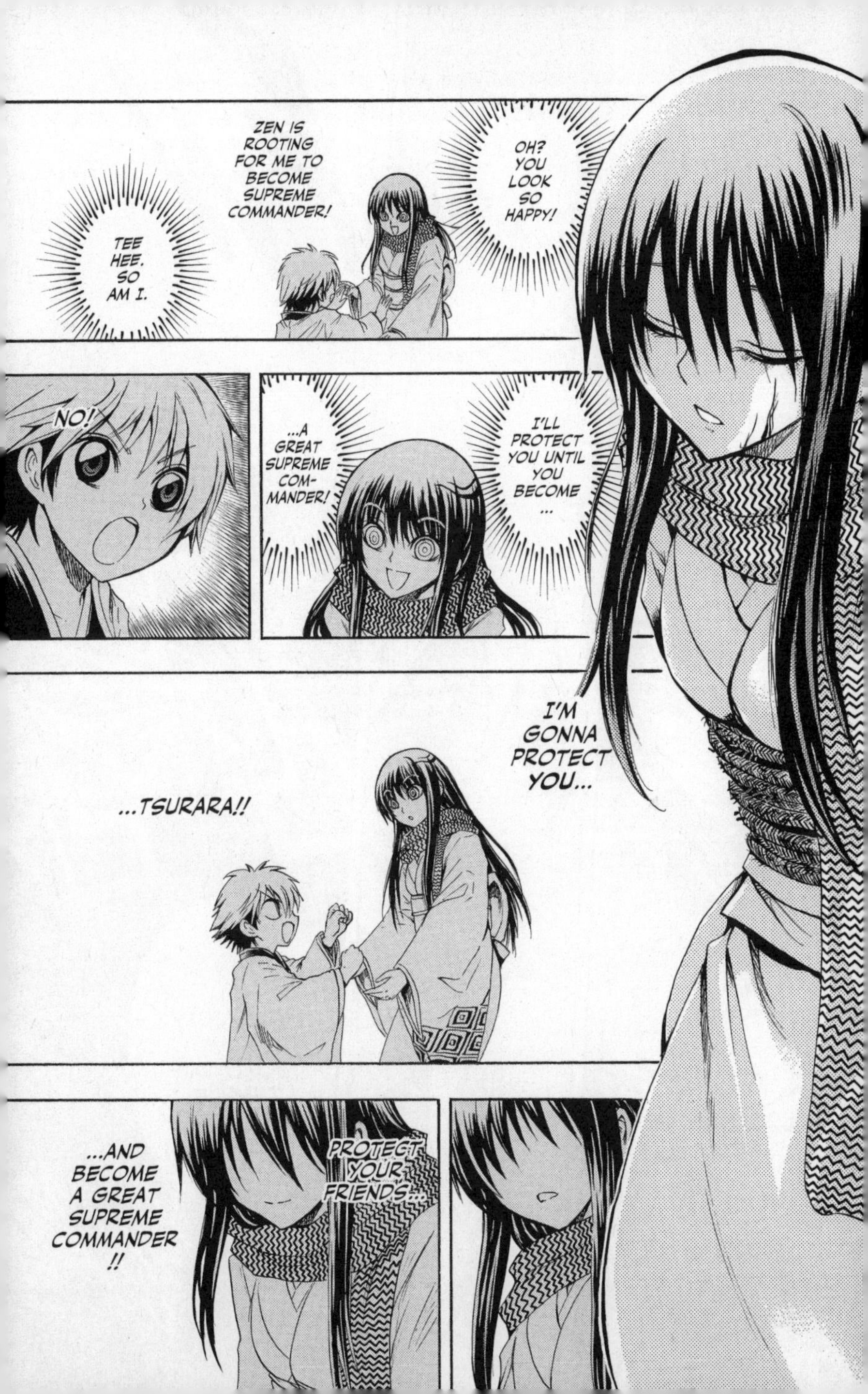
I'M GONNA PROTECT YOU...
OH? YOU LOOK SO HAPPY!
ZEN IS ROOTING FOR ME TO BECOME SUPREME COMMANDER!
TEE HEE. SO AM I.
I'LL PROTECT YOU UNTIL YOU BECOME ...
...A GREAT SUPREME COM-MANDER!
NO!
...TSURARA!!
PROTECT YOUR FRIENDS...
...AND BECOME A GREAT SUPREME COMMANDER !!

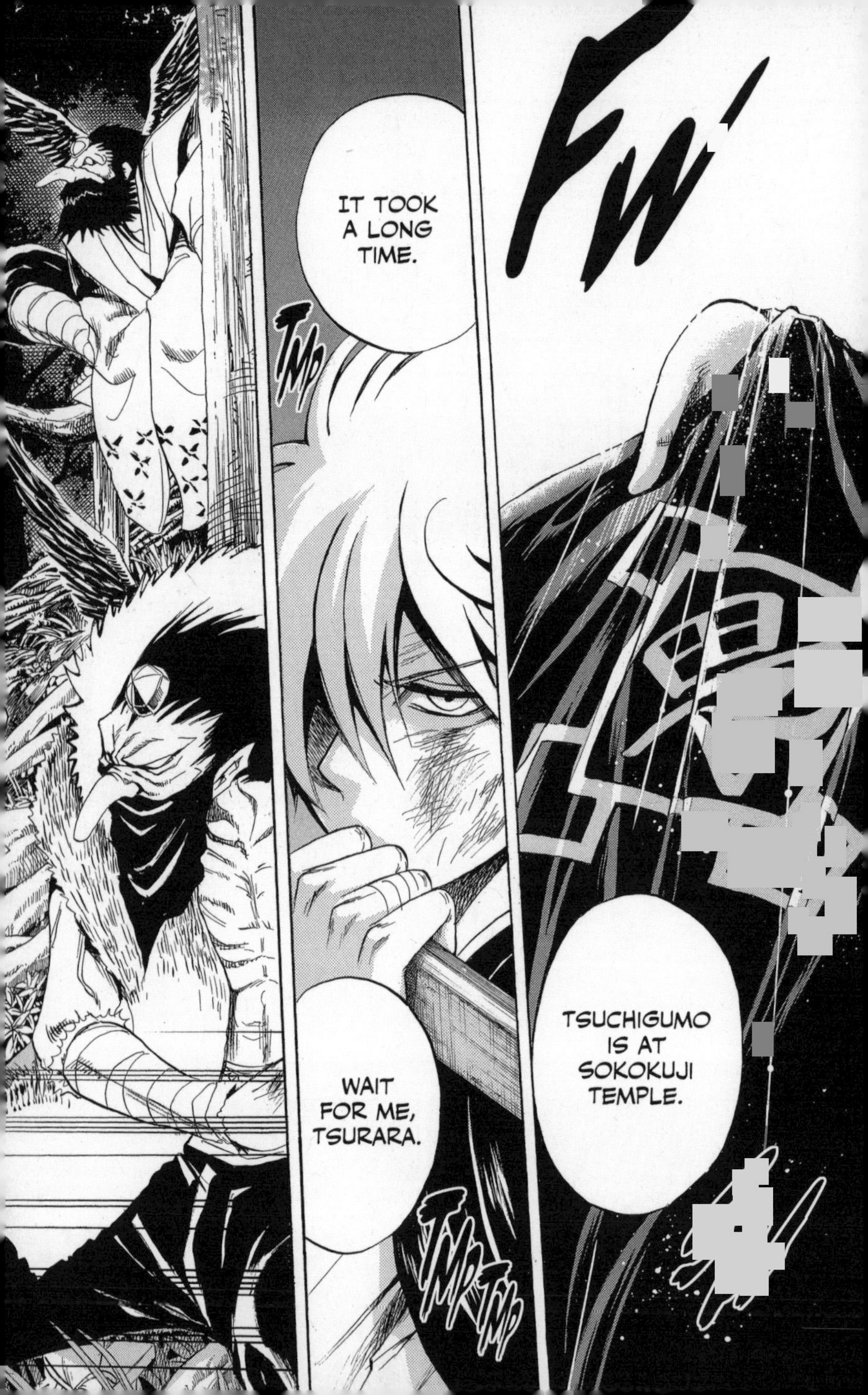
FWI
TSUCHIGUMO IS AT SOKOKUJI TEMPLE.
IT TOOK A LONG TIME.
TMP
WAIT FOR ME, TSURARA.
TMP TMP

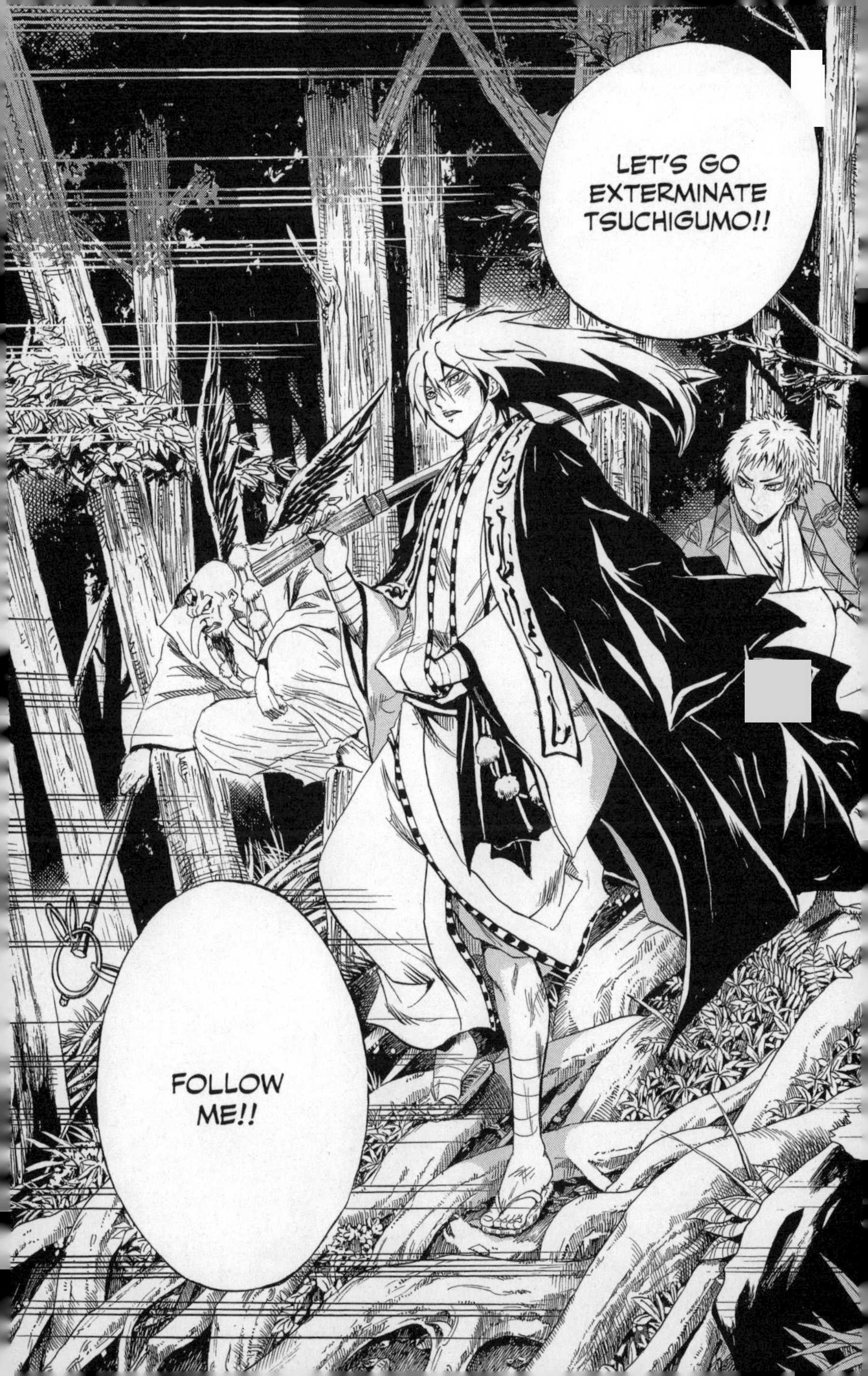
LET'S GO EXTERMINATE TSUCHIGUMO!!
FOLLOW ME!!

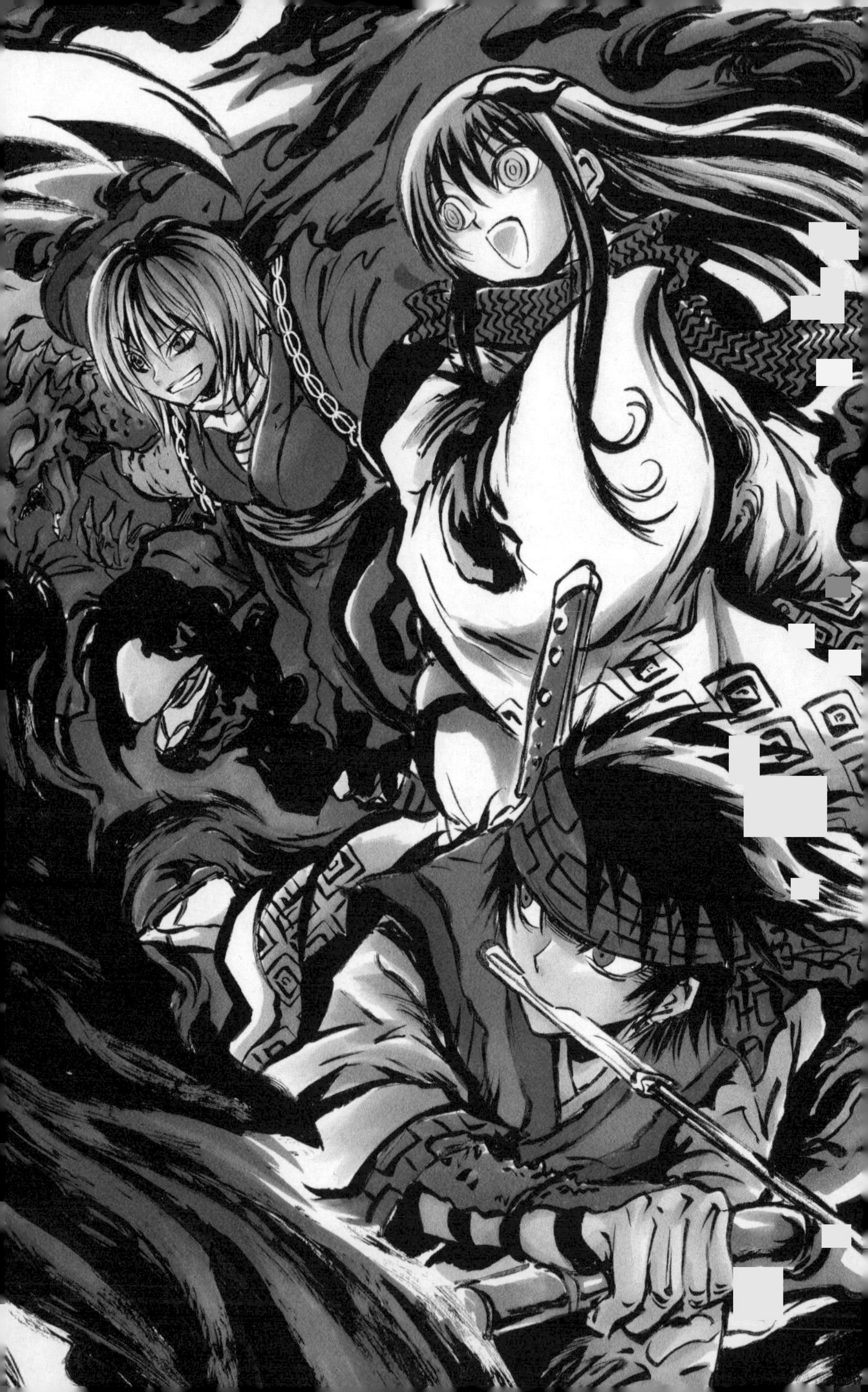

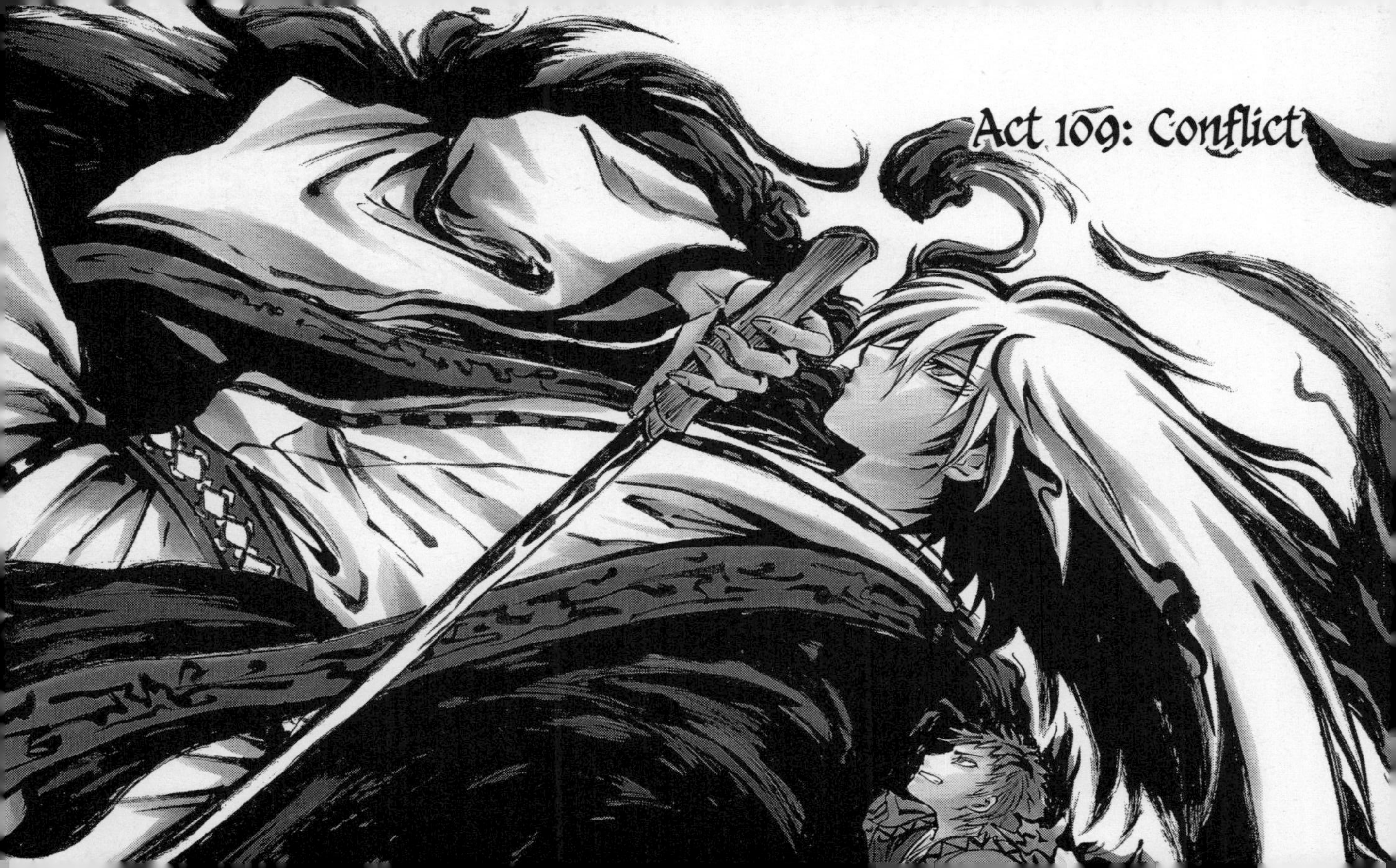
Act 109: Conflict

NURA: RISE OF THE YOKAI CLAN

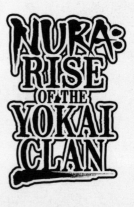

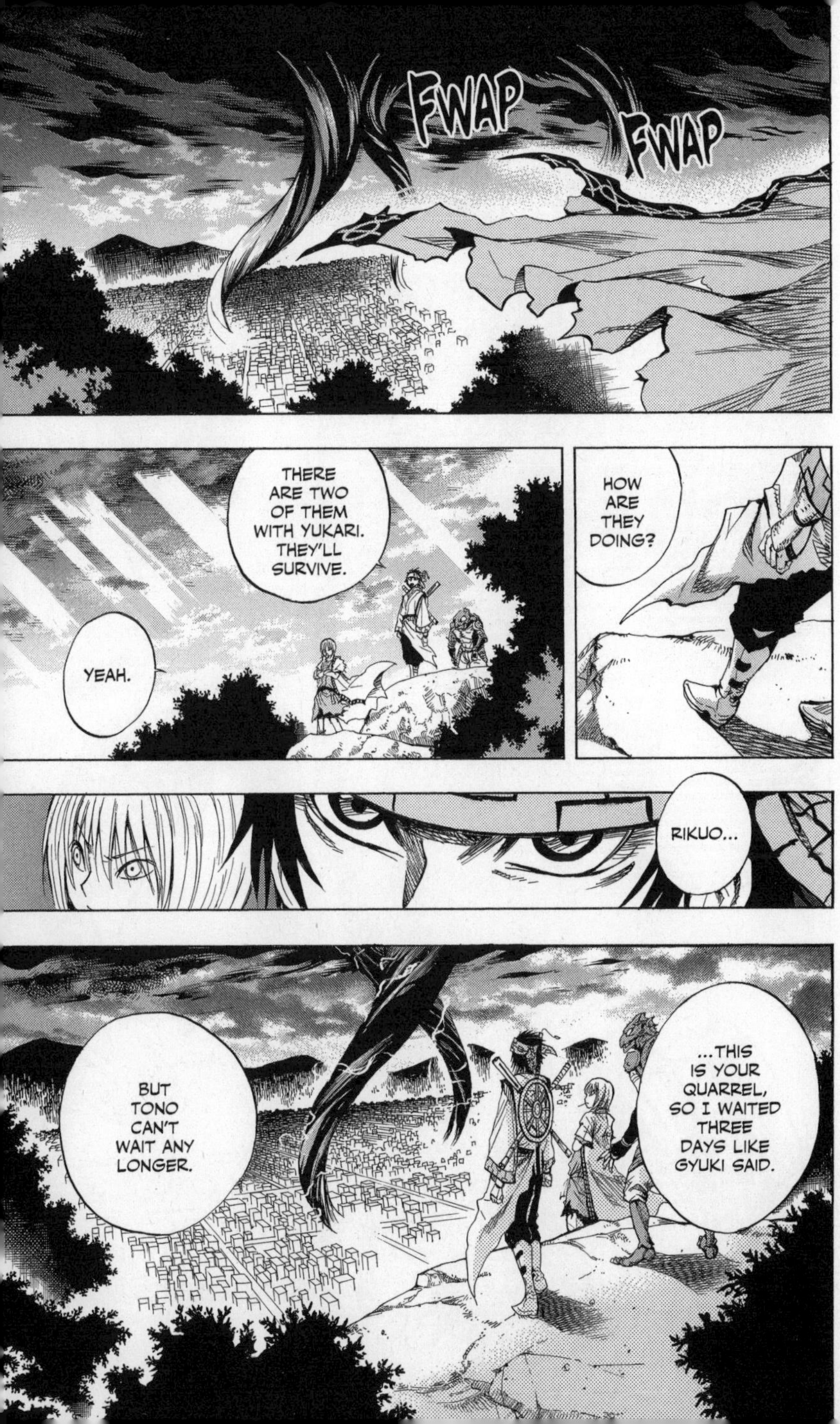
FWAP
FWAP
HOW ARE THEY DOING?
THERE ARE TWO OF THEM WITH YUKARI. THEY'LL SURVIVE.
YEAH.
RIKUO...
...THIS IS YOUR QUARREL, SO I WAITED THREE DAYS LIKE GYUKI SAID.
BUT TONO CAN'T WAIT ANY LONGER.

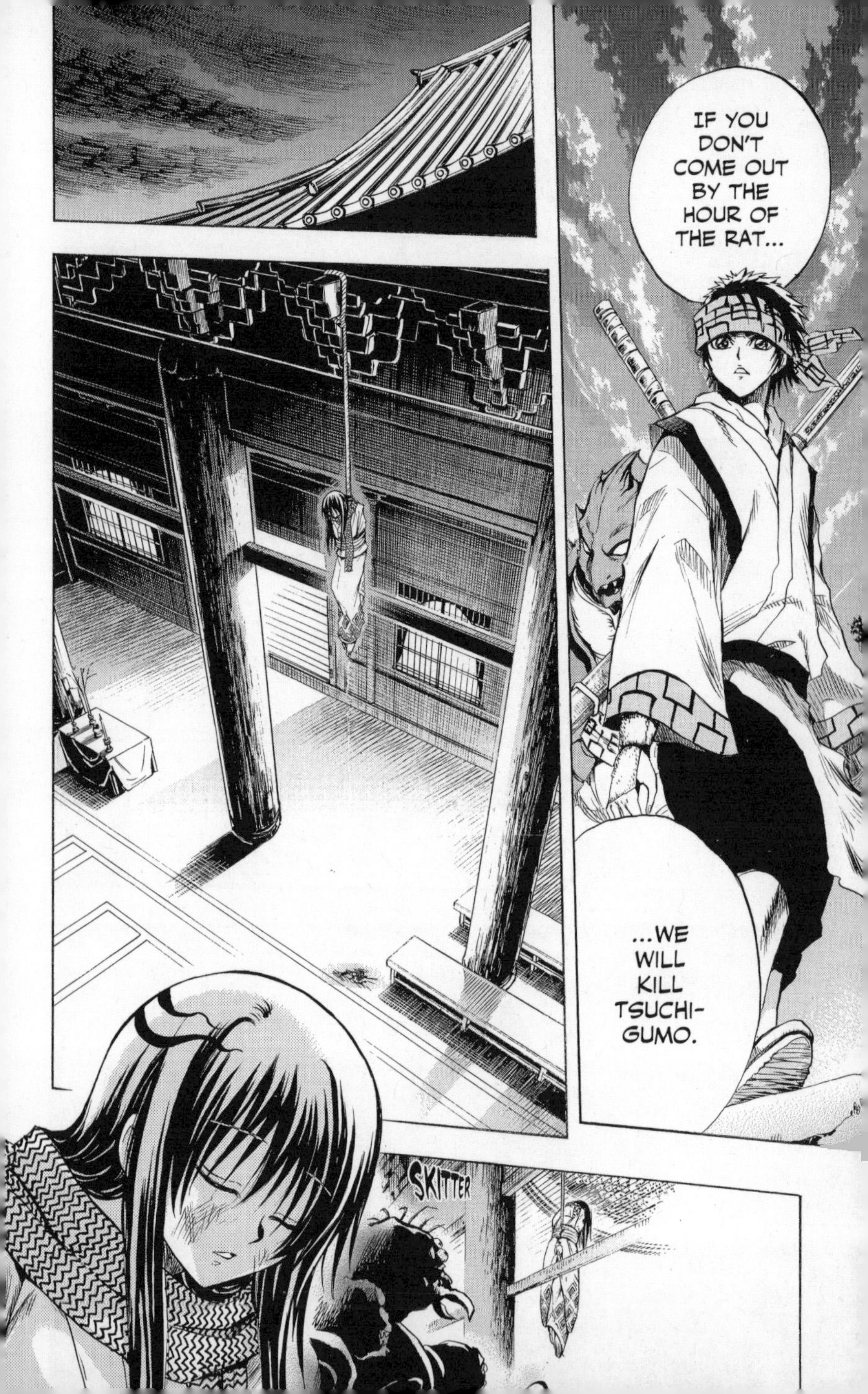
IF YOU DON'T COME OUT BY THE HOUR OF THE RAT...
...WE WILL KILL TSUCHI-GUMO.
SKITTER

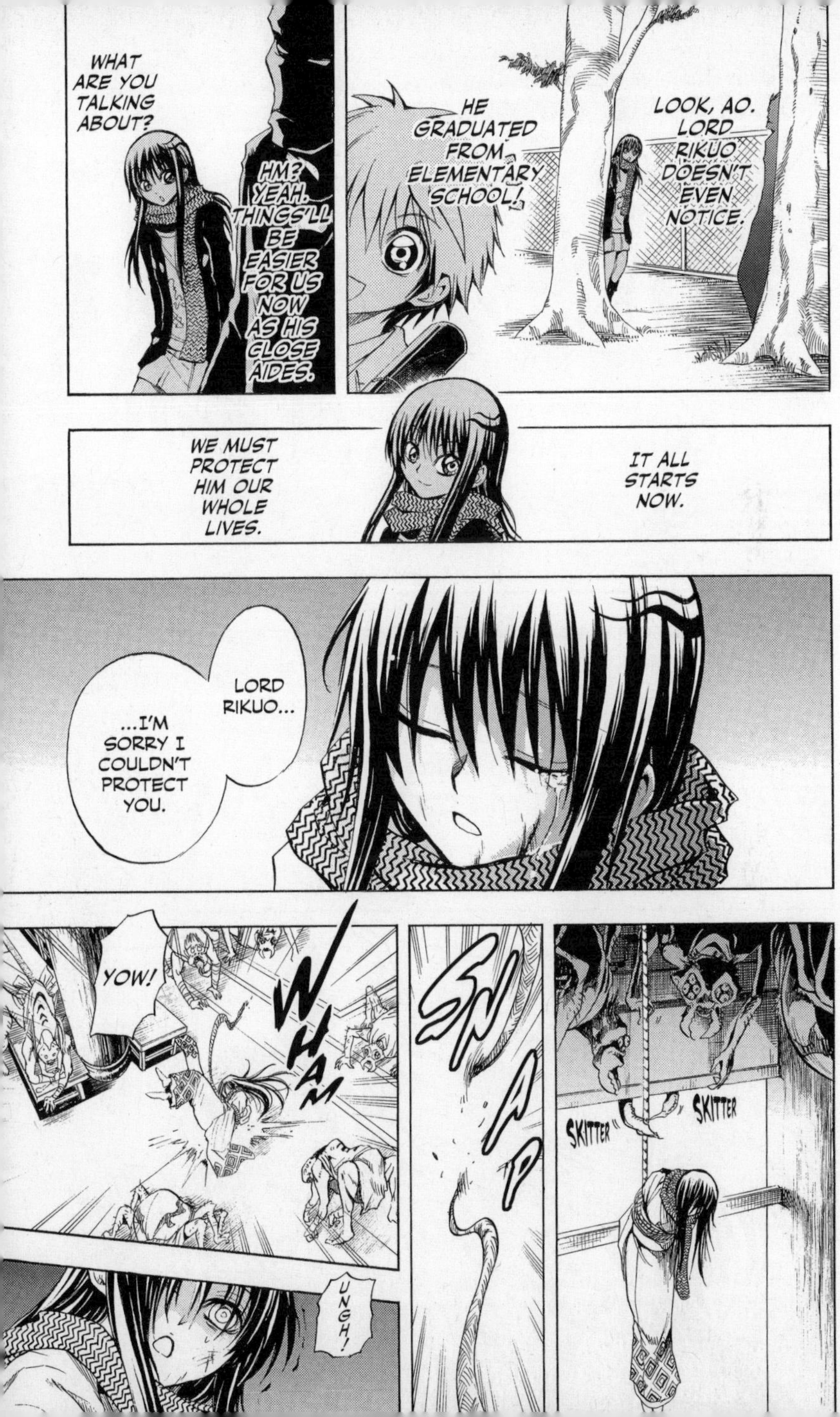

LOOK, AO. LORD RIKUO DOESN'T EVEN NOTICE.
HE GRADUATED FROM ELEMENTARY SCHOOL!
WHAT ARE YOU TALKING ABOUT?
HM? YEAH. THINGS'LL BE EASIER FOR US NOW AS HIS CLOSE AIDES.
IT ALL STARTS NOW.
WE MUST PROTECT HIM OUR WHOLE LIVES.
LORD RIKUO...
...I'M SORRY I COULDN'T PROTECT YOU.
SKITTER
SKITTER
SNAP
WHAM
YOW!
UNGH!

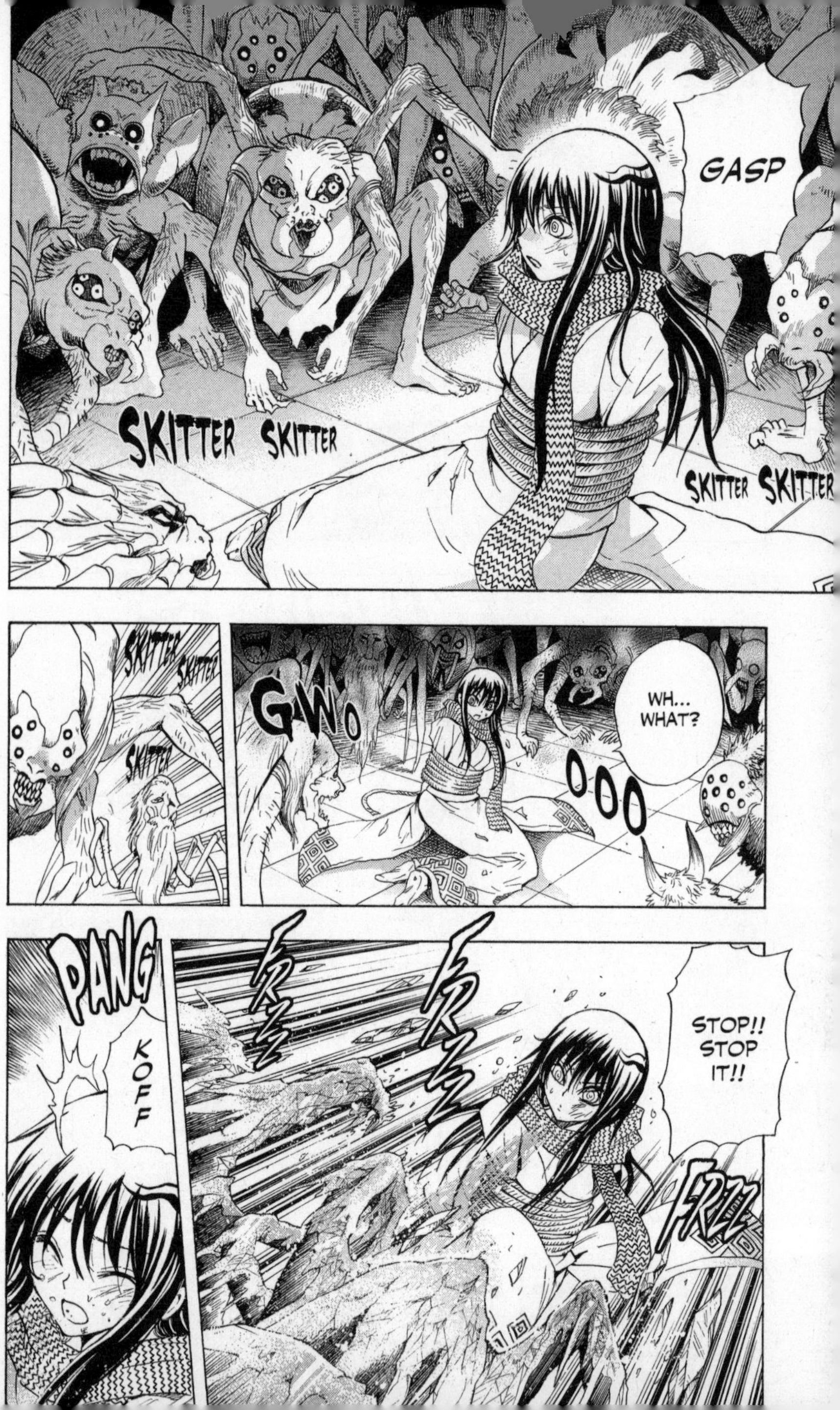
GASP
SKITTER SKITTER
SKITTER SKITTER
WH... WHAT?
GWOOO
SKITTER SKITTER
SKITTER
STOP!! STOP IT!!
FRZZ
PANG
KOFF

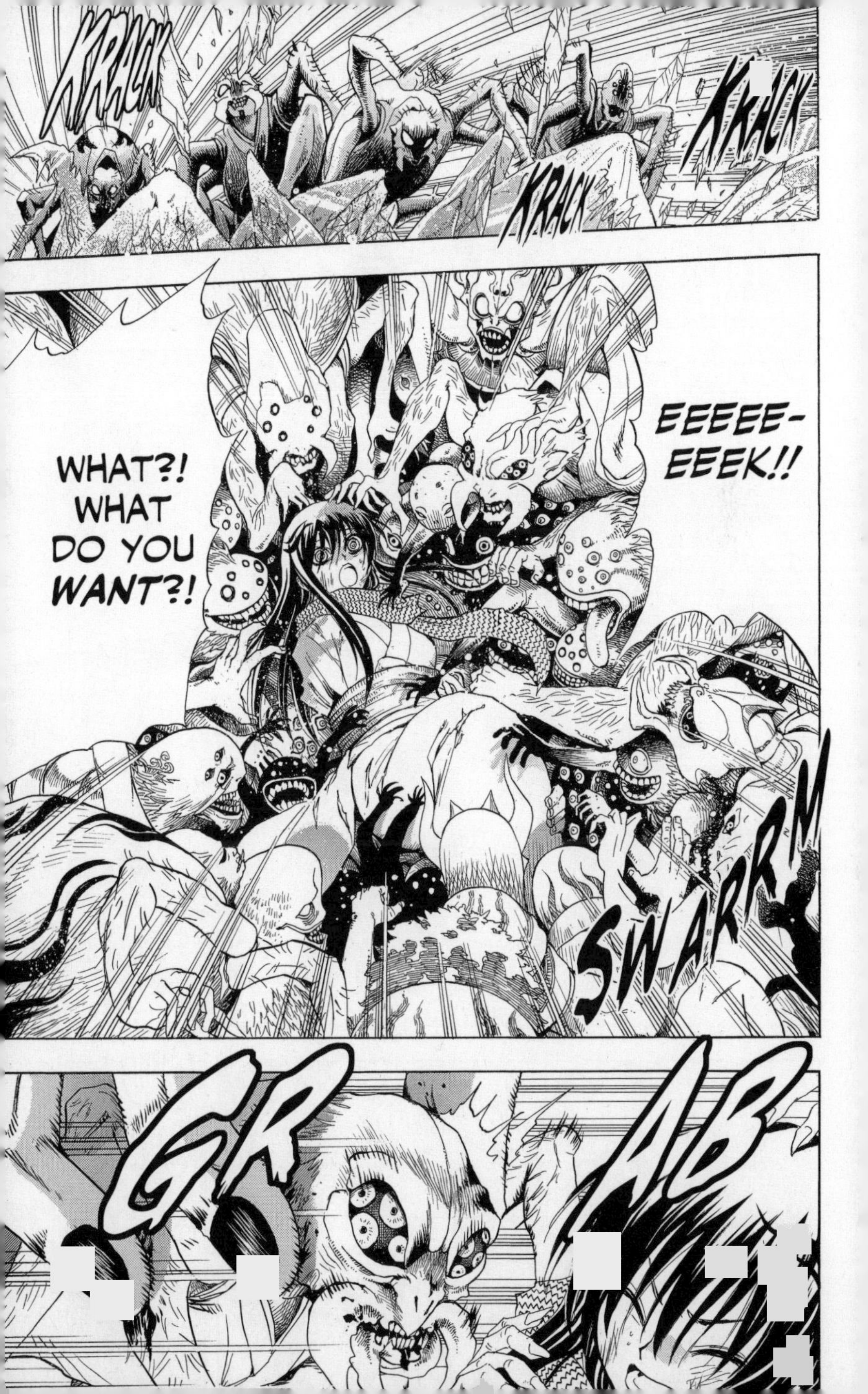
KRACK
KRACK
KRACK
EEEEE-
EEEK!!
WHAT?!
WHAT
DO YOU
WANT?!
SWARRM
AB
GR

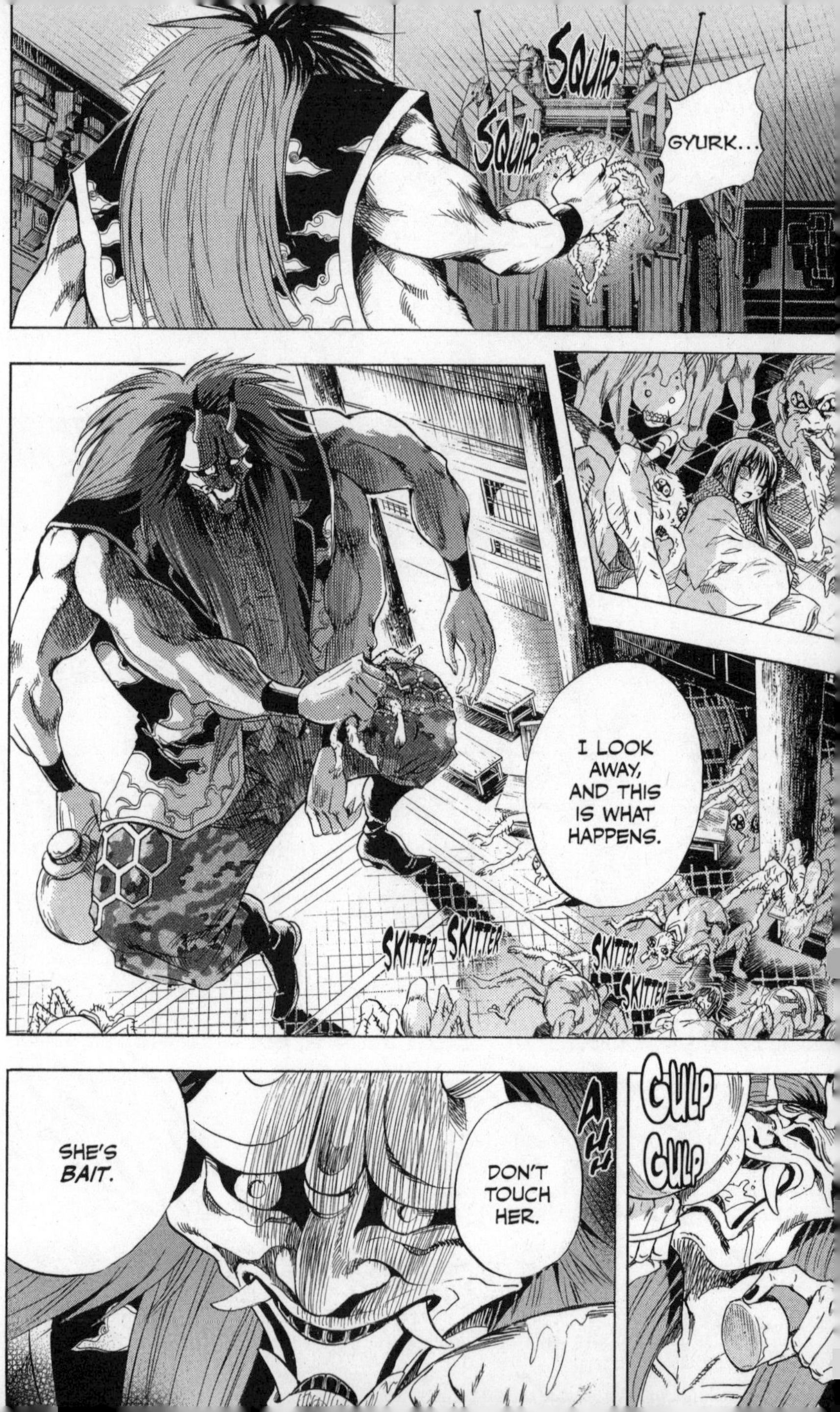
GYURK...
SQUIR
SQUIR
SQUIR
I LOOK AWAY, AND THIS IS WHAT HAPPENS.
SKITTER
SKITTER
SKITTER
SKITTER
GULP
GULP
AHH
DON'T TOUCH HER.
SHE'S BAIT.

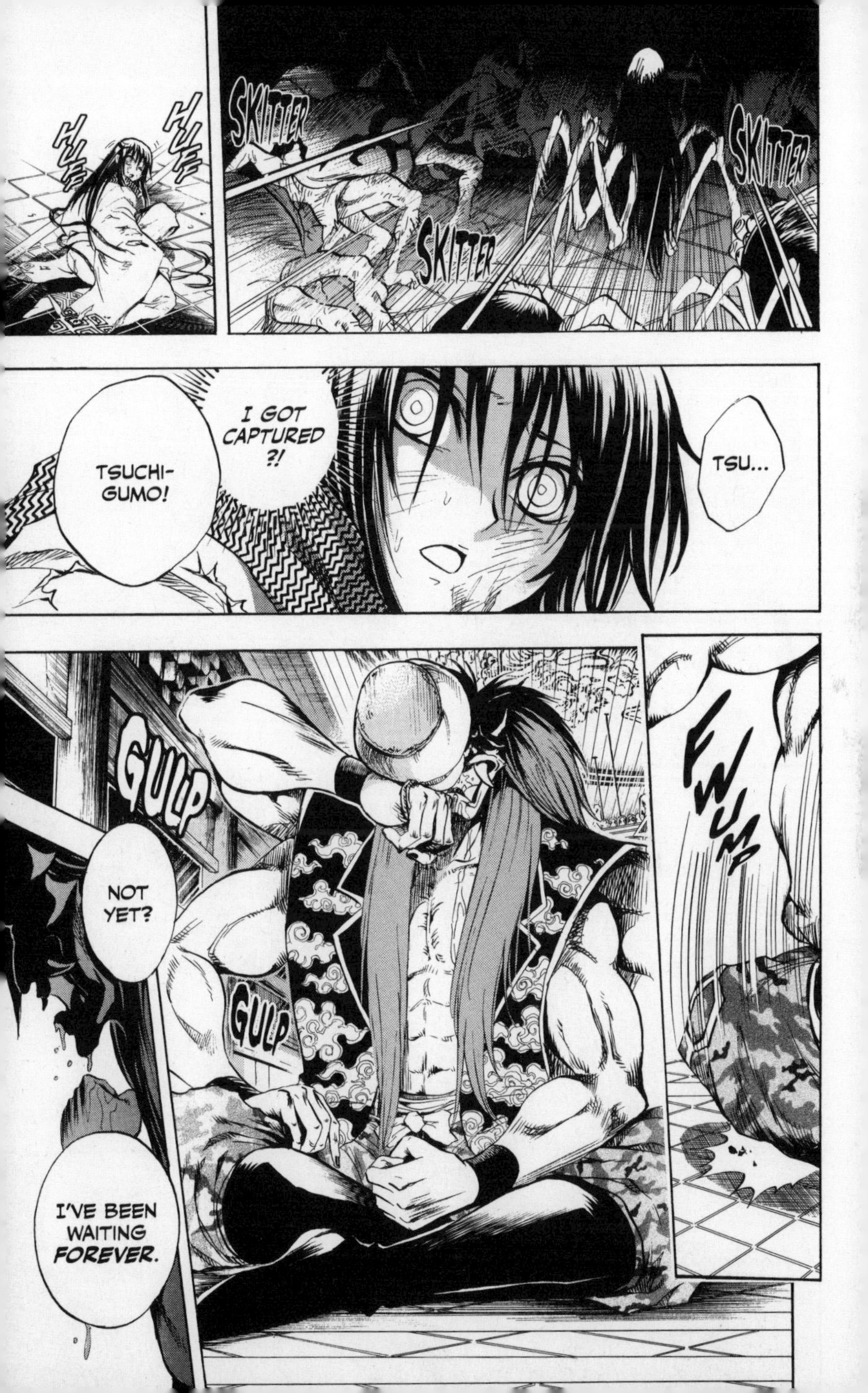
SKITTER
SKITTER
SKITTER
HUFF
HUFF
TSU...
I GOT CAPTURED ?!
TSUCHI-GUMO!
FWUMP
GULP
NOT YET?
GULP
I'VE BEEN WAITING FOREVER.

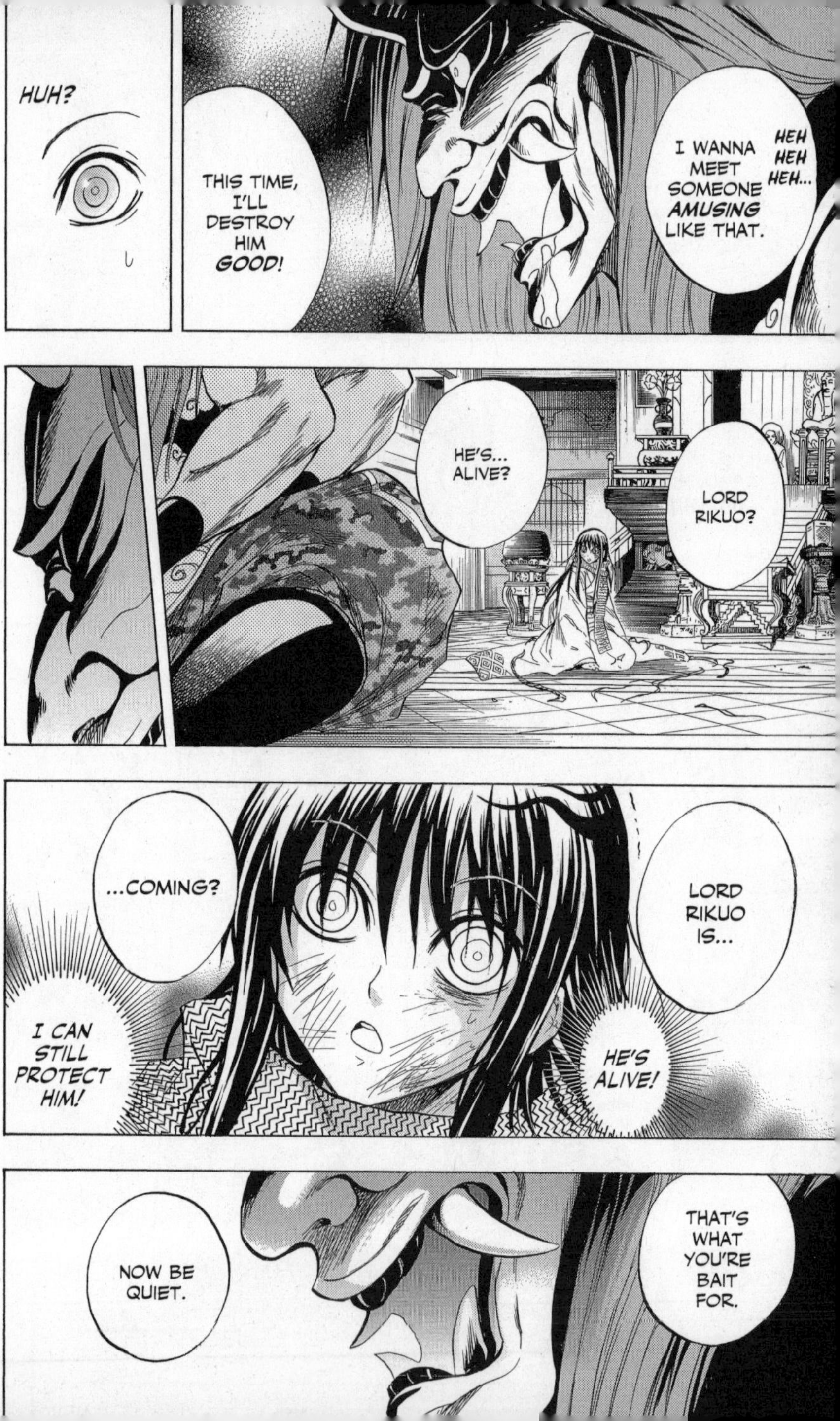
HEH HEH HEH...
I WANNA MEET SOMEONE AMUSING LIKE THAT.
THIS TIME, I'LL DESTROY HIM GOOD!
HUH?
LORD RIKUO?
HE'S... ALIVE?
LORD RIKUO IS...
HE'S ALIVE!
...COMING?
I CAN STILL PROTECT HIM!
THAT'S WHAT YOU'RE BAIT FOR.
NOW BE QUIET.

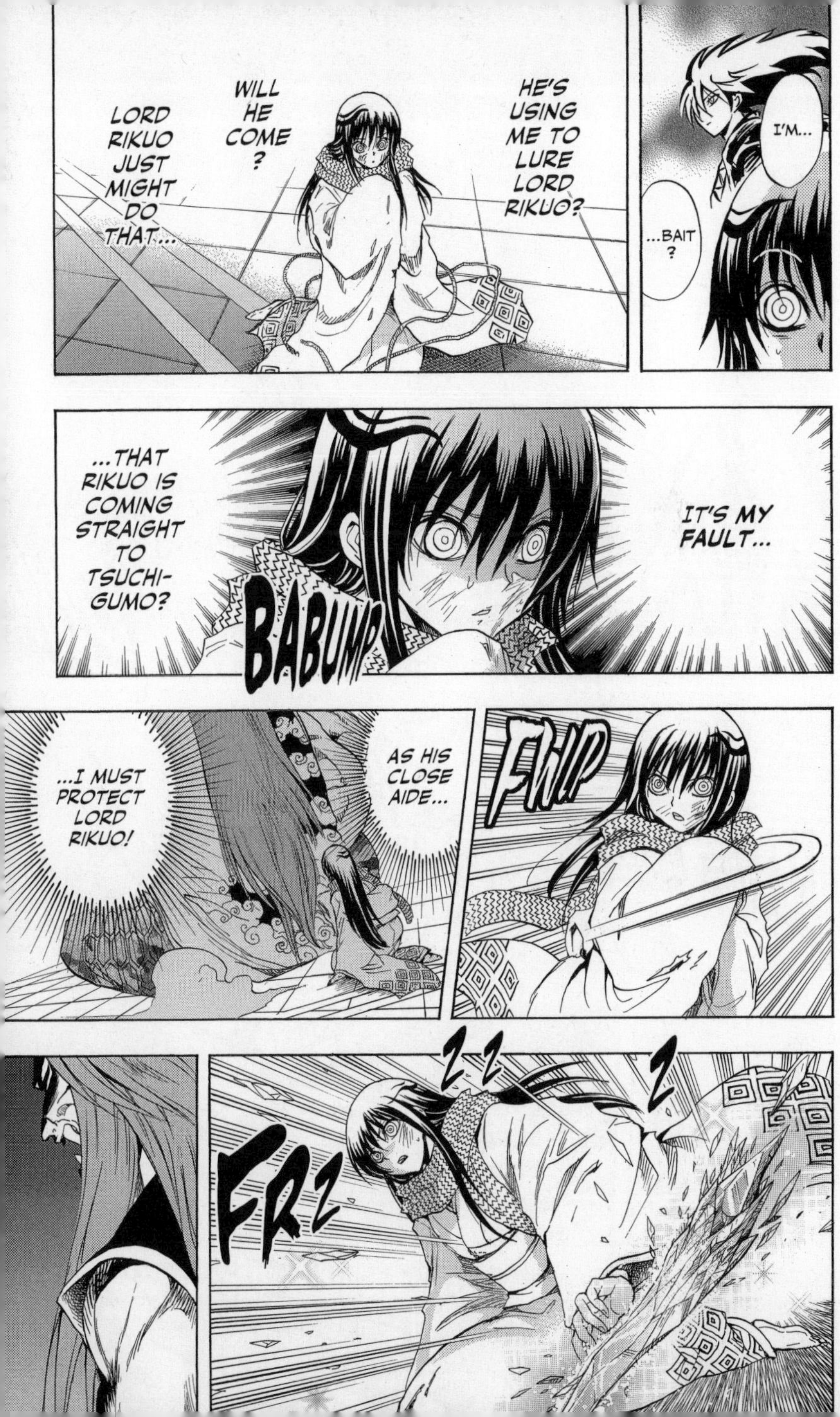
I'M...
...BAIT?
HE'S USING ME TO LURE LORD RIKUO?
WILL HE COME?
LORD RIKUO JUST MIGHT DO THAT...
IT'S MY FAULT...
...THAT RIKUO IS COMING STRAIGHT TO TSUCHIGUMO?
BABUMP
FWIP
AS HIS CLOSE AIDE...
...I MUST PROTECT LORD RIKUO!
Z Z
Z
FRZ

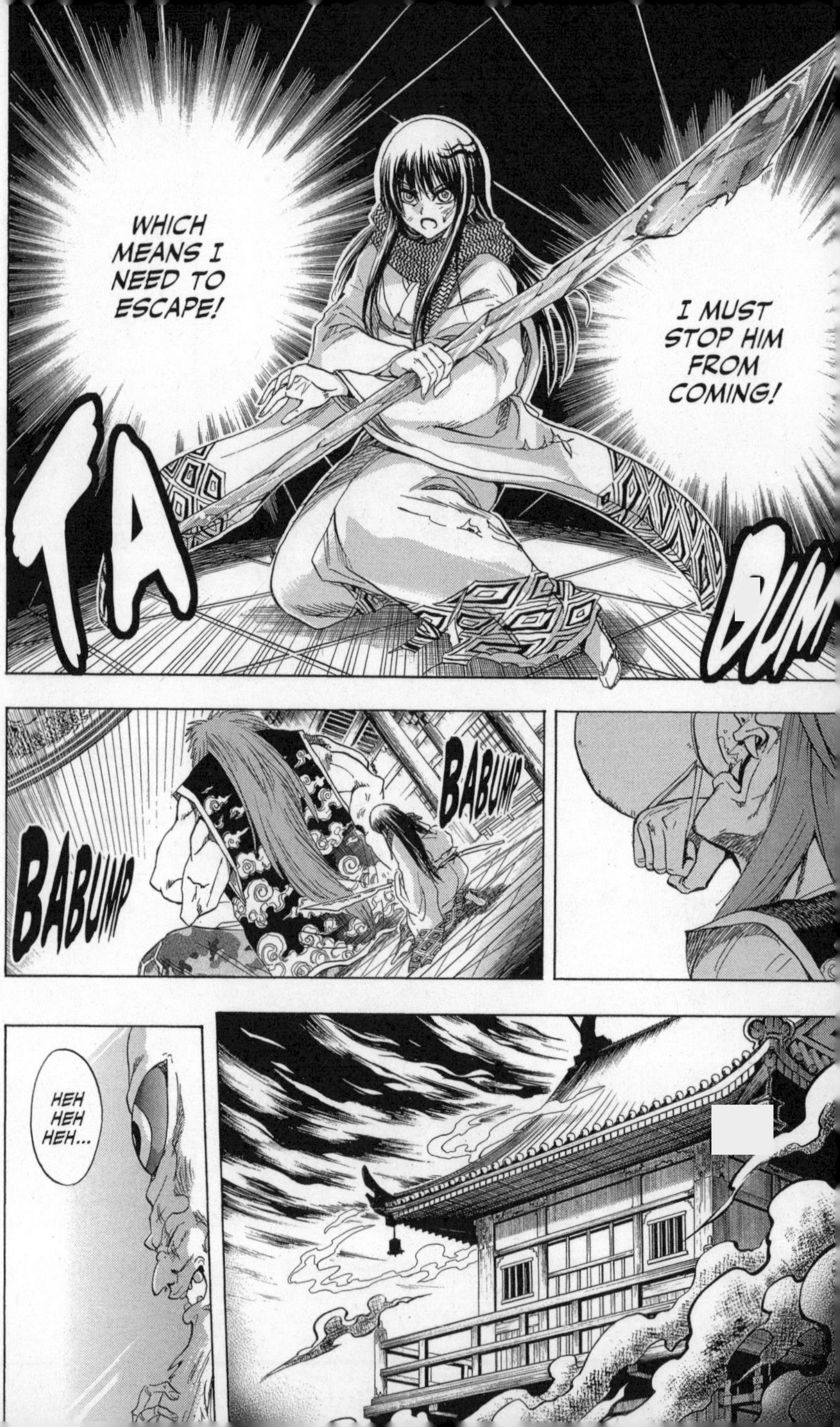
I MUST STOP HIM FROM COMING!
WHICH MEANS I NEED TO ESCAPE!
DUM
TA
BABUMP
BABUMP
HEH HEH HEH...

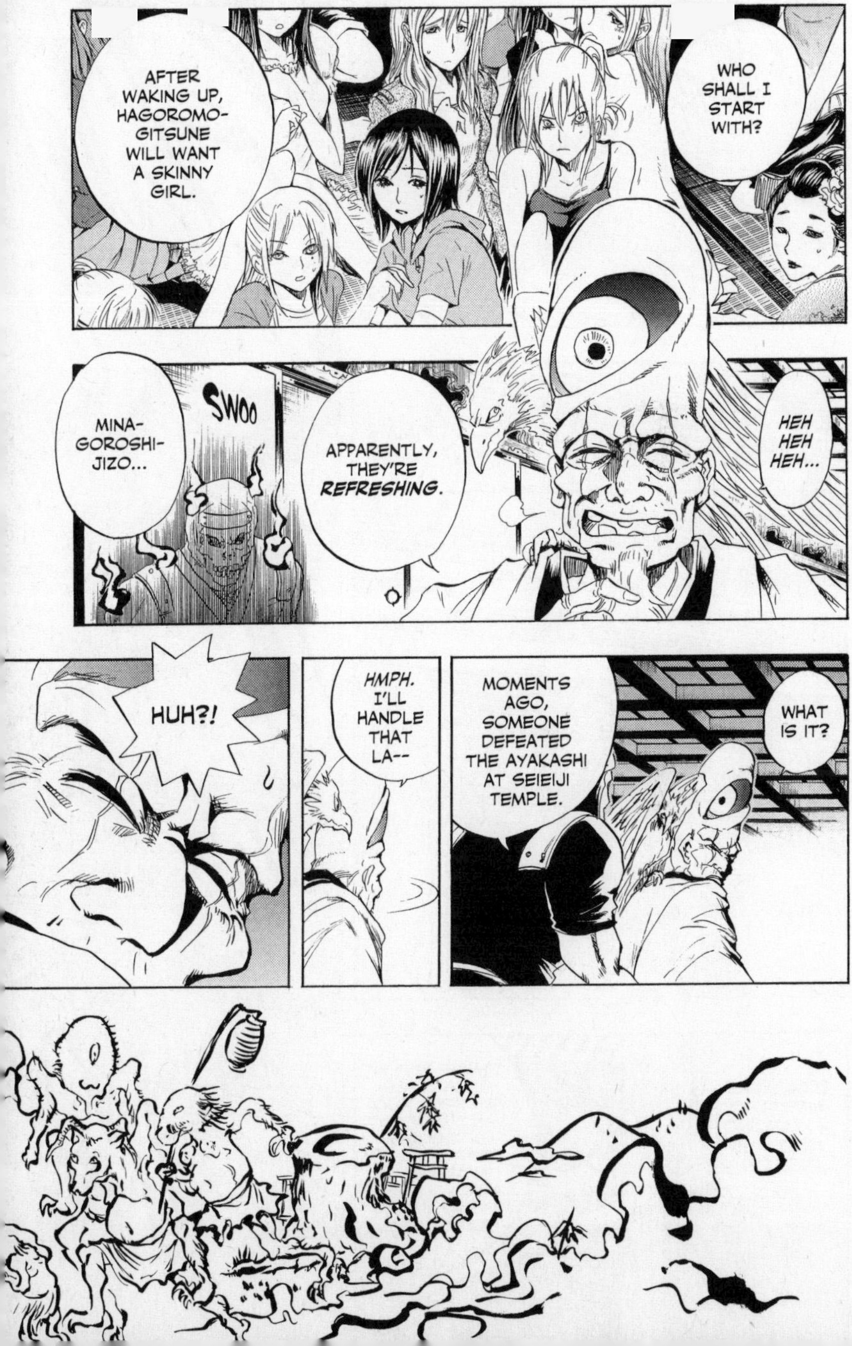
WHO SHALL I START WITH?
AFTER WAKING UP, HAGOROMO-GITSUNE WILL WANT A SKINNY GIRL.
HEH HEH HEH...
APPARENTLY, THEY'RE *REFRESHING*.
SWOO
MINA-GOROSHI-JIZO...
WHAT IS IT?
MOMENTS AGO, SOMEONE DEFEATED THE AYAKASHI AT SEIEIJI TEMPLE.
HMPH. I'LL HANDLE THAT LA--
HUH?!

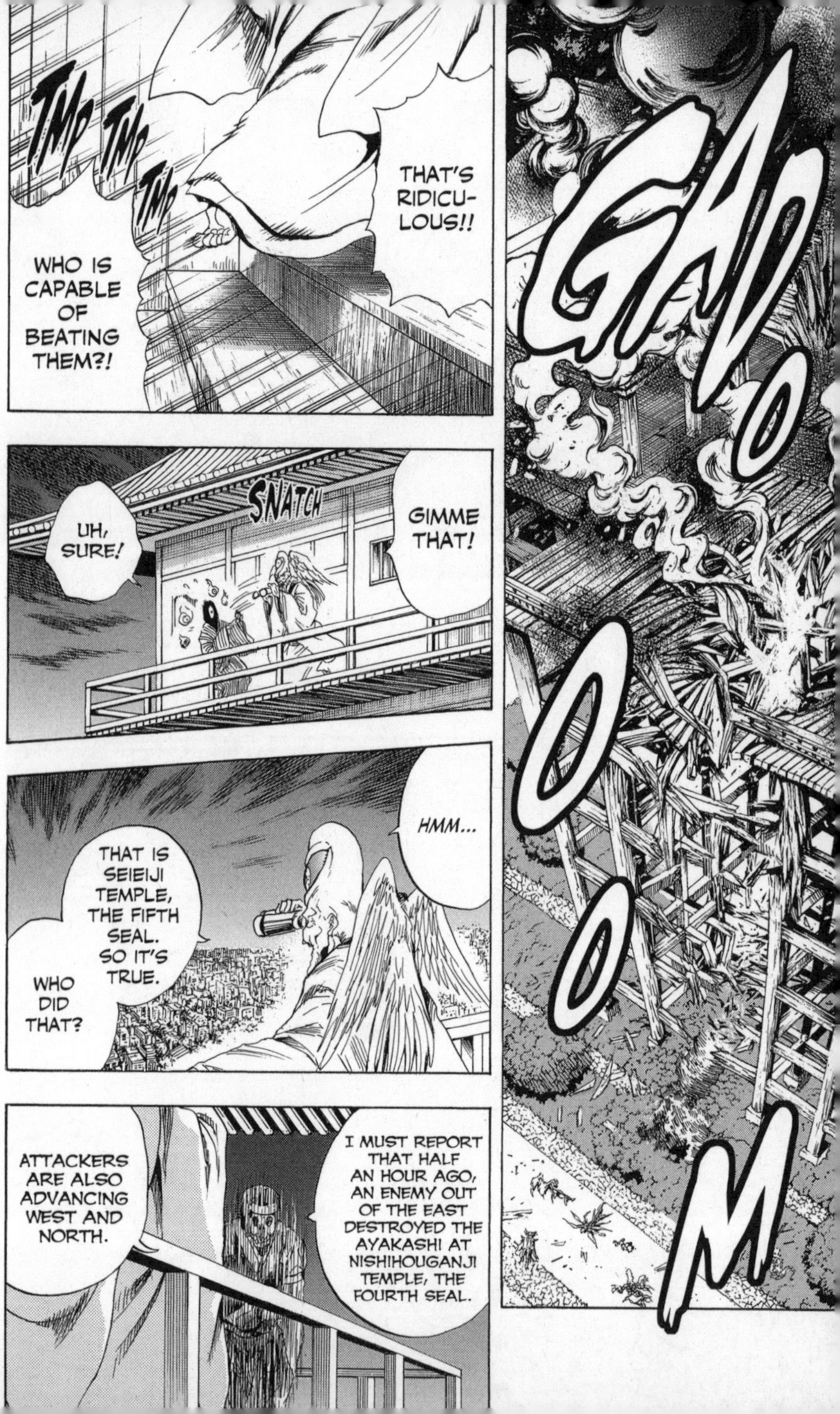
THAT'S RIDICULOUS!!
TMP TMP TMP
WHO IS CAPABLE OF BEATING THEM?!
GIMME THAT!
SNATCH
UH, SURE!
HMM...
THAT IS SEIEIJI TEMPLE, THE FIFTH SEAL. SO IT'S TRUE.
WHO DID THAT?
I MUST REPORT THAT HALF AN HOUR AGO, AN ENEMY OUT OF THE EAST DESTROYED THE AYAKASHI AT NISHIHOUGANJI TEMPLE, THE FOURTH SEAL.
ATTACKERS ARE ALSO ADVANCING WEST AND NORTH.

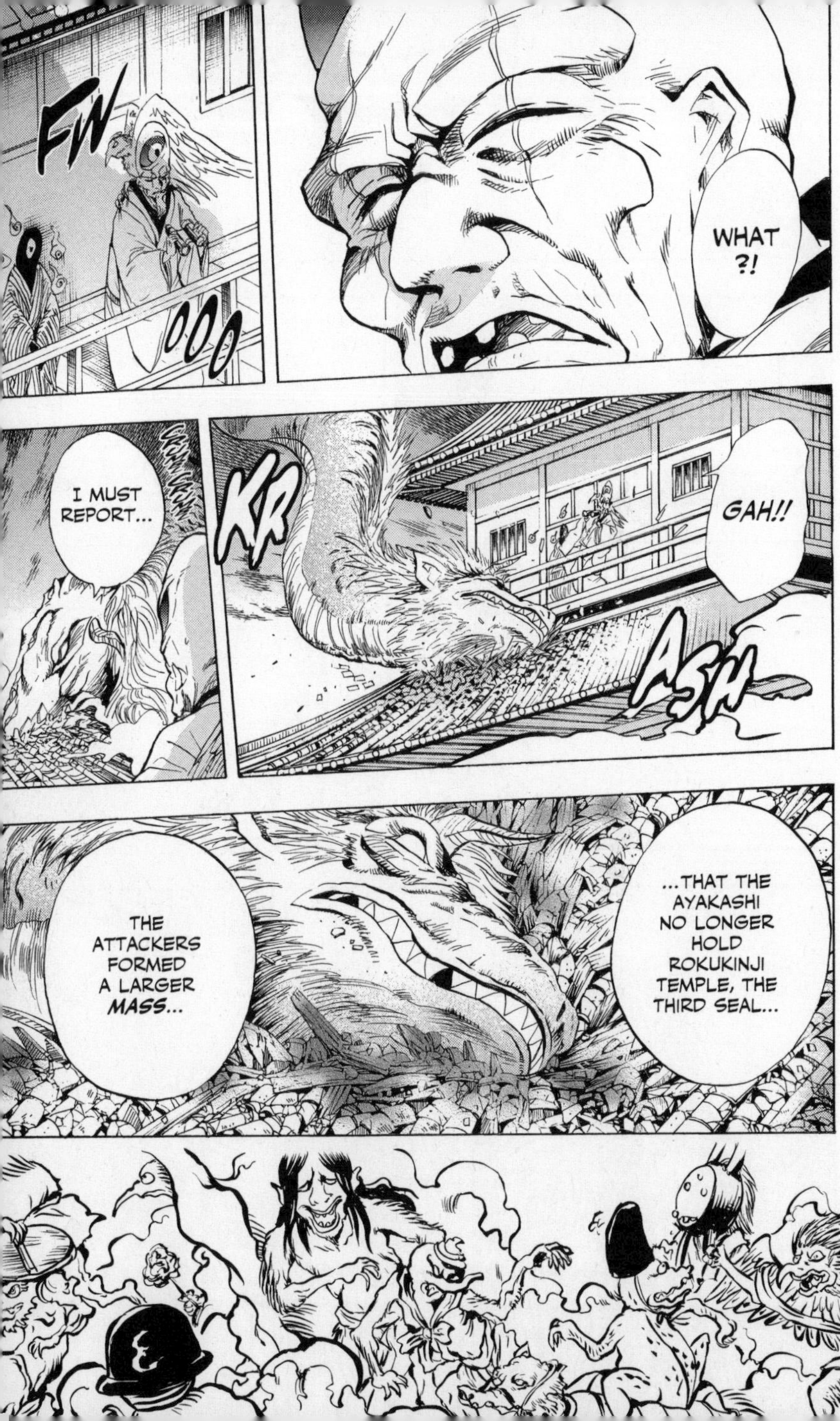
WHAT ?!
FW
OOO
GAH!!
KR
ASH
I MUST REPORT...
...THAT THE AYAKASHI NO LONGER HOLD ROKUKINJI TEMPLE, THE THIRD SEAL...
THE ATTACKERS FORMED A LARGER *MASS*...

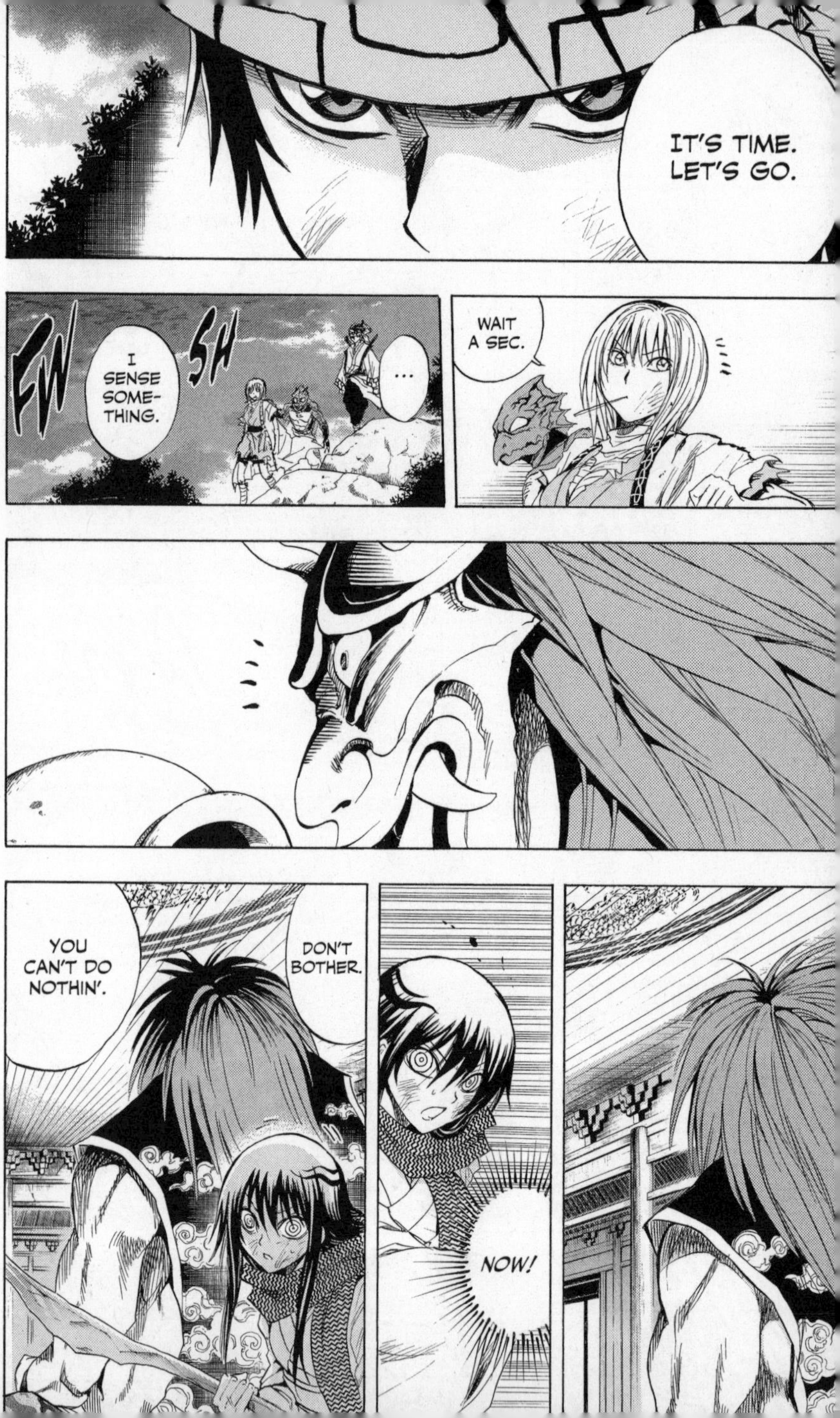
IT'S TIME. LET'S GO.
WAIT A SEC.
...
I SENSE SOMETHING.
FWSH
NOW!
DON'T BOTHER.
YOU CAN'T DO NOTHIN'.

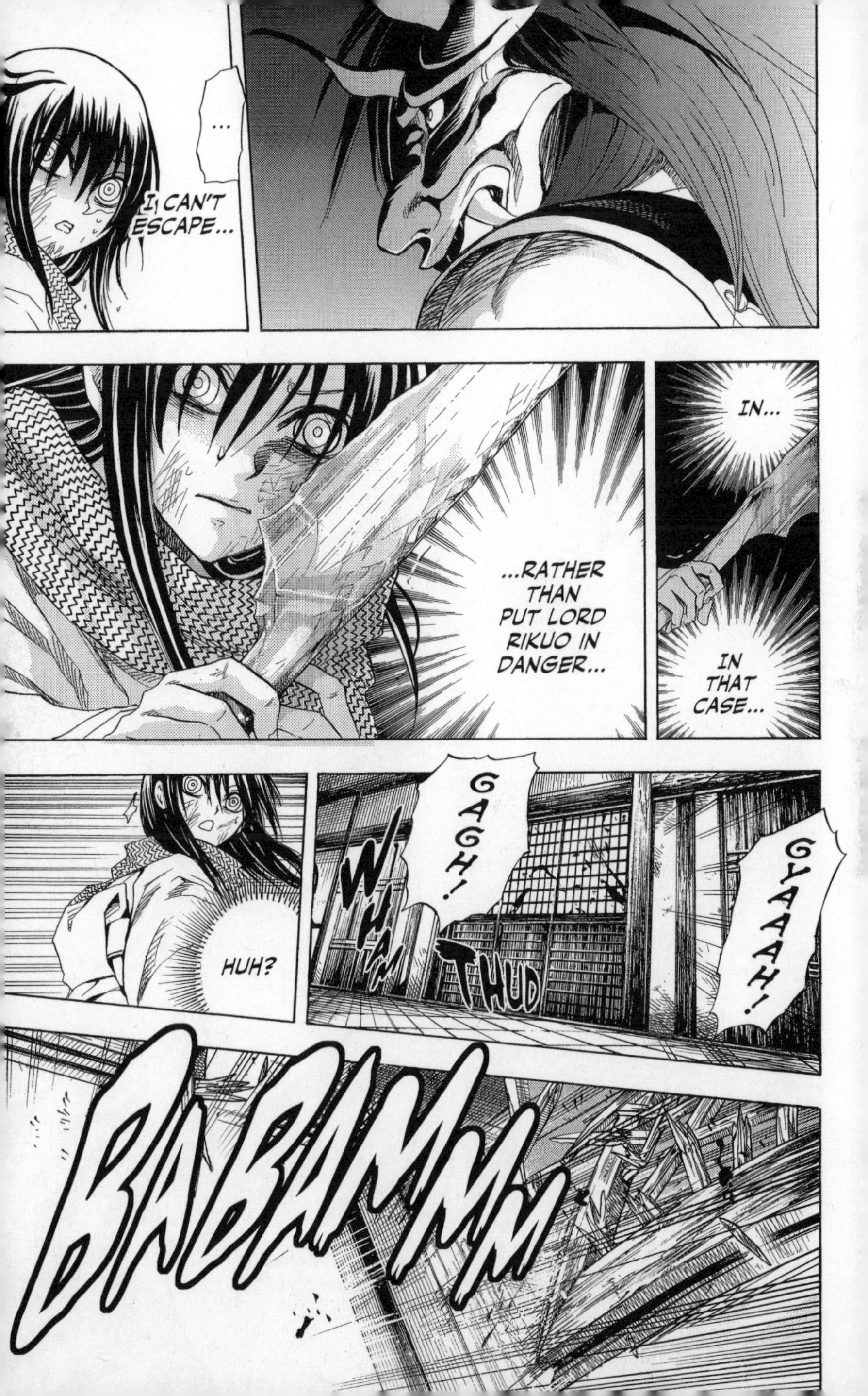
...
I CAN'T ESCAPE...
IN...
IN THAT CASE...
...RATHER THAN PUT LORD RIKUO IN DANGER...
GYAAAAH!
GAGH!
WHAM
THUD
HUH?
BABAMMM

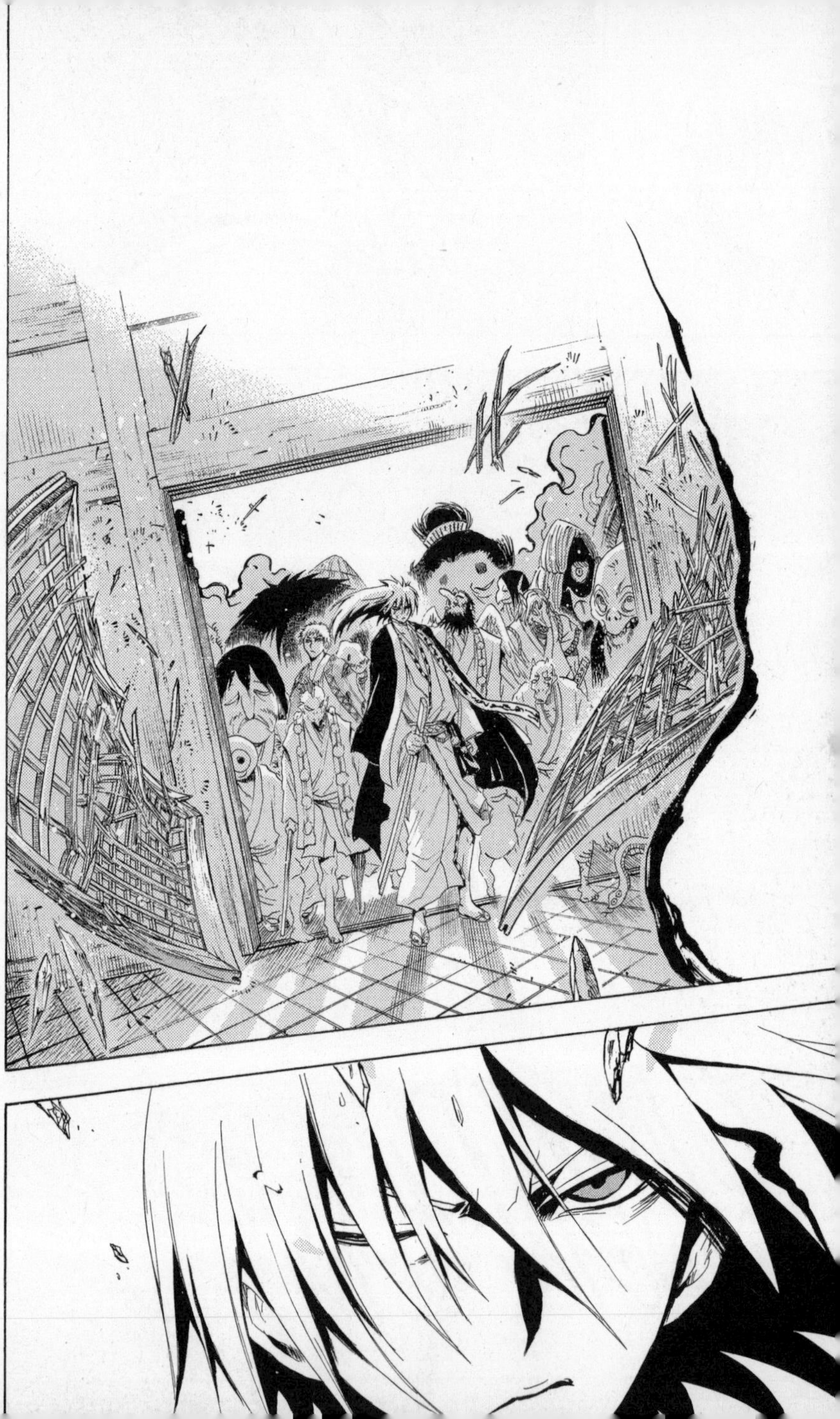

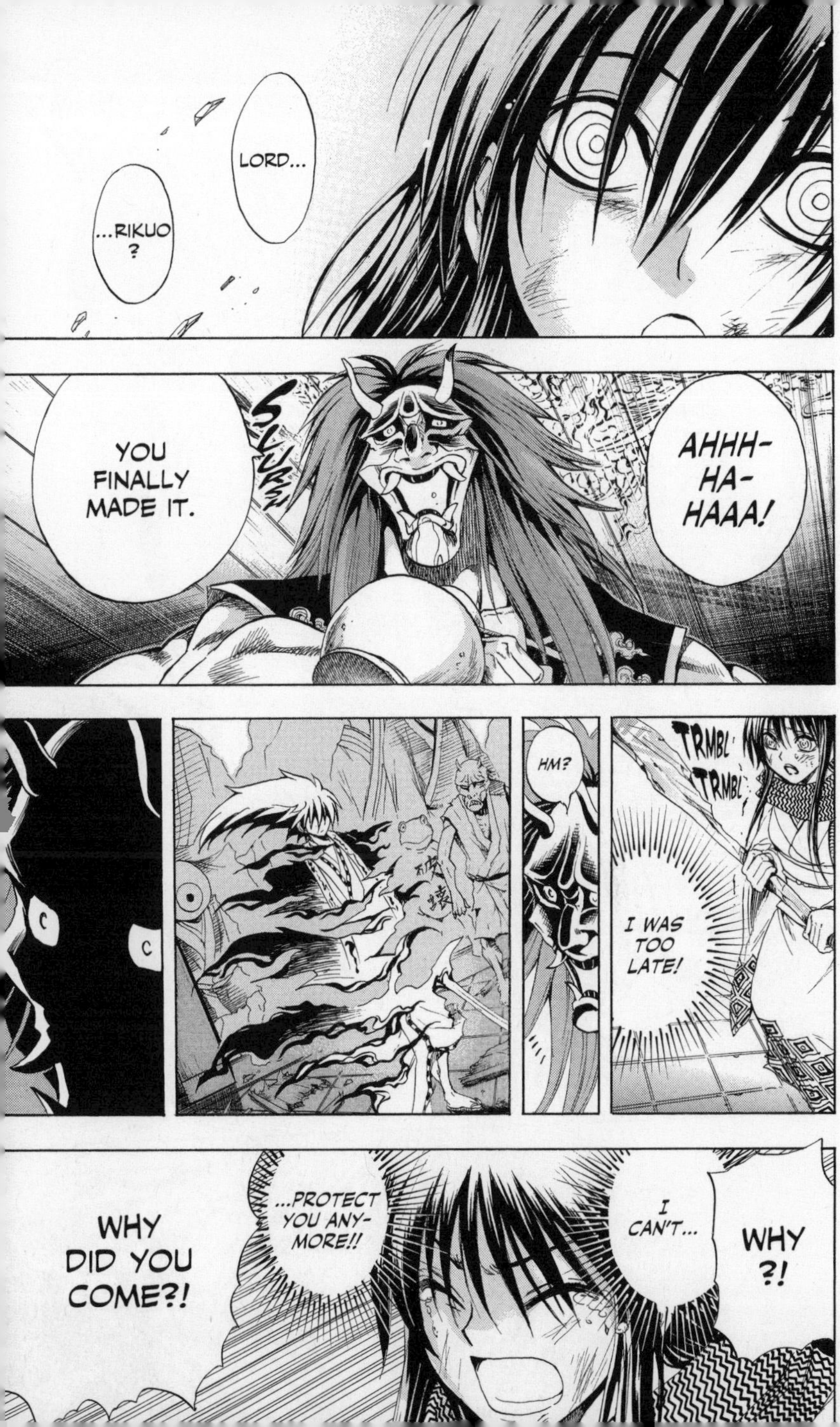
LORD...
...RIKUO?
AHHH-HA-HAAA!
YOU FINALLY MADE IT.
TRMBL TRMBL
I WAS TOO LATE!
HM?
WHY?!
I CAN'T...
...PROTECT YOU ANY-MORE!!
WHY DID YOU COME?!

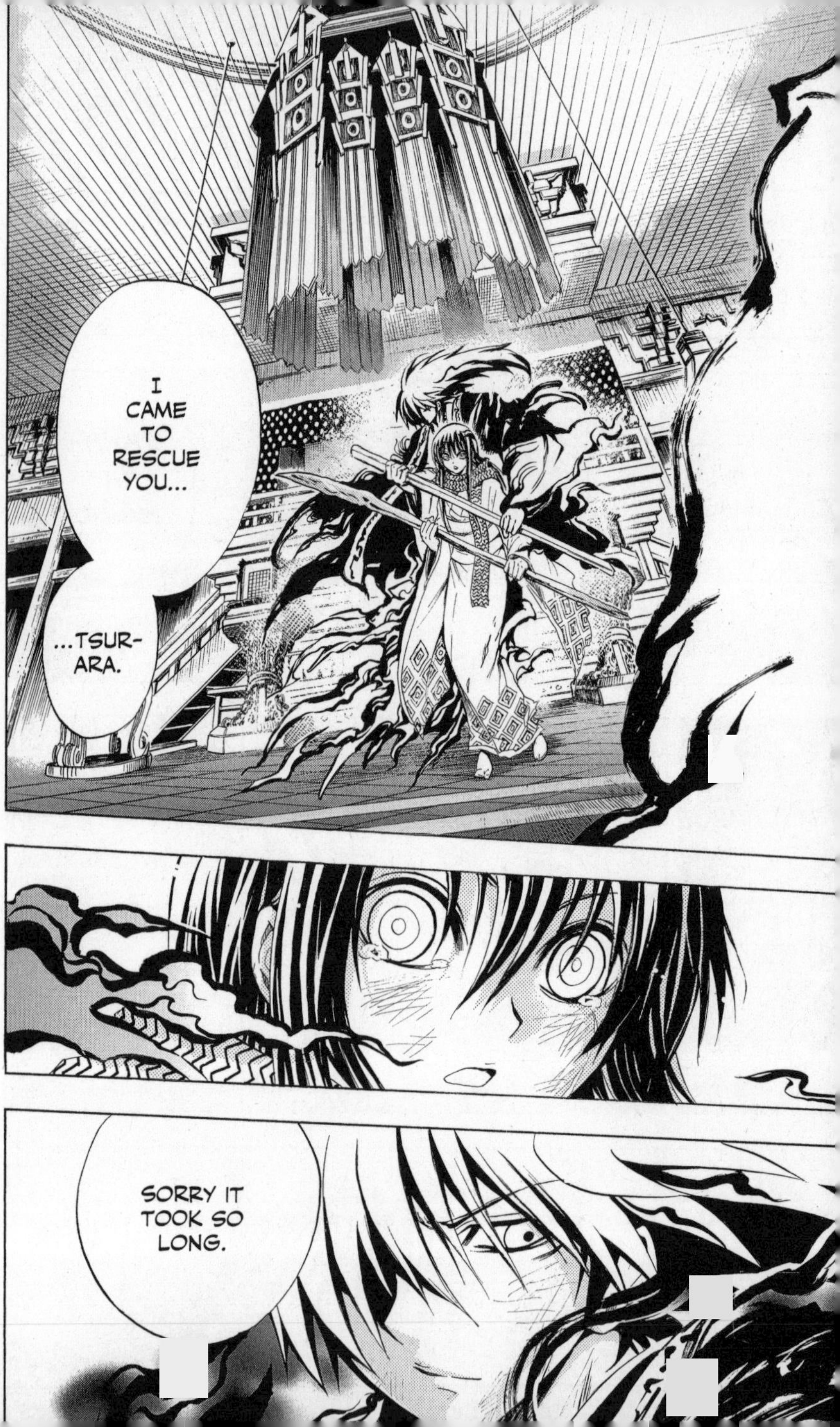
I CAME TO RESCUE YOU...
...TSUR-ARA.
SORRY IT TOOK SO LONG.

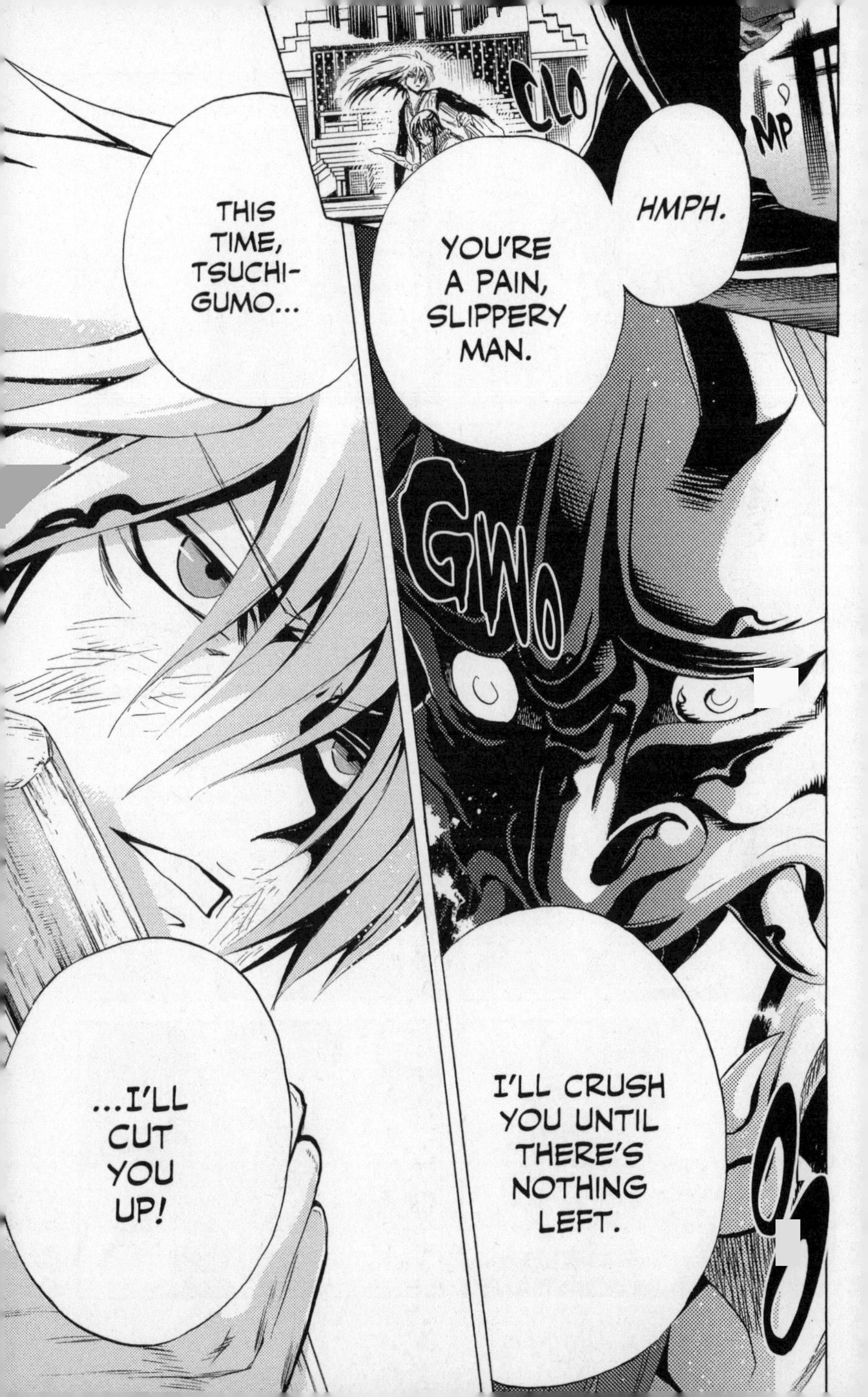
CLOMP
HMPH.
YOU'RE A PAIN, SLIPPERY MAN.
GWO
I'LL CRUSH YOU UNTIL THERE'S NOTHING LEFT.
THIS TIME, TSUCHI-GUMO...
...I'LL CUT YOU UP!

HAGOROMOMOMOMOMO!!

Kyoto Comic Strips!!

By Kana Yoshimura

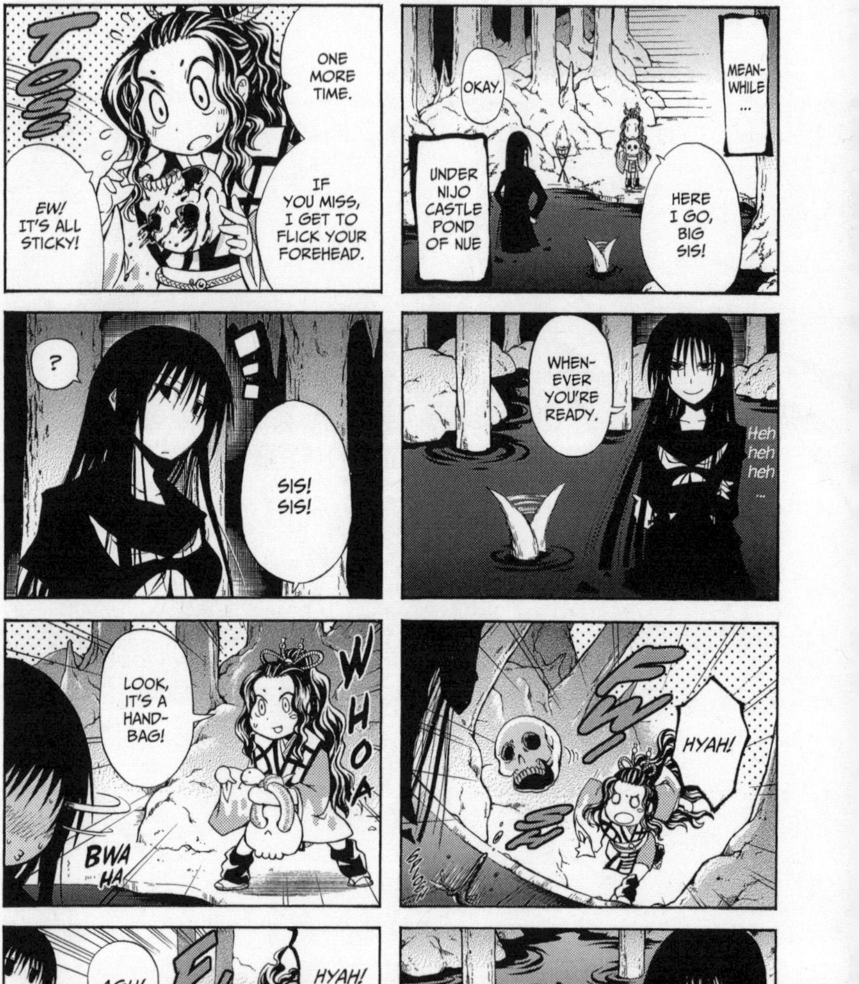
MEAN-WHILE...
OKAY.
HERE I GO, BIG SIS!
UNDER NIJO CASTLE POND OF NUE
WHEN-EVER YOU'RE READY.
Heh heh heh...
HYAH!
YOU'LL NEVER HIT MY TAIL THAT WAY.
MISSED AGAIN.
PLOK
SPLISH
ONE MORE TIME.
IF YOU MISS, I GET TO FLICK YOUR FOREHEAD.
EW! IT'S ALL STICKY!
TOSS
?
SIS! SIS!
LOOK, IT'S A HAND-BAG!
WHOA
BWA HA
HYAH!
AGH!
SMAK

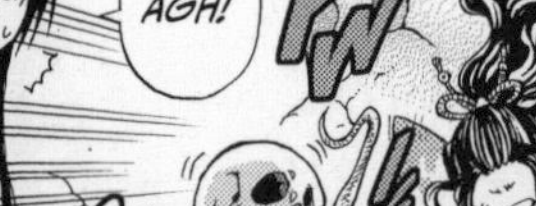
We had free time this volume...

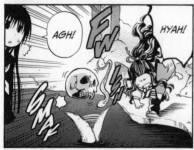

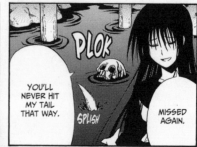

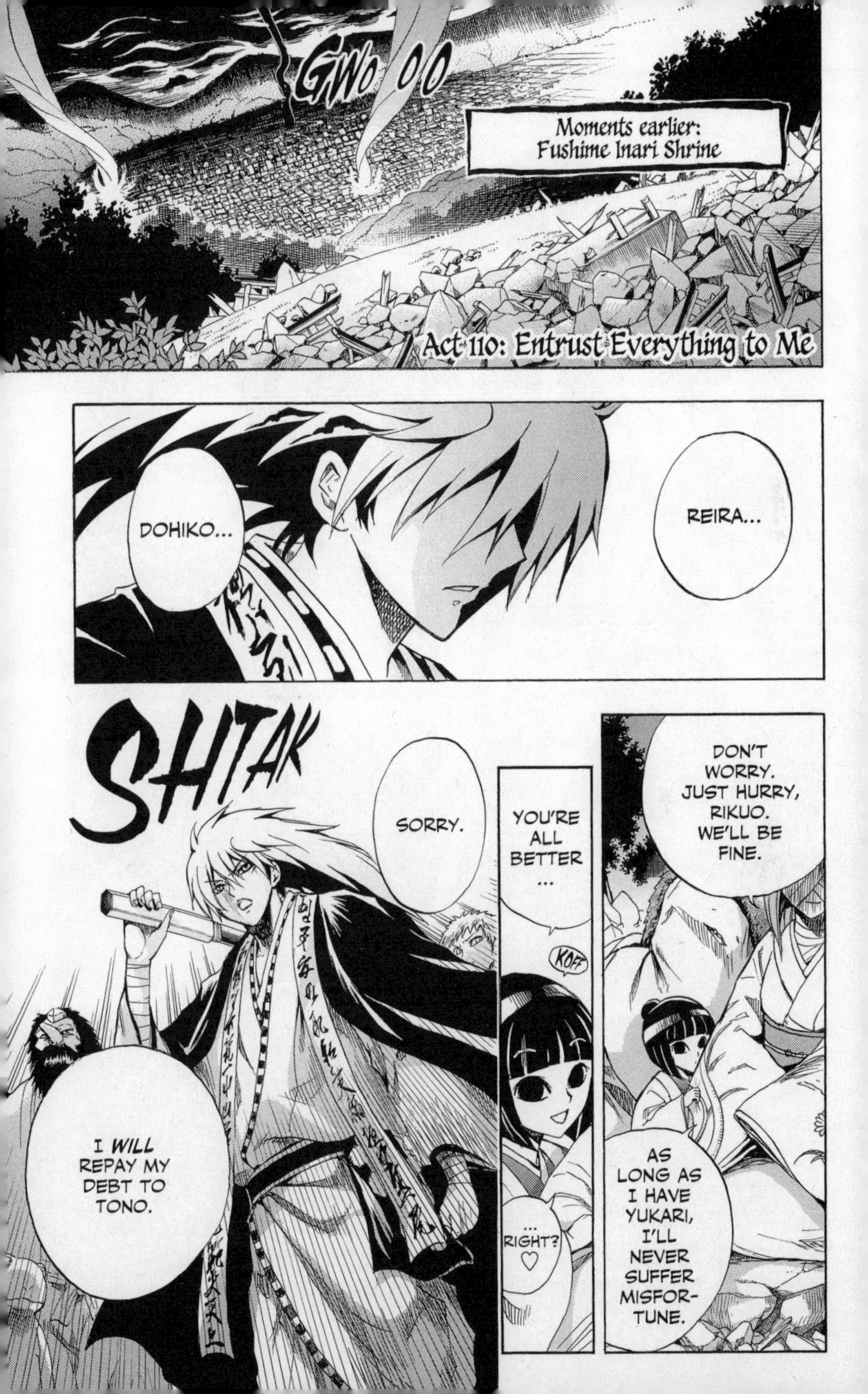
GWOOO
Moments earlier:
Fushime Inari Shrine
Act 110: Entrust Everything to Me
REIRA...
DOHIKO...
DON'T WORRY. JUST HURRY, RIKUO. WE'LL BE FINE.
AS LONG AS I HAVE YUKARI, I'LL NEVER SUFFER MISFORTUNE.
YOU'RE ALL BETTER ...
KOFF
... RIGHT? ♡
SHITAK
SORRY.
I WILL REPAY MY DEBT TO TONO.

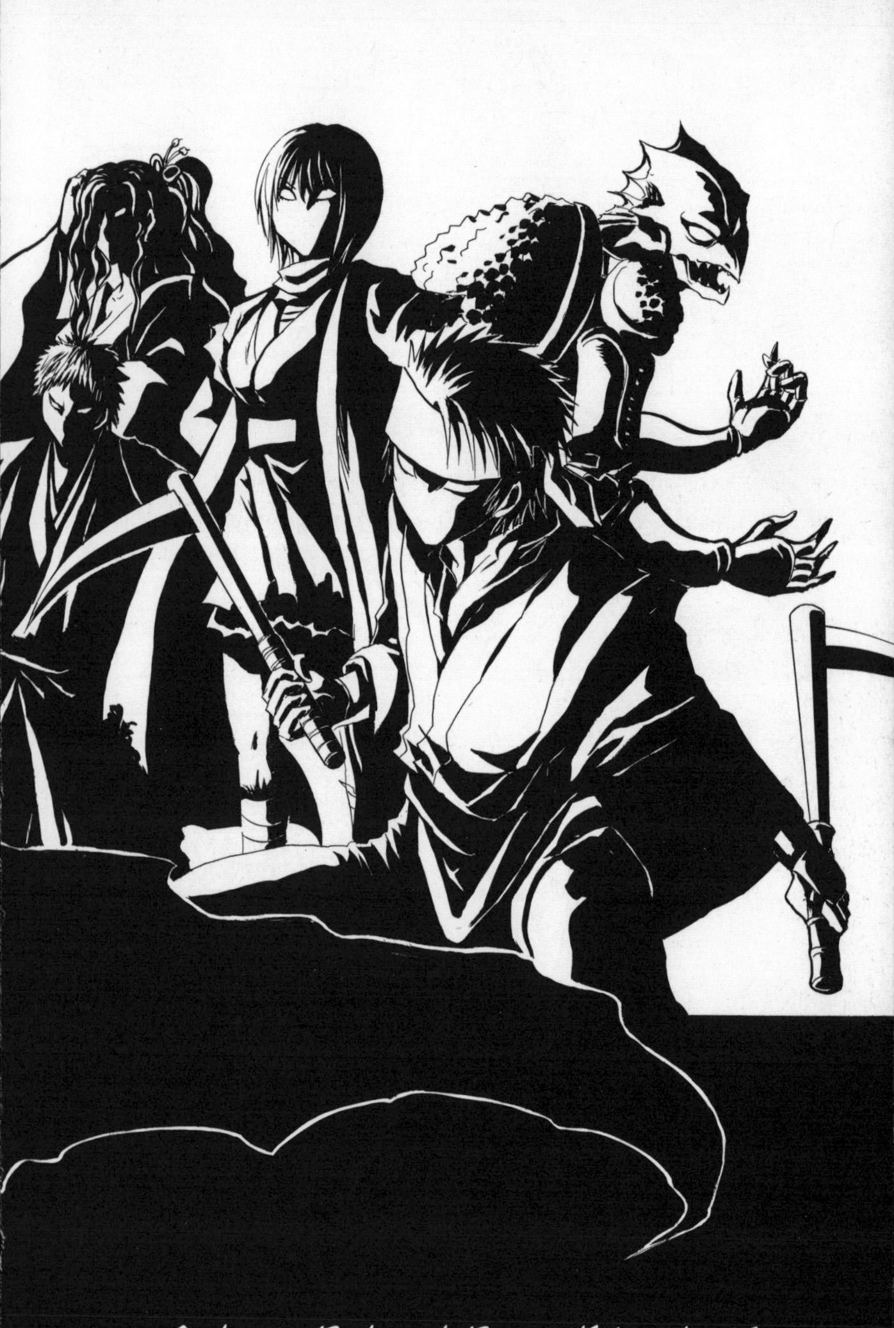

Act 110: Entrust Everything to Me

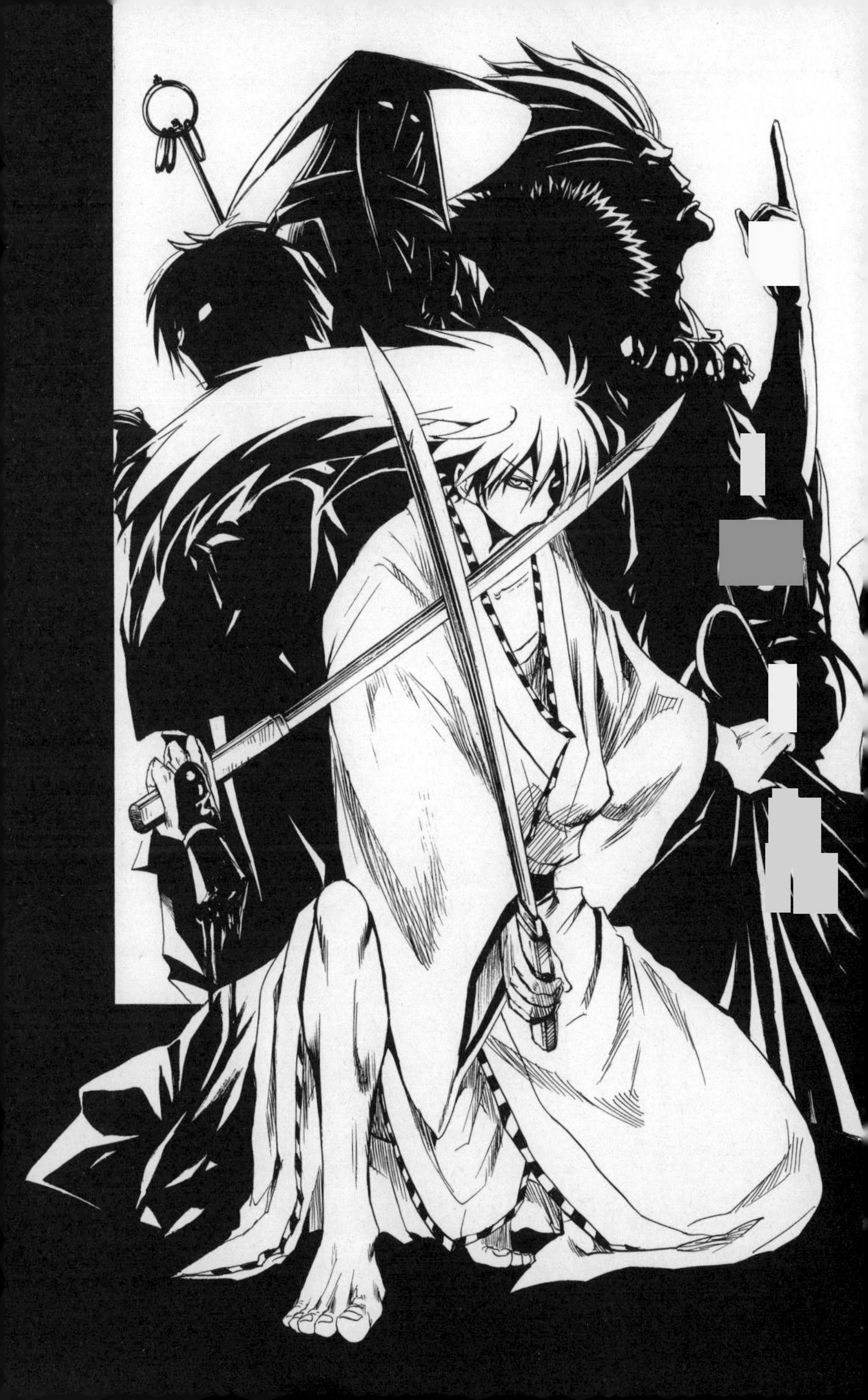

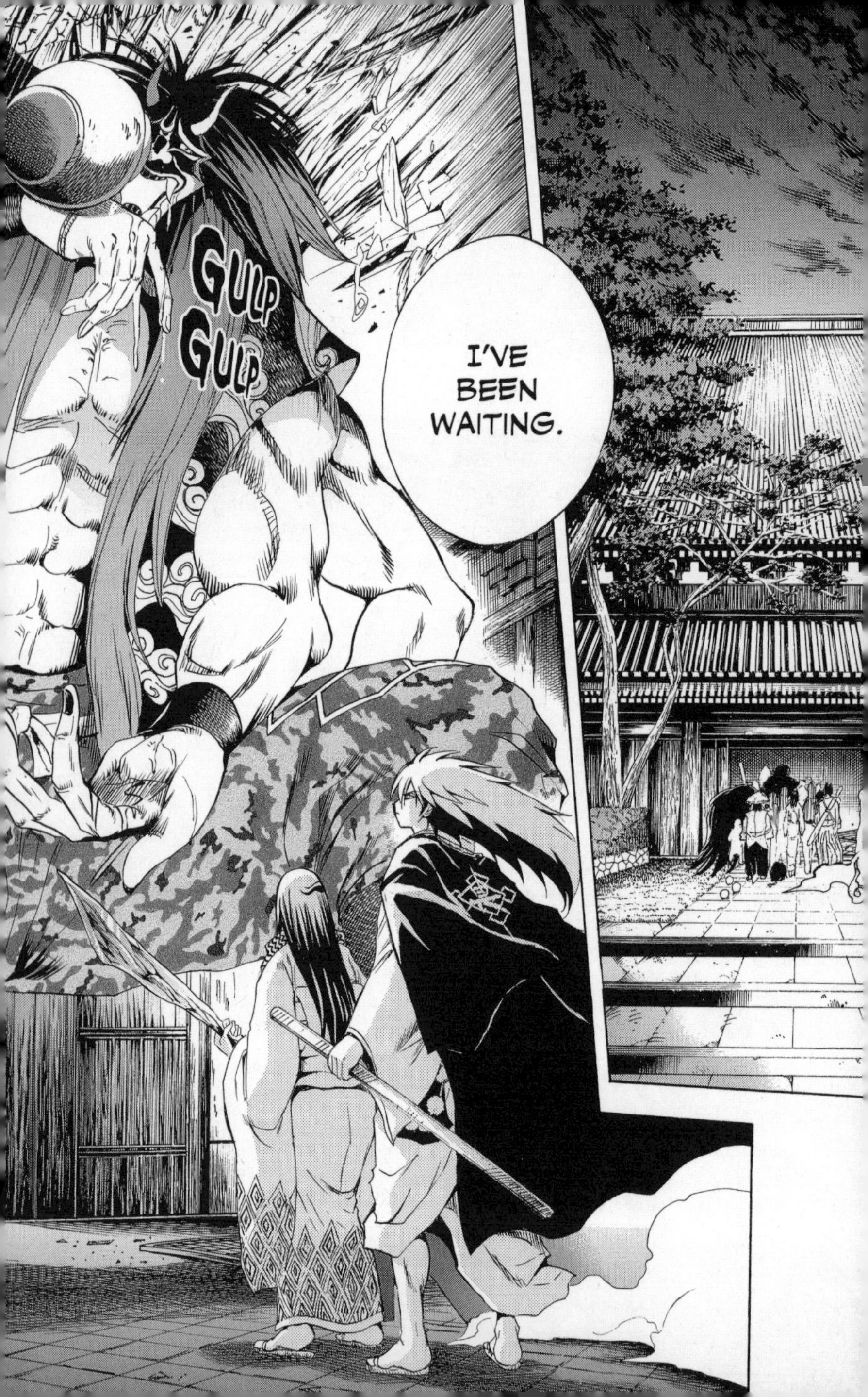
I'VE BEEN WAITING.
GULP GULP

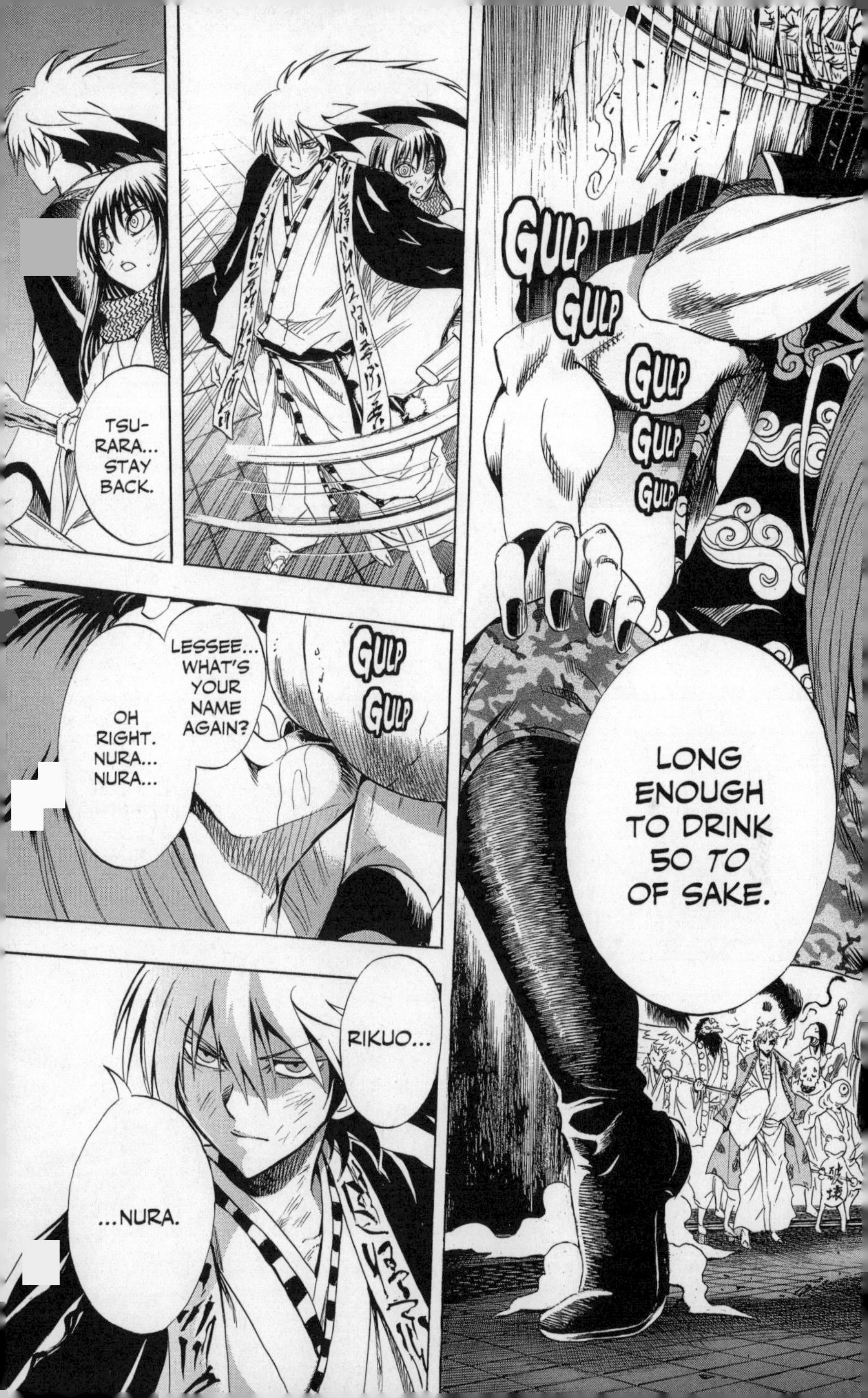
GULP
GULP
GULP
GULP
GULP
LONG ENOUGH TO DRINK 50 *TO* OF SAKE.
TSU-RARA... STAY BACK.
GULP
GULP
LESSEE... WHAT'S YOUR NAME AGAIN?
OH RIGHT. NURA... NURA...
RIKUO...
...NURA.

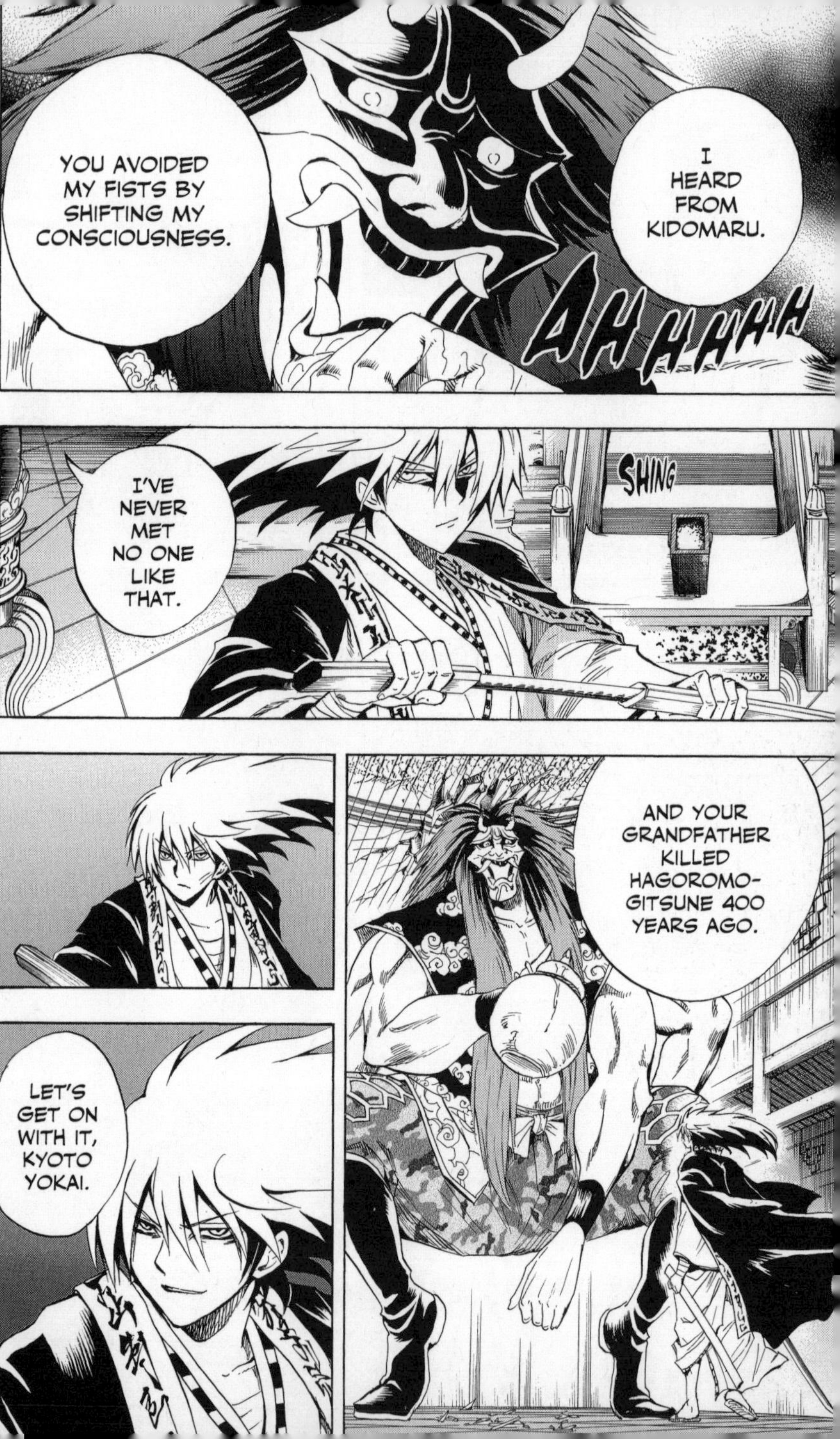
I HEARD FROM KIDOMARU.
YOU AVOIDED MY FISTS BY SHIFTING MY CONSCIOUSNESS.
AHHHHHH
SHING
I'VE NEVER MET NO ONE LIKE THAT.
AND YOUR GRANDFATHER KILLED HAGOROMO-GITSUNE 400 YEARS AGO.
LET'S GET ON WITH IT, KYOTO YOKAI.

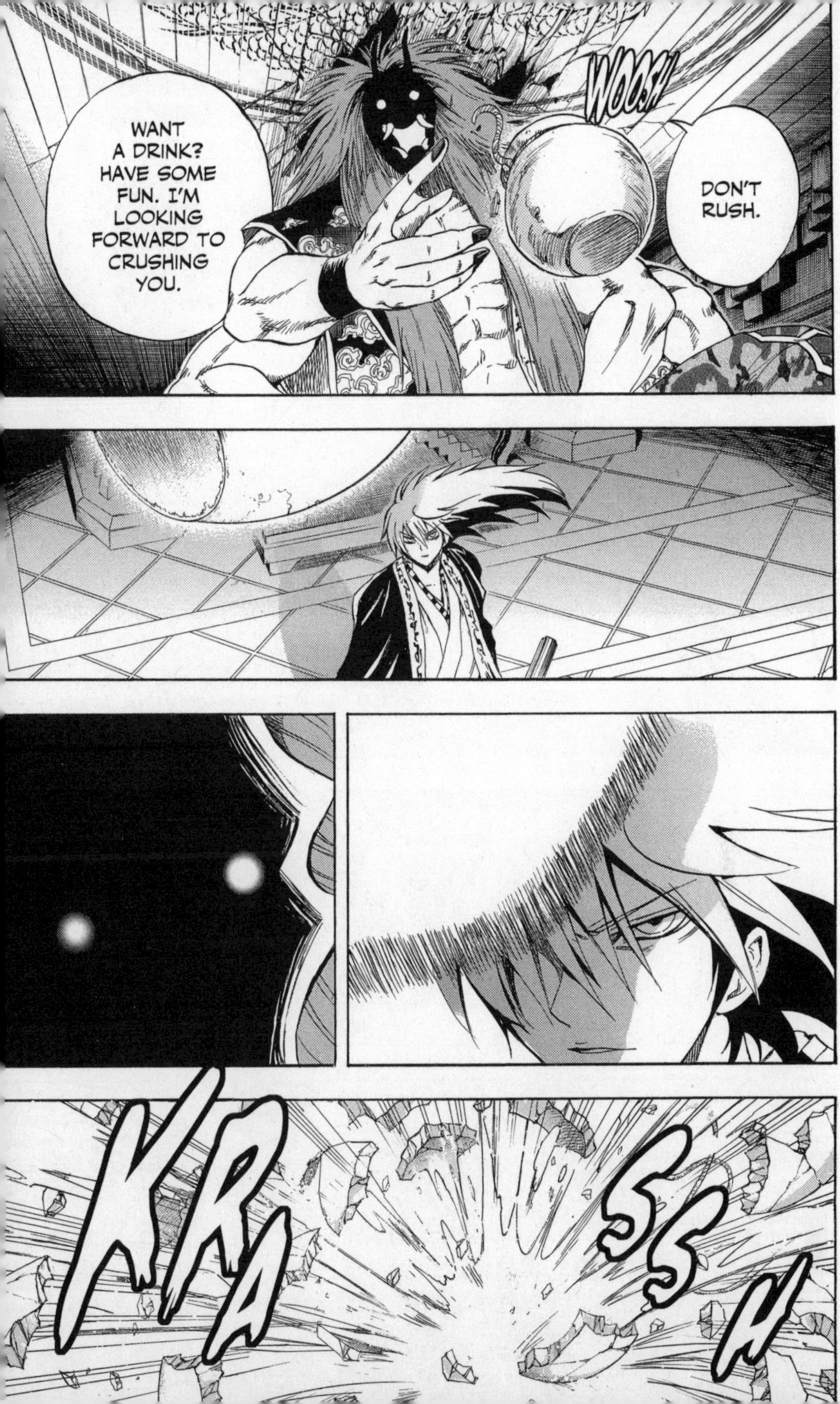
WOOSH
DON'T RUSH.
WANT A DRINK? HAVE SOME FUN. I'M LOOKING FORWARD TO CRUSHING YOU.
KRASSH

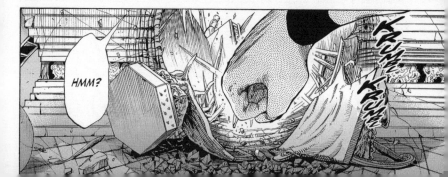

HMM?

KRUMB
KRUMB

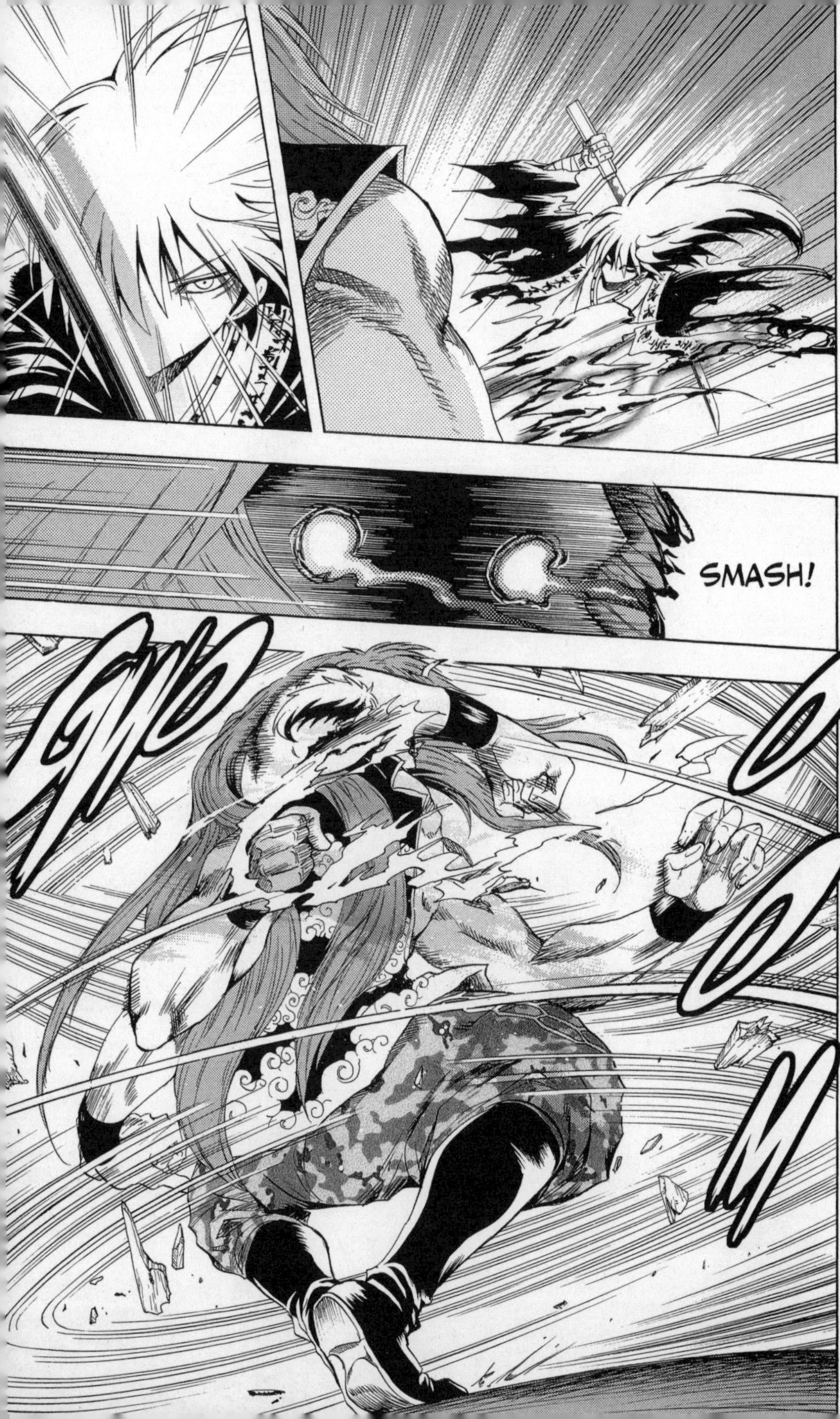
SMASH!

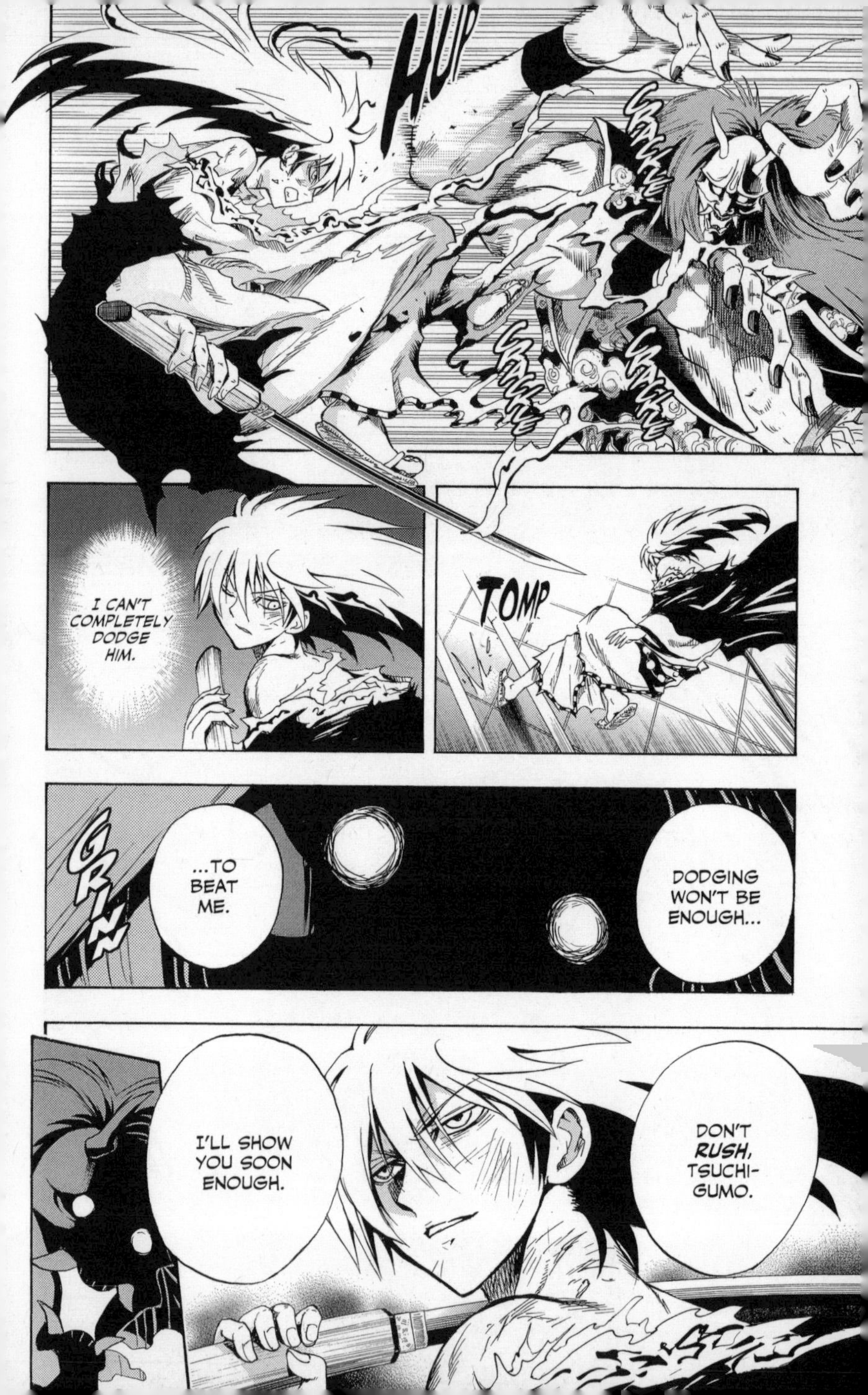
HUP
TOMP
I CAN'T COMPLETELY DODGE HIM.
DODGING WON'T BE ENOUGH...
...TO BEAT ME.
GRINN
DON'T *RUSH*, TSUCHI-GUMO.
I'LL SHOW YOU SOON ENOUGH.

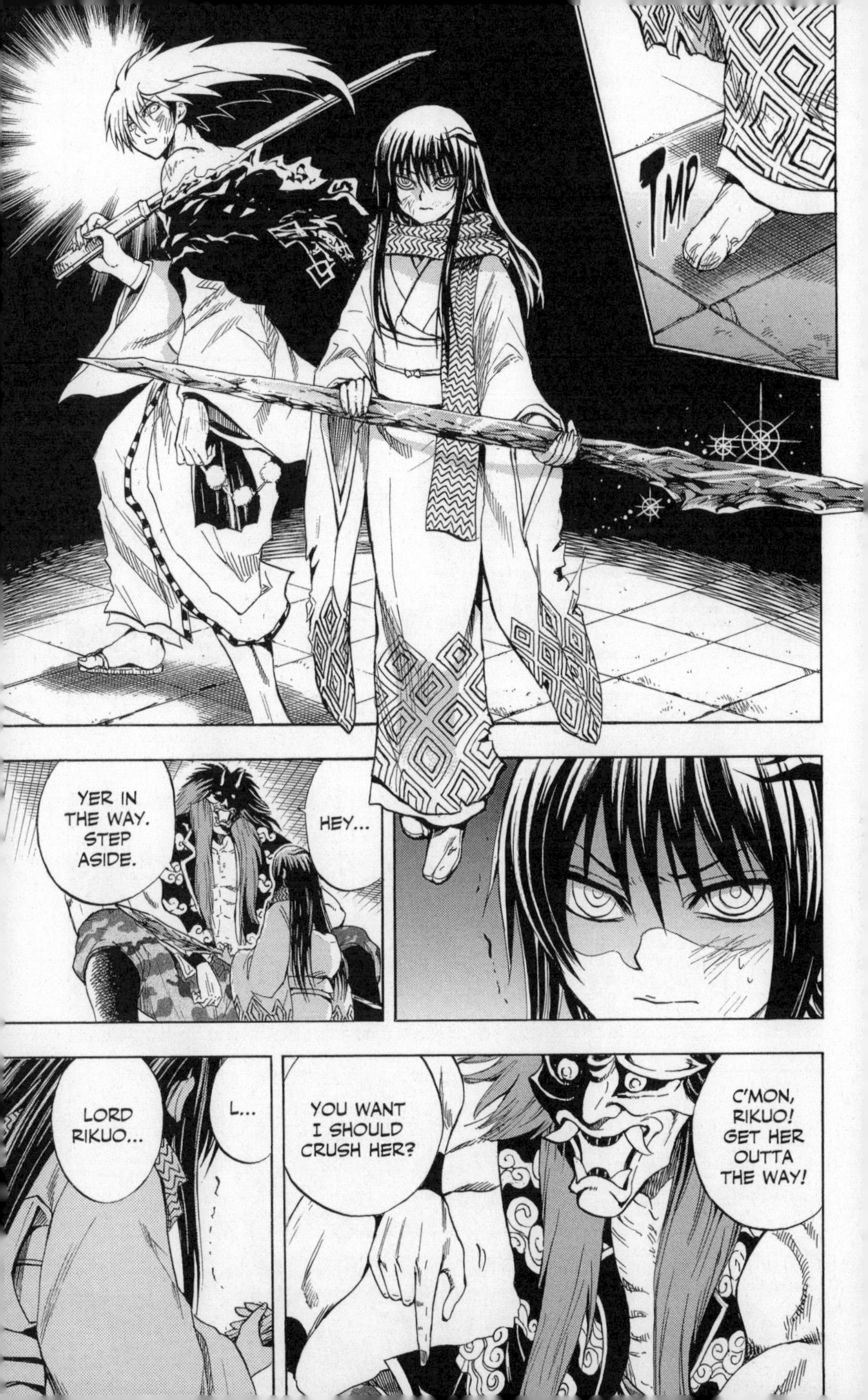
TMP
HEY...
YER IN THE WAY. STEP ASIDE.
C'MON, RIKUO! GET HER OUTTA THE WAY!
YOU WANT I SHOULD CRUSH HER?
L...
LORD RIKUO...

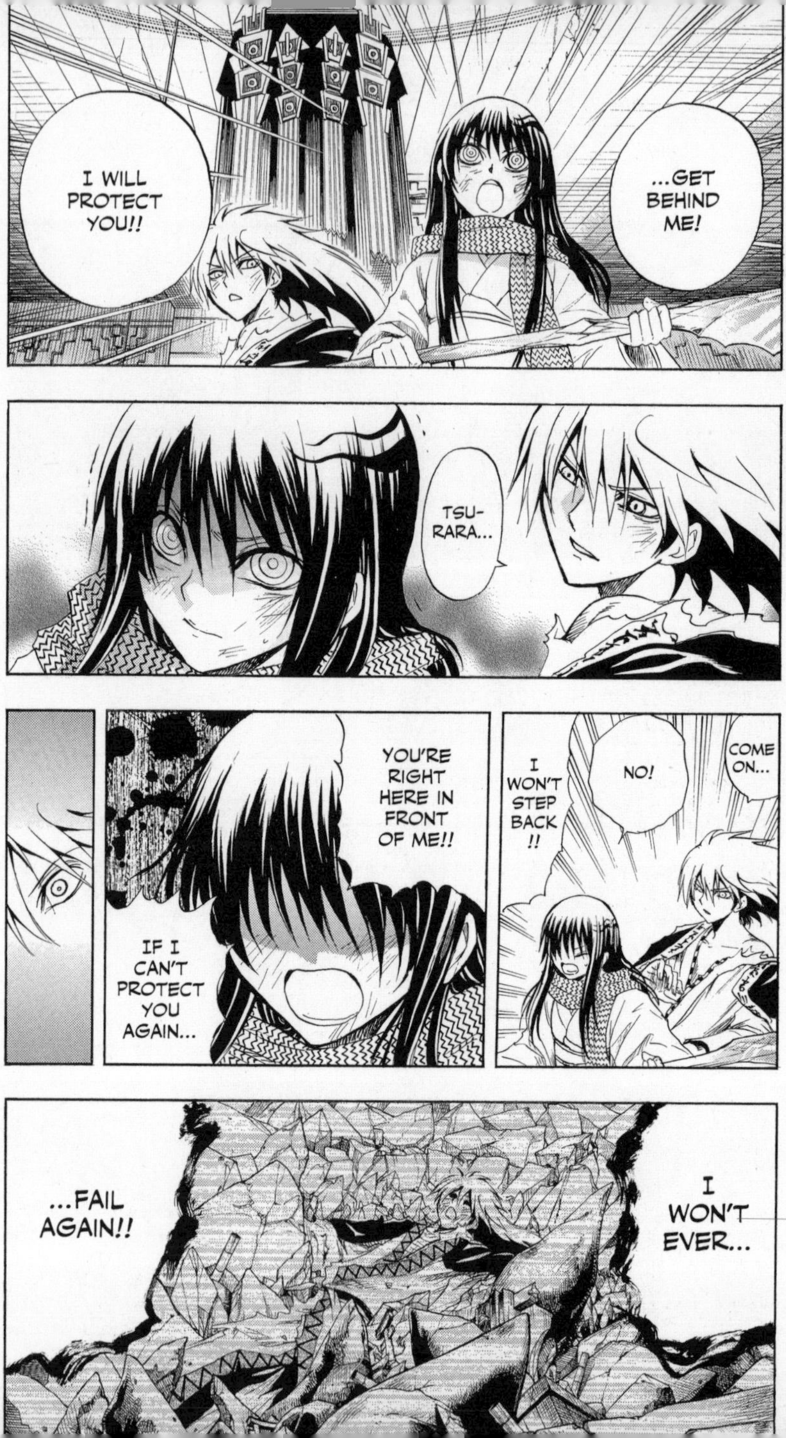
...GET BEHIND ME!
I WILL PROTECT YOU!!
TSU-RARA...
COME ON...
NO!
I WON'T STEP BACK !!
YOU'RE RIGHT HERE IN FRONT OF ME!!
IF I CAN'T PROTECT YOU AGAIN...
I WON'T EVER...
...FAIL AGAIN!!

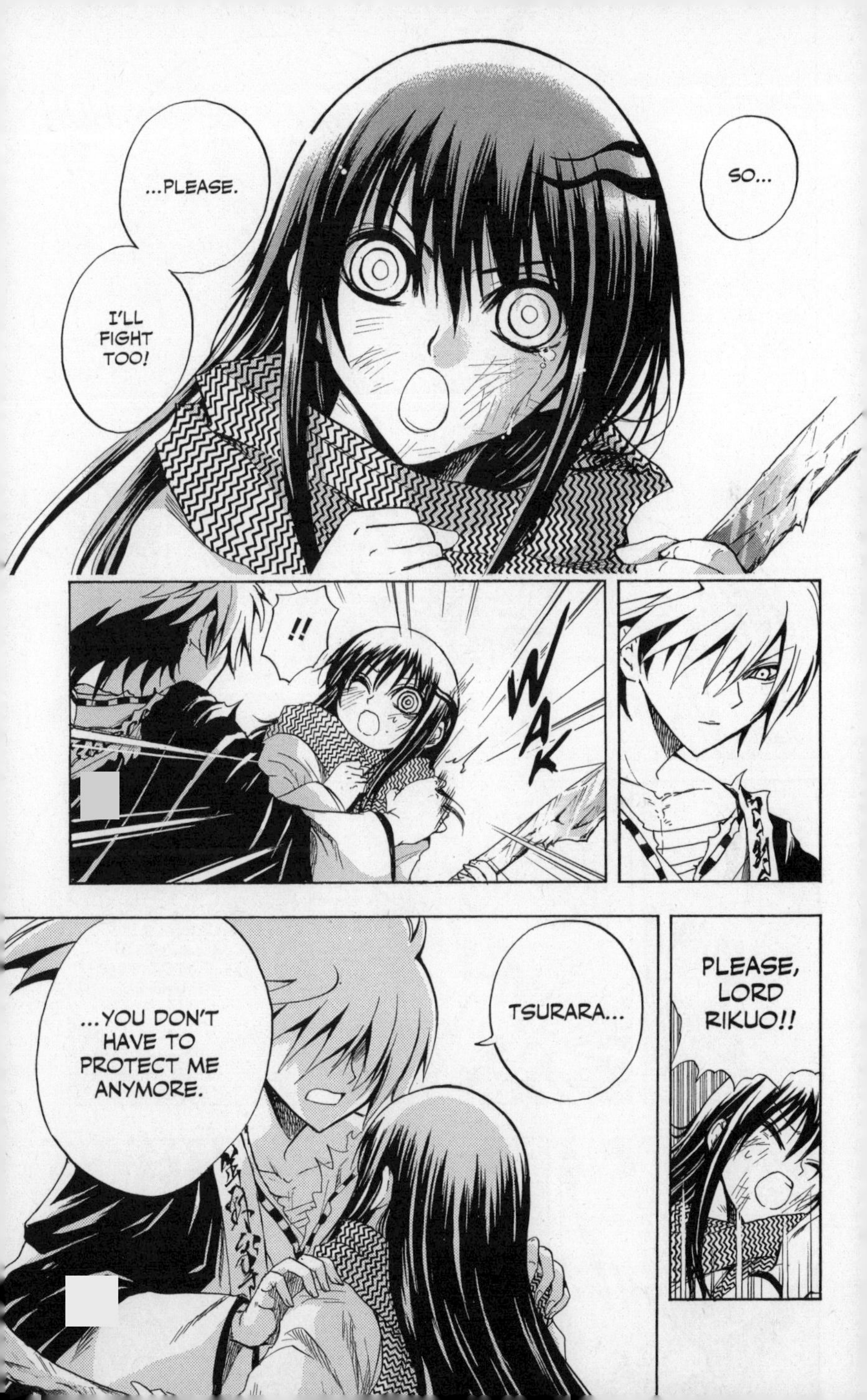
SO...
...PLEASE.
I'LL FIGHT TOO!
!!
WAK
PLEASE, LORD RIKUO!!
TSURARA...
...YOU DON'T HAVE TO PROTECT ME ANYMORE.

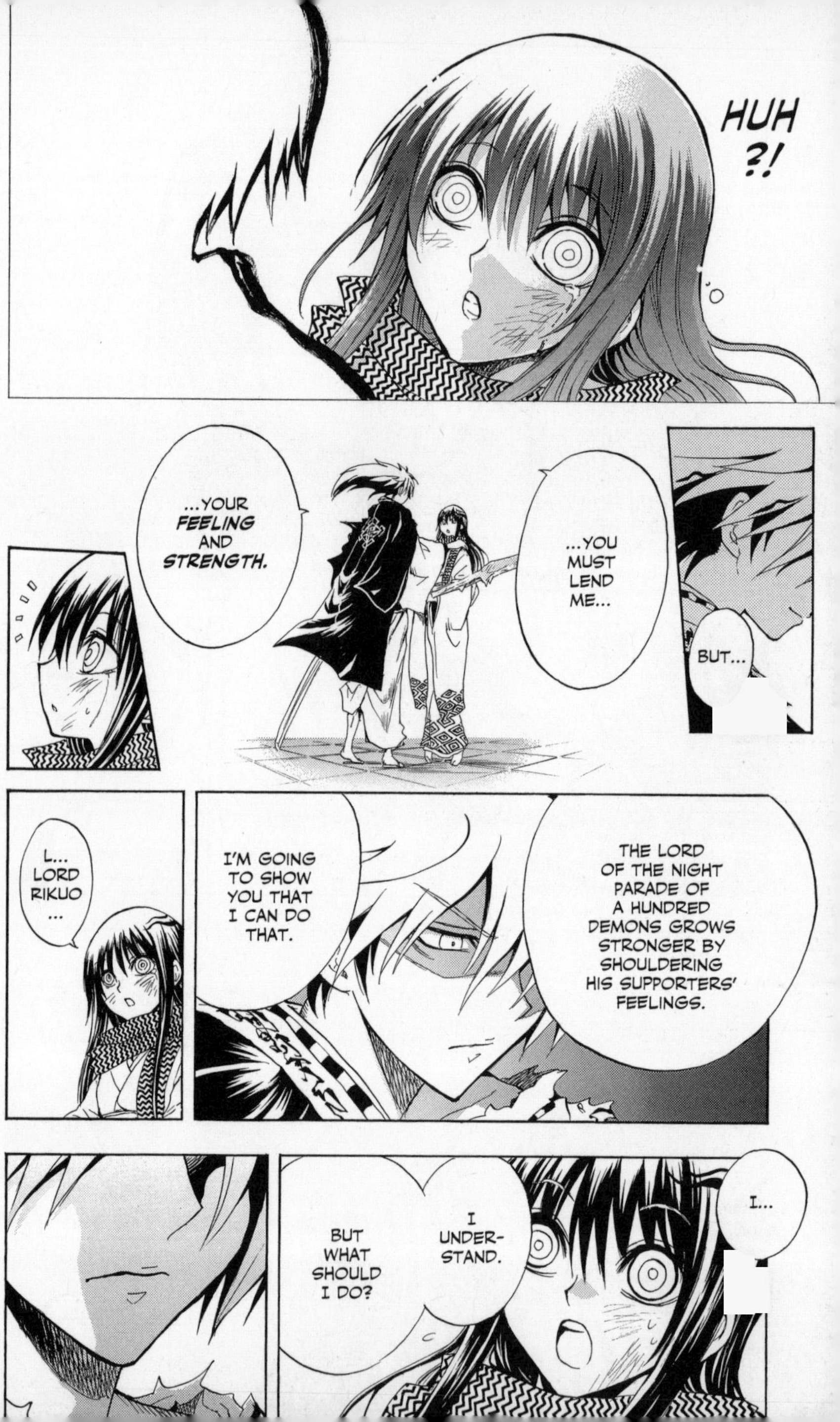
HUH ?!
BUT...
...YOU MUST LEND ME...
...YOUR FEELING AND STRENGTH.
THE LORD OF THE NIGHT PARADE OF A HUNDRED DEMONS GROWS STRONGER BY SHOULDERING HIS SUPPORTERS' FEELINGS.
I'M GOING TO SHOW YOU THAT I CAN DO THAT.
L... LORD RIKUO ...
I...
I UNDER-STAND.
BUT WHAT SHOULD I DO?

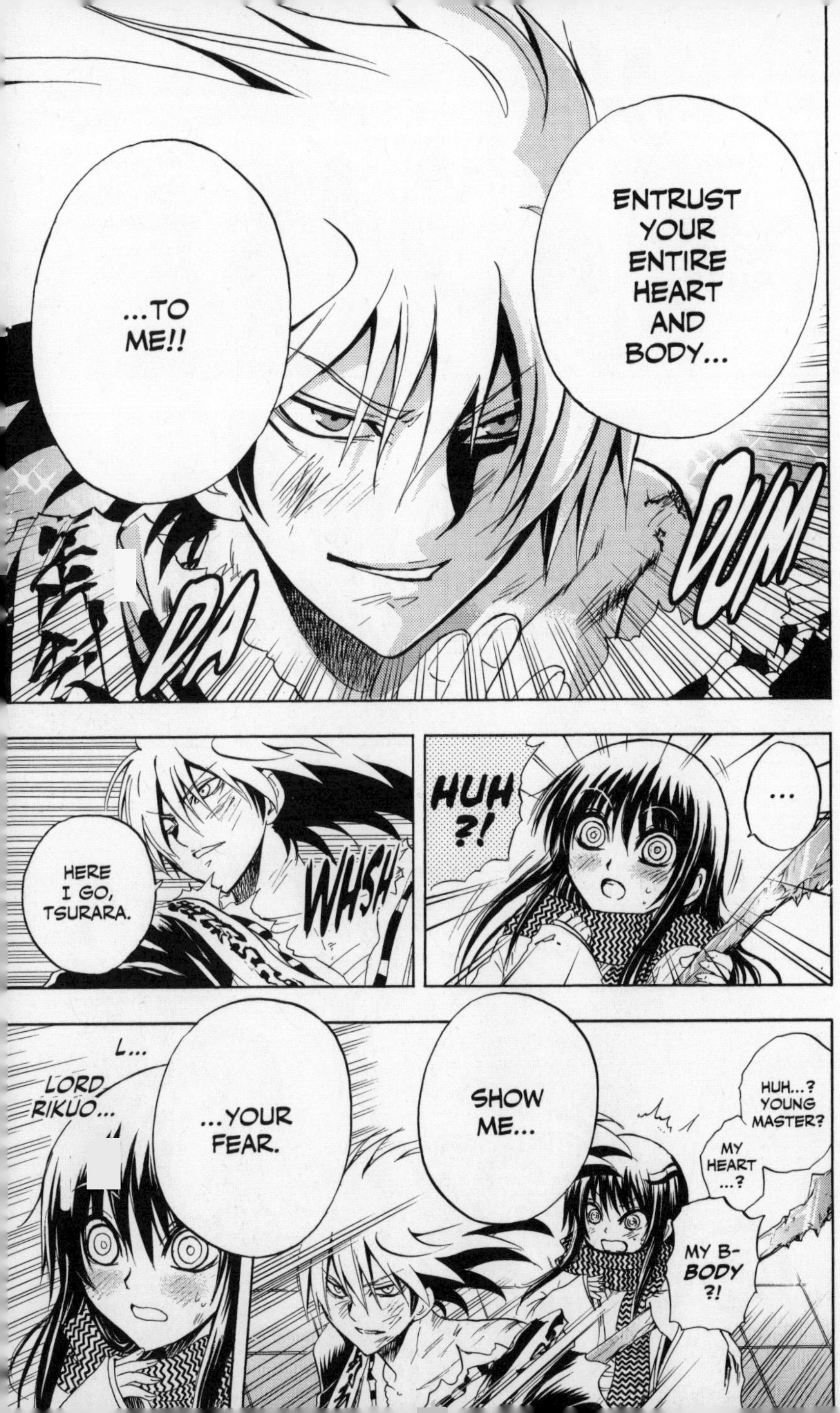
ENTRUST YOUR ENTIRE HEART AND BODY...
...TO ME!!
...
HUH ?!
HERE I GO, TSURARA.
WHSH
HUH...? YOUNG MASTER?
MY HEART ...?
MY B-BODY ?!
SHOW ME...
...YOUR FEAR.
L...
LORD RIKUO...

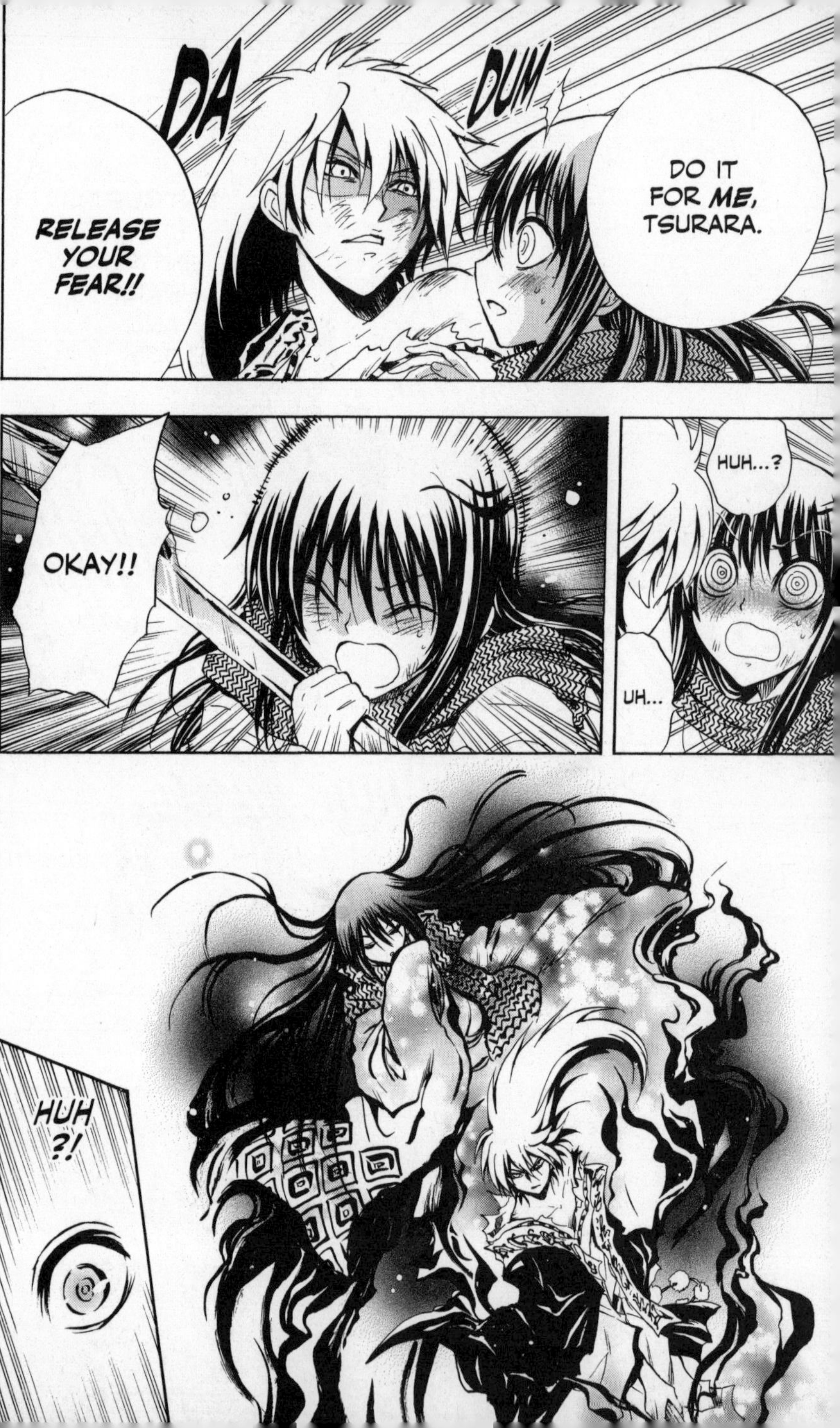
DA DUM
DO IT FOR ME, TSURARA.
RELEASE YOUR FEAR!!
HUH...?
UH...
OKAY!!
HUH ?!

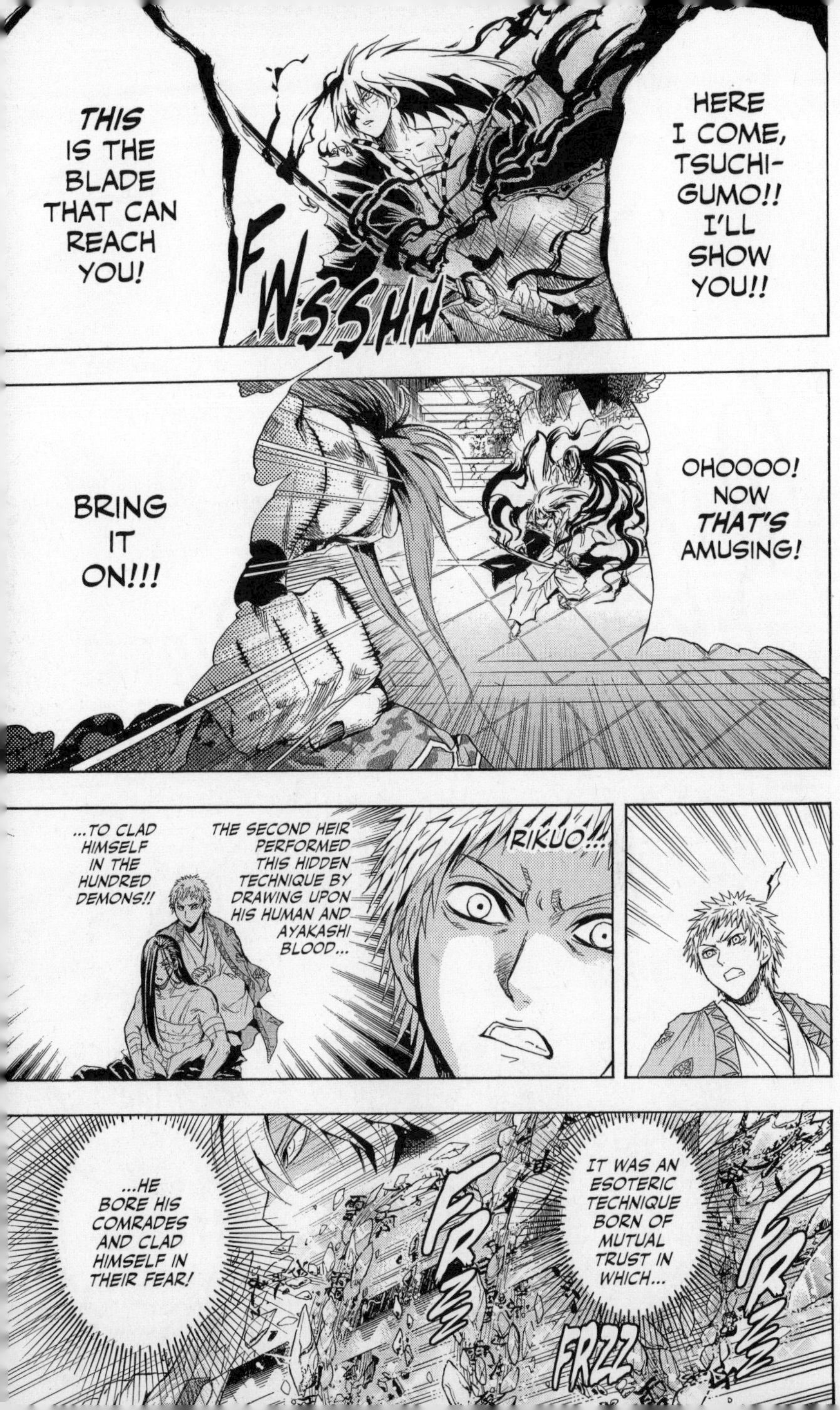
HERE I COME, TSUCHIGUMO!! I'LL SHOW YOU!!
THIS IS THE BLADE THAT CAN REACH YOU!
FWSSHH
OHOOOO! NOW THAT'S AMUSING!
BRING IT ON!!!
RIKUO!!
THE SECOND HEIR PERFORMED THIS HIDDEN TECHNIQUE BY DRAWING UPON HIS HUMAN AND AYAKASHI BLOOD...
...TO CLAD HIMSELF IN THE HUNDRED DEMONS!!
IT WAS AN ESOTERIC TECHNIQUE BORN OF MUTUAL TRUST IN WHICH...
...HE BORE HIS COMRADES AND CLAD HIMSELF IN THEIR FEAR!
FRZZ

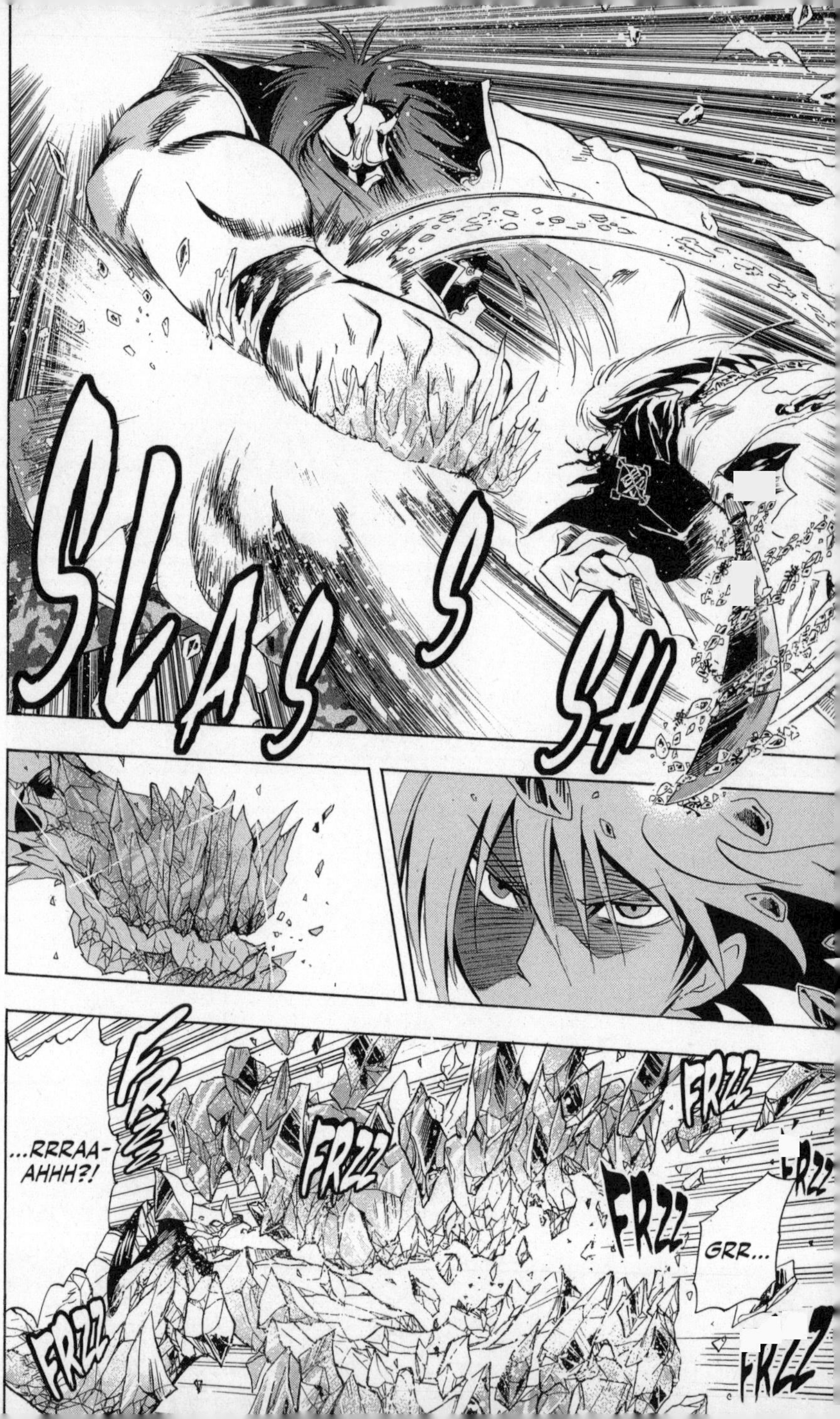
SLASSSH
FRZZ
FRZZ
GRR...
FRZZ
...RRRAA-AHHH?!
FRZZ

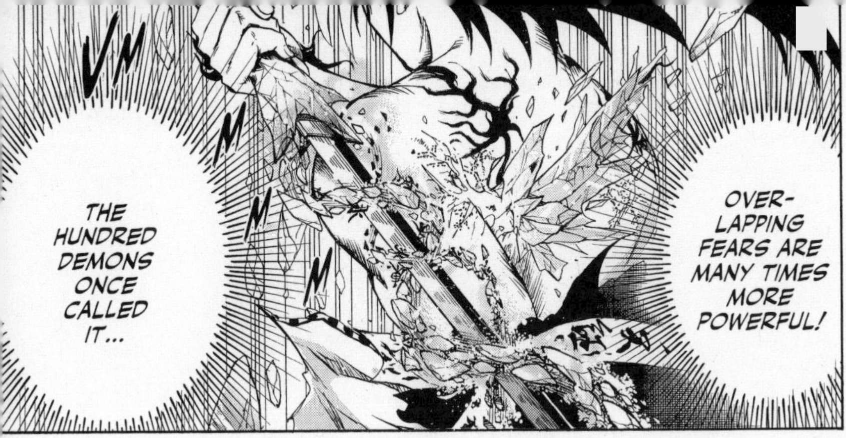
OVER-LAPPING FEARS ARE MANY TIMES MORE POWERFUL!
THE HUNDRED DEMONS ONCE CALLED IT...
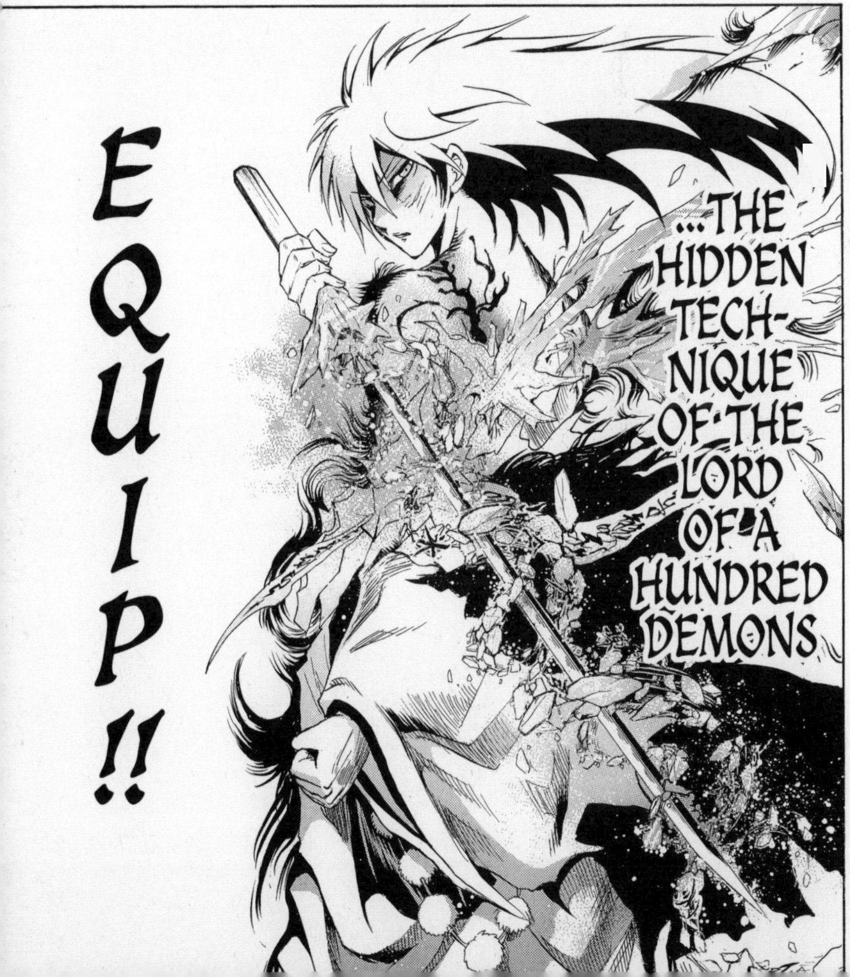
...THE HIDDEN TECH-NIQUE OF THE LORD OF A HUNDRED DEMONS
EQUIP!!

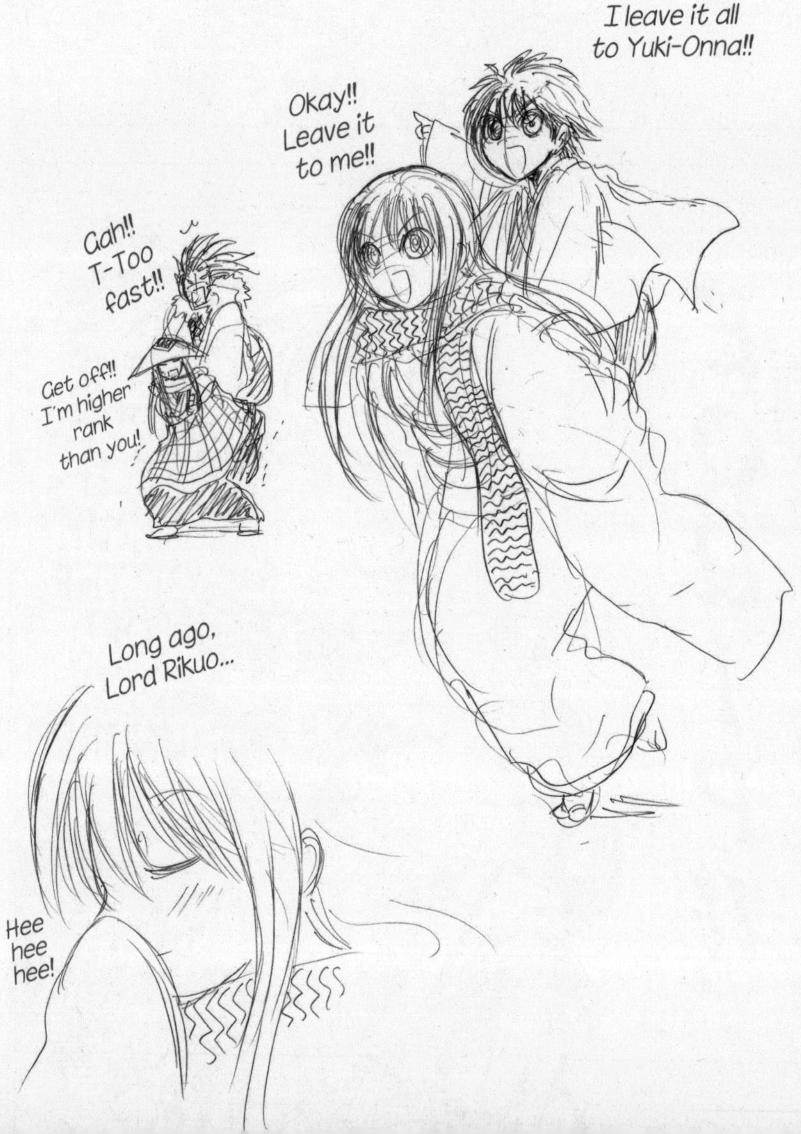
I leave it all to Yuki-Onna!!
Okay!! Leave it to me!!
Gah!! T-Too fast!!
Get off!! I'm higher rank than you!
Long ago, Lord Rikuo...
Hee hee hee!

Act 111: Pink Blossoms Under the Snow

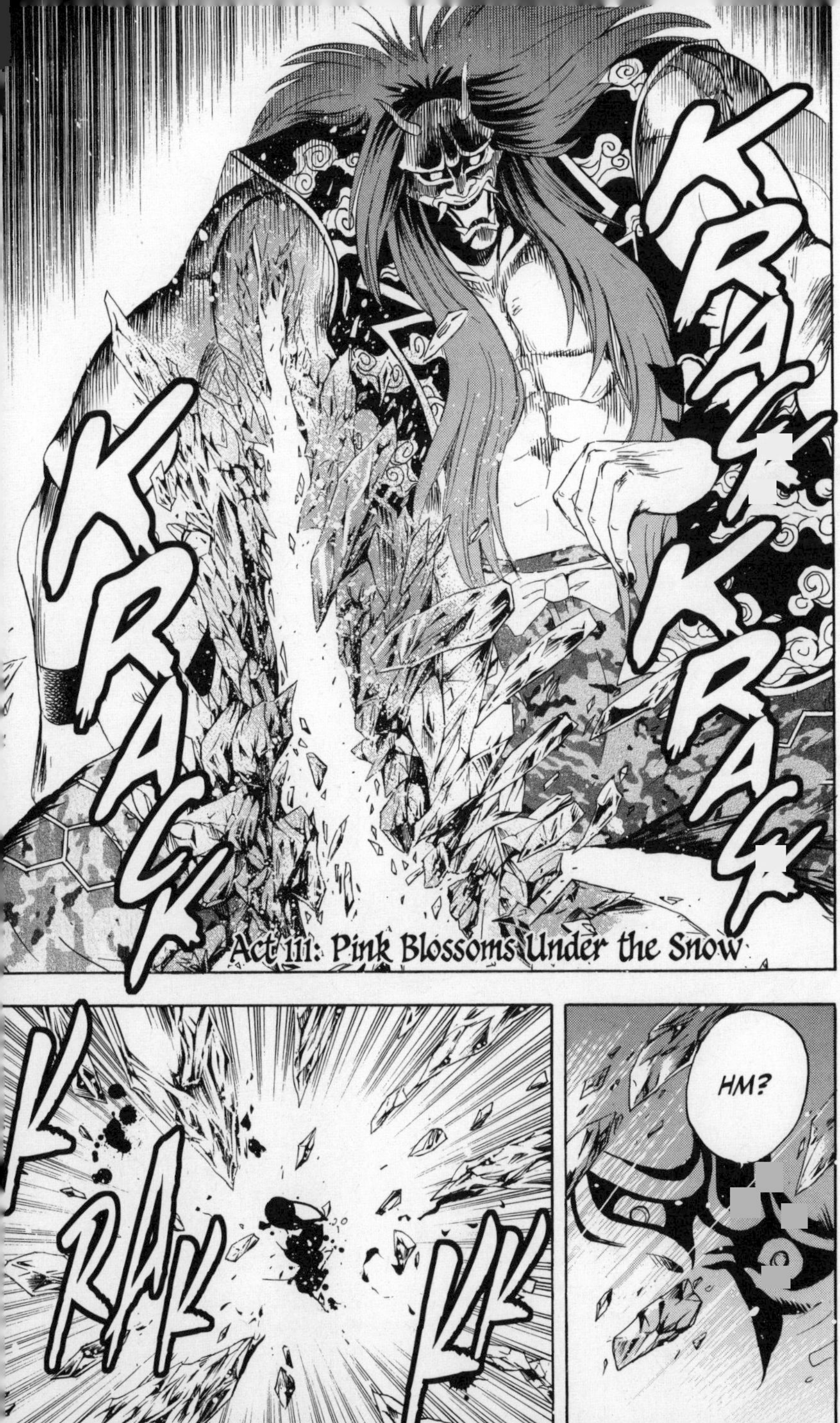
KRACK
KRACK
KRACK
HM?

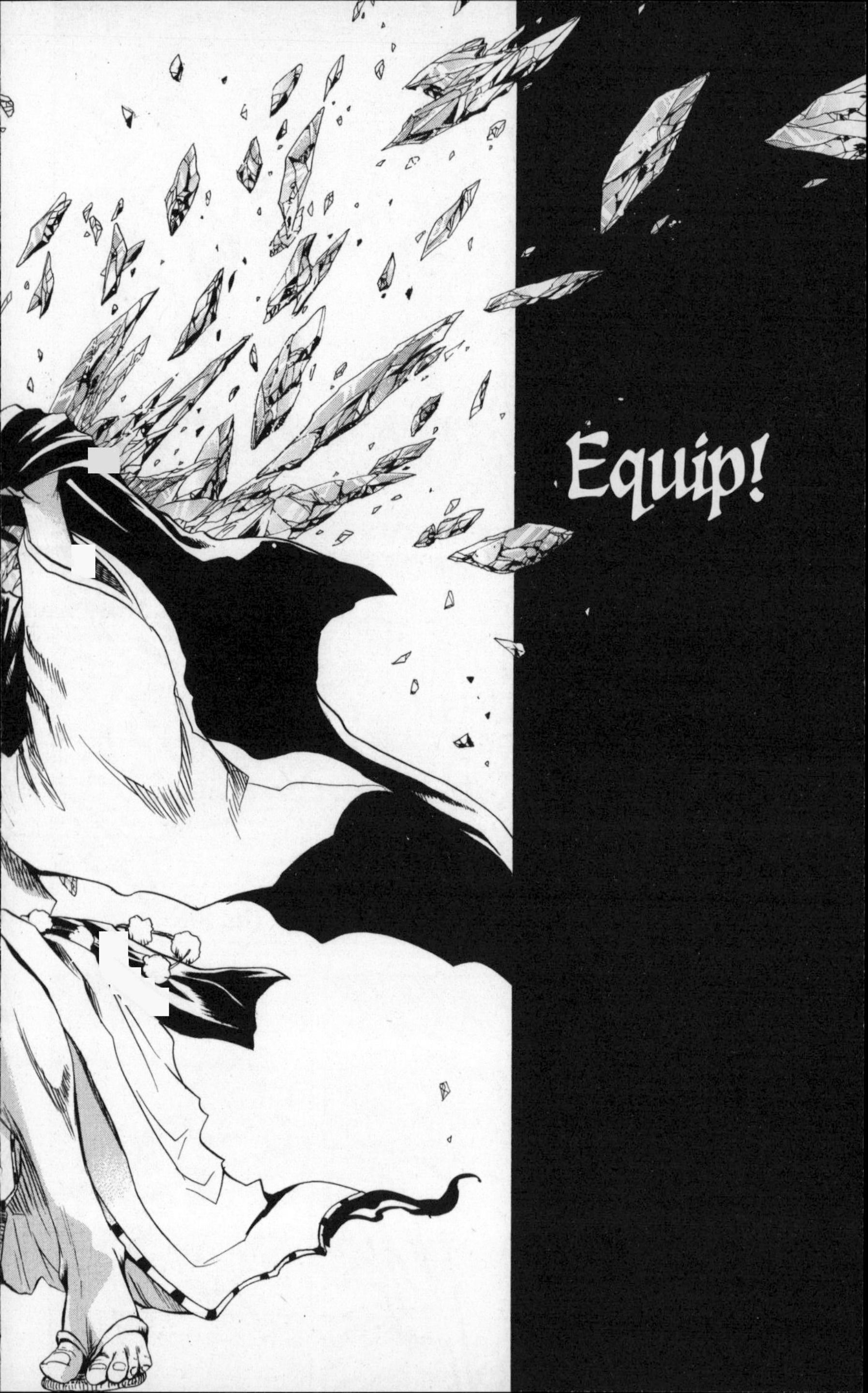
Equip!

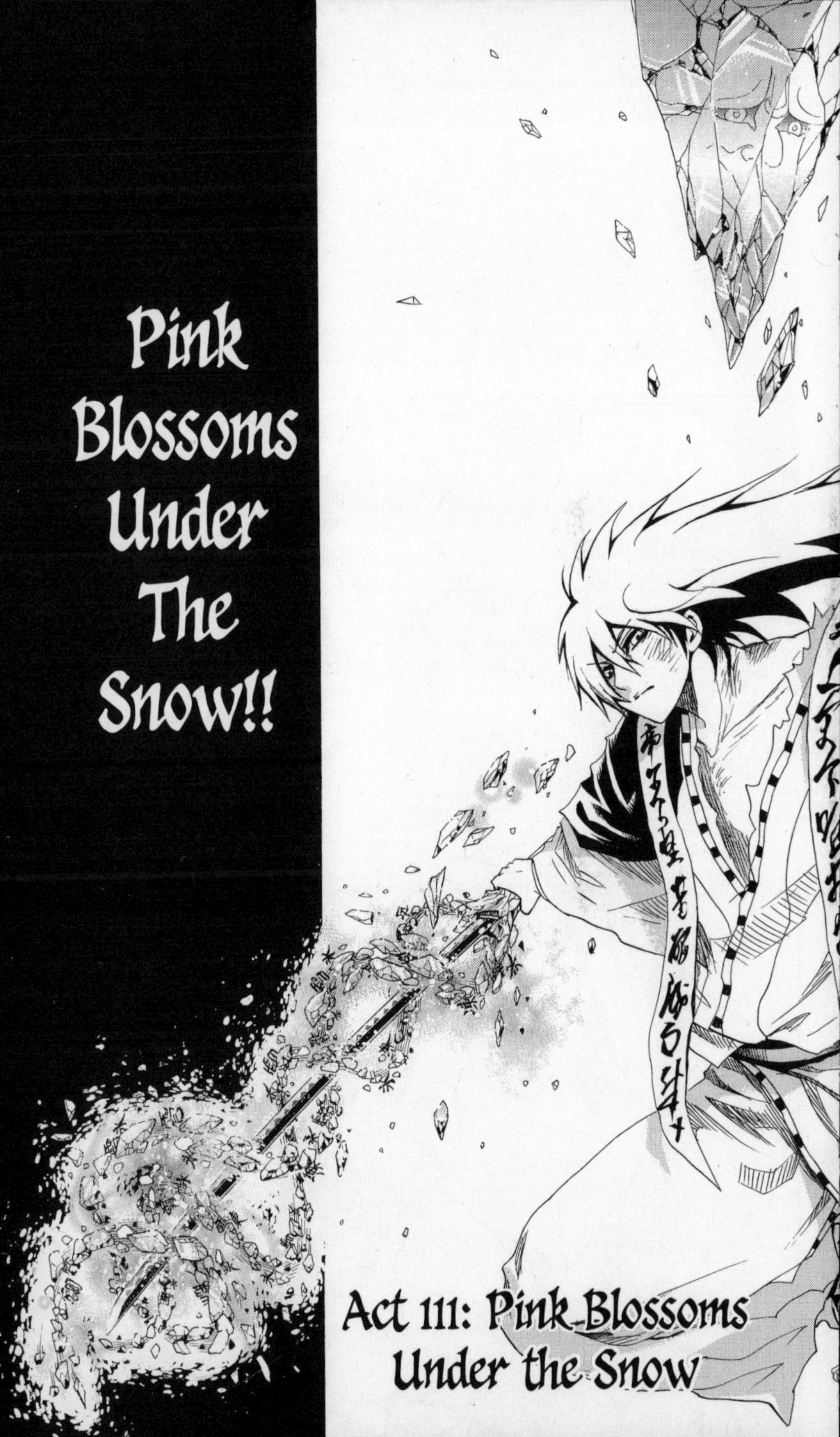
Pink Blossoms Under The Snow!!
Act 111: Pink Blossoms Under the Snow

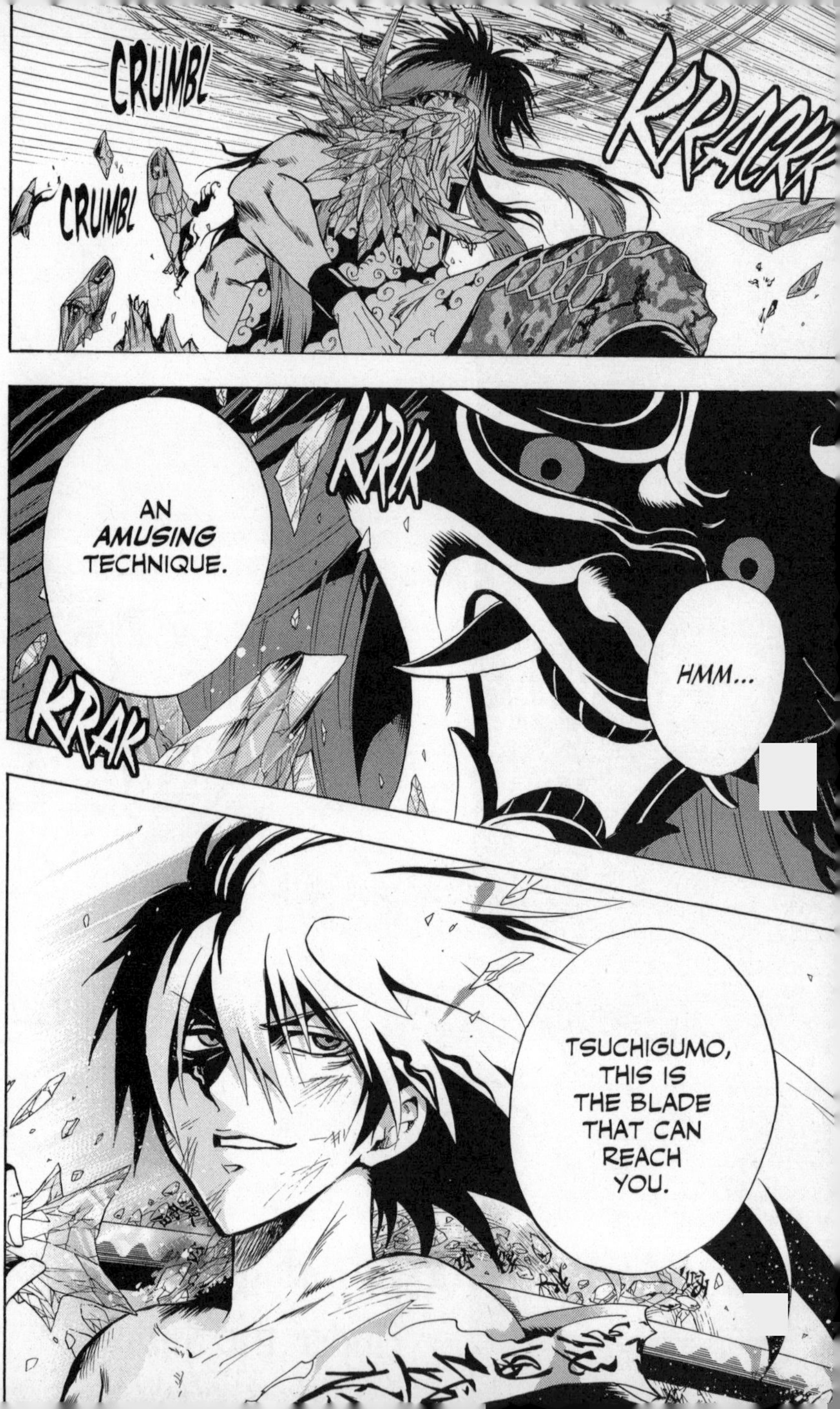
KRACKK
CRUMBL
CRUMBL
HMM...
KRIK
AN AMUSING TECHNIQUE.
KRAK
TSUCHIGUMO, THIS IS THE BLADE THAT CAN REACH YOU.

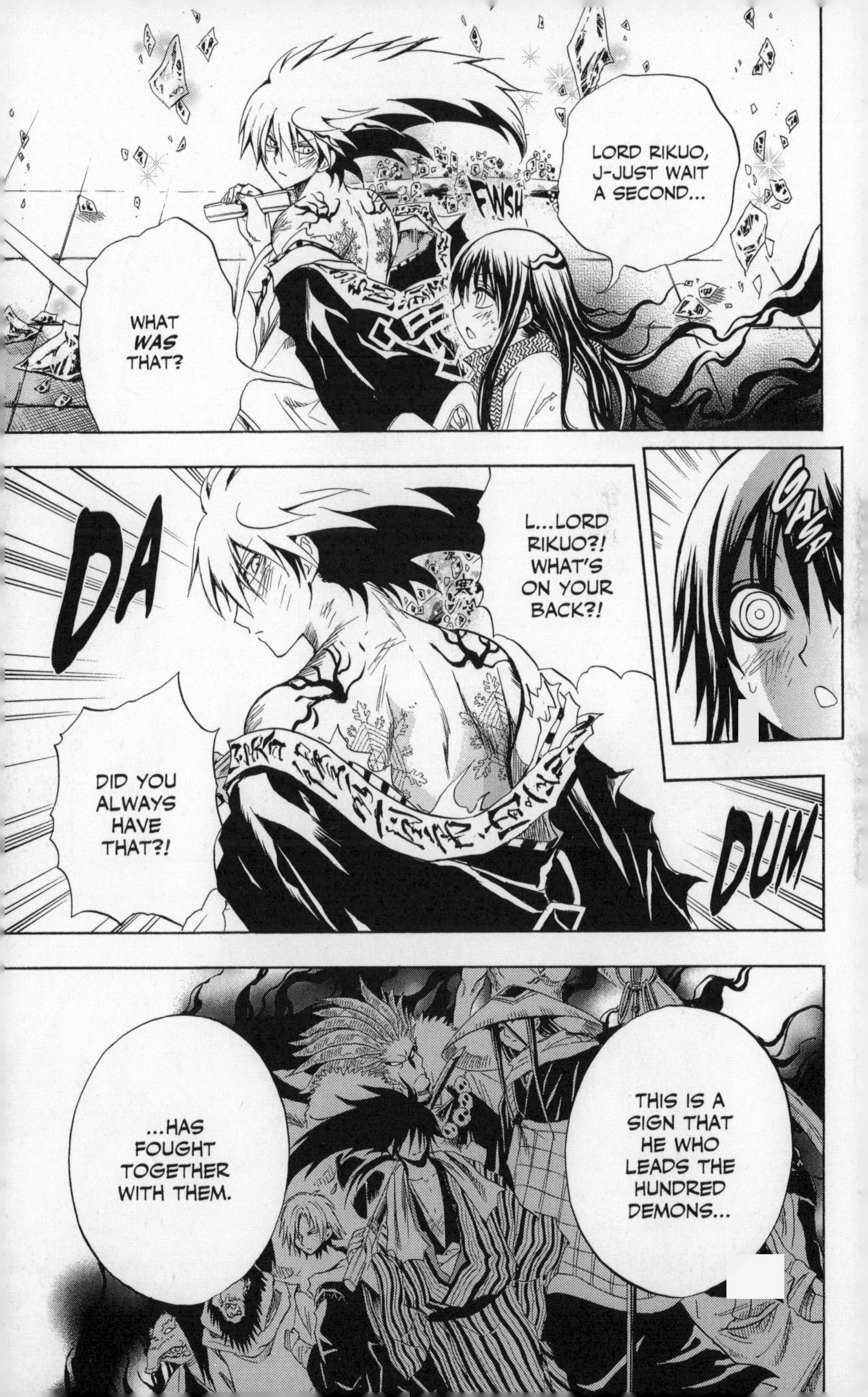
LORD RIKUO, J-JUST WAIT A SECOND...
FWSH
WHAT *WAS* THAT?
GASP
L...LORD RIKUO?! WHAT'S ON YOUR BACK?!
DUM
DA
DID YOU ALWAYS HAVE THAT?!
THIS IS A SIGN THAT HE WHO LEADS THE HUNDRED DEMONS...
...HAS FOUGHT TOGETHER WITH THEM.

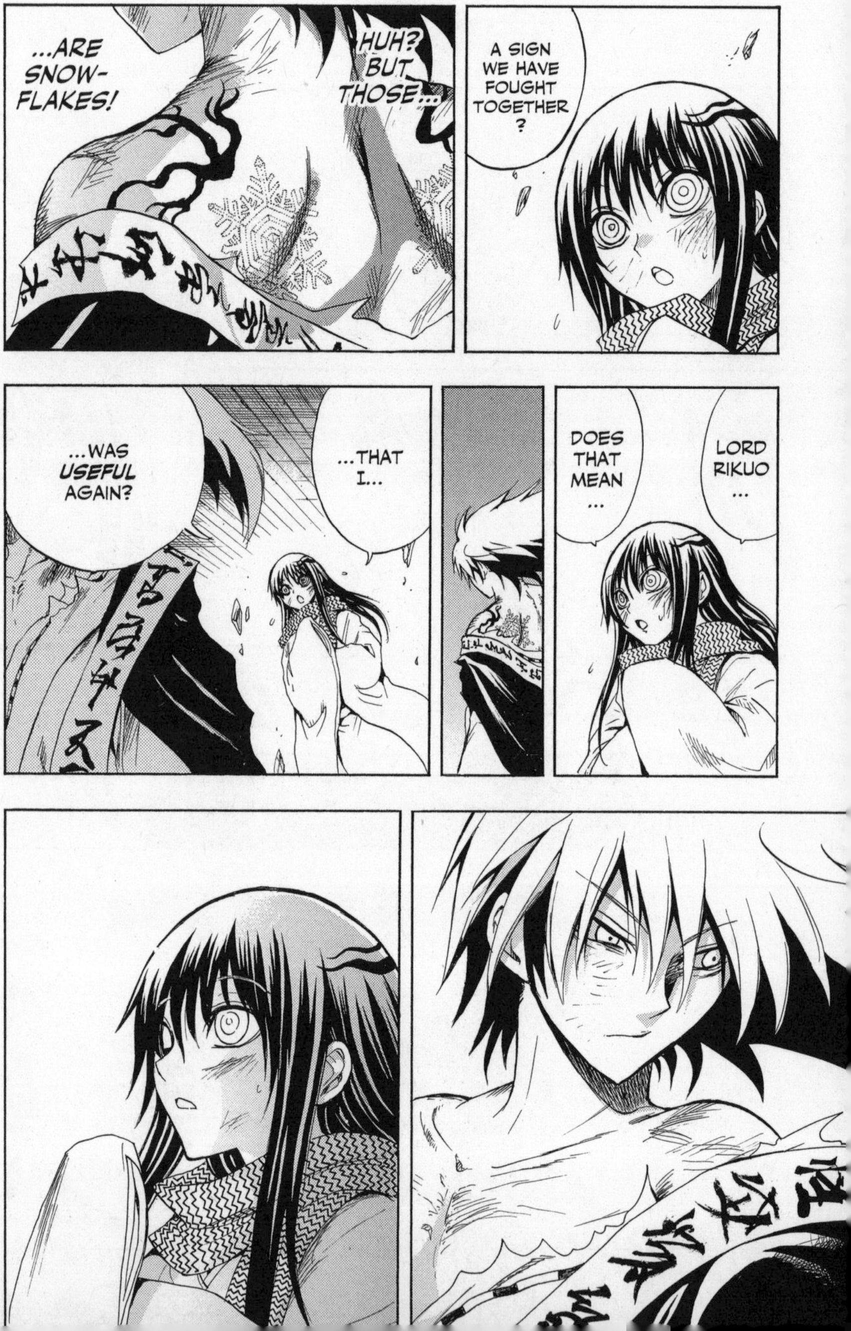
A SIGN WE HAVE FOUGHT TOGETHER?
HUH? BUT THOSE...
...ARE SNOW-FLAKES!
LORD RIKUO...
DOES THAT MEAN...
...THAT I...
...WAS USEFUL AGAIN?

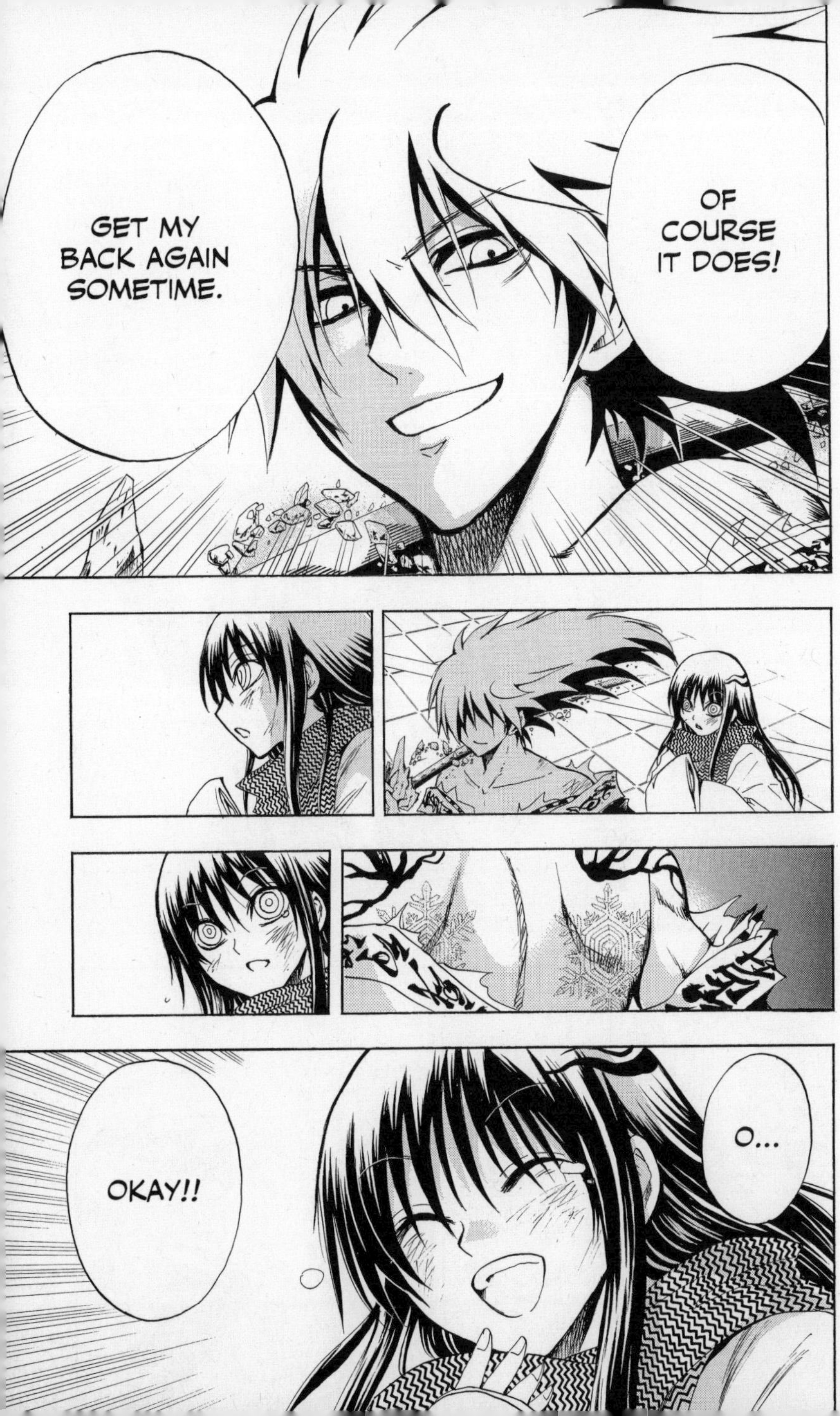
OF COURSE IT DOES!
GET MY BACK AGAIN SOMETIME.
O...
OKAY!!

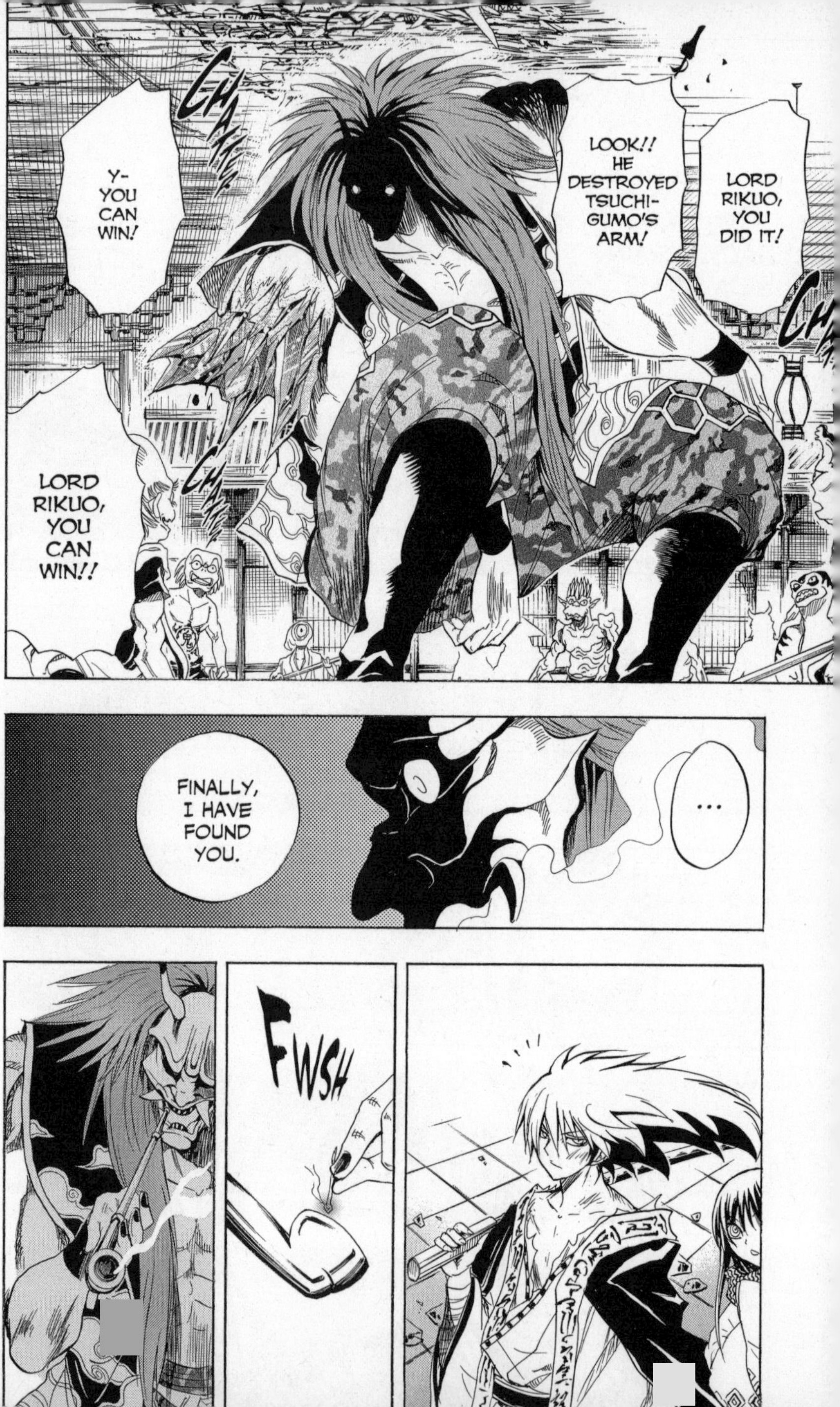
LORD RIKUO, YOU DID IT!
LOOK!! HE DESTROYED TSUCHI-GUMO'S ARM!
Y-YOU CAN WIN!
LORD RIKUO, YOU CAN WIN!!
...
FINALLY, I HAVE FOUND YOU.
FWSH

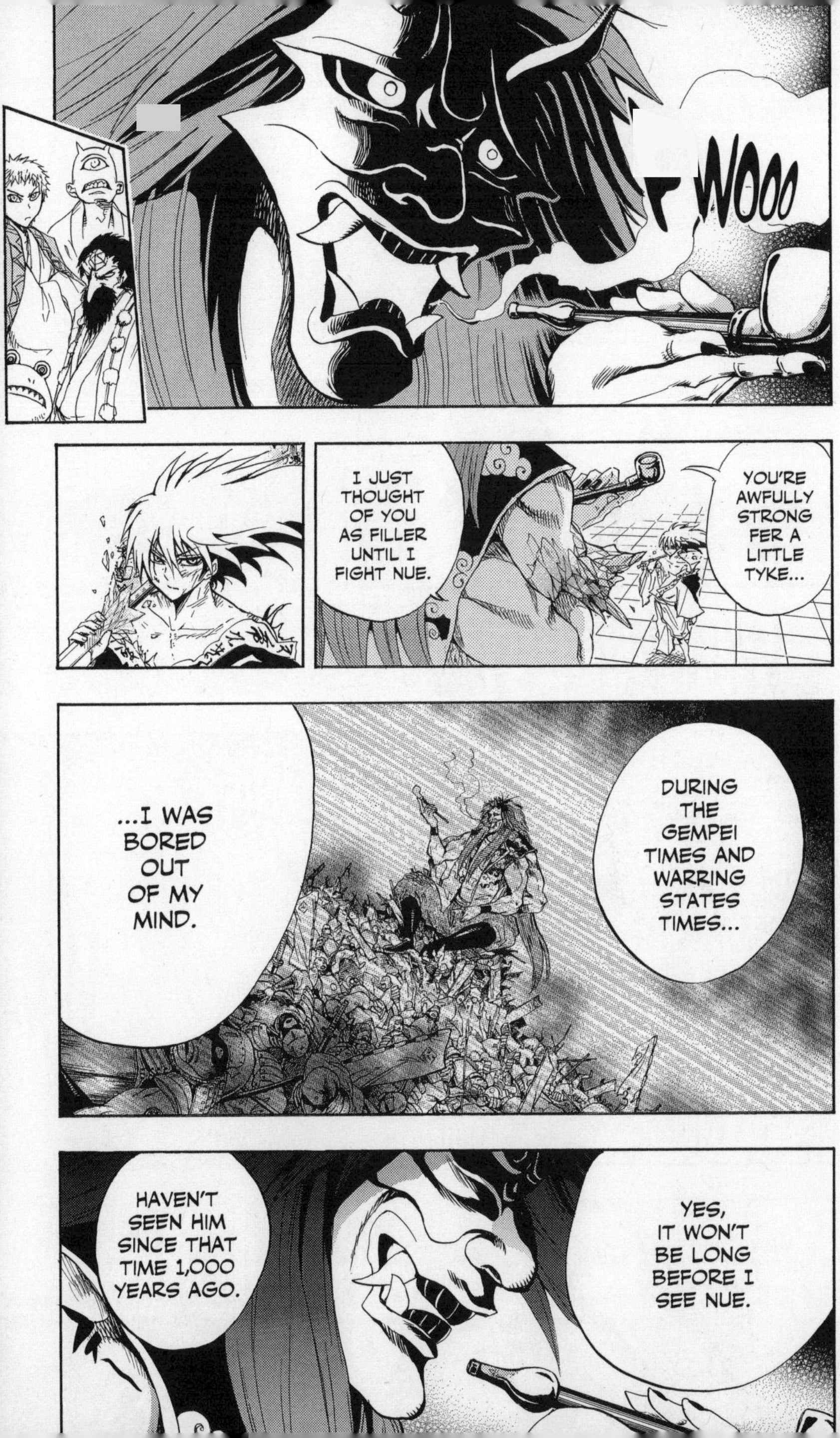
FWOOO
YOU'RE AWFULLY STRONG FER A LITTLE TYKE...
I JUST THOUGHT OF YOU AS FILLER UNTIL I FIGHT NUE.
DURING THE GEMPEI TIMES AND WARRING STATES TIMES...
...I WAS BORED OUT OF MY MIND.
YES, IT WON'T BE LONG BEFORE I SEE NUE.
HAVEN'T SEEN HIM SINCE THAT TIME 1,000 YEARS AGO.

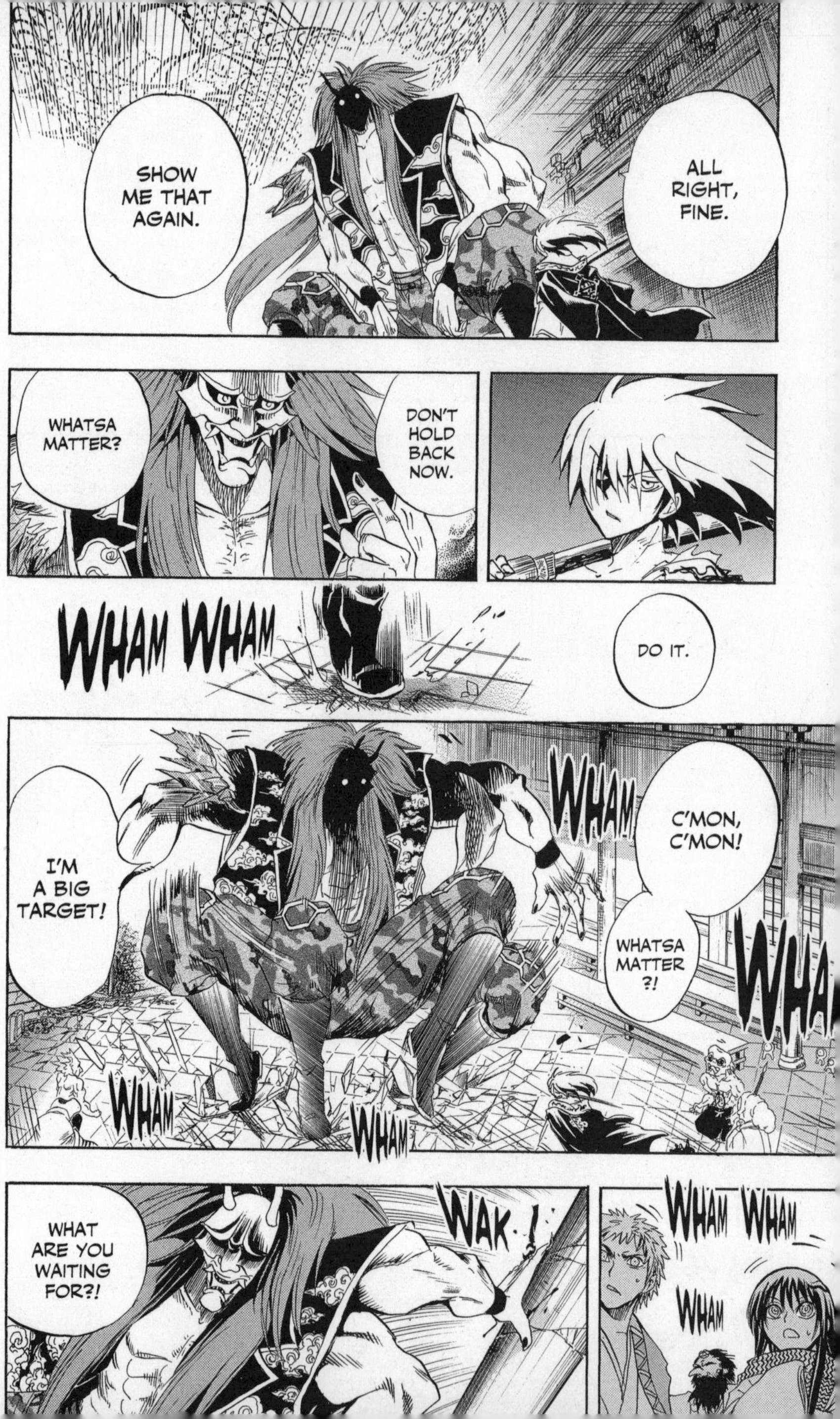
ALL RIGHT, FINE.
SHOW ME THAT AGAIN.
DON'T HOLD BACK NOW.
WHATSA MATTER?
DO IT.
WHAM WHAM
WHAM
C'MON, C'MON!
WHATSA MATTER?!
WHA
I'M A BIG TARGET!
WHAM
WHAM
WHAM WHAM
WHAM
WAK!
WHAT ARE YOU WAITING FOR?!

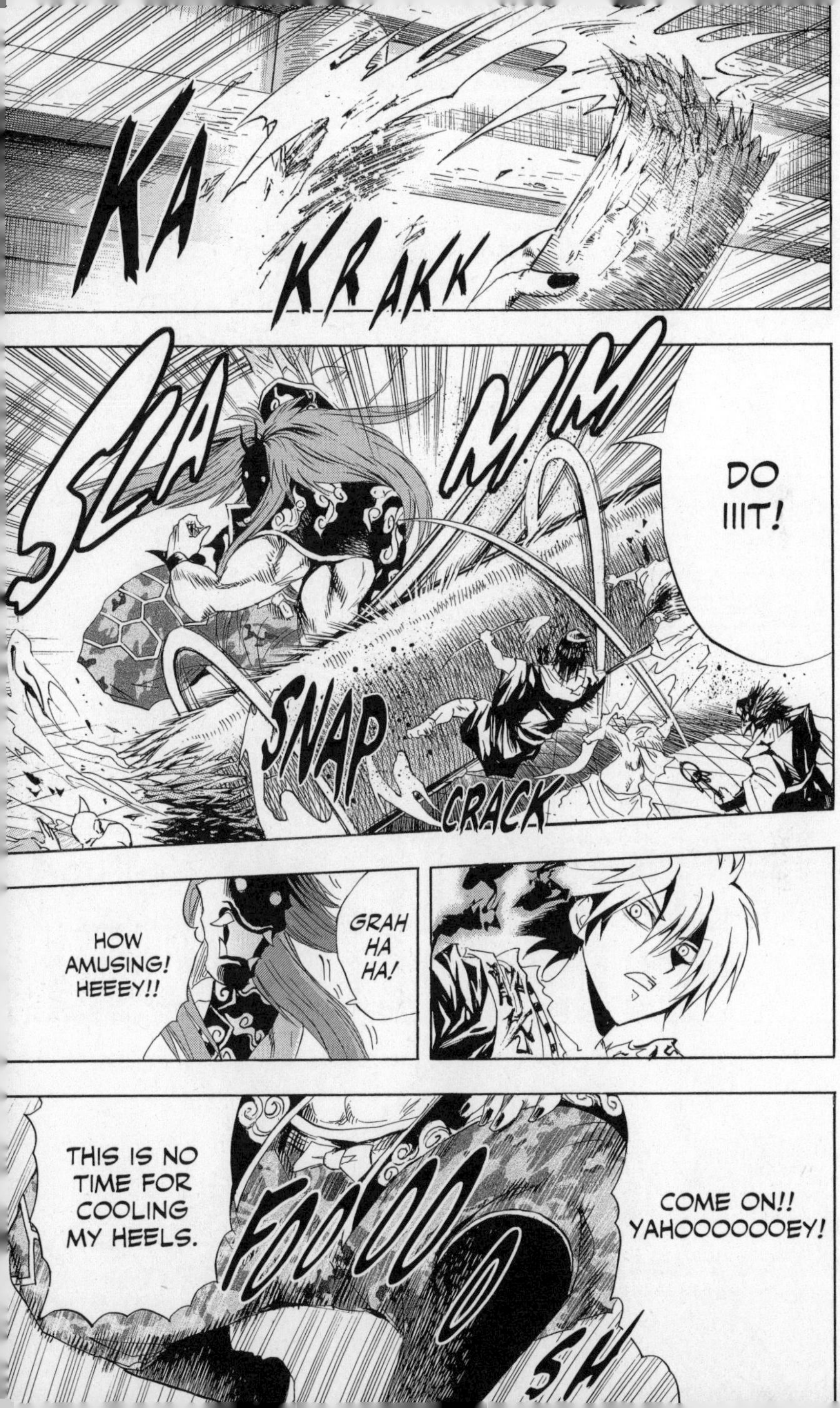
KA KRAKK
DO IIIT!
SLAMM
SNAP
CRACK
GRAH HA HA!
HOW AMUSING! HEEEY!!
COME ON!! YAHOOOOOOEY!
THIS IS NO TIME FOR COOLING MY HEELS.

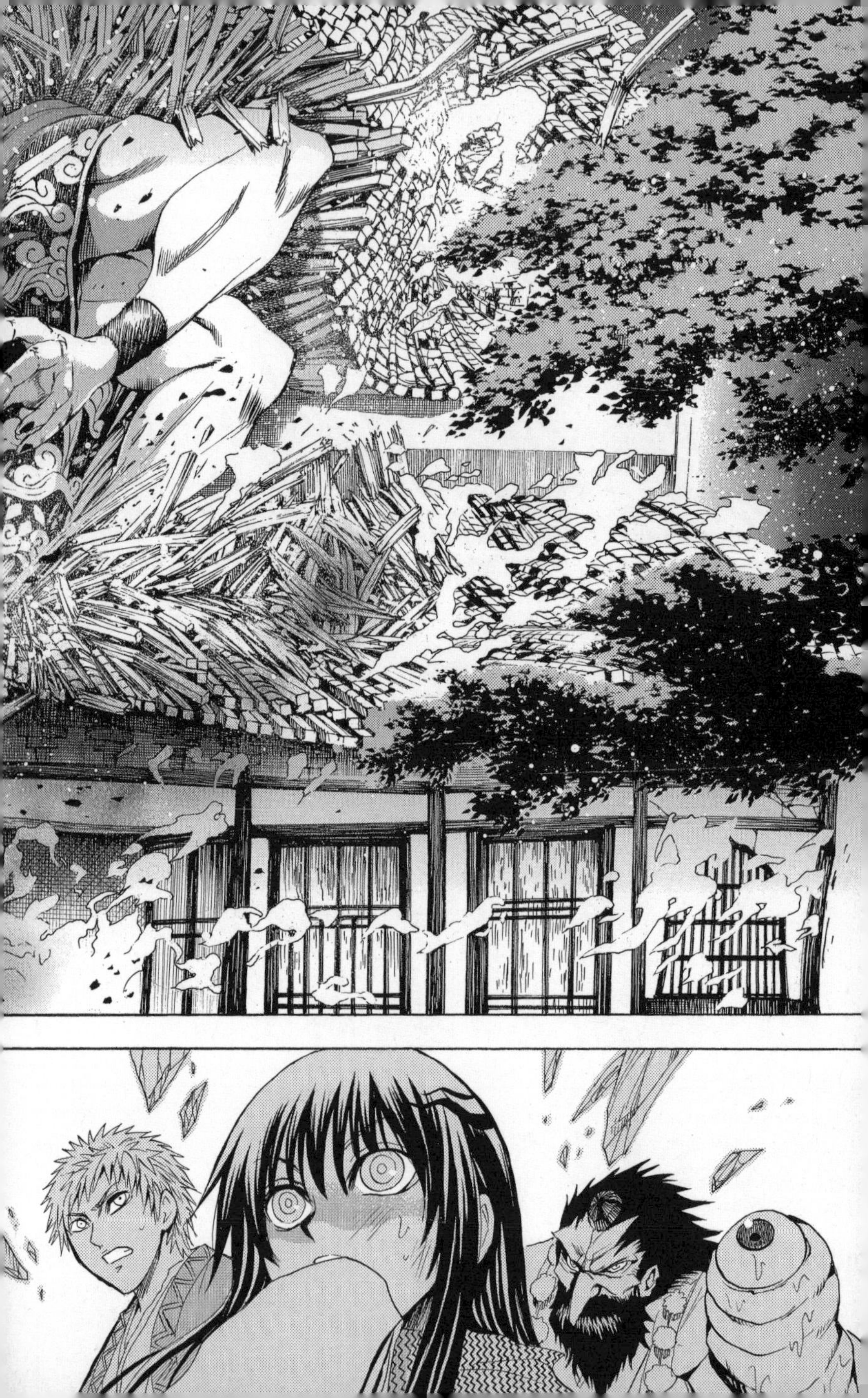

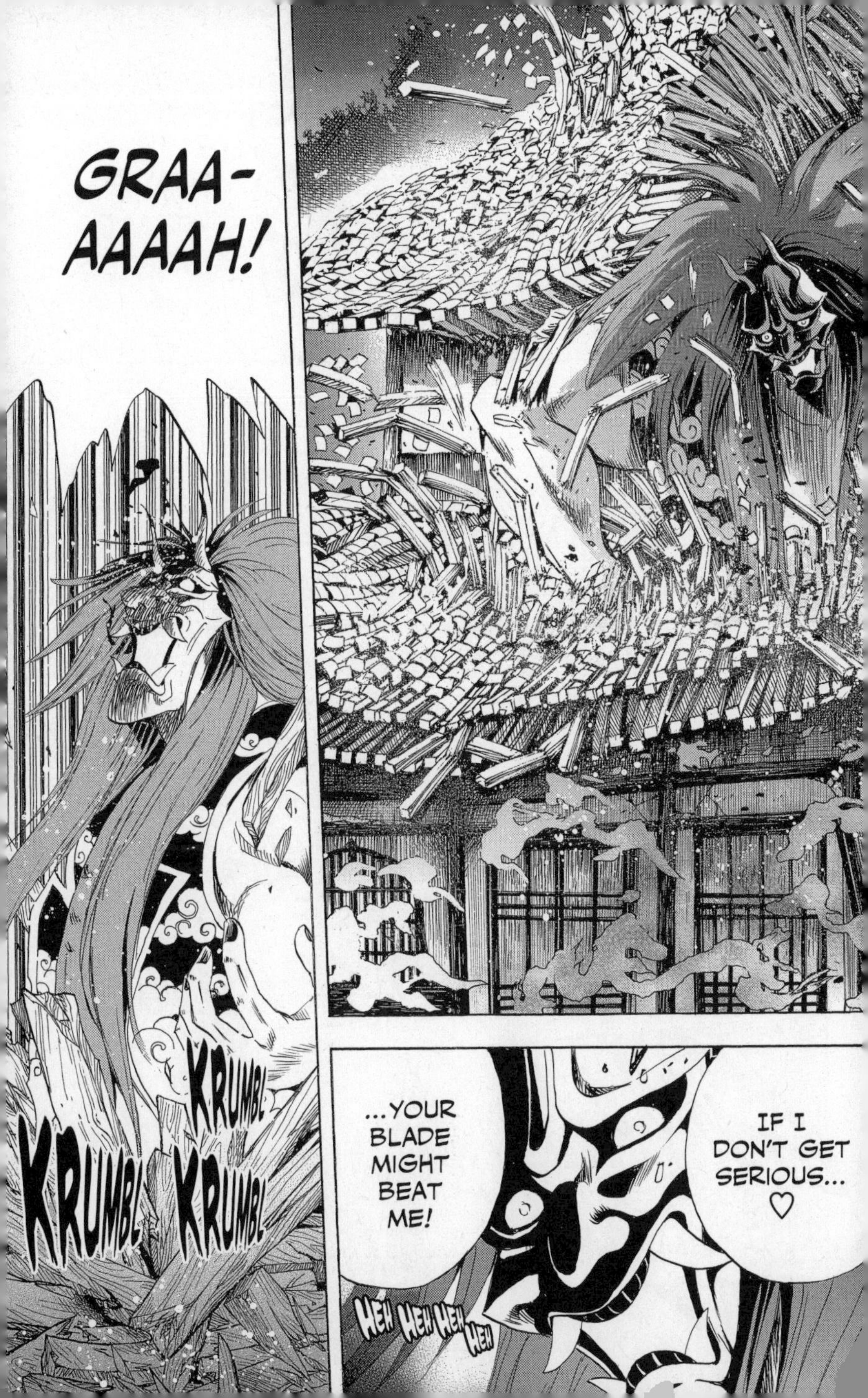
IF I DON'T GET SERIOUS... ♡
...YOUR BLADE MIGHT BEAT ME!
HEH HEH HEH HEH
GRAA-AAAAH!
KRUMBL
KRUMBL KRUMBL

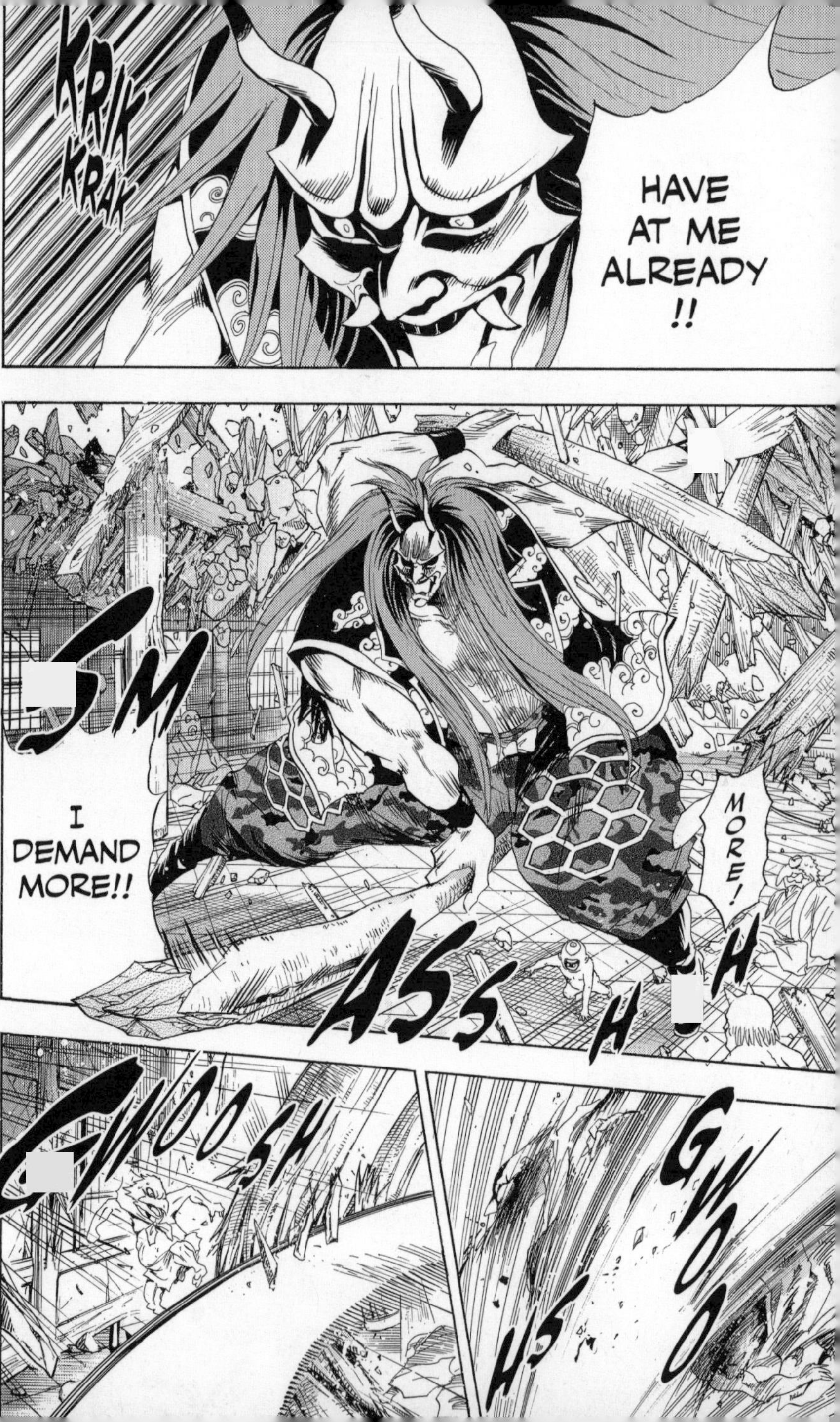
HAVE AT ME ALREADY !!
KRIK KRAK
MORE!
I DEMAND MORE!!
SM
ASS
H H H
GWOOOSH
GWOOSH

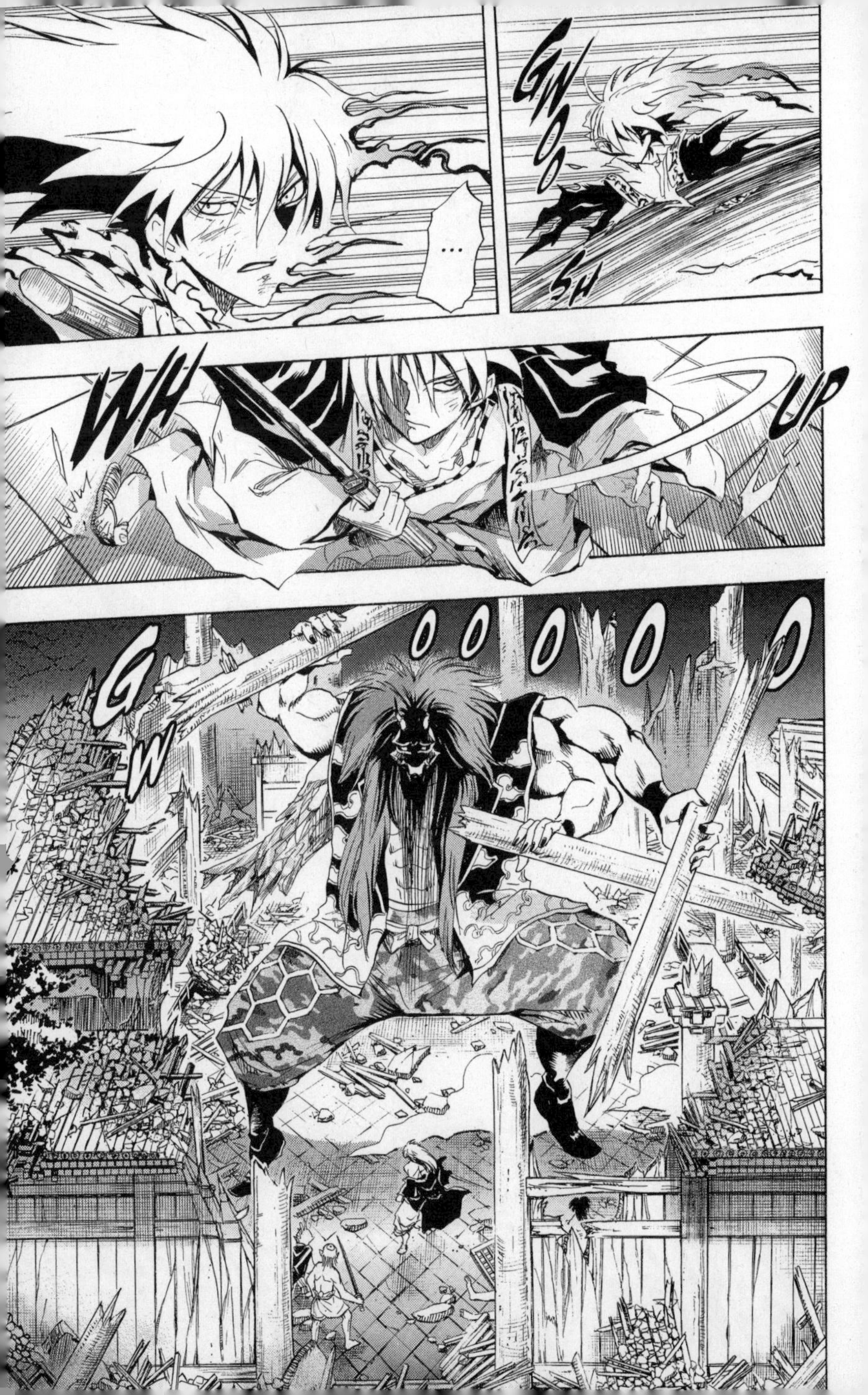

GWOOOSH
...
WHUP
GWOOOOO

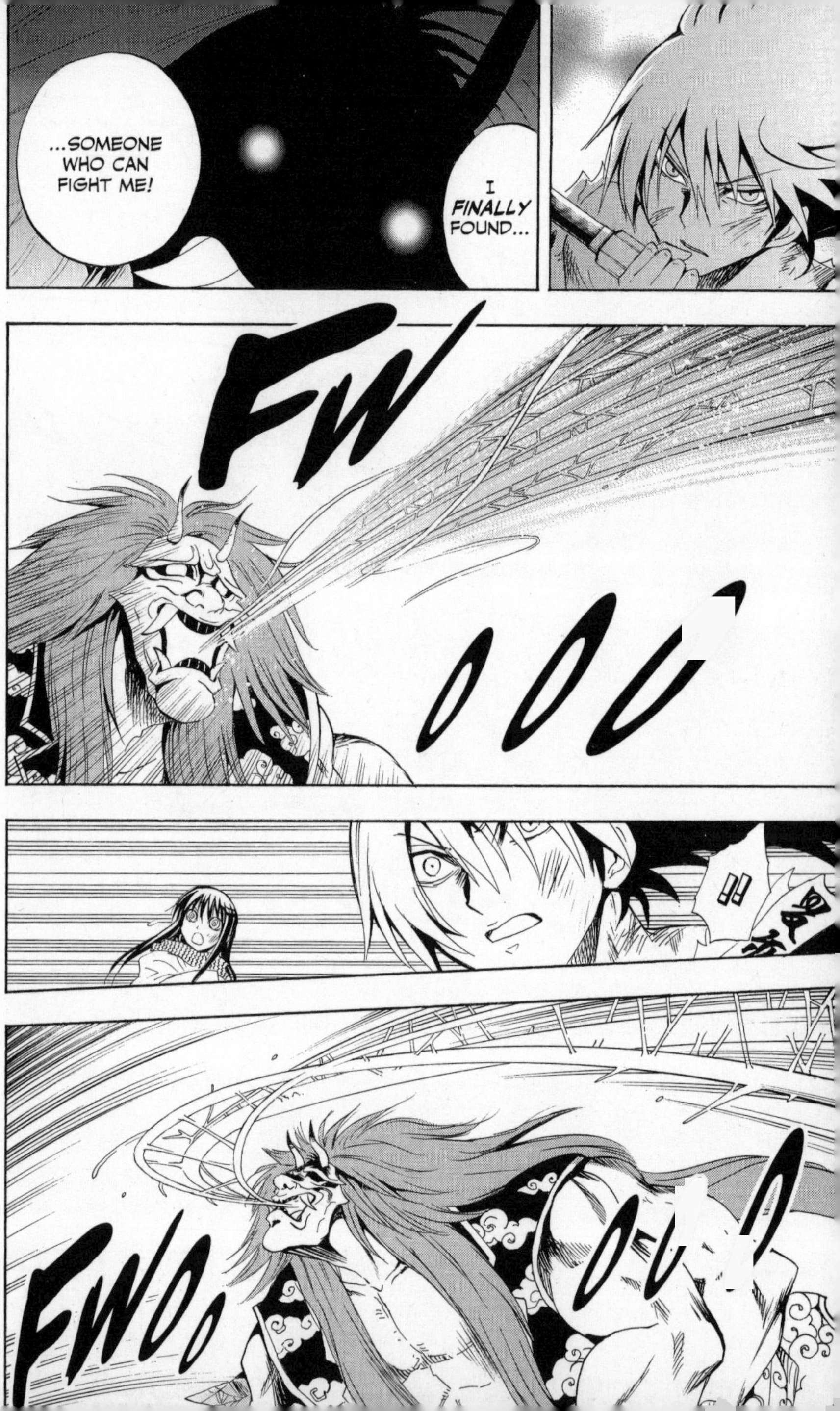
I FINALLY FOUND...
...SOMEONE WHO CAN FIGHT ME!
FWOOO
!!
FWOOO

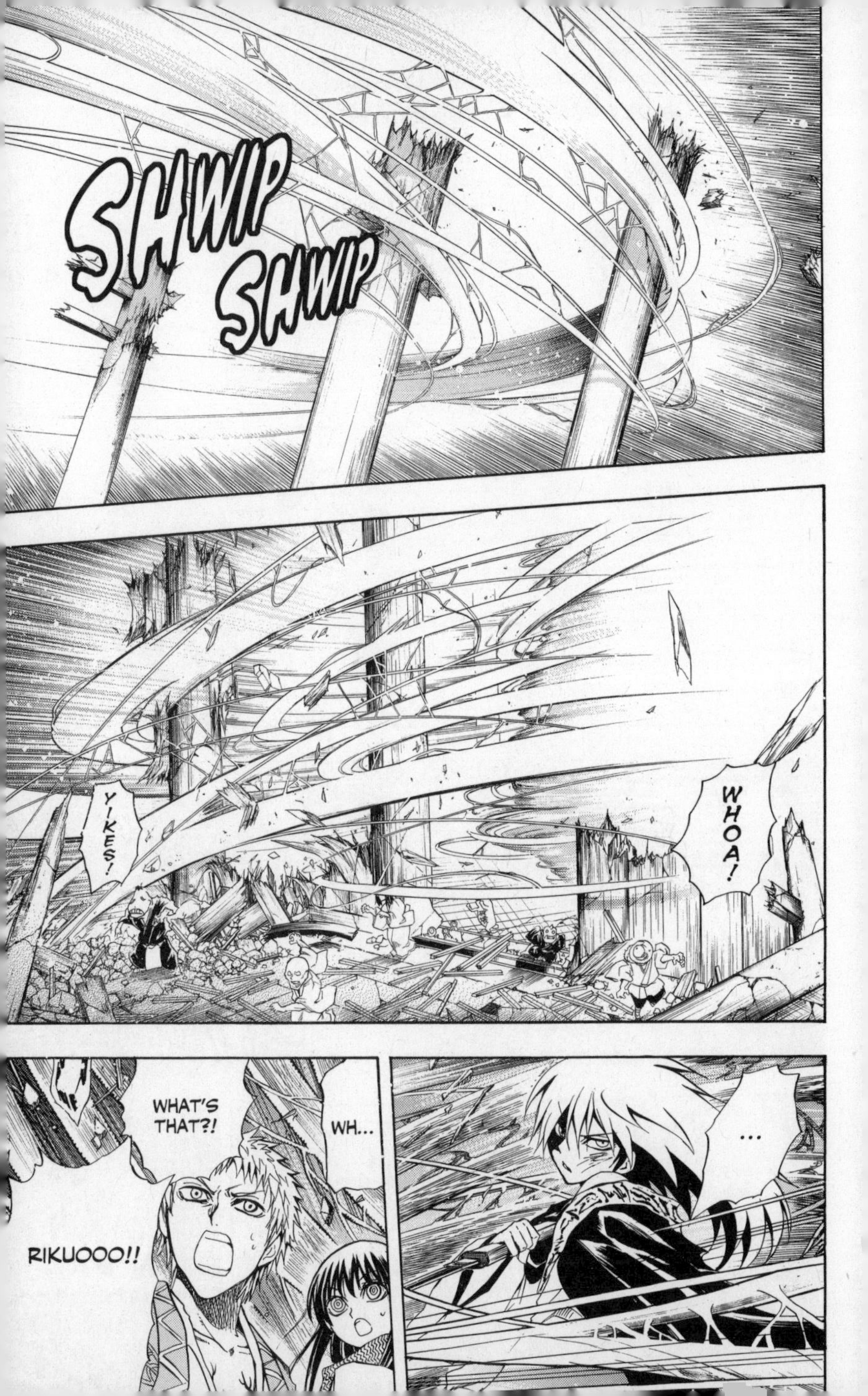
SHWIP
SHWIP
WHOA!
YIKES!
...
WH...
WHAT'S THAT?!
RIKUOOO!!

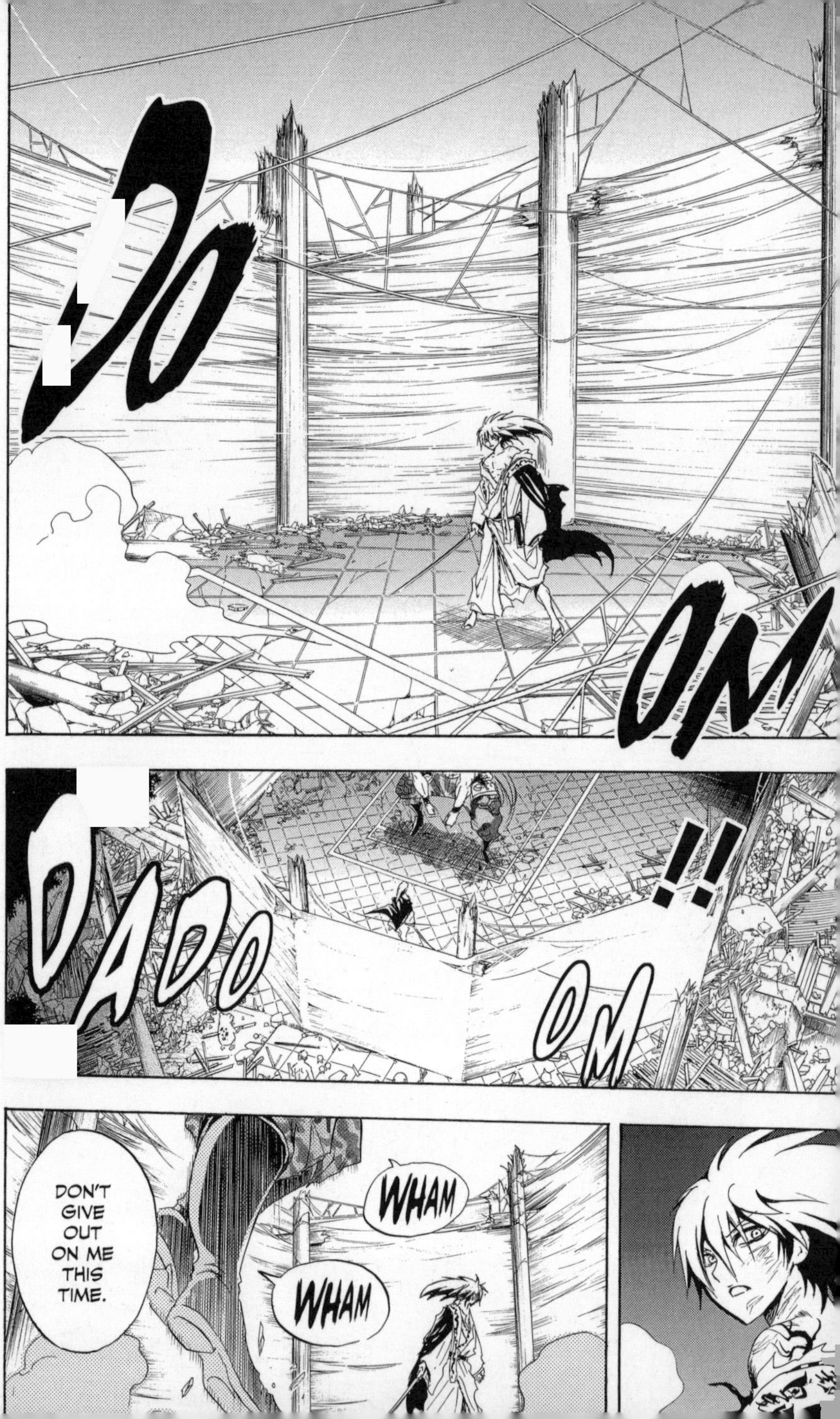
DOOM
DADOOOM
!!
WHAM
DON'T GIVE OUT ON ME THIS TIME.
WHAM

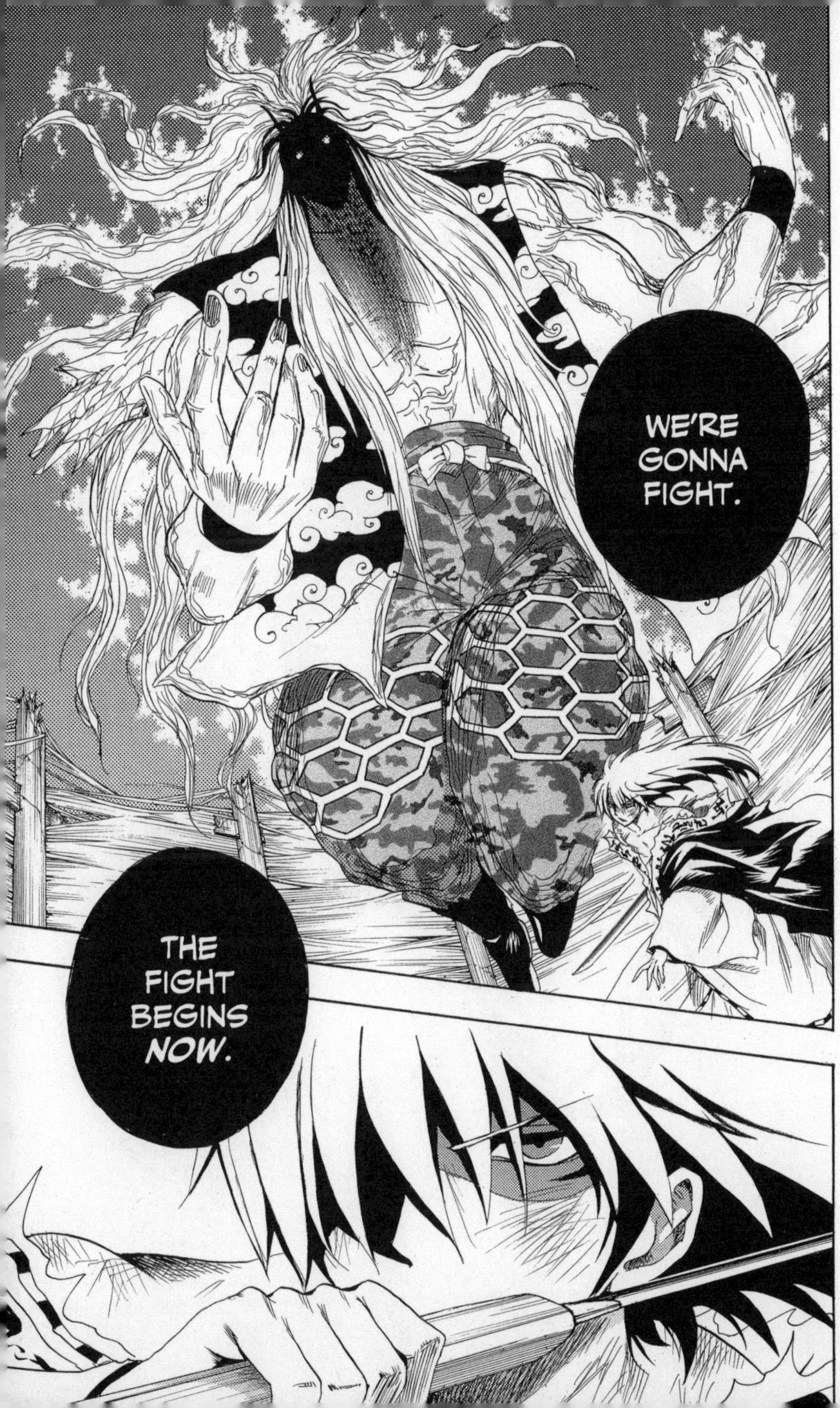
WE'RE GONNA FIGHT.
THE FIGHT BEGINS NOW.

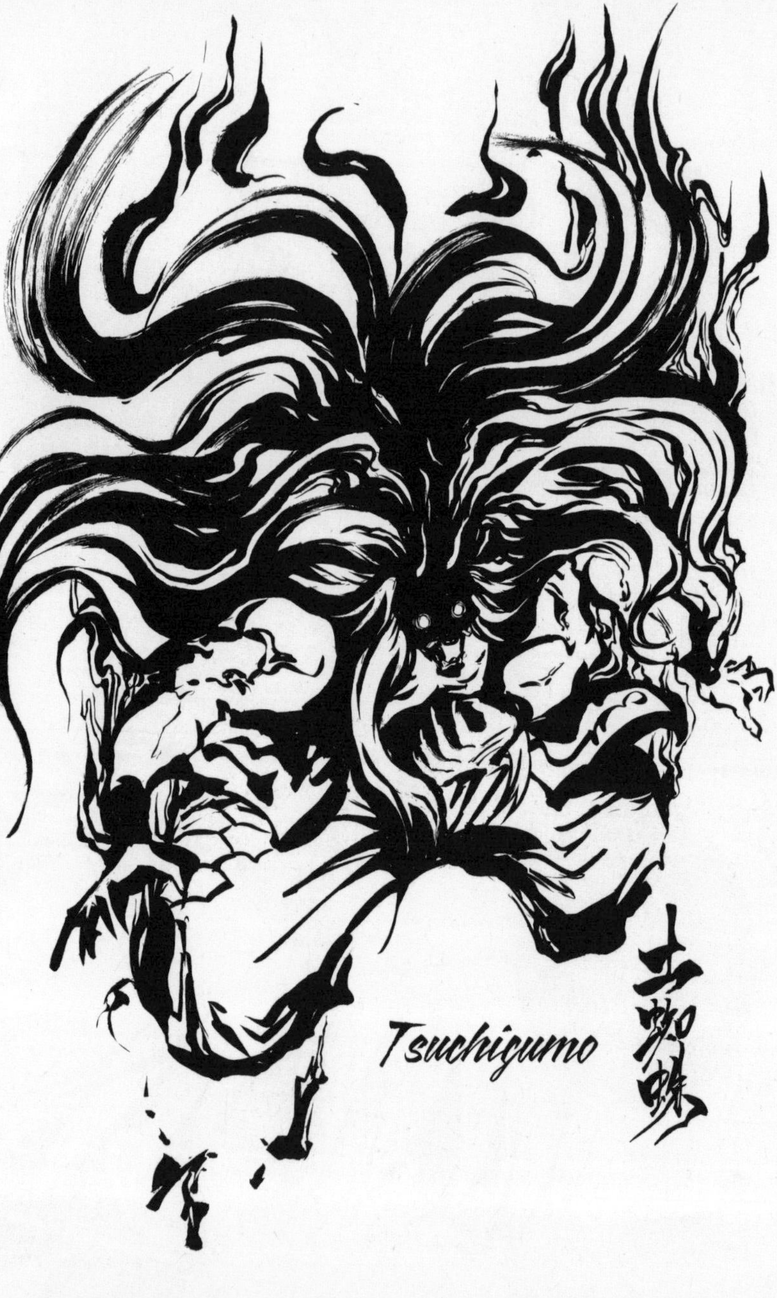
Tsuchigumo
土蜘蛛

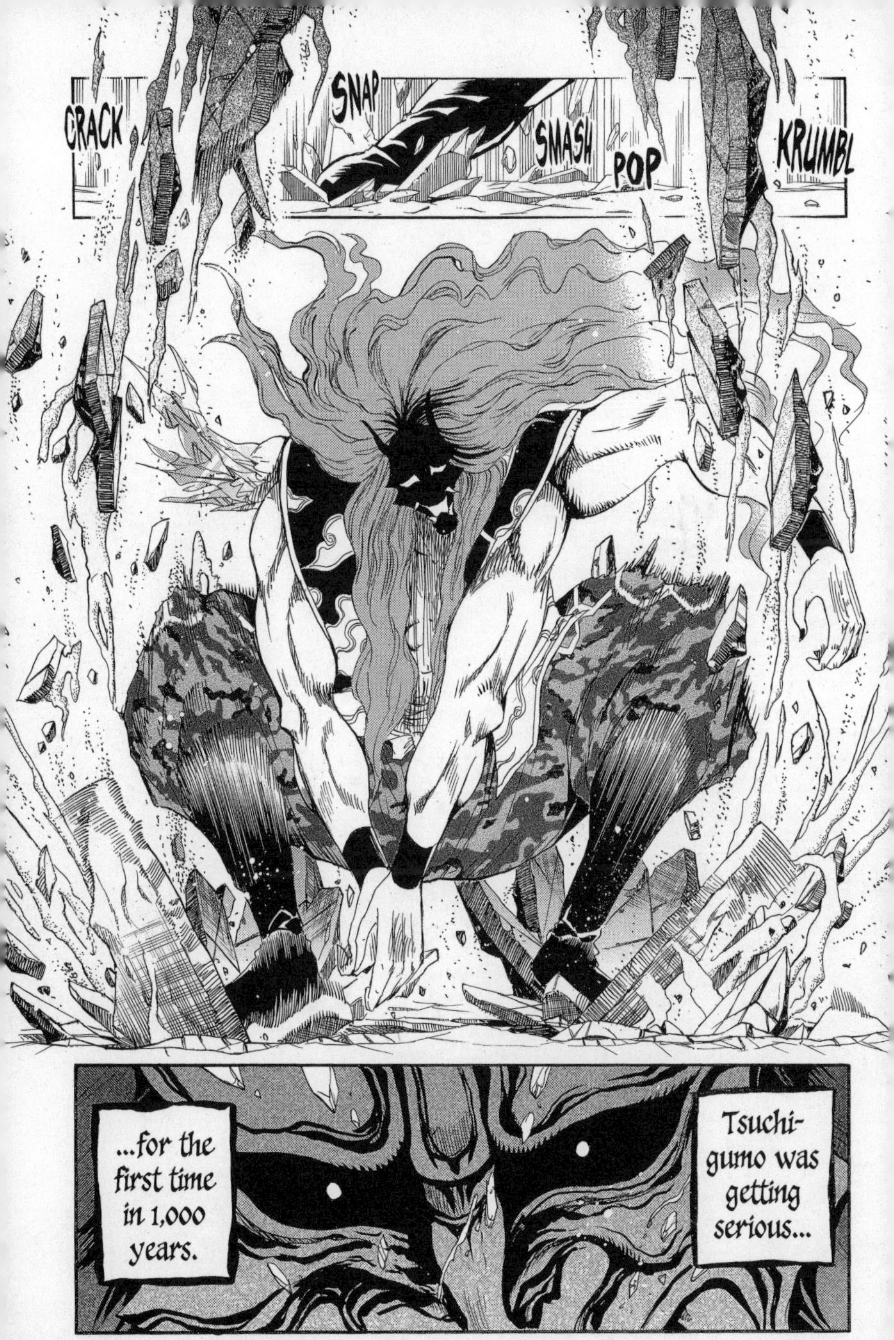
KRUMBL
POP
SMASH
SNAP
CRACK
Tsuchi-gumo was getting serious...
...for the first time in 1,000 years.

Act 112: Full Blast

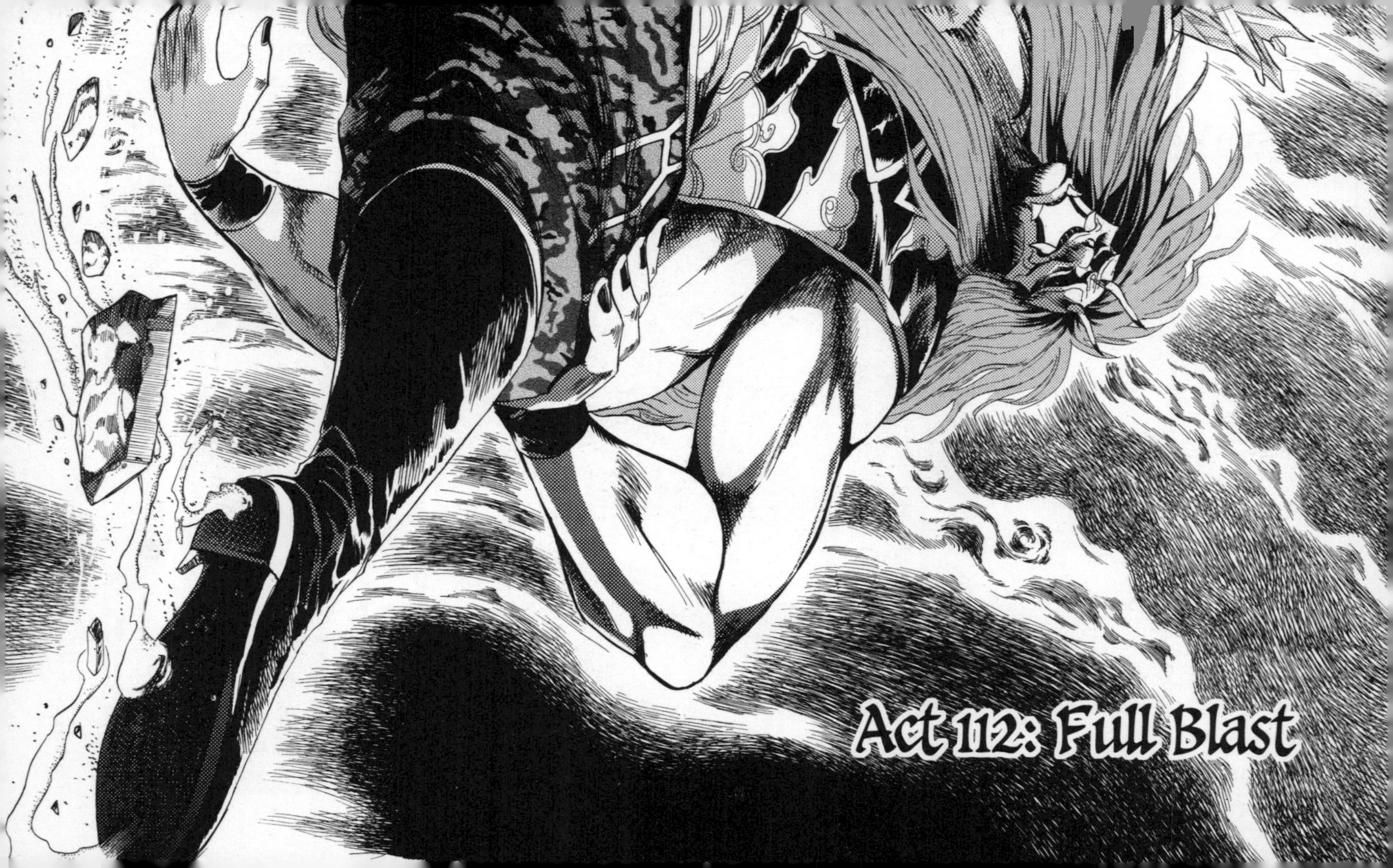
Act 112: Full Blast

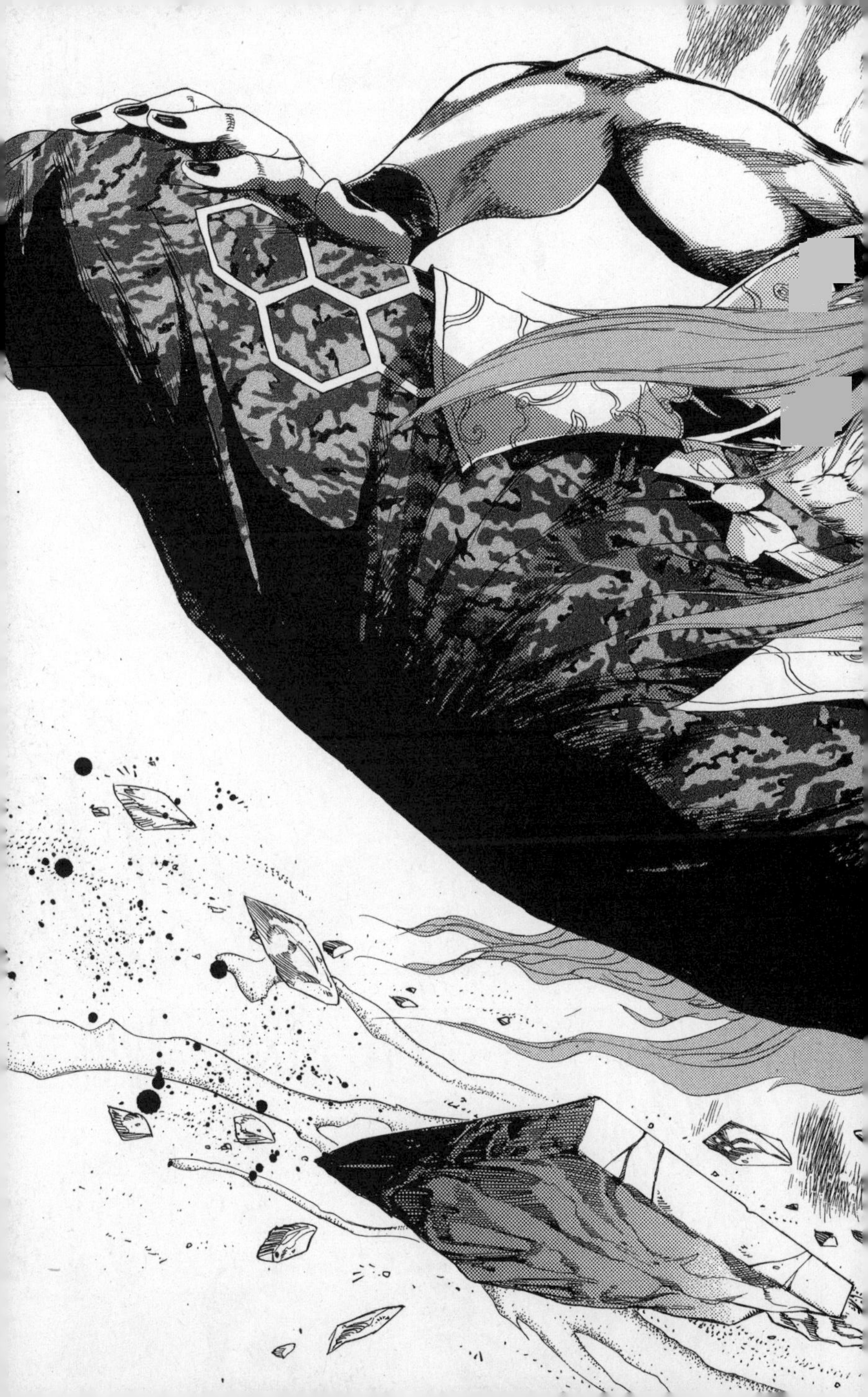

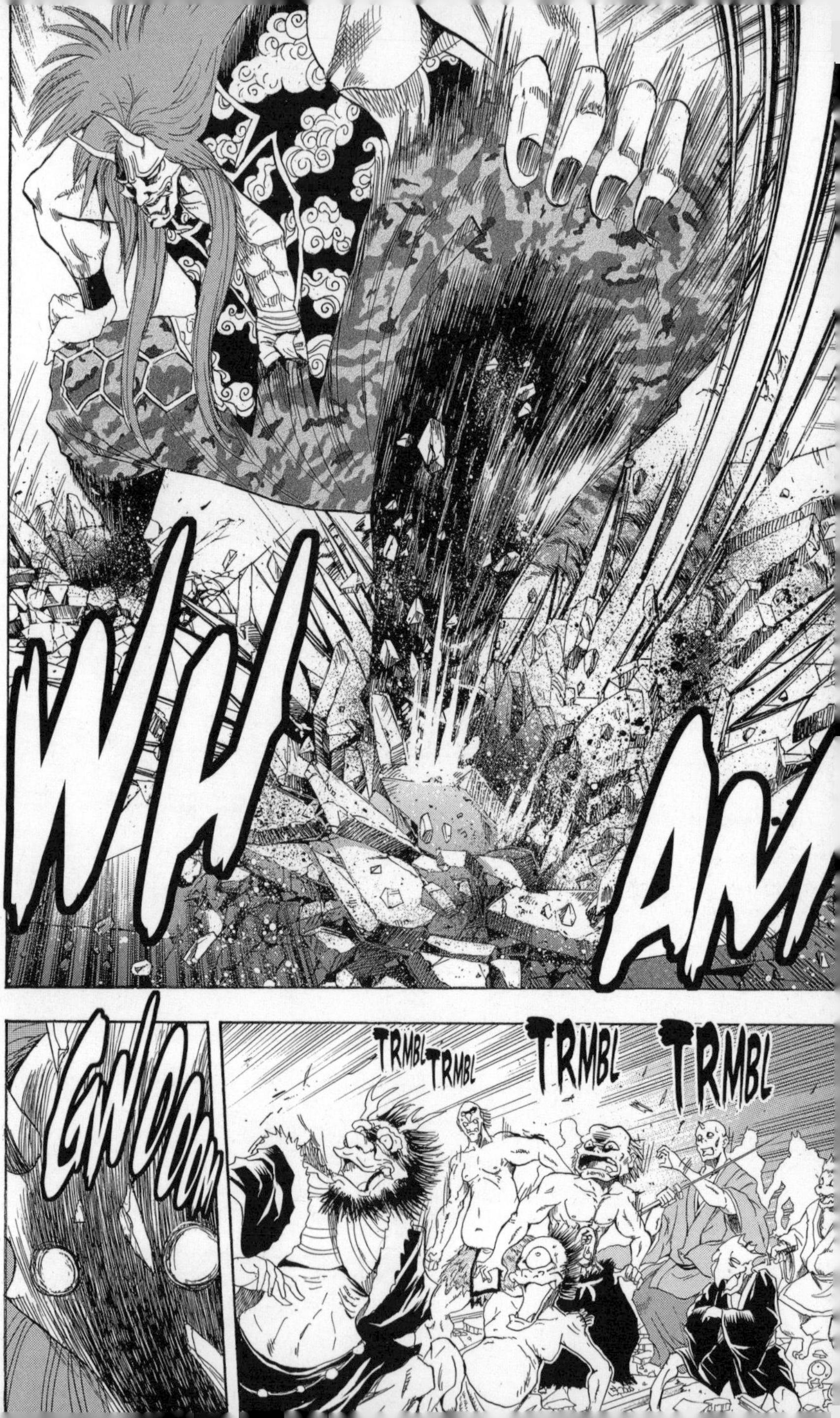
WHAM
TRMBL TRMBL
TRMBL
TRMBL
GWOOM

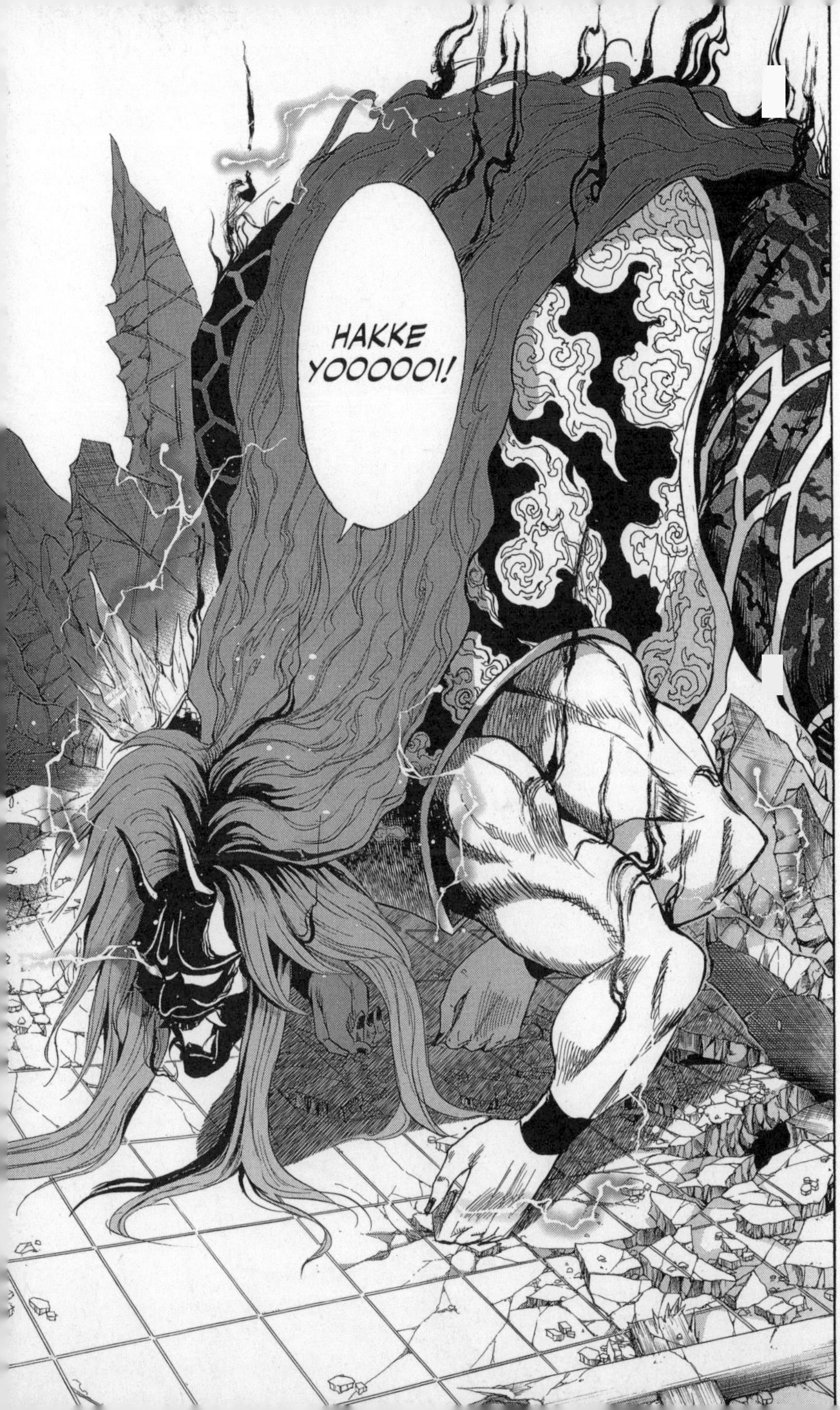
HAKKE YOOOOOI!

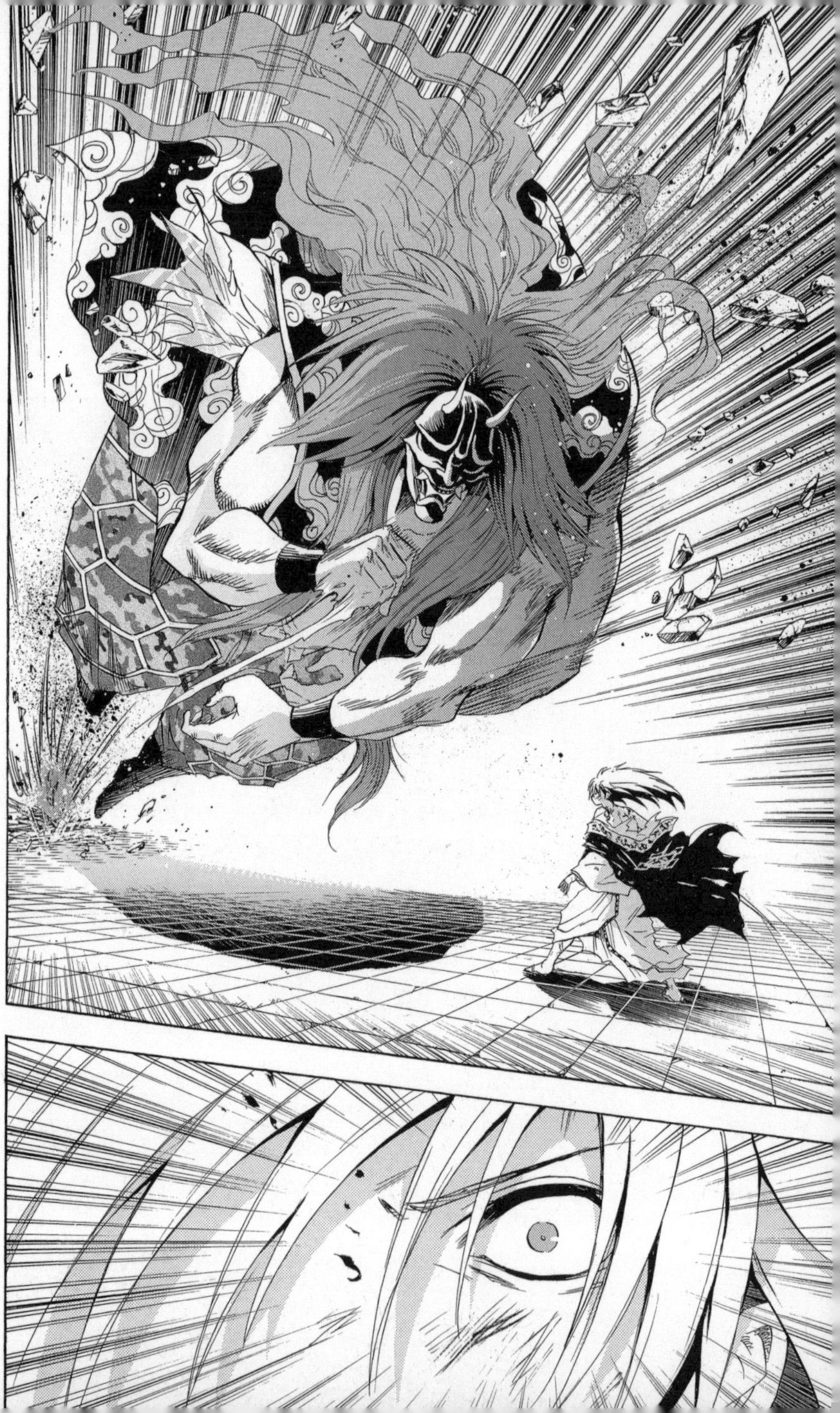

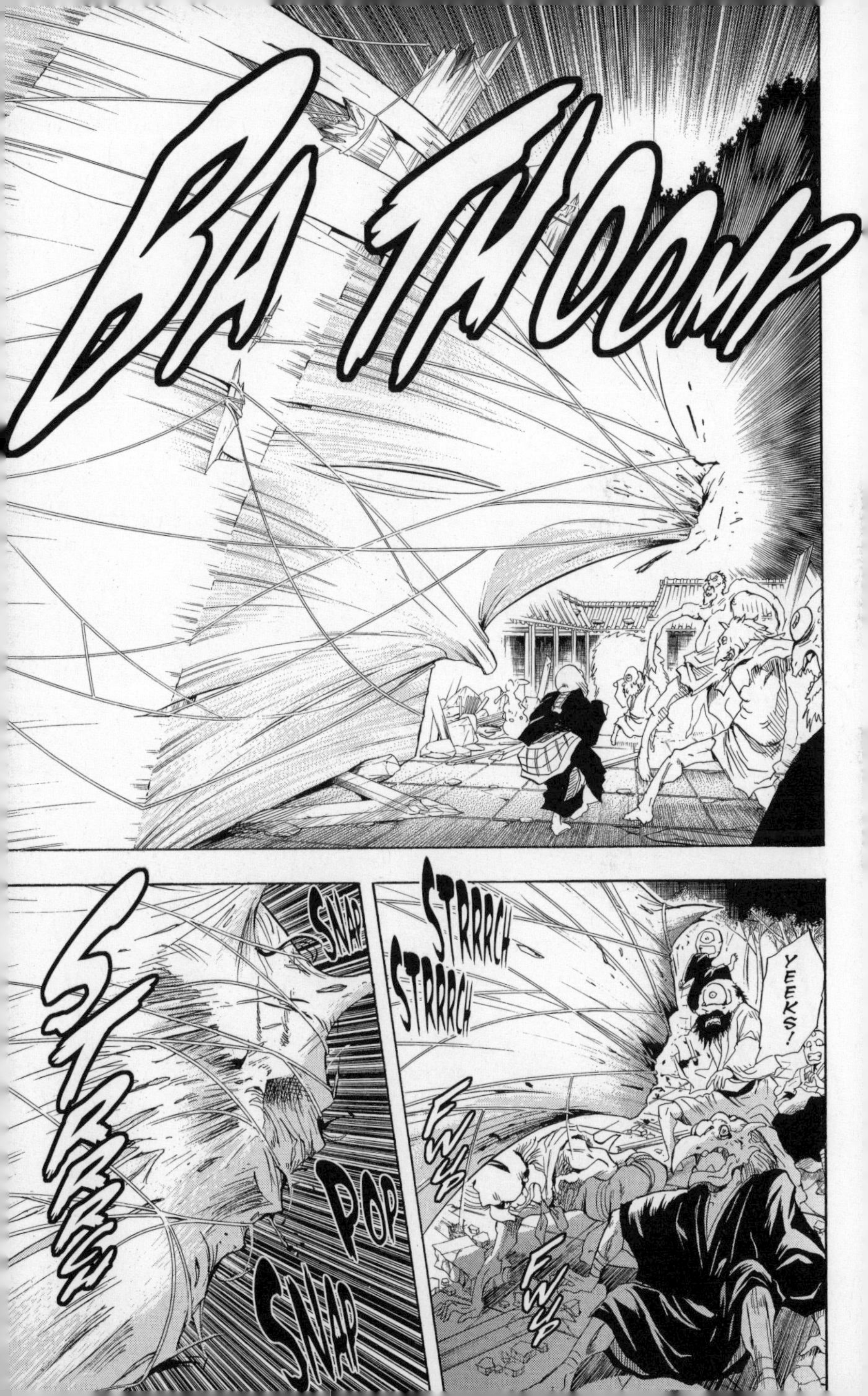
BA THOOM
YEEKS!
STRRRCH
STRRRCH
FWIP
FWIP
SNAP
POP
SNAP

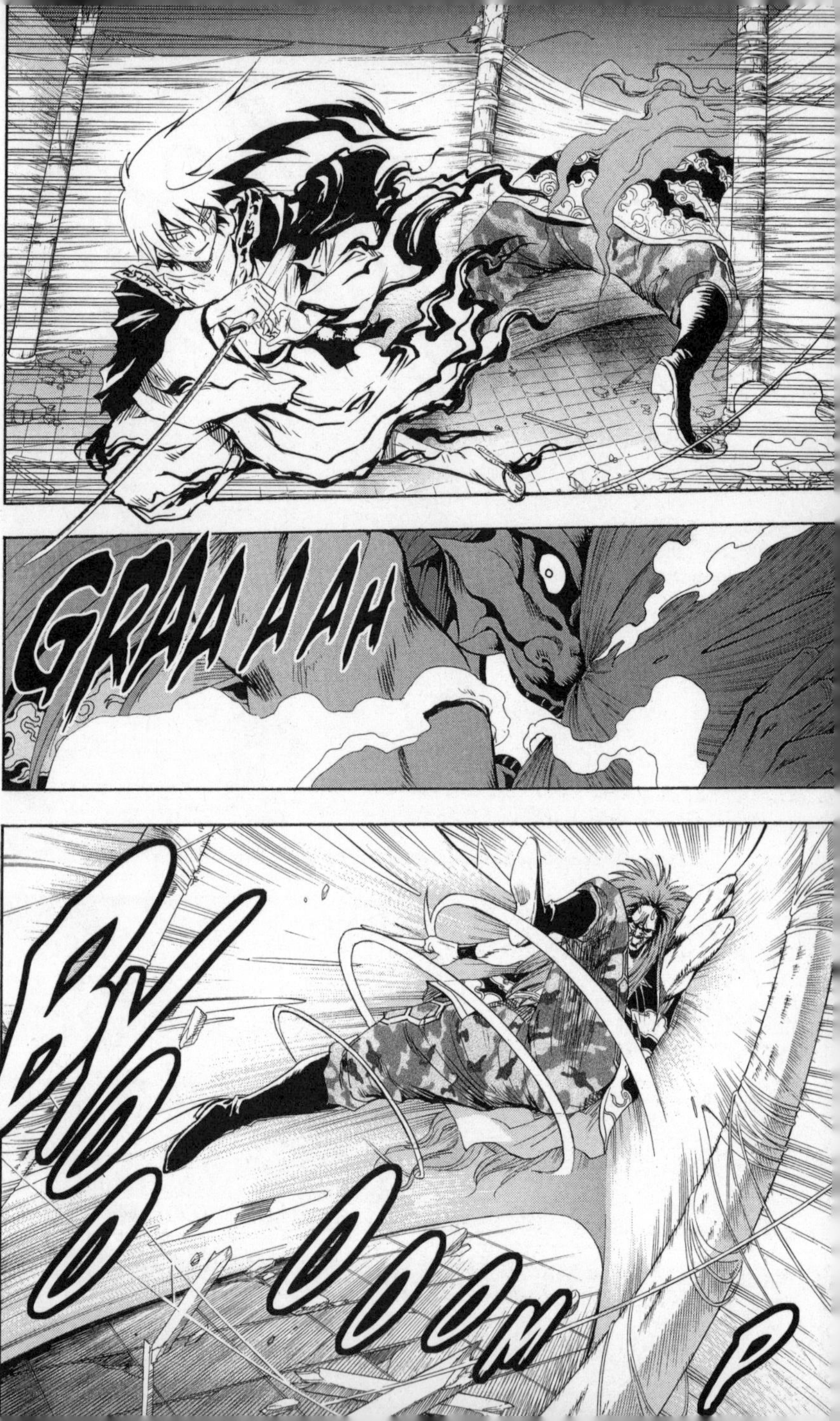
GRAAAAH
BWOOOOOOMP

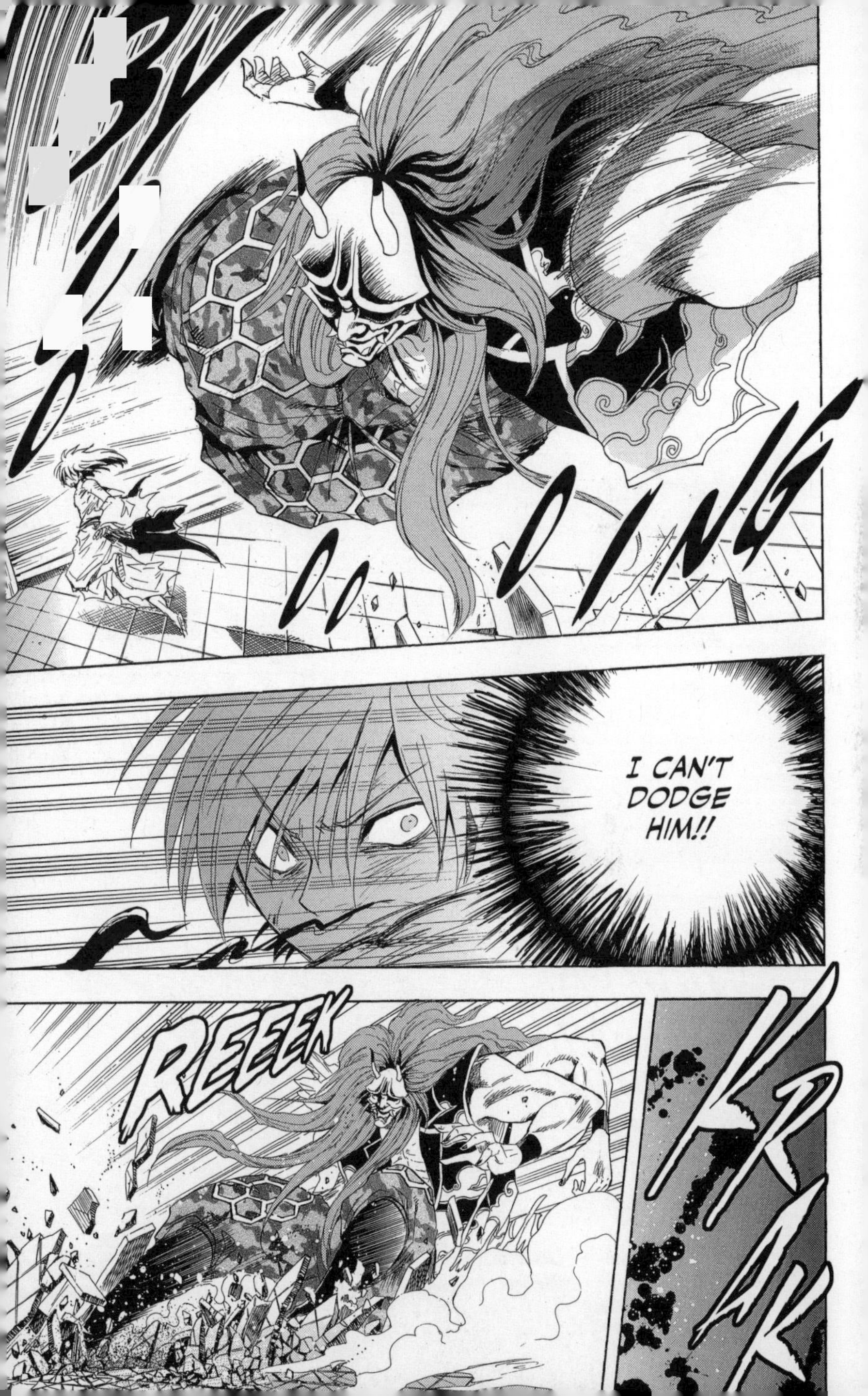
I CAN'T DODGE HIM!!
KRAK
REEEK

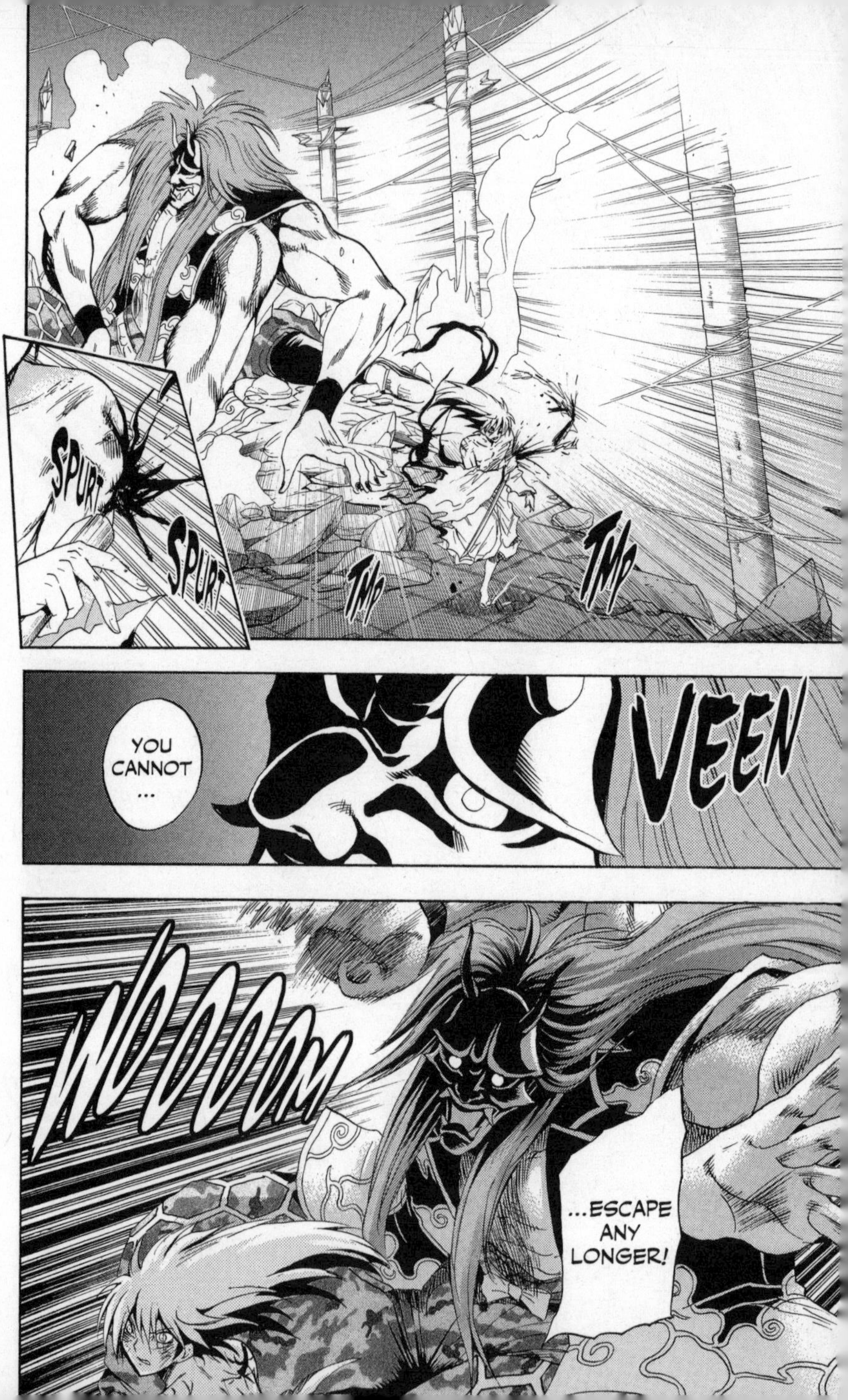
TMP
TMP
SPURT
SPURT
VEEN
YOU CANNOT ...
WOOOOM
...ESCAPE ANY LONGER!

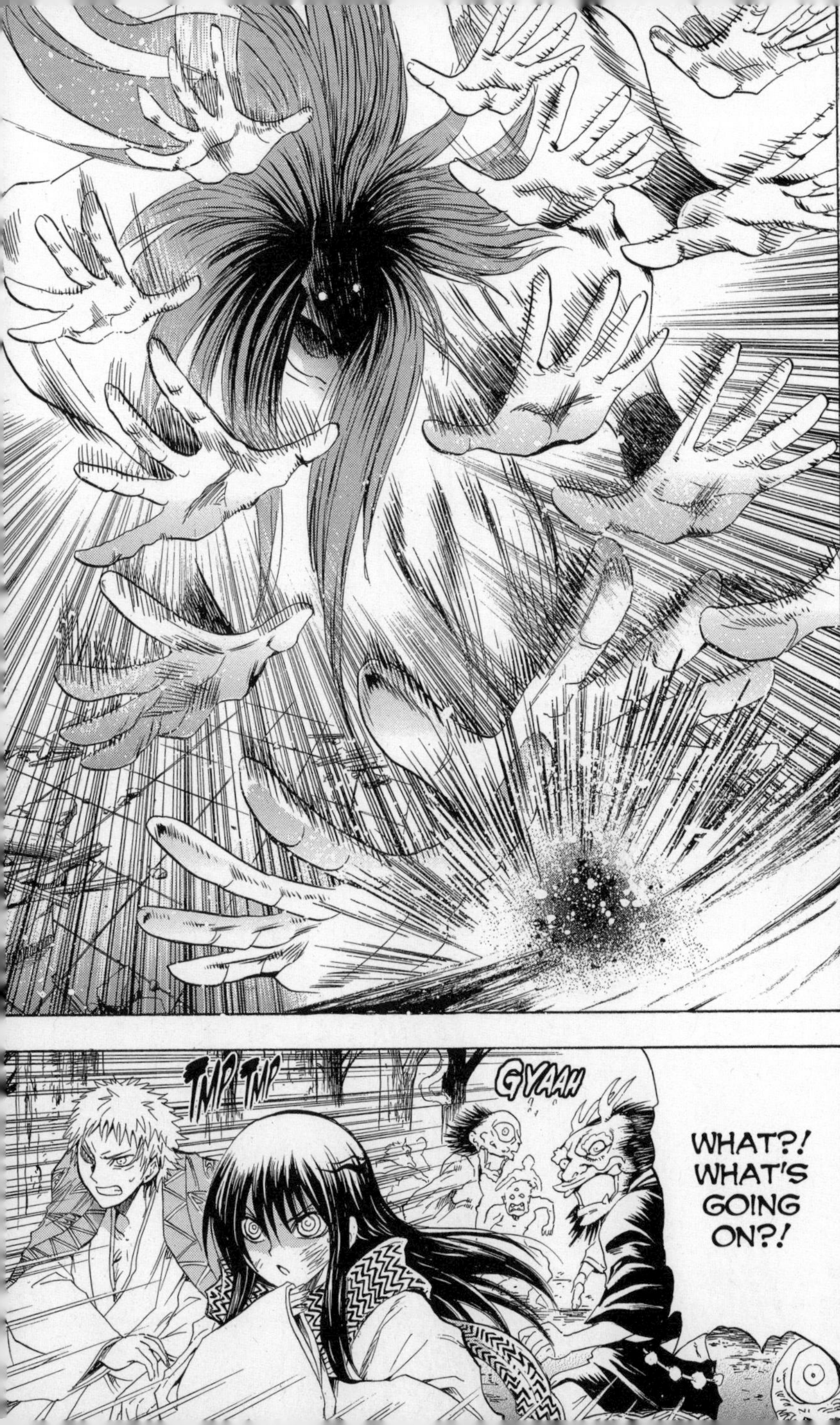
WHAT?! WHAT'S GOING ON?!
GYAAH
TMP TMP

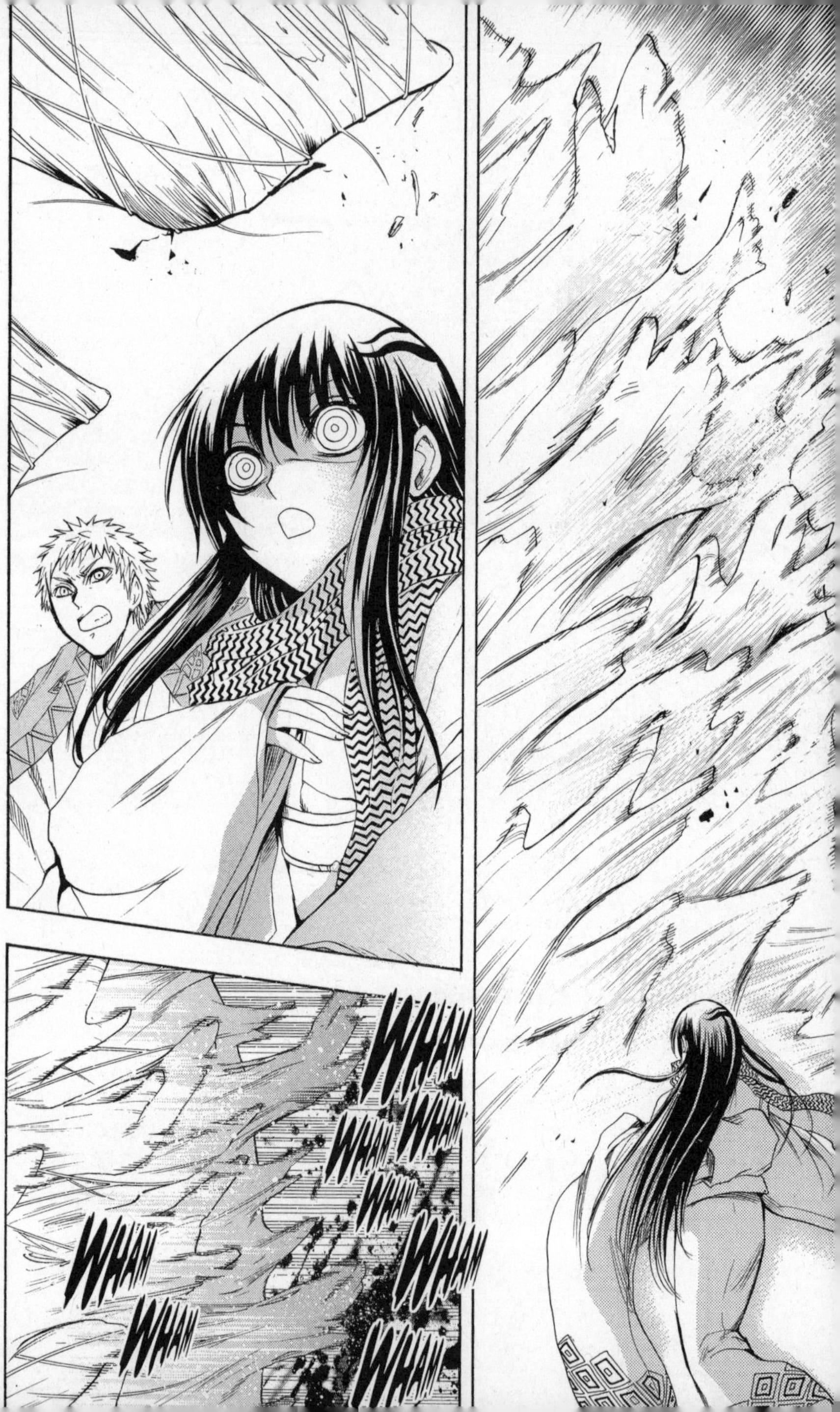
WHAM
WHAM
WHAM
WHAM
WHAM
WHAM
WHAM
WHAM

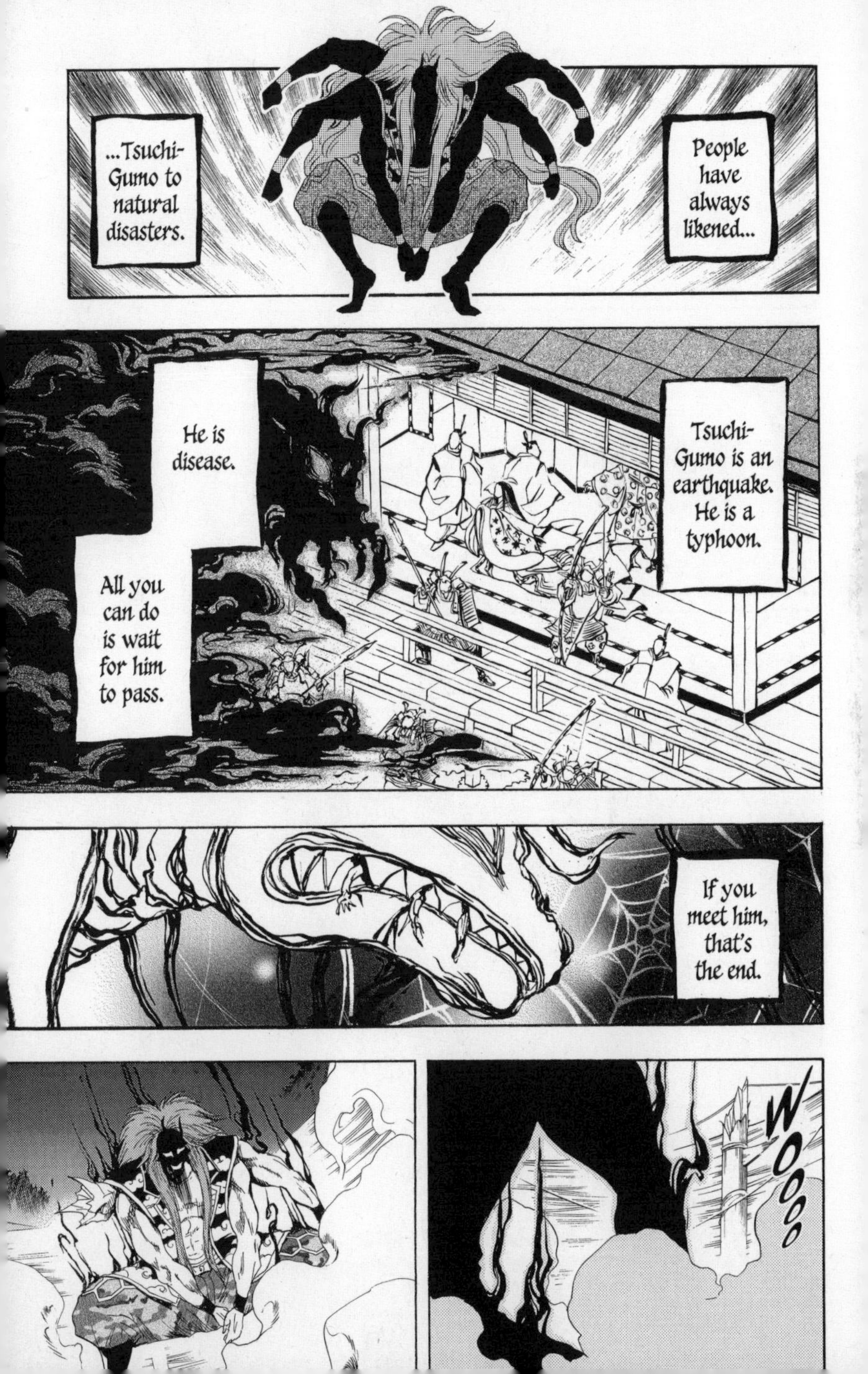
People have always likened...
...Tsuchi-Gumo to natural disasters.
Tsuchi-Gumo is an earthquake. He is a typhoon.
He is disease.
All you can do is wait for him to pass.
If you meet him, that's the end.
WOOOO

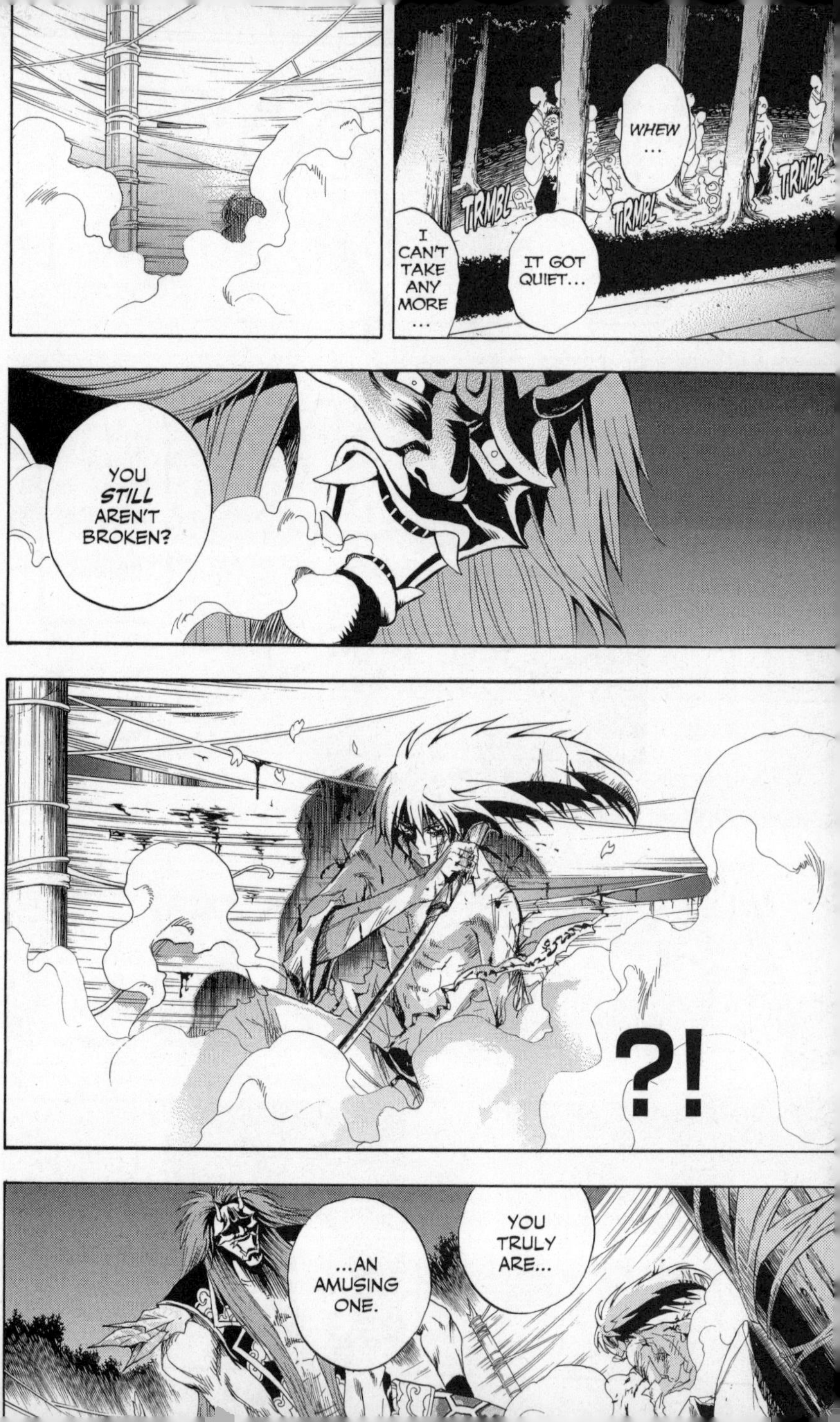
TRMBL
WHEW...
TRMBL
TRMBL
IT GOT QUIET...
I CAN'T TAKE ANY MORE...
YOU *STILL* AREN'T BROKEN?
?!
YOU TRULY ARE...
...AN AMUSING ONE.

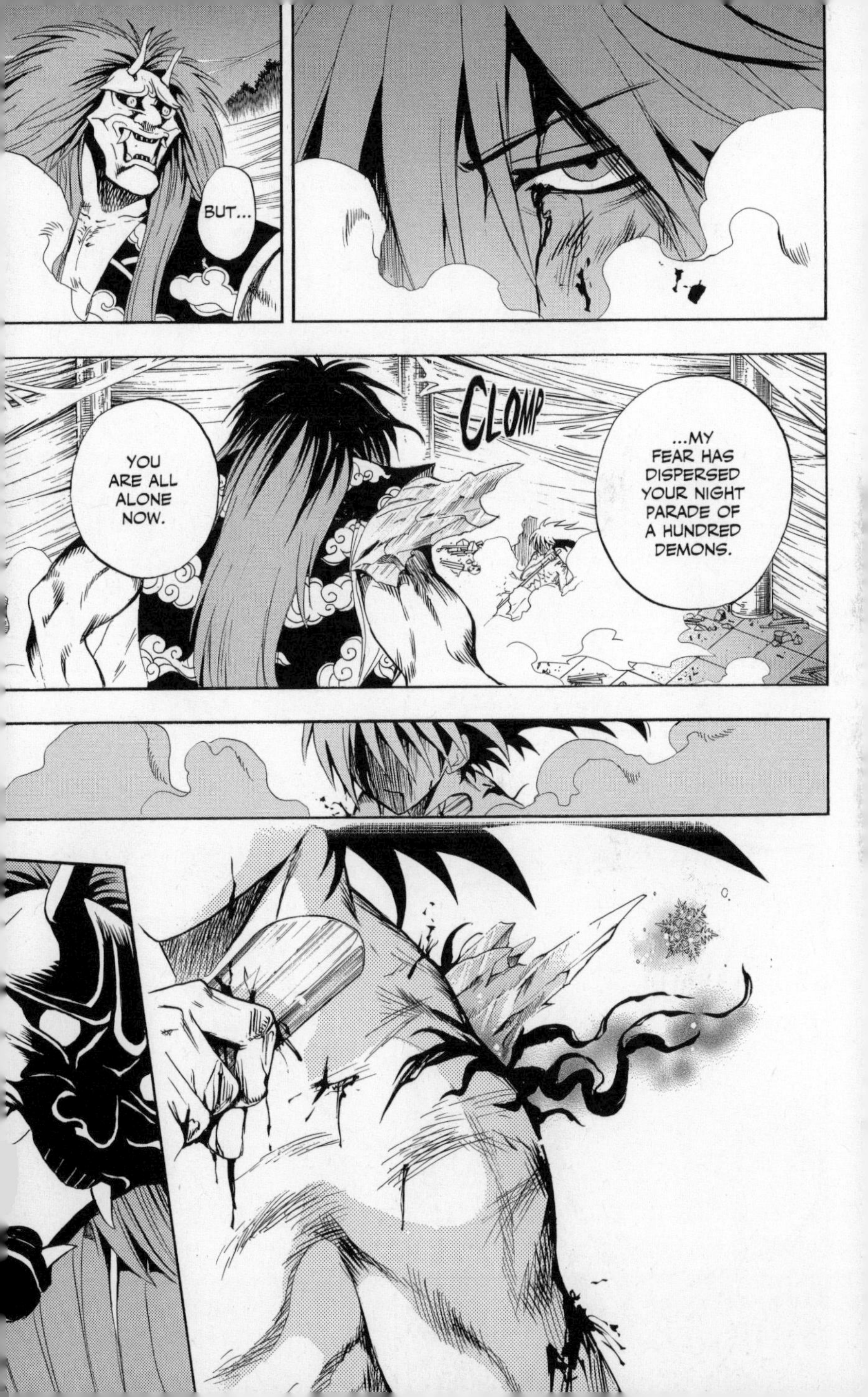
BUT...
CLOMP
...MY FEAR HAS DISPERSED YOUR NIGHT PARADE OF A HUNDRED DEMONS.
YOU ARE ALL ALONE NOW.

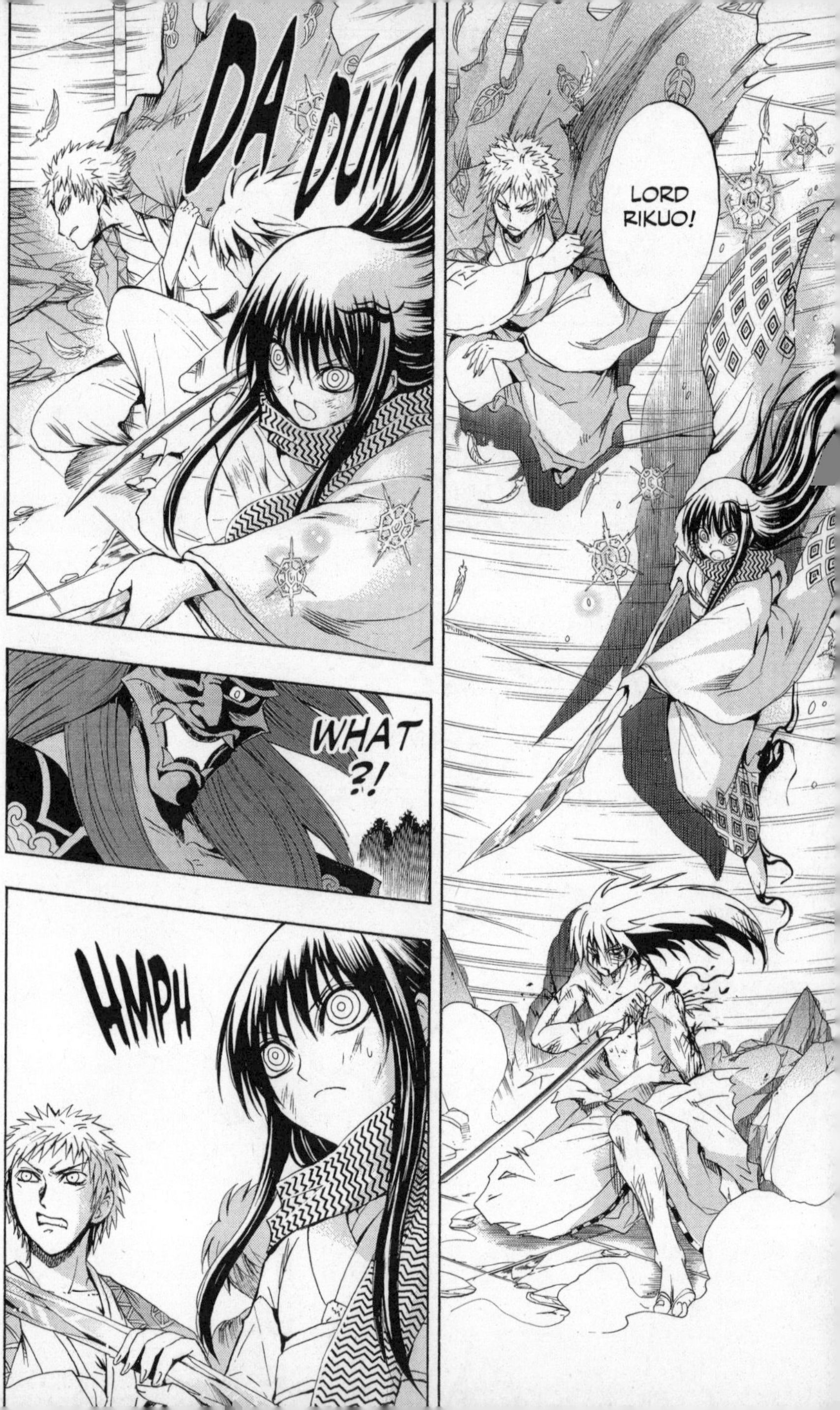
LORD RIKUO!
DA DUM
WHAT ?!
HMPH

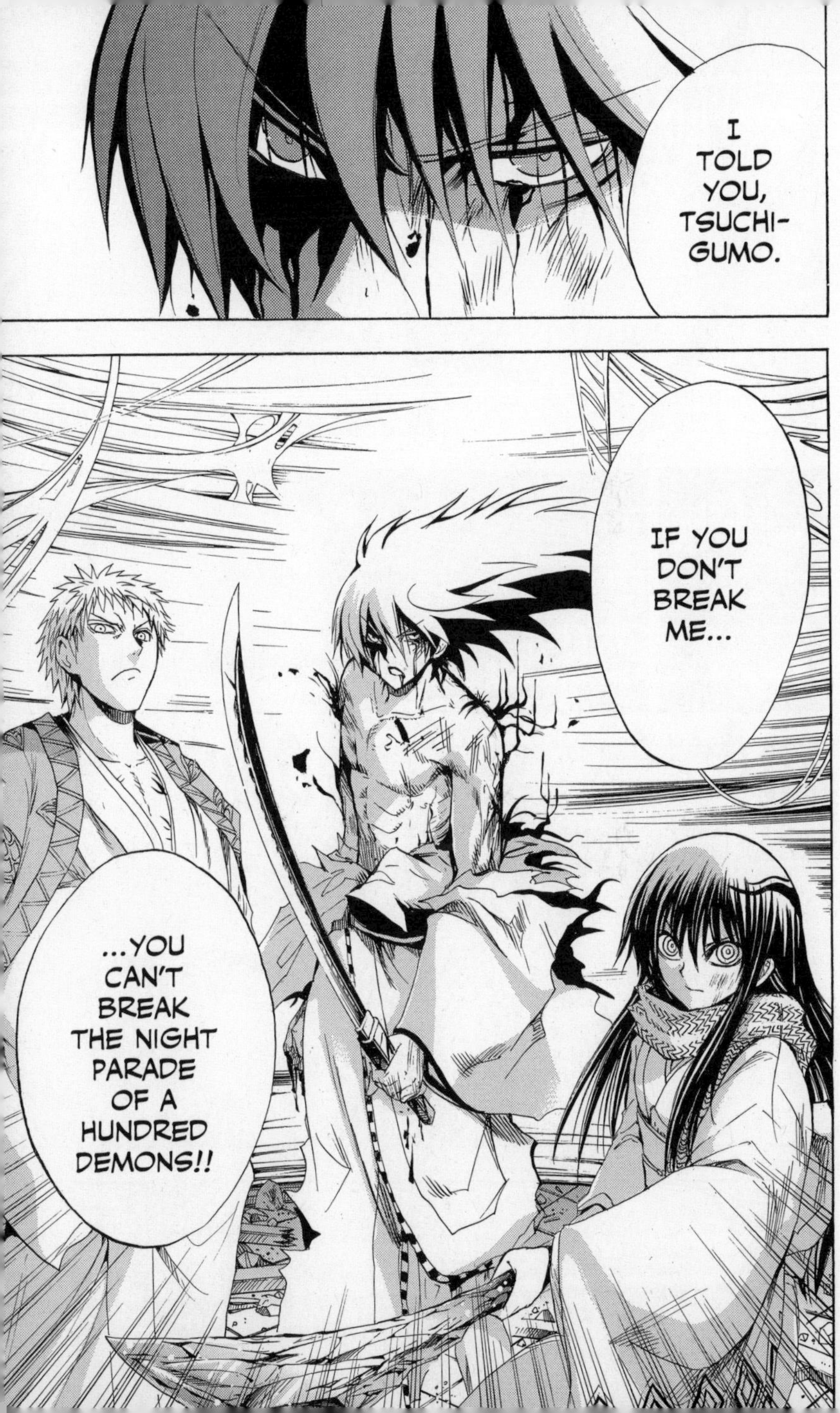
I TOLD YOU, TSUCHIGUMO.
IF YOU DON'T BREAK ME...
...YOU CAN'T BREAK THE NIGHT PARADE OF A HUNDRED DEMONS!!

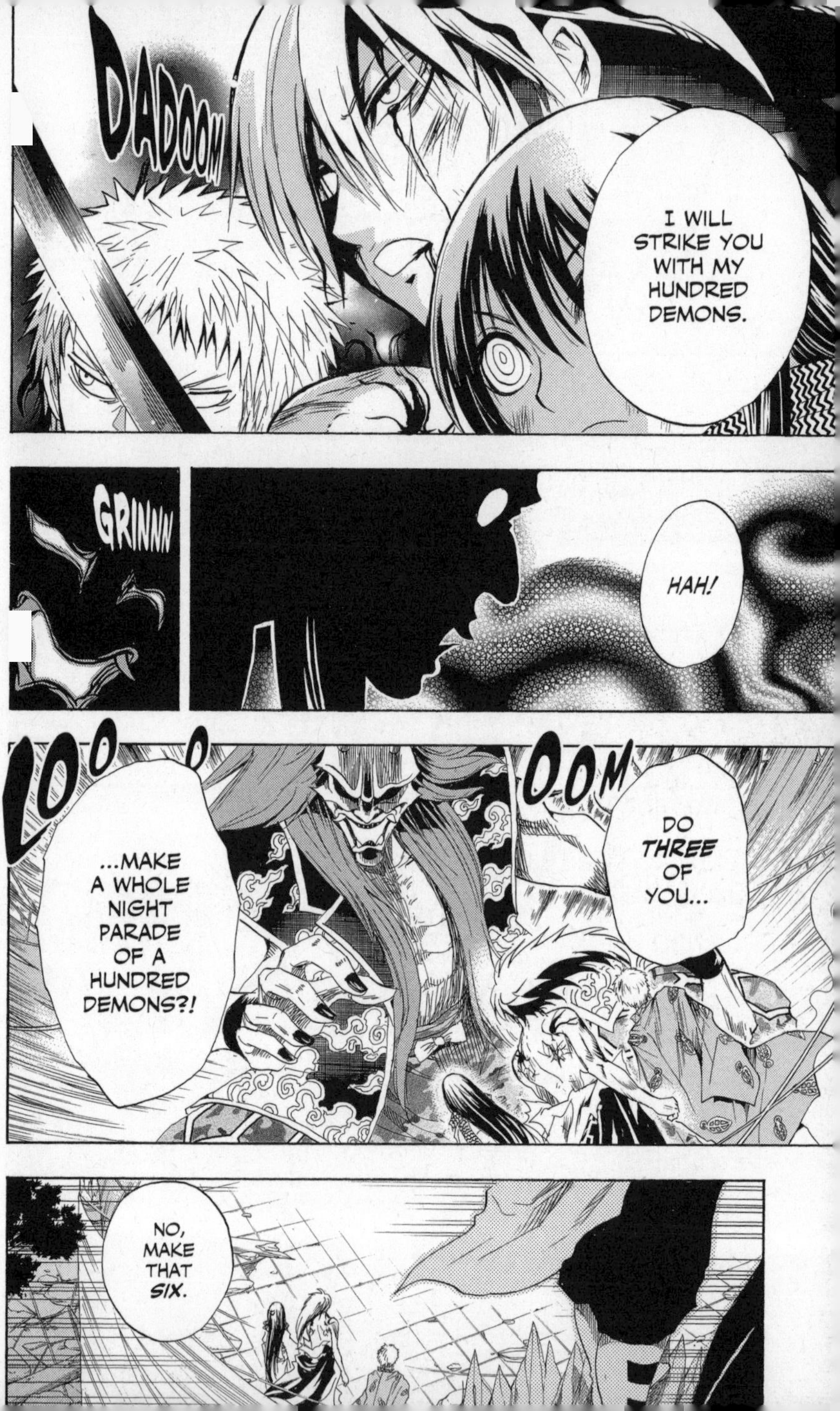
I WILL STRIKE YOU WITH MY HUNDRED DEMONS.
DADOOM
HAH!
GRINNN
DO *THREE* OF YOU...
...MAKE A WHOLE NIGHT PARADE OF A HUNDRED DEMONS?!
LOO O O O-OOM
NO, MAKE THAT *SIX*.

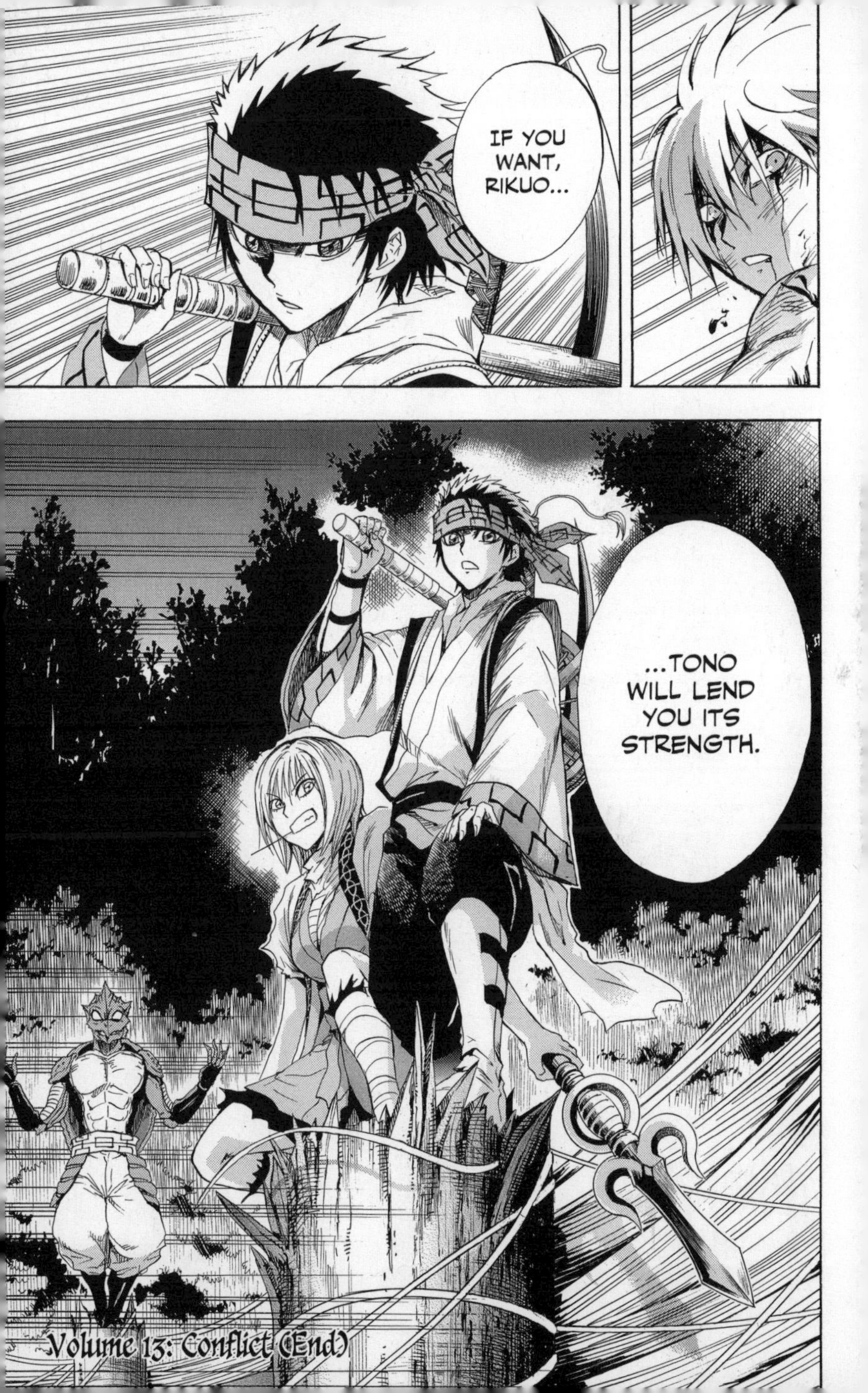
IF YOU WANT, RIKUO...
...TONO WILL LEND YOU ITS STRENGTH.
Volume 13: Conflict (End)

Dried Aconite Root

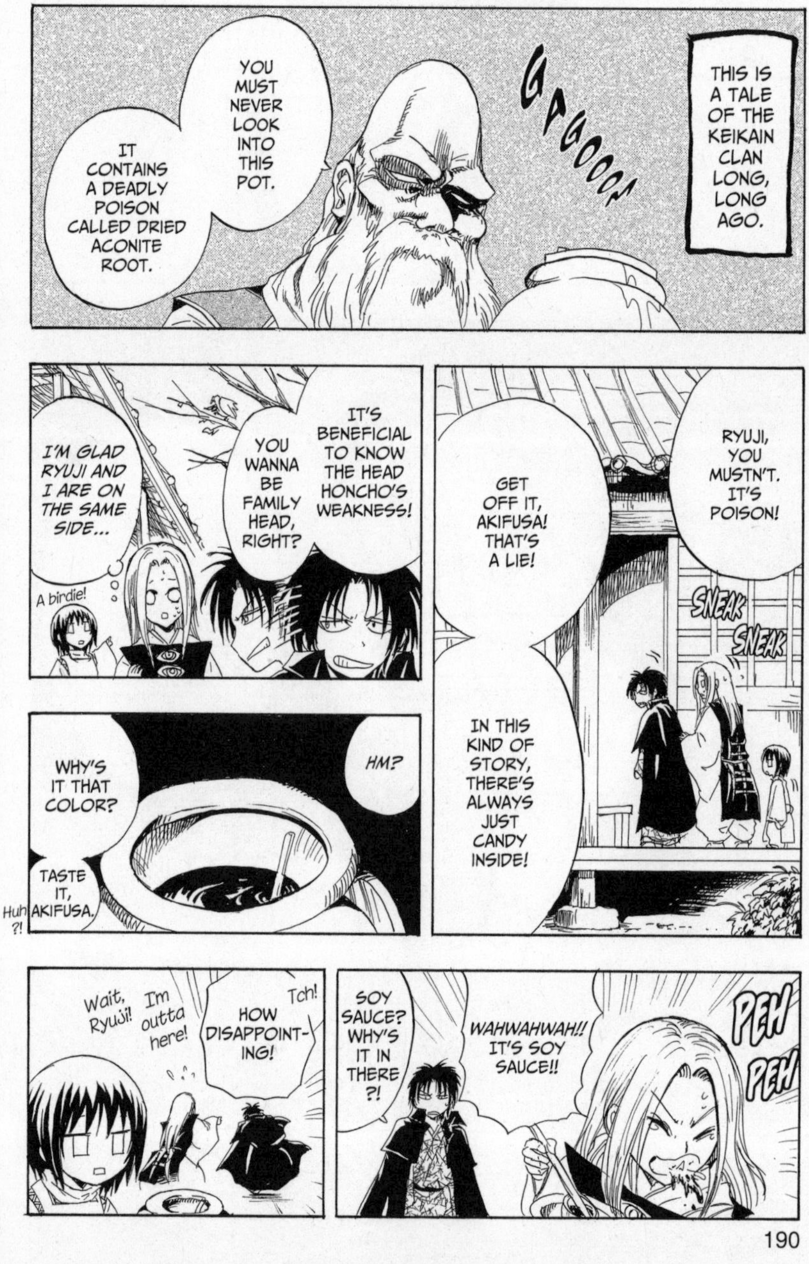
THIS IS A TALE OF THE KEIKAIN CLAN LONG, LONG AGO.
GAGOOON
YOU MUST NEVER LOOK INTO THIS POT.
IT CONTAINS A DEADLY POISON CALLED DRIED ACONITE ROOT.
RYUJI, YOU MUSTN'T. IT'S POISON!
GET OFF IT, AKIFUSA! THAT'S A LIE!
SNEAK SNEAK
IN THIS KIND OF STORY, THERE'S ALWAYS JUST CANDY INSIDE!
IT'S BENEFICIAL TO KNOW THE HEAD HONCHO'S WEAKNESS!
YOU WANNA BE FAMILY HEAD, RIGHT?
I'M GLAD RYUJI AND I ARE ON THE SAME SIDE...
A birdie!
HM?
WHY'S IT THAT COLOR?
TASTE IT, AKIFUSA.
Huh?!
PEH PEH
WAHWAHWAH!! IT'S SOY SAUCE!!
SOY SAUCE? WHY'S IT IN THERE?!
Tch!
HOW DISAPPOINTING!
I'm outta here!
Wait, Ryuji!

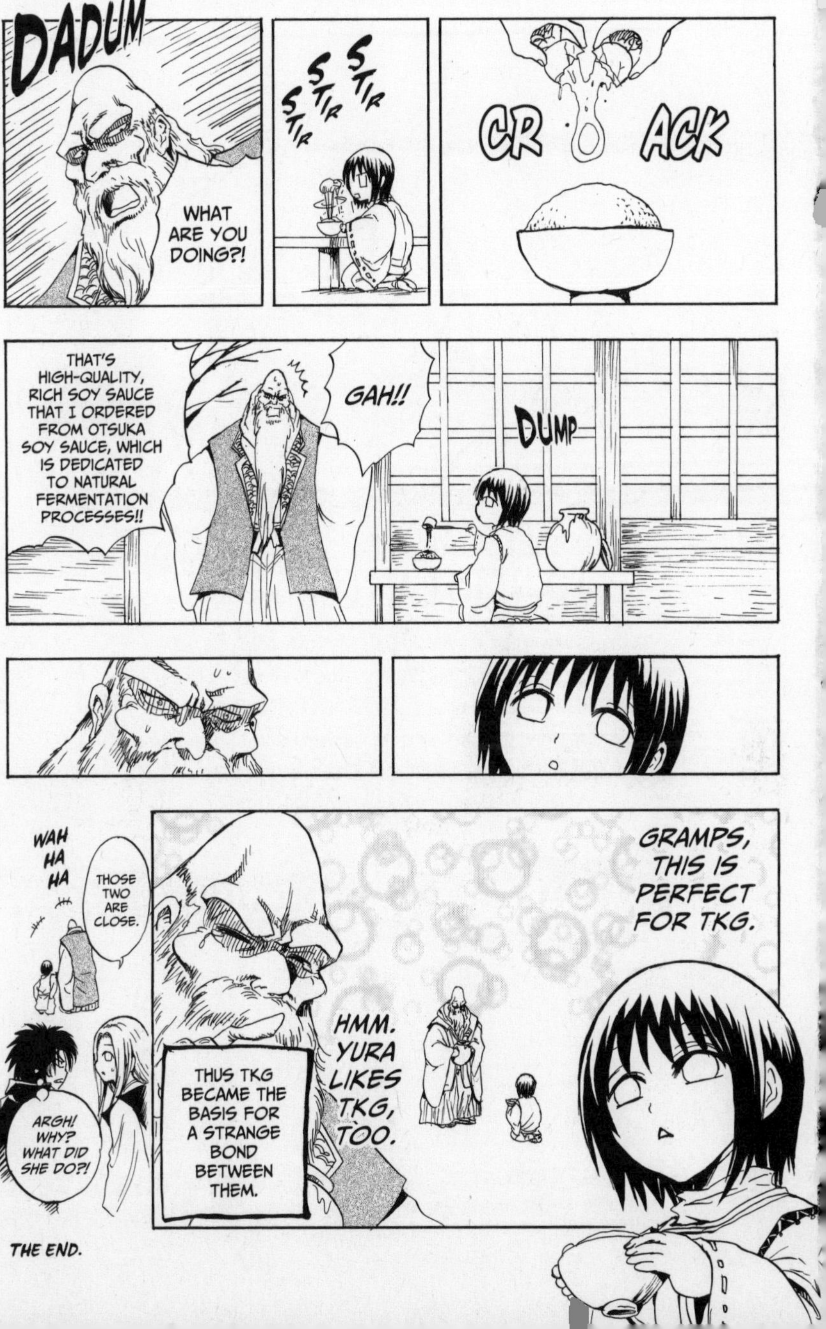
CR ACK
STIR STIR STIR
DADUM
WHAT ARE YOU DOING?!
DUMP
GAH!!
THAT'S HIGH-QUALITY, RICH SOY SAUCE THAT I ORDERED FROM OTSUKA SOY SAUCE, WHICH IS DEDICATED TO NATURAL FERMENTATION PROCESSES!!
GRAMPS, THIS IS PERFECT FOR TKG.
HMM. YURA LIKES TKG, TOO.
THUS TKG BECAME THE BASIS FOR A STRANGE BOND BETWEEN THEM.
WAH HA HA
THOSE TWO ARE CLOSE.
ARGH! WHY? WHAT DID SHE DO?!
THE END.

ABE NO SEIMEI?

IN THE NEXT VOLUME...
TO NIJO CASTLE

As Nurarihyon is attacked by hordes of angry Kyoto yokai, Rikuo and his hundred demons arrive to attempt to take down Hagoromo-Gitsune, a yokai about to give birth to a dangerous dark-arts yokai from the past! A massive battle ensues that reveals secrets of Rikuo's family history... and puts him in some serious risk of bodily harm!

AVAILABLE APRIL 2013!